Luckiest Man

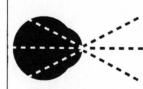 This Large Print Book carries the
Seal of Approval of N.A.V.H.

Luckiest Man

The Life and Death of Lou Gehrig

Jonathan Eig

Thorndike Press • Waterville, Maine

Published in 2005 by arrangement with Simon & Schuster, Inc.

Thorndike Press® Large Print Biography.

The tree indicium is a trademark of Thorndike Press.

The text of this Large Print edition is unabridged.
Other aspects of the book may vary from the original edition.

Set in 16 pt. Plantin by Carleen Stearns.

Printed in the United States on permanent paper.

Library of Congress Cataloging-in-Publication Data

Eig, Jonathan.
    Luckiest man : the life and death of Lou Gehrig / by Jonathan Eig.
        p. cm.
    ISBN 0-7862-7638-X (lg. print : hc : alk. paper)
    Includes bibliographical references.
    1. Gehrig, Lou, 1903–1941. 2. Baseball players — United States — Biography. 3. Amyotrophic lateral sclerosis — Patients — United States — Biography.
    I. Title.
GV865.G4E54 2005
796.357′092—dc22   2005005050

For Jennifer

As the Founder/CEO of NAVH, the only national health agency solely devoted to those who, although not totally blind, have an eye disease which could lead to serious visual impairment, I am pleased to recognize Thorndike Press* as one of the leading publishers in the large print field.

Founded in 1954 in San Francisco to prepare large print textbooks for partially seeing children, NAVH became the pioneer and standard setting agency in the preparation of large type.

Today, those publishers who meet our standards carry the prestigious "Seal of Approval" indicating high quality large print. We are delighted that Thorndike Press is one of the publishers whose titles meet these standards. We are also pleased to recognize the significant contribution Thorndike Press is making in this important and growing field.

Lorraine H. Marchi, L.H.D.
Founder/CEO
NAVH

* Thorndike Press encompasses the following imprints: Thorndike, Wheeler, Walker and Large Print Press.

CONTENTS

PROLOGUE

Lou Gehrig stepped onto the field at Yankee Stadium wearing a pinstriped uniform that no longer fit. His pants were bunched at the waist. His jersey billowed in the wind. The crowd hushed as they watched him walk, head bowed, feet shuffling, arms hanging weakly at his sides. They had seen him make the trip from the dugout to home plate thousands of times, but never like this, never with a look of dread creasing his face.

It was July 4, 1939, Lou Gehrig Appreciation Day at Yankee Stadium, a hot and sticky afternoon. For the first time in his life, Gehrig was afraid to be on a ballfield. He was thirty-six years old and dying. His Yankee teammates and their opponents that day, the Washington Senators, were lined up on the infield grass, waiting for the ceremony to begin. His wife and parents watched from box seats along the third-base line. More than 61,000 people sat elbow to elbow in the stands.

Gehrig never looked up. When he finally reached home plate, he stopped and scratched at the dirt with his feet. The master of ceremonies introduced some of the special guests in attendance, including Gehrig's former teammate Babe Ruth and New York mayor Fiorello H. La Guardia. Gehrig twisted his blue cap in his hands and tottered from side to side as he listened to a series of short speeches. Next came the presentation of gifts: a fishing rod, some silver plates, a trophy with an eagle on top. He accepted them without saying a word.

The crowd applauded, but only politely. Here was Gehrig, the greatest first baseman the game had ever seen. Yet for all his accomplishments, his movie-star looks, and his gentlemanly manner, fans, somehow, had never shown overwhelming enthusiasm for him. Sportswriters said he lacked color. He was no Babe Ruth, they complained. The Babe was the Bambino, their child, and people loved him unconditionally. Gehrig's nickname — the Iron Horse — was inspired by a train, and it was perfectly apropos. Most people don't appreciate a train's strength and reliability until they're standing on the platform one day and it doesn't show up.

When the presentations were over, the emcee, Sid Mercer, asked if the guest of honor had anything to say. Gehrig answered with a slight, almost imperceptible shake of the head, no. He was afraid he'd collapse if he tried to speak. Workers moved into position, ready to roll up the wires and pull down the microphones. Only then did it dawn on the men and women in the stands that he was going away. Cries of protest rang out. The shouting grew louder and spread like a fever through the stadium. Soon, all the fans were on their feet. Their voices came together in a chant that shook the grandstand: "We want Lou! We want Lou!"

Gehrig stood still. His shoulders hung limp and heavy. At last, Joe McCarthy, manager of the Yankees, walked over and whispered in his ear. Gehrig nodded, ran his fingers through his hair, and stepped hesitantly toward home plate. The chanting stopped. Silence blanketed the stadium again.

Ever so slowly, Gehrig leaned toward the microphones and drew a deep breath. He was about to deliver one of the saddest and strongest messages an American audience had ever heard.

CHAPTER 1

THE SURVIVOR

Baseball at the turn of the century was a game for poor immigrants and high school dropouts. The same brawny men who forged steel, built outhouses, and swept the streets through the winter turned to baseball in spring, hoping for a shot at wealth and glory. Henry Louis Gehrig was born to a poor family of immigrants, same as so many other professional ballplayers. But in many important ways he was different, and the difference had a great deal to do with his parents.

When Gehrig talked about his childhood, he rarely mentioned his father. Heinrich Gehrig stood mostly in the background of his son's life, a distant object obscured by his generously proportioned and fiercely stubborn wife. Heinrich didn't spend much time in the family apartment. When the old man wasn't working, he was looking for work. When he wasn't looking for work, he was usually at the local tavern, talking about looking for work.

Wilhelm Heinrich Gehrich was born in 1867 in Adelsheim, Germany, the seventh of nine children. He grew up in poverty. His father, Johann Philipp, was a carpenter. His mother, Sophia Johanna Pfeiffer, also came from a poor family. When Johann and Sophia married in November of 1856, they did so with a sense of urgency. Sophia gave birth to their first child three weeks after the wedding. By 1870, the Gehrichs were identifying themselves as the Gehrigs. As Heinrich grew up, he trained as an ornamental metal worker, pounding intricate patterns into iron and steel, making grilles for doors, railings, and balustrades. Metal work paid better than a lot of the grueling labor typically assigned to young men who lacked formal education, but it rarely provided a steady paycheck, at least for Heinrich. Throughout much of his life, his distaste for hard labor guided him.

Heinrich left Germany at the age of twenty. He may have emigrated illegally, since there appear to be no records of his journey in either Germany or the United States. He settled first in Chicago, didn't like his prospects there, and soon tried New York. Long after most men his age had married, Heinrich remained single. No doubt his pokey work habits made him something short of a princely catch. He had no known family in the United States and probably lived alone, renting a bed or sofa from a family that needed whatever pittance he could afford to pay. In 1901, at the age of thirty-four, he finally met the woman he would marry.

Anna Christina Fack was born in 1882 in Schleswig-Holstein, a German province near the Danish border. When Christina was one year old, her mother died after delivering a stillborn son. Her father, a carpenter, quickly remarried. It's not clear whether Christina continued to live with her father's new family or moved in with her grandparents. She grew into a tall, sturdy woman, with powerful hands and forearms, like her father, and no waist whatsoever. Her hair was curly and blond, but there was nothing cute or girlish about her. As soon as she was old enough, she began working as a servant around Schleswig-Holstein, saving her money and plotting her escape.

She left home in May 1900, five months after her eighteenth birthday, sailing from Hamburg to New York in third-class steerage on a ship called the *Pennsylvania*. She had no friends or relatives waiting for her in the United States, no job and no place to live. As she stepped off the boat at Ellis Island, she told the clerk recording her arrival that she had twenty-five dollars to her name. She may well have been lying. Immigrants often exaggerated their wealth for fear of being turned away, and twenty-five dollars was a considerable sum for a new arrival traveling in third-class steerage.

Heinrich and Christina seemed like an unlikely couple. Both were German Lutherans, and neither was particularly religiously observant, but the similarities more or less ended there. He was mild-mannered and relaxed — maybe too relaxed — with a childish sense of humor. She was humorless and stern, single-minded in her determination to make a better life than the one she had inherited. Heinrich was an inch or so taller than his wife, but it was Christina, at 5 feet 8 inches and two hundred pounds, who filled the frame when they posed together, most often stone-faced, for photographs. Why did she choose a man almost twice her age with a weakness for the bottle and no regular source of income? The couple never mentioned in later interviews how they met or why they married. But the calendar offers one compelling piece of information: Their first child, Anna Christina, was born on May 26, 1902 — just six months after her parents' wedding.

The Gehrigs made their first home together in a German neighborhood in

Manhattan called Yorkville, which was so far north that many New Yorkers didn't think of it as part of the city. Yorkville had been populated by Germans from as early as 1850, and by the time Heinrich and Christina moved in, it had the distinct feel of a bustling Deutschland village. Some referred to 86th Street where it met Second Avenue as Sauerkraut Avenue. Butchers hung hams and sausages in their shop windows. Polka music pulsed through the walls of the local beer halls. The smell of hops from the neighborhood's giant breweries turned the air sweet on warm days, though not sweet enough to cover the smell of the countless horses that pulled carts along the cobblestone streets.

The Gehrigs began raising their family at one of those moments in history when everything seemed to be changing. Electric lightbulbs were beginning to shine in some of New York's wealthier homes, replacing the gas lamps that had stained the city's walls and polluted its air for so long. The energetic Theodore Roosevelt had just become the youngest president in the history of the United States. The Wright brothers were at work on their four-cylinder, gasoline-powered flying machine. Henry Ford founded his motor company in 1903 on an investment of $100,000. The Flatiron Building, one of the world's tallest skyscrapers, had just gone up on 23rd Street in New York. Below ground, workers were digging miles of tunnels for subway trains. Horse racing was still the nation's most popular sport, but baseball, a game that adapted nicely to the city's alleys and sandlots, was coming on fast.

Anna Christina was born in her parents' apartment at 242 East 94th Street, in a building that later made way for a commercial laundry. The Gehrigs moved several blocks north after her birth, to 1994 Second Avenue at East 102nd Street. But they were not moving up. The family's growth put more strain on an already lean budget, in all likelihood forcing them to head for Yorkville's edge, a dozen blocks from the neighborhood's best shops. So many new buildings were going up on the city's northern frontier that landlords often offered several months of free rent to attract new tenants. On Second Avenue the family was exposed to the deafening rattle of the elevated trains, a sound so loud that people halted their conversations at the first hint of a tremor. The Gehrigs were not listed in any of the city directories during the first decade of the twentieth century, an indication that they might have been sharing apartments with other poor families, or else that they were moving so often that city record-keepers couldn't keep up.

Brick tenement buildings sprouted along Second Avenue, row after row, block after block. Shops on the ground floor sold coal, firewood, and groceries. Horse-drawn ice wagons clunked down the streets. Even the poorest immigrants were astounded by the variety and steady supply of available products. What they couldn't get in the stores arrived, almost magically, by pushcart. The Gehrigs were poor, but they were fortunate to be poor in a land of abundance. Christina, like most immigrants, knew how much her new home had to offer because she could see it every day — the fresh fruits, the fat hams, the warm coats — for sale on the street where she lived.

Above the shops on Second Avenue were apartments, their hallways dark, rooms glowing orange at night from gas lamps. Two-bedroom apartments sometimes accommodated three or four families. Windows stayed shut to keep out the noise and stench of the streets. A trip to the toilet meant a walk down the hall. Many tenement buildings had no bathtubs; instead cities built public baths. In warm weather, families crowded onto rooftops and fire escapes to sleep. Fresh air was a luxury.

For all her strength, there were some things Christina Gehrig could not control.

As a child, she had lost her mother and her only brother. Now, despite her obsessive nurturing as a wife and mother, her daughter became sick. In New York at the start of the twentieth century, there was no shortage of dangers to an infant's health. Tuberculosis, diphtheria, cholera, pneumonia, scarlet fever, and whooping cough were a few of the more common ones. Germs found fertile breeding grounds in the cramped, dirty apartments and tenement buildings overstuffed with coughing and sneezing children. Couples often planned for big families, anticipating that one or two children might not survive to adulthood. At three-thirty in the afternoon on September 5, 1902, Anna Gehrig died in the family apartment. A doctor in the neighborhood declared "convulsions" the cause of death and noted on the death certificate that the child had been bottle-fed. She was three and a half months old.

Christina's second child was born on June 19, 1903, nine months after the death of her first. By some unconfirmed accounts the baby boy weighed in at a whopping fourteen pounds. Eight days later, a woman named Phillipine Jandas — probably the midwife — filled out the birth certificate. Jandas apparently assumed that the Gehrigs' first son would be named Heinrich, after his father, and he very nearly was. But as she dipped her fountain pen and began to write the child's name at the top of the city-issued form, "H-e-i-n . . . ," her hand suddenly stopped. She went back, struck a line through the "i," connected the "e" directly to the "n," and then added an "ry." The baby was named Henry Louis — Louie, his mother would call him — and the Gehrig family took a giant step toward assimilation.

The Gehrigs and the Upper East Side were both growing. When the elevated train tracks along Second and Third Avenues were completed late in the nineteenth century, they cast thick, crazy-quilt shadows on the streets, blocking what little light had managed to sneak into adjacent apartments. The steel and iron tracks were ugly, and the trains were so loud they frightened horses. Even so, the Upper East Side became a very attractive neighborhood.

While the poor clustered near the train lines, the wealthy began lining up a few blocks to the west, along Central Park. In 1901, the same year the Gehrigs were married, Andrew Carnegie built a massive house at 91st Street and Fifth Avenue (now the home of the Cooper-Hewitt Museum), a short walk from some of the poorest parts of Yorkville. Jacob Ruppert

— who owned the brewery that made Knickerbocker beer and who would eventually come to own the Yankees — lived at Fifth Avenue and 93rd Street in a castle-like mansion on a hill. All around these massive homes were rocky, vacant lots, shantytowns, and a growing number of tenement buildings. The Ruppert home had a buffer against the city's grimy side: a densely planted apple orchard. Children from the tenements would look down the street to check for cops and then hop the fence and grab all the fruit they could stuff in their pockets. Adults from the tenements near the Ruppert estate learned quickly that there were legitimate opportunities available within the walls of the nearby mansions. There were tea sets to shine, horses to shoe, clothes to mend, and windows to wash. It wasn't high-paying work, but there was an awful lot of it. The Gehrigs needed money, Heinrich wasn't coming up with much, and Christina didn't have any relatives to help take care of the children so that she might go to work. Still, she found a way. She began cooking and cleaning for her neighbors, most of whom were too busy cooking and cleaning in the mansions to take care of their own homes.

Thirteen months after the birth of their son, the Gehrigs' family grew again. Sophie Louise, named for Heinrich's mother, was born on July 27, 1904. Heinrich continued working sporadically. Christina continued to pick up the slack. Stacks of laundry piled up on her kitchen counters and tabletops. The apartment smelled of soap and coal and sugar and flour and, sometimes, a nice beef stew. A neighbor walking into her cluttered kitchen might have had a difficult time determining where Christina's own housework ended and her paid labor began.

Lou was always Lou, or Louie — never Henry. A picture at age four shows a solidly built fireplug of a boy, one foot on the sidewalk, the other on the macadam curb, his hands placed rakishly on his hips. He wears a turtleneck, a hooded sweater that's several sizes too big, three-quarter-length knickers, and square-toed shoes. His wavy blond hair is a mess. The sun gleams in his right eye, and his lips almost form a smile.

Christina put her son to work as her second in command, delivering stacks of folded laundry and picking up supplies from nearby stores. Even as a small boy he proved remarkably reliable. The prize, when he returned to the apartment, was a cut of roast beef and a slice of homemade pie. But the real reward for Lou must have been Christina's approval, something Heinrich rarely received.

As her two children got older, Christina began leaving the house in search of more work. The teeming tenements were no-body's idea of an ideal place to raise a family, but they at least provided a steady supply of babysitters. More mansions kept popping up in the neighborhood, which meant more jobs, which meant Christina was able to find work mopping, dusting, and cooking. To earn extra money, she often brought home laundry from the mansions and washed it in her apartment. Tenement units had no plumbing, of course, so water had to be hauled up the stairs, heated on the stove, and poured into the tub. Dirty water had to be carried back downstairs and out of the building. Washing and rinsing a single load of laundry required about fifty gallons of water. Christina Gehrig had a body built for manual labor, but her shoulders surely must have grown rounder and her legs thicker as she toted water, laundry, groceries, wood, and ice, not to mention children.

Heinrich and Christina argued often and at impressive volume. One morning, after Heinrich had been out late drinking the night before, Christina discovered a stash of seventeen dollars in crumpled bills, the result of her husband's good luck at the pinochle table. While Heinrich slept, Christina hustled Lou out of the house and took him by train to Coney Island, where she let him ride the roller coaster and eat hot dogs and ice cream until the money was gone. The day became a cherished memory, one they would laugh about for years, remembering not only the fun but also that it came at Heinrich's expense. Many years later, Lou's wife, Eleanor, would write that Christina and Lou "resented the fact that he [Heinrich] spent too much time over pinochle and beer, and he resented the fact that they were subtly allied against him."

In the winter of 1906, Sophie, not yet two years old, became sick. Her parents took her to Riverside Hospital on February 15, but the doctors there couldn't help. Sophie, diagnosed with measles, diphtheria, and broncho-pneumonia, held on for five weeks. She died on March 22, just before dawn. With no money to bury her, the Gehrigs allowed the hospital to send her body to Fresh Pond, a crematorium in Queens.

At some point during these seasons of loss, Christina became pregnant and gave birth to another boy. But the child died too quickly to acquire a name. There is no birth or death certificate on file with New York City.

By the time he was three years old, Henry Louis Gehrig, like his mother, was an only child. Later, when he became one of the nation's most famous athletes and the subject of countless newspaper and magazine articles, Christina would boast that Lou had been better off than most of the poor immigrants in their neighborhood. Inasmuch as she made sure he never missed a meal, she was right. But she usually neglected to mention that her son's special circumstance came at great cost. The Gehrigs were just as poor as their neighbors — poorer than many. Their sole advantage, if it can be called an advantage, was that they had only one child to clothe and feed. Lou would never speak in detail of his lost siblings. He acknowledged the deaths but not how deeply his family had been hurt.

Christina devoted herself more fiercely than ever to work. She used her extra income to help move the Gehrigs out of Yorkville and into an apartment in the neighborhood of Washington Heights, at 2266 Amsterdam Avenue, far uptown under the old Washington Bridge, which crossed the Harlem River. The Gehrigs enrolled their son at Public School 132, a massive rectangle of brick built in the same year he had been born. Though the boy threw with his left hand and kicked with his left foot, he learned to write with his right hand. Schoolteachers in those days didn't give lefties a choice.

Gehrig was the subject of a crushing degree of attention. Christina fed him as if he were a runt, as if every bite he took were an immunization, as if every ounce of flesh on his chunky frame might provide further protection from the invisible germs choking New York City's air. "I don't pretend Lou was born with a silver spoon in his mouth," she said. "But he never left the table hungry, and I can say he had a terrible appetite from the first time he saw daylight. Maybe his clothes were torn, dirty and rumpled after playing baseball and football, but he was always clean and neatly dressed when I sent him off to school."

When he left the house, Gehrig burst forth like a furloughed soldier, starved for recreation. He played marbles, hitched sleigh rides, and threw snowballs at anything that moved up on Deep Grass Hill. He stole potatoes from grocery stores and roasted them over trash fires in vacant lots. Once, when he was eleven, he swam across the Hudson River, from Manhattan to Fort Lee, New Jersey. He begged to be included in baseball games, even when the boys at play were bigger and older. The children in the neighborhood soon discovered that Gehrig, while not especially coordinated, had an arm like a slingshot. He wasn't bad with his fists, either.

But back in his family apartment, Gehrig

did what he was told and ate what was in front of him. Christina cooked so much food that her table sometimes looked as if it were set for four children. It was thick and greasy stuff — stews and wursts and potato pancakes and pickled herring — and Little Louie kept eating until no one but his mother called him "little" anymore. The Gehrig family had been pounded by poverty and wrecked by disease, but Christina emerged as a hero to her only surviving child. She was not the most lovable hero. She was a muscular, unemotional figure. But with Heinrich so often gone, it was Christina who explained to her son what would be expected of him. It was she who set the example. Her devotion was never in doubt.

"I'm like one of those Al Smith cigars — up from the streets," Gehrig once said. "And if it had not been for my mother, well, I'd be a good-natured, strong-armed and strong-backed boy, pushing a truck around New York, loading and unloading boxes that less powerful truck drivers could not handle."

Henry Louis Gehrig would grow into a soft-spoken and enigmatic man, sensitive and kind, and yet unfathomable in many ways. But some elements of his personality were easier to read than the big "NY" he would come to wear across his chest as a member of the New York Yankees. He was a worrier, obsessed with pleasing others. As an adult, he was fortunate enough to earn terrific sums of money for playing a game he adored. He found himself a part of the greatest baseball team of all time, consorting with some of the most extraordinary men to ever lift bat or beer bottle, during one of the nation's most exuberant eras. Yet he always approached his job with a grim determination and a deep fear of disappointing his employers, his teammates, and his fans.

Throughout his career, Gehrig would dote on his mother. He would write her when the team went on the road, and when he returned from a long trip, he would greet her on the train platform with long hugs and tender kisses. His public displays of affection for his mother earned him a fair bit of ribbing from his teammates, and much more no doubt went on behind his back. But he was never ashamed. He loved her, and he didn't care who knew it. If there were a Hall of Fame for mama's boys, Gehrig would have been a shoo-in.

CHAPTER 2

"BABE" GEHRIG

Lou Gehrig was picked on as a child — for his poverty, for his shyness, for his ethnicity, and not the least for his bulging rear end. The children on the playgrounds awarded him the plainest of all nicknames: "Fat."

He was nervous and aloof. He kept his thoughts and feelings in check. But action was a critical part of his otherwise timid life. "We kids used to get up and play baseball at six and seven o'clock in the morning," he recalled, "so that by the time the sun was good and hot we'd have our fill of the game and could bum our way up to 181st Street and go swimming. . . . We'd swim and eat cookies all day, return home late for supper and get the devil whaled out of us for waywardness."

At play, his shyness gave way to a joyful sense of adventure and a powerful competitive drive. He grew angry when he lost, and shouted when he thought he'd been cheated. He teased and ran from the neighborhood policemen, same as the other children, but never landed in serious trouble. He was too cautious to cause real problems, too frightened by his mother's stern look and his father's occasional slap. Some children find their greatest joy in books, others in the company of friends. Gehrig found his in the physical, in the digging and jumping and tackling and punching, in the reassuring feel of a leather ball with raised stitches squeezed in his left hand.

At play in the northernmost reaches of Manhattan, he would have had almost constant views of the city's waterways. He would have taken long walks past harbors full of tugs and freighters that puffed black smoke and churned oily, gray water. But for a young man who loved games, the neighborhood's centerpiece was an enormous wooden stadium called the Polo Grounds, home of baseball's New York Giants. The Polo Grounds sat in Coogan's Hollow, a North Harlem meadow framed by a large bluff to the west and the Harlem River to the east. Fans who couldn't afford twenty-five cents for admission would scramble up to the top of Coogan's Bluff and catch glimpses of the games for free. There was no better place than the bluff for a boy to turn his back on the place where he grew up and lose himself for a while in baseball.

"Back in the days when a quarter was a

fortune and we had to save for weeks to get the price of a bleacher seat," Gehrig once wrote, "the Giants had been our favorites. And our quarters had all gone for a seat in the left field bleachers — the 'George Burns bleachers' we always called them in the good old days." George Burns — not the comedian — played left field for the Giants from 1911 to 1921.

Gehrig's neighborhood was also home to Hilltop Park, home of the Highlanders, the team that would later become the Yankees. Hilltop Park sat on one of the highest pieces of ground in Manhattan, between Broadway and the Hudson River at West 165th Street, overlooking the New Jersey Palisades. The stadium had been built in only six weeks, at a cost of $300,000, after the Highlanders were purchased from Baltimore in 1903. There were seats enough for 16,000, but many more squeezed in for big games. Fans would bring their own chairs and set them up deep in the outfield or along the foul lines. Fences were so deep — at 542 feet to center field — that there is no record of a ball ever leaving the park for a home run.

Baseball in the first part of the twentieth century was vastly different from the game played today — vastly different even from what it would become by the time Lou

Gehrig began his professional career. Games started late in the afternoon so that fans could work nearly a full day, spend two hours at the ballpark, and still get home for dinner. Men with megaphones announced the starting lineups. A small army of vendors sold steamed sausages (they were not yet widely known as hot dogs), peanuts, and — as "Take Me Out to the Ball Game," the nation's number-one hit song in 1908, noted — Cracker Jack. As the games wore on, fans in the upper reaches of the grandstand found themselves looking down at the action through a halo of cigarette and cigar smoke, but city dwellers at the time were accustomed to smoke and foul odors.

Players wore heavy flannel uniforms with no names or numbers on the back. "You can't tell the players without a program!" vendors at the stadiums shouted. Fielders' gloves were not much bigger than those worn by blacksmiths or carriage drivers. The gloves helped soften the sting on hard-hit balls, but they were nothing like the giant baskets that players use today to grab fly balls. Back then, a one-handed catch was something special. When a ball was slapped foul into the stands, fans tossed it back onto the field. Few spectators paid to sit in the outfield because balls were seldom hit to the deepest part of the park.

At the time, great swaths of outfield grass were seen as a boon to offense, allowing balls to roll a while before they were retrieved and tossed back.

In the first decade of the century, the game was built largely on speed and daring. The most exciting play was the inside-the-park home run. Pitchers spat upon and scuffed the baseballs to make them break more sharply. By the end of nine innings, the balls were often lopsided and soggy, their red stitches frayed, their white skins brown and gray. "We didn't have a baseball to hit in those days," recalled Raymond "Rube" Bressler, who played the game from 1914 to 1932. "We had a squash." Today a bat goes "Crack!" when it meets the ball; then it went "Plunk."

"The only way you could hit a home run was if the outfielder tripped and fell down," said Edd Roush, who played from 1913 to 1931. "The ball wasn't wrapped tight and lots of times it got mashed on one side." Good old George Burns, for example, came to bat more than 7,000 times in his career, yet he hit only forty-one home runs. Scoring occurred about as often as it does today in a World Cup soccer match. When a batter reached first base, even with one out, managers, desperate for runs, often instructed the next man to lay down a sacrifice bunt.

Not long after Lou Gehrig's seventh birthday, the Highlanders and Giants engaged for the first time in a short-lived spectacle called the City Series. The Manhattan Bridge had just been completed. The light opera *Naughty Marietta* was a big hit downtown. And somewhere to the west, the Philadelphia Athletics and Chicago Cubs were competing in the baseball event that was meant to capture the attention of fans nationwide: the seventh annual World Series. But in October of 1910, most of the baseball hawks in Gehrig's neighborhood were more interested in the competition between the Highlanders and Giants, with games alternating between the Polo Grounds and Hilltop Park. The teams played purely for bragging rights (and, in the case of the owners, for the thousands of dollars in ticket revenues generated by the games). The Giants, with pitcher Christy Mathewson, winner of twenty-seven games that year, were the heavy favorites. Ballplayers in 1910 didn't win huge national celebrity — there was no TV or radio yet to spread their fame — but Mathewson was the closest thing to a superstar the game possessed. He was one of baseball's few college men and its finest role model. He lived cleanly and spoke eloquently. Only his pitches were nasty.

The Highlanders, counting on a bunch

of no-names like John Wesley Knight and Harry Meigs Wolter, never had a chance. The Giants not only won the series, four games to two, but also won the ongoing loyalty of Gehrig and most of his friends.

Baseball was growing up fast, and young immigrants like Gehrig took to the sport with fervor. This was no country club game. Most baseball fans had little interest in tennis or golf or badminton. Theirs was a game played in the grass and dirt by men with European surnames and beer breath. It became America's pastime not merely because it was invented here but because it embraced the nation's egalitarian ideals — except, of course, for the fact that African American players were not permitted to play in the major leagues. On streets filled with a dozen or more accents, baseball offered a universal vocabulary. And there was no better neighborhood to witness the enthusiasm than the one in which Lou Gehrig grew up.

On April 14, 1911, flames swept through the Polo Grounds' wooden grandstand. A watchman from the nearby railroad track spotted the fire and sounded an alarm, but too late. Clouds of orange and gray smoke choked the night air over northernmost Manhattan as neighbors stepped out of their apartments to watch the ballpark burn.

Months later, baseball's finest palace rose from the ashes, a giant bowl of concrete and steel, with Italian marble boxes around the front of the upper-deck grandstand, balustrades decorated with American eagles, and a cantilevered roof topped with blue and gold banners. The grandstand was embellished with a series of ornate male and female figures, each holding a shield emblazoned with the logo of one of the National League's eight teams: New York, Brooklyn, Boston, Philadelphia, Pittsburgh, Chicago, Cincinnati, and St. Louis. But putting aside all the frilly detail, the single most impressive thing about the stadium was its size. It had 16,000 seats when it reopened and expanded weeks later to 34,000.

As fans arrived by a network of subways, trolleys, and elevated trains from far beyond Gehrig's working-class neighborhood, the Polo Grounds became a muscular symbol of New York's growth and a testament to the increasingly important role of sport in American culture. It was the first ballpark with pretensions. The owners guessed, correctly, that a baseball stadium could function in much the same way as a city park — as an escape, a cool wedge of green grass in an otherwise gray and grimy city, a place people would set out to visit when they wanted brief refreshment from their cramped and sooty lives.

Still, the men who rebuilt the Polo Grounds failed to foresee some of the changes that would affect their business. They didn't anticipate the advent of the automobile, for example. The Polo Grounds offered no parking. More important, they failed to predict that fans would soon clamor to see home runs smashed over outfield walls. The Polo Grounds' horseshoe shape encouraged people to sit along the foul lines, not in the outfield. The stadium's design also created a vast outfield. To a batter standing at home plate, center field at the Polo Grounds looked like it ended somewhere in the Hamptons.

Young Lou Gehrig learned about baseball's famous players by collecting the glossy gray baseball cards that came in packages of his father's Sweet Caporal cigarettes. Like most of the children who used broomsticks for bats and rags for bases, he indulged the dream of becoming a professional athlete, even though he showed few natural abilities. He was slow on the bases and even slower to learn. Games that came naturally to others required long hours of practice for him. "Some ballplayers have natural born ability," he once said. "I wasn't one of them." The fact that he threw left-handed made him something of a misfit, too, because no one in his neighborhood owned a left-hander's glove. When Heinrich finally bought his son a mitt one year for Christmas, he bought it for the wrong hand. He never considered that a left-handed boy would need a mitt for his right hand. Gehrig jammed it on backwards and used it as best he could.

Though the Gehrigs had their own apartment on Amsterdam Avenue, they were far from comfortable. When census takers knocked on his door in 1910, Heinrich claimed that he had worked almost continuously in 1909, but that just then he happened to be between jobs. The Gehrigs lived among Irishmen, Englishmen, Italians, and Jews; seamstresses, proofreaders, bricklayers, and clerks. Most families had at least two incomes. Their neighbors, the Gallaghers, for example, had three adults living in their apartment, and all three had jobs. Mr. Gallagher was a porter, and his two daughters were telephone operators.

When his mother was working, Lou sometimes followed his father to the nearest *turnverein,* a German gymnastics club and social hall at 156th Street in the Bronx. Gehrig lacked confidence in many ways, but he began at an early age to believe in his physical strength. At the *turnverein* he fell in love with exercise, with the parallel bars, pulleys, and free weights, with the musty smell of the locker room and the quiet company of men. Everything about it appealed to him. It was solitary work, grueling at times, but exercise offered a clear system of rewards. The harder he worked, the stronger he got. By the time he was twelve, his chest and shoulders had begun to catch up to his belly and backside. The firm line of his powerful jaw had begun to emerge from beneath those fleshy cheeks.

In 1917, the United States declared war on Germany. As American soldiers began shipping out, anti-German sentiment in the United States swelled. The Gehrigs might have wished they were back in Yorkville, where there were enough of their own people to provide a buffer. Gehrig, in his last year at P.S. 132, came in for more taunting than ever. Even in America's ballparks, German immigrants sought to distance themselves from their native land. Heinie Groh, an infielder for Cincinnati, and Heinie Zimmerman, who played third base that year for the Giants, both let it be known that they preferred from then on to be called Henry.

For many of Gehrig's classmates at P.S. 132, graduation day marked the end of their formal education. They were ready to begin working full-time, in the family store, at home, or at any of the low-paying service jobs available at the time to minors. But Christina Gehrig wanted her son to go to high school. She wanted him to be an architect or an engineer. So she dressed him for his grade-school graduation as if he were an up-and-coming aristocrat, in a high-collared shirt buttoned to the chin, a long coat with a thick sash around the waist, and a baggy pair of knickers. He combed his blond hair straight back, which added at least an inch or two to his already impressive height. As he posed for a photograph, he managed a tight-lipped smile.

At the time Lou Gehrig entered the High School of Commerce, at 155 West 65th Street — a long ride along elevated train tracks from home — his cheeks were still pale and smooth. Even with the baby fat gone, he had the expression of an innocent child, a face waiting for its lines to be written. His mother continued to tell him how to dress. Christina Gehrig insisted on knickers for her son. Maybe they were his best pants, or maybe she wanted to go on thinking of him as Little Louie. In any case, Heinrich said nothing on his son's behalf. So Lou, afraid of making trouble, bought a pair of long pants with the money he made at one of his jobs, hid them in the dumbwaiter, and changed every day on his way in and out of the apartment building.

Those who knew Gehrig as a young man used words such as "worried" and "harassed" to describe him. They said he seemed from an early age to be carrying with him a sense of his own worthlessness.

He kept to himself at Commerce High, making few close friends. If the girls in his school or neighborhood were attracted to this strong and handsome young man, Gehrig didn't seem to notice. His classmates said they never saw him with a girl. Gehrig didn't play on any athletic teams during his first year at Commerce. In one interview, he said it was his mother's decision not to let him play. In another, he said the choice was his own. "I wanted to play ball on the high school team, but lacked the courage to try out for a position until my junior year," he said.

Later, when Gehrig was famous, several of his former classmates would attempt to take credit for discovering the young athlete. Oliver Gintel, for one, who went on to make a nice living selling furs, claimed that he had been trying out for the soccer team when he accidentally kicked a ball in the direction of a beefy young man at the edge of the field. The stranger took a short step, swung his left leg at the ball and sent it flying almost the entire length of the practice field. "I then went to work on him in earnest," recalled Gintel in a letter to one of Gehrig's early biographers.

When Gehrig did finally begin to compete, he did so with hurricane-force energy, as if making up for lost time. He played soccer, football, and baseball, sometimes two out of three on the same day. Baseball, at the outset, was his weakest game, by some accounts. But he was too big and strong for his coach, Harry Kane, to give up on him. Kane put Gehrig at first base, where his clumsiness seemed likely to do the least damage. The coach drilled his infield by hitting ground balls to every position and having the fielders throw over and over again to first. The fields at Commerce were a mess, more rock than grass. Balls skidded in the dirt and bounced off his glove, shins, and chest. Gehrig kept practicing.

He also pitched in high school. Though he lacked control, he threw the ball harder than anyone on his team. But it wasn't Gehrig's pitching that excited his coaches. By the spring of his junior year, it was clear that Gehrig was one of the most powerful hitters — if not *the* most powerful hitter — ever to emerge from the city's public schools. Long-distance home runs were still a relatively new phenomenon, and there were only a few grown men in the big leagues capable of hitting them with regularity. When Gehrig started launching balls over fences in high school games, word spread quickly. His biggest weakness as a hitter, Kane said, was an inability to hit curve balls from left-handed pitchers. So Kane, a left-handed pitcher who had won two games and lost seven as a big-league pitcher before becoming a coach, began tossing his star pupil curve after curve. "We set to work together," Kane recalled years later, "and after a few weeks of practice, day in and day out, he completely overcame his fault."

While his son attended Commerce, Heinrich Gehrig became ill. Some accounts said he was stricken with some sort of temporary paralysis; others suggested that the disability was more mundane, possibly alcohol-induced. In either case, the result was the same: He couldn't work. The family moved from Amsterdam Avenue to another apartment building in the same neighborhood, at 2079 Eighth Avenue.

Christina turned to the help-wanted section of the newspaper and found a full-time job as a cook and housekeeper for Sigma Nu Theta, a fraternity at Columbia University. Her son helped out by taking whatever jobs he could get — working in butcher shops and grocery stores, delivering newspapers, mowing lawns in summer, and shoveling snow in winter. Sometimes he dug for clams on the banks of the Hudson River, selling his catch to the nearby Connor's Hotel. One day, he showed up for high school football practice covered in soot, explaining that he'd been doing janitorial work in place of his father. And sometimes, when practice was over, he would head to the Sigma Nu house at Columbia to help his mother serve dinner or clean up after it. Weekends and holidays provided a chance to work longer hours and make more money.

Schoolwork did not seem to get in the way much. By most accounts, Gehrig was a solid but unspectacular student. As with sports, he had to work hard to get by.

By the start of his senior year, he stood nearly six feet tall and weighed more than 180 pounds. In his orange and blue football jersey and skin-tight pants, Gehrig stood out on the gridiron like a skyscraper among row houses. His size was not the only thing classmates noticed: "No one who went to school with Lou can forget the cold winter days and Lou coming to school wearing khaki shirt, khaki pants and heavy brown shoes, but no overcoat, nor any hat," wrote classmate Arthur Allen Narins in a letter to biographer Paul Gallico. "He was a poor boy." Until well into his thirties, when he had become one of the nation's wealthiest and best-known athletes, Gehrig consistently refused to wear an overcoat, no matter how cold the weather.

For all his insecurities, Gehrig the teenager surely must have realized that he was becoming a fine athlete. If his coaches and peers didn't convince him, then perhaps the law of supply and demand did. By the time he turned seventeen, strangers were offering him money to play a game that his mother had long deemed a worthless trifle. The Minqua Assembly District, a political club on 181st Street, fielded a semiprofessional baseball team and recruited Gehrig to play as they competed with squads from other political districts in New York and New Jersey. Each team was paid thirty-five dollars, the cash to be divided evenly among its players at the end of a game. But pitchers and catchers received special stipends of five dollars each, perhaps intended to help the assemblymen recruit a couple of talented ringers at key positions. Gehrig told the Minqua managers he was a pitcher. Five dollars was enough to feed his family for a week.

On June 24, 1920, a few days after Gehrig's seventeenth birthday, more than 8,000 fans gathered at Grand Central Terminal to bid farewell and good luck to the Commerce baseball team as it departed for a big game in Chicago. The steam engines hissed, and the crowd shoved and screamed. Security guards, afraid that they might lose control of the mob, sent for help. The police arrived. Violence was avoided.

Commerce was New York's best baseball team that year. With each win that spring, the excitement had climbed. The athletes became campus heroes, and Lou Gehrig, bashing the ball harder than any high school coach or player had seen, became the biggest hero of all. There is no evidence to suggest, however, that he took advantage of his celebrity to forge friendships or to sweep young women off their feet. He enjoyed the company of his teammates, but he otherwise kept to himself.

The boys from Commerce had beaten every top team in New York, and now came their reward — a trip to Chicago, all expenses paid, and the chance to compete against Chicago's best high school team, Lane Technical, in a game played at Cubs Park, soon to be renamed Wrigley Field. It was Gehrig's first long journey, his first glimpse of the small towns and big farms and crooked rivers that stretched out over the western states. The New Yorkers wouldn't get much sleep on the train. They were too excited.

Even before Gehrig and his teammates departed, newspapers in Chicago had warned readers that Commerce would be tough to beat. "The Gotham boys have a first baseman, Louis Gehrig, who is called the 'Babe Ruth' of the high schools," wrote the *Chicago Tribune*. "If he gets hold of one, it is quite likely to be driven over the right wall at the Cubs' park." Gehrig, of course, would spend the next twenty years facing comparisons to Ruth. The first may well have been the sweetest.

For a short time it appeared that Commerce might have to make the trip without its leading power hitter. Christina Gehrig didn't want to let her son leave home for five days. Lou assured his mother that he would make up whatever work he missed, but Christina was unmoved at first. She didn't understand why a young man needed to go to Chicago to play ball. Her son's busy after-school schedule suggested that there were more than enough games in the New York metropolitan area. Lou tried to explain that this was a special game, a championship game, but he wasn't able to budge his mother. He asked Coach Kane to intervene. Kane visited the Gehrigs and promised that he would look after their boy. Only then did Christina relent. For Lou, it was a small but crucial victory. Perhaps he felt his mother's hold on him loosen as his train sped west. He rode in a train car full of new things: crisp white sheets and extra blankets and uniformed servants. The entire trip must have felt like a spectacular gift. He couldn't see much as he stared out the window into the darkness, but he could feel the movement, the gentle rocking. His life until then had been one of fixed geography. Now he was going somewhere.

The young athletes from Commerce High were treated like celebrities. Former President William H. Taft, also on his way to Chicago, stopped into their car to wish them well. So did Joe Frisco, a stuttering comedian, who tried out some of his jokes and showed the boys a brand new dance he called "The Shimmy." The engine sighed to a stop in Chicago on a warm Friday morning. A soft Lake Michigan breeze greeted the boys as they stepped onto the platform and squinted into the sun. More than 2,000 people met them at the station. The crowd included the Lane Tech High School marching band, dressed in khaki uniforms with wide-brimmed hats. As the band began to play, President Taft slipped away virtually unnoticed. Gehrig and his twelve teammates whispered and laughed as they climbed into convertibles and joined a parade through the city's downtown Loop. Streets were not closed for the parade, so the marchers had to slide out of the way of rumbling delivery trucks and

48

horse-drawn carriages. The procession continued along Madison Street to State Street, where the tall buildings threw shadows and amplified the sounds of the screeching trumpets and snapping snare drums. It would have been nearly impossible to be in downtown Chicago that Friday morning and not know the young men from New York had arrived and that tickets were still on sale for the next day's game — one dollar for box seats and fifty cents for general admission.

After a stop for lunch, the team traveled by car to Comiskey Park on the city's South Side, where the White Sox were playing the Cleveland Indians. The boys tucked their uniforms under their arms and carried them into the stadium so they could change out of their other clothes and begin practicing when the game ended. The young athletes had looked forward to seeing the White Sox and Indians almost as much as they had looked forward to their own game. The great Shoeless Joe Jackson patrolled the outfield for the Sox, and the boys from Commerce scrutinized his every move. They had terrific seats, courtesy of Mr. Comiskey, and Chicago pounded Cleveland for a 6-3 win. (Scoring had gone up somewhat since 1911, when the league started using balls with cork centers.) Shoeless Joe proved every bit as good as advertised, with two hits in three at-bats, one run batted in, and one run scored. A year later, Jackson and seven of his teammates would be banned for life from baseball for allegedly throwing the 1919 World Series.

After the game, the high school players slipped into their uniforms and walked to Armour Park, just north of the big-league stadium. The park, named for one of Chicago's meatpacking titans, sat within sniffing distance of the city's massive slaughterhouses. The smell of blood and burnt hair and excrement was awful, "an elemental odor," the muckracking novelist Upton Sinclair had once written, "raw and crude." But the boys from New York were probably too keyed up to care. Jimmy Archer, who had retired just two years earlier after a long career with the Pirates, Tigers, Cubs, Dodgers, and Reds, stood in the shade and watched the teenagers practice. The shortstop, Bobby Bunora, made some smooth moves around the middle of the infield, and third baseman Sewell Johnson fired the ball convincingly from third base to first.

"These kids can play ball," Archer said to a reporter standing beside him.

After taking a few throws at first base, Gehrig tossed his mitt in the dirt and picked up a bat. Though it was only practice, his performance was impressive enough to make the next day's paper — though not impressive enough that reporters would double-check the spelling of his name: "Louis Gherig . . . ," wrote the *Tribune*, "displayed a bit of batting prowess that made the spectators gasp. Twice, when taking his turn, he poled a long drive to right field that probably would have cleared the right field wall at the Cubs park."

By now the players and coaches at Lane surely knew that Gehrig was a dangerous hitter. His size, if nothing else, would alert them when he stepped to the plate. If Saturday's game got tight, Lane's pitchers would probably walk him rather than take a chance that he might hit a home run.

The team stayed downtown at the Hotel Sherman and woke to another cloudless blue sky. They used the players' entrance at Cubs Park, walking down a long ramp to the cool, dank locker room. They chatted nervously as they changed into their uniforms. The Lane Tech band led them onto the field before playing the national anthem. The stands were packed with more than 6,000 fans, the biggest crowd anyone could recall for a high school game. Lane brought its cheerleading squad, but the fans hardly needed any encouragement to make noise.

Bobby Bunora struck out to start the game. Sewell Johnson followed with a single. Gehrig fouled off two pitches, then took a walk. With two men on, Lane's slender young pitcher, Tom Walsh, lost his cool. He hit the next batter and walked the one after that, forcing in a run. By the end of the first inning, the New Yorkers led, 3-0.

The "binglefest," as one writer called it, had begun. Between innings, singers raised megaphones to their lips and serenaded the crowd. Joe Frisco dropped by and once again presented his "Shimmy," this time to a much bigger audience. As the game stretched on, though, Gehrig didn't do much bingling, shimmying, or anything else. He grounded back to the pitcher in the second inning, struck out in the fourth with a man on base, then walked again and scored in the sixth. In four at-bats, he put the ball in play only once, and even then hit it feebly.

"The crowd was beginning to wonder if the stories of his batting prowess were all myths," one Chicago writer noted.

With Commerce leading 8-6 in the top of the ninth inning, Gehrig came to bat for the last time. The bases were loaded, with two outs. He stepped into the batter's box, spread his feet in a wide stance, and looked hard at Lane's new pitcher, a right-hander

52

named Norris Ryrholm.

If Ryrholm could retire Gehrig, Lane would make it to the bottom of the ninth trailing by only two runs. They would still have a chance. Ryrholm made up his mind not to give this man-sized boy standing before him anything he could pull hard to right field. *Keep it away from him,* he told himself as he stepped on the rubber, swung his arms, and reared back to throw.

But his delivery was not as good as his intent. The pitch floated just where Gehrig liked it, high and inside. Gehrig squeezed the bat and swung, shifting his weight from back to front, channeling the full force of his growing body through his wrists.

He knew in an instant that he'd hit it well. He dropped his bat and ran toward first, watching the ball soar higher and higher, over the brick wall in right field and out of sight. It bounced once on Sheffield Avenue and came to rest on the wooden porch of a house across the street. The Commerce boys leapt from the dugout, screaming and waving their caps. When Gehrig crossed the plate, his dimpled grin visible even from the cheap seats, his teammates slapped his back and hugged him and laughed.

"I couldn't believe I had knocked a ball out of a big-league park until our first base coach told me I could take it easy and I saw the Lane right fielder looking help-lessly up at the fence," Gehrig recalled in an interview more than a decade later.

The next day, his photo appeared for the first time in the New York *Daily News.* "The bright star of the inter-city high school championship game . . . ," the paper reported, "was 'Babe' Gehrig."

Back home, Christina Gehrig was eager for her son's return. Though still not a fan of the game, she must have recognized when she saw his picture in the paper that baseball was not entirely frivolous. She clipped the article and stuffed it in a drawer.

CHAPTER 3

AT COLUMBIA

If Babe Ruth had not arrived in New York City at the start of the Roaring Twenties, some aspiring comic-strip artist would have invented him. He was wild, heroic and lovable, equal parts Tarzan, Buck Rogers, and Orphan Annie. He spoke his mind and devoured everything he could get his hands on — especially food, booze, and women.

He joined the Yankees and almost instantly became much more than a ballplayer. To the Yankees, he became a huge source of revenue, attracting enormous crowds even for meaningless games. To the reporters who covered the team, he was a dream come true. To the fans, he was a source of never-ending wonder. The roaring economy was producing an endless array of bigger, faster, and slicker products. Bold advertisements promised that mechanization would soon transform American life. Toasters, irons, and vacuum cleaners would free women of their domestic labors. When Ruth came along, bigger and stronger and brassier than anyone who had ever played the game, he seemed to many Americans like another of these fabulous innovations. There was no telling what he could do.

Never before had one man so radically changed the way a game was played and so thoroughly energized its fans. Michael Jordan, sixty-five years later, would elevate basketball with his explosive leaps and gyrating dunks, but he would be preceded by incremental reformers such as Julius Erving and George Gervin. Muhammad Ali would bring a combination of style, speed, and power to heavyweight boxing, but his gifts would be rare, not revolutionary. Ruth, on the other hand, was doing things no one had foreseen. In 1919, he hit a record-breaking twenty-nine home runs. The next year, when he hit fifty-four — thirty-five more than his nearest competitor — baseball had been remade in the Babe's image. As he stepped into the batter's box, he joked with the umpire and took a few practice swings, giving the crowd time to adore him and the opposing pitcher more time to fret. When he connected for a homer, the ball floated high in the air, giving fans more time to stare in awe. The Babe would chuckle and tip his cap as he rounded the bases. He was the sport's first showman, the first to fully appreciate that sporting events produced not just winners and losers, but also stars — and that stars could be winners even when their teams lost. Young men with dreams of playing professional baseball, if they were smart, started swinging for the fences. So what if they struck out? No one struck out more than the Babe.

Ruth not only changed the approach of young athletes; he also changed how coaches and scouts assessed talent. They began paying more attention to some of the lumbering men who might previously have been left to football. To Henry Louis Gehrig, seventeen years old and still very much under his mother's watch, Babe Ruth became an unlikely but powerful role model.

Gehrig's mother wanted him to be a collegian — or a "collision," as she pronounced it. But Gehrig now was obsessed with baseball, so he began looking at colleges with strong baseball programs. Dartmouth and the University of Pennsylvania were high on his list. But Christina wasn't ready to let her son leave town.

On Thanksgiving Day, 1920, Commerce High School met DeWitt Clinton High School in a football game played at Columbia University's South Field. More than 10,000 fans overflowed the bleachers. Sitting high above the field that day were

Robert W. Watt, Columbia's graduate manager of athletics, and Frank "Buck" O'Neill, the university's football coach. The game was a dud, Clinton winning easily. Yet Watt and O'Neill focused their attention on a member of the Commerce team, a well-built young man with light-brown hair poking out from beneath his brown leather helmet. He seemed to be everywhere — tackling, running with the ball, even punting. O'Neill asked Watt if he knew the kid's name. Watt looked at his program and said it was Gehrig. The name should have registered with Watt. A few years earlier, when Watt was a student, he'd hired Christina Gehrig to clean his fraternity house. Lou Gehrig had probably washed Watt's dishes and wiped down the tables where he'd eaten dinner. Now, the name didn't mean a thing to him.

When the game was over, Watt and O'Neill crossed the field and talked to the young man. Heinrich Gehrig, who had been in the stands, joined them and reminded Watt of the family's connection to Columbia. As a result, Gehrig never visited the other schools that might have offered him athletic scholarships. He graduated from Commerce on January 27, 1921, and in February he enrolled in Columbia's extension program. He needed the extension program, in all likelihood, because he lacked some of the high school credits required of Columbia's freshmen. In the extension program, he completed courses in general chemistry, elementary algebra, intermediate German, and literature and composition.

When the weather warmed, he began practicing with the school's baseball team. On April 5, Columbia played an exhibition game against the Hartford Senators, a team of minor-league professionals from the Class A Eastern League. Gehrig, wearing a sweatshirt instead of a proper baseball uniform, smashed two home runs. The second shot, according to *The Hartford Times*, "went sailing out over the enclosure past a big sundial and almost into the School of Mines. It was a mighty clout and almost worthy of Babe Ruth's best handiwork."

That spring, scouts for the New York Giants tried to persuade Gehrig to quit college and jump to the big leagues. Gehrig wasn't sure. His mother wanted him to get an education. The scouts urged him at least to attend a tryout, promising that the legendary manager of the Giants, John McGraw, would be there to watch him play. Gehrig reached the Polo Grounds at eleven in the morning. It was probably the first time he had ever stepped into the dugout or onto the field. He stared out to the "George Burns bleachers," at the ornate façade that rimmed the roof, at the seemingly endless rows of empty seats.

McGraw was a stumpy and pale Irishman. He had black eyes and black hair. Perched on a dugout step, gazing out from beneath the brim of a cap, he looked like a stern general commanding his troops. He was the sporting world's Teddy Roosevelt, or perhaps its Napoleon — stubborn and cocky, a natural leader of men. McGraw's life had been filled with illness and despair. His mother and stepmother had both died young. So had four of his seven brothers and sisters. By the age of twelve he had essentially left both school and home to devote his life to baseball. By the time he came to manage the Giants, he had remade himself completely. He'd read Shakespeare and traveled the world. But nothing he encountered in his studies or travels enthralled him so much as the art of baseball. He probably knew the game better than any man alive. "Life without baseball had very little meaning to him," his wife Blanche said. "It was his meat, drink, his dream, his blood and breath, his very reason for existence." He was driven to win and pushed his players as hard as he pushed himself. That intensity made him one of the best-paid and best-loved men in the game, especially among the game's working-class fans, the immigrants who were fighting to find their place. To a young man like Gehrig, to try out for the great McGraw was to stand before baseball's preeminent deity. This was judgment day.

The tryout started well. Gehrig hit seven balls into the short right-field stands, according to a batboy who recalled the day years later in an interview with a newspaper reporter. Gehrig must have been feeling good as he grabbed his glove and jogged to first base. Almost immediately, though, a ground ball skipped through his legs. After only a few minutes, McGraw announced that he had seen enough of the first baseman.

McGraw was still wedded to the bunt and the steal. He wasn't looking for bruisers who couldn't field their positions, no matter how far they might hit the ball. He told one of his assistants to get rid of the kid. Years later, Gehrig would write that McGraw "did not give me too much attention, nor did he seem to be impressed with my possibilities."

Gehrig's muffed grounder turned into one of McGraw's most profound errors. He let the greatest first baseman of all time get past him. In the years ahead, McGraw would watch Gehrig's Yankees supplant his Giants as baseball's dominant team — but if he remembered giving the young man a tryout, he didn't talk about it much.

Gehrig never forgot. "I have often thought," he once said, "because of later developments, if he had given me a real opportunity to make good and taken pains with me, the baseball situation in New York perhaps would have been a lot different in the years that were to come."

The scouts were not about to challenge the great McGraw's judgment, but neither were they prepared to give up on this muscular prospect. They offered Gehrig a chance to join the Hartford Senators: They said he could play during the summer until he started at Columbia in the fall, with the understanding that he might get another chance to play for McGraw if he performed well. Gehrig agreed, and in so doing committed the most scandalous act of an otherwise squeaky-clean career. He almost certainly knew that college athletes were not allowed to play for money. The story of Eddie Collins was familiar to most baseball fans, and Gehrig identified Collins as one of his childhood heroes. Fifteen years before Gehrig arrived at Columbia, Collins had been the school's finest player. He would go on to a Hall of Fame career as a second baseman with the Philadelphia Athletics and the Chicago White Sox. But Collins played semiprofessional ball in the summer before his senior year at Columbia, using the name Sullivan in an attempt at camouflage, and it cost him his final year of college eligibility.

On June 2, 1921, the local papers in Hartford reported the arrival of a hard-hitting first baseman by the name of "Lefty Gehrig." But after the first mention, someone must have made it clear to the local papers that this player's stay in Hartford was meant to be hush-hush and that he would need a better alias. The next day, the papers reported that "Lew Lewis" had played first base for the Hartford Senators, going hitless with a sacrifice fly in four at-bats. "After he gets used to the surroundings, he may develop," *The Hartford Courant* noted. Gehrig banged a triple in his second game, then two more hits in the following contest. On June 8, when he lined a double off the "B" in the Buick sign on the right-field fence, the Babe Ruth comparisons surfaced again in the press.

While young Mr. Lewis proved himself a strong hitter, the rest of his game needed refinement. He flubbed some easy plays at first and took foolish chances running the bases. On June 10, with his team trailing in the bottom of the ninth, he was picked off first base, snuffing a potential rally. The Senators lost, 4-2.

A few days later, word of Gehrig's adventures in Hartford got back to New York. Andy Coakley, Columbia's baseball coach, was furious. He took the train to Hartford and told his first baseman that if he quit right away, his scholarship and college playing career might be salvaged. Gehrig agreed to come home. He was suspended from collegiate competition for one year. Later, he would claim that he didn't know he had done anything wrong when he signed on to play in Hartford. No one ever pressed him to explain why an innocent man would play under a pseudonym.

Gehrig's guiding force was his physical strength. Even at Columbia, surrounded by great books, sharp minds, and learned instructors, he was focused most on the power of his own body. He was an average student. He had not been raised on literature or even on the intellectual concepts connected with organized religion. There is no indication that he or his parents ever practiced as Lutherans. But his mother had pressed on him the importance of ambition and hard work, and his father had taught him at the *turnvereins* that some measure of confidence could be built through physical conditioning. Now more than ever, these two influences merged as Gehrig began to recognize the possibilities for success in his life. If college provided the vehicle, sports gave him the fuel.

Why didn't he quit school and turn pro after his Hartford escapade? For one thing, it wasn't clear that he was ready. He batted only .261 and hit no home runs in twelve games at Hartford. He still struggled to hit the curve, especially against left-handed pitching. His defense was sloppy, his baserunning atrocious. No doubt the Senators would have kept him for the season, but they were not about to offer him a big bonus. Neither were the Giants. Gehrig might have also felt he owed a debt of loyalty to Columbia, which had agreed to pay his tuition and had already paid for his classes in the extension program. He also didn't want to do anything to jeopardize his mother's job at the fraternity.

Christina and Heinrich had never seen a professional baseball game. They could tell that the sport was taken seriously in the United States simply by watching the huge crowds that swarmed through their neighborhood to get to the Polo Grounds and by the growing stash of press clippings concerning their son, which Christina dutifully saved. Still, Christina did not believe the game could offer a respectable career. She intended for her son to become something more serious, something more suitable for a second-generation

American. So Gehrig settled in for his first year as a college man.

By the age of nineteen, Gehrig was more handsome than ever. He kept his wavy hair cut short, which accentuated his strong jaw, deep dimples, and bright blue eyes. But while some of his more well-to-do classmates wore starched shirts and ties, Gehrig often dressed in baggy pants and a drab white shirt, topping off the outfit with a tattered gray sweatshirt. He didn't own a dinner jacket and still refused to wear a heavy coat, even on the coldest of winter days. Sam Dana, one of his classmates, met him on campus one freezing day and asked why Gehrig didn't have anything warmer to wear. "Oh, this is all I need," Gehrig said.

That fall, Gehrig pledged Phi Delta Theta. He had enough independence, at least, not to join Sigma Nu, the fraternity that employed his mother. He would eat dinner with the Phi Delts, then rush over to Sigma Nu to help his mother clear tables and wash dishes. No wonder he had trouble making friends. Columbia men came mostly from wealthy families and elite private schools, not from tenements. Their families employed women like Christina. Yet Gehrig aligned himself not with his frat brothers but with his mother, as he would most of his life. Gehrig was among the best-looking men on campus, and an athlete to boot, but he never went out on dates. "Handsome as he was, the campus flames simply couldn't afford to be seen with a boy who didn't even have decent clothes," wrote Paul Gallico, a Columbia graduate who was still hanging around the school when Gehrig attended.

He made little effort to make friends of either sex. He was Lou Gehrig, campus jock, as plain as the gray sweatshirt on his back.

"He was sorta shyish," Dana recalled.

One night in one of the campus dormitories, Dana, Walter Koppisch, and a few other members of the Columbia football team were shooting craps. Gehrig stood at the perimeter, watching over their shoulders.

"Would somebody lend me a quarter so I can get in the game?" he asked, according to Dana.

"I gave him a dollar," Dana said. "He put it in, faded it, and that was the end of the game."

Dana never asked Gehrig to pay him back, and Gehrig never offered.

Gehrig studied contemporary civilization, English literature, trigonometry, advanced German, and physical education in his freshman year. He flunked English and German. Though he and his parents were fluent in German, Gehrig probably didn't get much practice writing in that language. He had to take deficiency exams to get credit for the two failed classes and earned Cs on both exams. But in passing contemporary civilization he survived one of the most challenging college courses in the country. The syllabus alone ran 148 pages, covering everything from the Renaissance to the recent works of Sigmund Freud. In his sophomore year, Gehrig took more German, more English literature, and more physical education. He added navigational astronomy, business administration, and principles of economics. His grades have not been made public, but he did well enough at least to avoid taking more deficiency exams. Later in life, as he traveled the country by rail with the Yankees, he would sometimes excuse himself from his teammates and retire with a book. While news reporters would note that some of the team's more outgoing members had been spotted with beautiful young women and even the occasional Hollywood starlet, Gehrig, according to their reports, was seen with Nietzsche and Voltaire. Sportswriters had a tendency to exaggerate, however. Although Gehrig may have read philosophy from time to time, he preferred a good ten-cent western.

Though banned from competition during his first year at Columbia, Gehrig wasn't banned from practice. He spent every spare moment with the baseball and football teams. He fielded grounders and thrashed at curves and kicked punts and lobbed spirals. Still, he never felt the electrifying jolt of real competition. His life was a practice field. He bounced with enthusiasm when the team played an exhibition game, but when the games that counted got under way, he stood on the sidelines and watched.

With the onset of his sophomore year, he finally got his chance, beginning with football in the fall of 1922. "Buck O'Neill always wanted me to play in the line, at guard or tackle, but I wanted to play in the backfield, where I could carry the ball," Gehrig once said. "Carrying the ball was my idea of fun in football."

"Lou was stubborn and bull-headed," O'Neill told one writer. "He didn't like to do what he was told." In the end, it was O'Neill who backed down. Gehrig started at halfback, alongside Koppisch, the team's All-American captain. Gehrig proved to be a powerful runner, with surprising speed. When confronted with a tackler, he tended to bulldoze rather than dodge.

"I tackled him head-on in practice and

got a nice bone bruise," said Dana, a reserve running back. "Put me out of action awhile. After that I tried to tackle him from the side and go with him, let him have that extra yard or two."

Gehrig also played defensive tackle and punted. In his first game, a 48-3 victory over Ursinus College, he scored two touchdowns. The school's *Alumni News* noted: "Gehrig is the beef expert and has mastered the science of going where he is sent, for at least five yards. His plunges seem to carry force, for they invariably sent the defenders back when they tackled him." He may have been the school's finest athlete, but he somehow managed to make it seem utterly unglamorous. Yearbooks and newspapers routinely described him as "consistent."

In March, with the ground outside still frozen and spring not even teasing at its arrival, Gehrig ended his exile from college baseball and began practicing in the gymnasium with the Columbia team. He worked out mostly as a pitcher.

The spring of 1923 was a splendid time to live in New York. Men and women cranked their Victrolas and danced to "Tea for Two" and thumbed through magazine ads for new Maidenform bras. They managed with little effort to ignore the fact that the Ku Klux Klan was flexing its muscles in Indiana and Oklahoma and William Jennings Bryan was attacking evolution anywhere he could get an audience.

The most pleasant diversion of all in New York was the opening of Yankee Stadium at 161st Street between Jerome and River Avenues in the Bronx, directly across the river from the Polo Grounds. It was far and away baseball's greatest park, tailor-made to fit the game's greatest star, Babe Ruth. Colonels Tillinghast Huston and Jacob Ruppert had purchased the team in 1915, only about a year after its name was changed from the Highlanders to the Yankees. Once they had Ruth, they wanted a stadium big enough to host football games, boxing matches, and political rallies. It would be a profit center, not just a ballfield. Mass transit lines were already in place, and the Grand Concourse in the Bronx was beginning to develop into a sophisticated strip of homes and businesses, modeled after some of the broad streets of Europe. In selecting the Bronx, the team sent a message to fans in all five of the city's boroughs: If you want to see the Yankees, you'll have to come to us. And they did.

The stadium was spectacular. It had seating for about 58,000 fans, an elevator to carry team executives to their offices,

71

and an unprecedented sixteen "toilet rooms," eight for each gender. The most important feature of the field was its short right-field fence (294 feet, 9 inches), which ensured that there would be plenty of home runs for left-handed batters. It was no wonder that sportswriters would come to refer to it as "The House That Ruth Built."

Meanwhile, the men who actually built Yankee Stadium — Ruppert and Huston — were preparing to dissolve their partnership. Huston had never liked the team's manager, Miller Huggins, and had threatened publicly to fire him. Whenever Huggins and Ruth feuded, Huston sided with the slugger who had turned the Yankees into the nation's most profitable sporting franchise. But Ruppert, soft-spoken and stubborn, remained loyal to the manager. Ruppert wore his white hair slicked back neatly across the crown of his head. He had a great instinct for making money and no trouble devising ways to spend it. While his partner would use the newspapers to voice his complaints about Huggins, Ruppert kept quiet but refused to budge. Divorce became inevitable, but Huston and Ruppert agreed to keep their partnership intact until the new ballpark opened. Shortly after the start of the season, Ruppert purchased Huston's half of the team for about $1.25 million, roughly six times the amount Huston had paid eight years earlier.

On April 18, 1923, more than 74,000 fans crowded in and another 25,000 were turned away as the stadium opened its doors. John Philip Sousa led the Seventh Regiment Band in "The Star Spangled Banner," Governor Al Smith threw out the first pitch, and Ruth hit the first home run, a third-inning shot that landed ten rows deep in the bleachers. The Yanks won, 4-1 over the Boston Red Sox.

That same afternoon in Morningside Heights, Gehrig pitched for Columbia against Williams College. He had emerged that season as the team's best pitcher, but only because the rest of the staff was so shabby. Gehrig was a terrific hitter who needed work on the rest of his game. "Judged by college baseball standards," said Coach Coakley, "he was a fair outfielder and a good pitcher. In the outfield, he covered a lot of ground, got most of the drives hit his way, and had a strong arm. . . . As a pitcher, he didn't have much stuff, but he did have a better fast ball than most college pitchers and against certain teams he could just rear back and fire that fast ball all afternoon."

Against Williams that day, Gehrig's

fastball sizzled. He struck out seventeen, setting a school record. At bat he added a single and a double, driving in one run. Unfortunately, it was the only run Columbia scored, and the Lions lost, 5-1. Gehrig pitched in eleven of his team's nineteen games that season, winning six and losing four, with one no-decision. He struck out seventy-seven batters. He hit .444, with six doubles, two triples, and seven home runs. For decades, Columbia students and faculty would recall those home runs as if they had been rocket blasts. One bash reportedly broke a window in Hartley Hall, another was said to have smashed a sundial, dedicated by the class of 1885, 450 feet from home plate, and yet another was reported to have nearly knocked out a dean on the steps of the Low Memorial Library. South Field sat at the center of campus, between 114th and 116th Streets, bounded by Broadway and Amsterdam avenues. No doubt Gehrig's home runs shook the campus, but the damage assessments were almost certainly exaggerated.

At some point that spring, Coakley took Gehrig to see his first game at Yankee Stadium. The college star didn't recall any of the details of the game when interviewed years later. But it was the first time he saw Babe Ruth play, and it was that sight that made the most lasting impression. "And when I saw the way he swung, watched the perfect rhythm and timing," Gehrig said, "I made up my mind that there was one man to pattern after. I learned a lot from Babe Ruth in that one day."

But Babe Ruth was not the most important Yankee in Lou Gehrig's life, at least not yet. That honor would belong to a retired catcher named Paul Krichell, who appeared in only eighty-seven games in two seasons with the St. Louis Browns and compiled a lifetime batting average of .222. His most memorable performance was also his most embarrassing: In the fifth inning of a game against the Tigers, on July 4, 1912, he let Ty Cobb steal second, third, and home. After that, Krichell bounced around the minor leagues for a few years and coached one season for the Red Sox. In 1920, when Ed Barrow joined the Yankees as the team's general manager, he hired Krichell as one of his scouts.

Krichell began the spring of 1923 in New Orleans, watching the Yankees perform their spring training drills. He didn't have to go to New Orleans each spring, but it helped him do his job. He liked to hear the first pitches of a new season smacking the soft leather of the catchers' mitts. Sometimes he would crouch and catch a few himself, just to stay in shape and to remember what a good fastball looked and felt like. And he liked to see how some of the boys he had scouted in seasons past were holding up against big-league competition. When the Yankees broke camp and went north, Krichell did the same. He would scan the papers in New York every day and pick the games he wanted to see. He scouted not only college ball but also high school and semi-pro leagues. He went anywhere the railroads did.

Scouting was a wearisome business. Men such as Krichell traveled thousands of miles, stayed in dreary motels, ate in greasy diners, and watched hundreds of meaningless baseball games — all in the hopes of finding one good player, one shining nugget of gold. Find that player and you keep your job. Come up empty and you're finished. Krichell was one of the lucky ones. He would stay on the Yankee payroll for decades and would help deliver Tony Lazzeri, Mark Koenig, Leo Durocher, Phil Rizzuto, Vic Raschi and Whitey Ford. But at this point in his career he was still just a bush-beater among bush leaguers, trying to prove that he knew what he was doing.

On April 26, Krichell took the train to New Brunswick, New Jersey, to watch Columbia play Rutgers University. He knew little about either team. He happened to catch the same train as the Columbia squad, and he settled into a rear seat next to Andy Coakley for the short ride. Coakley, too, had struggled in the major leagues, pitching for the Philadelphia Athletics, the Cincinnati Reds, the Chicago Cubs, and the Yankees, compiling a record of 58–59, before quitting to become a coach. He knew that he didn't have much of a team at Columbia that year, so he was surprised to see the scout. As the train clattered south, the two men talked. Gehrig's name came up right away. Coakley described him as a left-handed pitcher who could hit — which was a bit like saying Charlie Chaplin was a composer and arranger who also made funny movies. Fortunately, Krichell had a chance to see for himself. Gehrig hit two homers in three at-bats against Rutgers that day. He played right field for the first time all year and looked uncomfortable on at least two of the three fly balls hit his way. But Krichell didn't care. That night, he phoned Barrow and announced that he had discovered the next Babe Ruth.

"I had a lot of confidence in Krichell," Barrow wrote in his autobiography, "but I thought he was going a bit overboard."

To confirm his instinct, the scout showed up at South Field for Columbia's next game, against New York University. Gehrig hit one of those homers that people would talk about for years, a shot that reportedly touched down on 116th Street and bounced out of sight. He went 2-for-3 and pitched a complete game, striking out eight in a 7-2 win.

Krichell wasted no more time. He chased down Gehrig after the game and asked him to show up the next morning at Barrow's Yankee Stadium office. When Gehrig arrived, Barrow offered him a contract. This time, it didn't take much to persuade the college sophomore to leave Columbia. He had made a few friends but felt no attachment to the school, and it was clear he was not destined for academic excellence. More important, his mother and father were sick at the time and unable to work. By some accounts, his mother was recovering from pneumonia. His father's illness was vague, as usual. In any case, the family needed money. Barrow offered $400 a month, or about $1,200 for the remainder of the 1923 season, plus a $1,500 signing bonus. It was a good deal, not a great one, at least by baseball standards. But for the Gehrig family, it was a life-altering payday. Campus legend has it that Gehrig consulted one of his professors, Archibald Stockder of the business school, before making his decision final. Stockder reportedly took a quick look

78

at Gehrig's grades and advised him to play ball.

Gehrig signed his first contract on April 30, 1923. His family would never be poor again. When Krichell died in 1957 at the age of seventy-four, he was remembered as the scout who discovered Lou Gehrig.

CHAPTER 4

THE BEHEMOTH
OF BING

Monday afternoon, June 11, 1923, was cool, but carried a strong hint of the long summer days to come. Lou Gehrig, toting his cleats and glove, traveled from his apartment in Morningside Heights to the Bronx. The streets around Yankee Stadium were clean and quiet. The ballpark gleamed like a giant sandcastle. The Yanks were scheduled to play the Indians that afternoon, but fans would not begin to arrive for hours.

Paul Krichell and Andy Coakley were waiting at the stadium to greet the newest Yankee. Gehrig, approaching his twentieth birthday, was stepping into the world of adults now, and Krichell and Coakley were tagging along to help ease the way — and, perhaps, to take some of the credit for having delivered him. The Yankees, after all, were not just any adults. "These were rough guys," recalled Bill Werber, a Duke University graduate who joined the team a few years after Gehrig. "They were swash-buckling, tobacco-chewing, cursing tough-guys. They were farmers, country boys." And they could be rough on rookies — particularly collegians.

Krichell led the way to the clubhouse, which looked like a partially finished base-ment, with wood floors, simple stools, tall metal lockers, and a couple of long tables used by the trainers for rubdowns. It smelled of talcum powder and tobacco smoke. Sunlight filtered in through streaky windows. The players were lounging in front of their lockers, slowly changing out of street clothes and into their uniforms, which were white with blue pinstripes. The interlocking "NY" on the chest and the numbers on the back had not yet been added. Bob Meusel, Joe Bush, Aaron Ward, and Everett "Deacon" Scott were playing cards in one corner. Babe Ruth sat closest to the door, half-dressed, oiling his glove. Miller Huggins, the manager, was in his office, sitting in front of a bat-tered rolltop desk. These were the men who would become Gehrig's second family and shape much of his adult life. They would teach him — or at least try to teach him — how to drink, seduce women, conduct interviews with the media, handle his finances, play cards, tell jokes, sign autographs, and doff his cap to the crowd after a big home run.

Huggins was all wrinkles and bones. He was overanxious and underfed, a victim of chronic insomnia. His false teeth fit him poorly. He looked like hell and felt worse most of the time. He'd grown up poor and gone to college, same as Gehrig. Huggins had a degree in law from the University of Cincinnati, which he had earned in his spare time while playing second base and batting leadoff for the Reds. As a player, he had been one of the smallest men in the league — 5 feet 4 inches and no more than 145 pounds — but he almost never backed down from a fight or a challenge. He played thirteen seasons in the big leagues, with the Reds and the Cardinals, batting .265 and hitting nine home runs. He drew a lot of walks and stole a lot of bases, earning a reputation as one of the scrappiest leadoff hitters of the dead-ball era. He managed the Cardinals for a few years, then took over the Yankees in 1918.

When Ruth joined the team two years later, he and Huggins clashed almost immediately. Huggins had no patience for baseball's biggest showboat. Ruth, who must have felt as if he were back at St. Mary's orphanage, saw no reason to be bossed around and nagged by a tightly wound disciplinarian. Like Ahab and the whale, or Billy Martin and Reggie Jackson, these two were destined to torment each other for years.

When the high-priced Yankees fell short of the pennant in 1920 and then lost to the Giants in the World Series the following year, Ruth began pushing for Huggins's removal. It was no surprise that most New York fans sided with the Babe. Huggins wasn't going to win any popularity contests, but he held on to his job courtesy of Colonel Jacob Ruppert. Even so, the steady diet of criticism and complaint seemed to eat away at the lining of his stomach. Even when his teams were winning, he worried almost constantly. He paced his hotel room when the Babe missed curfew. He bribed hotel clerks for information on his players' whereabouts. In a way, he had it worse than Ruth's wife, because Helen Ruth no longer seemed to care. The Babe was blessed with size, athletic grace, and a certain rough charm — all the things Huggins lacked — and the manager couldn't stand to see so much of it wasted. Huggins expected his players to show some respect, even fear, regardless of the fact that he looked so worn and weak.

Though it was early in the workday when Gehrig appeared in his office, Huggins had the look of a man who'd been through extra innings. He had just turned forty-five, but to Gehrig he probably seemed ancient.

The manager didn't bother to get out of his seat to greet his new player. He just looked up, said hello, and told Gehrig to go get a uniform.

As Gehrig left, Huggins chatted with Coakley. The men had been teammates for three years in Cincinnati. Huggins asked the Columbia coach if Gehrig was Jewish. The Yankees had Germans, Italians, and Irishmen on the roster. They would have liked a player to attract more of the city's Jewish population. But Coakley said Gehrig was German, not Jewish.

Doc Woods, the team's trainer, walked Gehrig through the humid clubhouse and introduced him to Ruth. The men shook hands; then Gehrig put on his uniform, hitched his black socks up to his knees, and tied the laces on his cleats. Huggins came out of his office and found the kid all alone, awaiting instructions.

Come on, Huggins said, follow me.

They marched down a long concrete corridor, Gehrig's metal spikes clacking, into the Yankee dugout. As he climbed the short set of steps onto the field for the first time, Gehrig gazed out at the bright green grass, the great white brow of battlement rimming the grandstand, the American flag far off in center field. Yankee Stadium's playing field had been built below street level, so that a player standing in the dugout felt as if he were at the base of a canyon, the grandest canyon in all of baseball. Even veteran players stepping onto the field for the first time often caught their breath.

As Gehrig trailed Huggins onto the field, Coakley found a seat in the stands behind home plate. Some of the Yankee players had taken their positions. They were scooping ground balls out of the dirt and circling under fly balls, practicing their throws and working on their footwork for double plays. Watching from behind the batting cage, getting ready to hit, were Ruth and third baseman Joe Dugan. Every few seconds, a cracking sound pierced the air and echoed among the empty seats. It was the sound of Wally Pipp, the first baseman, taking batting practice, spraying line drives around the field.

The story of what happened next may be apocryphal. Though it has been repeated in books and articles about Gehrig, its source is unclear, and it contains a hint of that too-good-to-be-true quality that infused a good deal of sports journalism in the 1920s and afterward.

"Get a bat," Huggins reportedly told the new arrival.

He got one and carried it to home plate. In the 1920s, most professional ballplayers favored big, heavy bats. The one Gehrig grabbed was probably thirty-six inches long and between forty and forty-four ounces, typical for big leaguers. He wrapped his palms around the handle of the bat, stepped into the batter's box and dug in.

The men who throw batting practice are baseball's humble servants. They serve up fastballs the way a waitress serves up steak — right down the middle of the plate. The name of this particular batting-practice pitcher has been forgotten, but by all accounts he did his job well. He started Gehrig with a juicy fastball. When Gehrig didn't swing, the pitcher threw another. Gehrig still didn't move. A third pitch whizzed by. Then a fourth. He should have creamed them all. Instead, the balls smacked against the screen and rolled around in the dust behind home plate.

Gehrig's fears usually disappeared when it came time to hit. In this case, however, his anxiety might have been a result of the bat he'd chosen. When a baseball player gets ready to hit, he usually checks to make sure the insignia of the bat's manufacturer — "Louisville Slugger," in most cases — faces either straight up or down, not out at the pitcher or back toward the catcher. Hitters believe that wooden bats break more easily if the bat isn't held properly. So as Gehrig stood in the batter's box and rotated the bat, he might have noticed the name etched in script at the fattest part of the barrel: "George 'Babe' Ruth." Most ballplayers are finicky about their bats, and Ruth was famously so. During some seasons, he notched lines in the barrel whenever he hit home runs. He liked to rub the wood with an animal bone to make its surface smoother and harder. The last thing Gehrig wanted to do was take a swing and risk breaking his idol's bat.

"Hit the ball," one of the Yankees shouted.

Another juicy fastball approached, as sweet as the others. This time Gehrig did swing, lining what would have been a solid single to right field. He hit a few more line drives. The bat didn't break. Then he found his range. Huggins, Ruth, and the others watched as Gehrig stepped into each pitch, his hips, torso, and shoulders rotating in a compact motion, weight shifting from left foot to right. Shots started clanging off the seats into the right-field bleachers. They were different from the long drives Babe Ruth usually hit. Ruth's homers were moon shots. Gehrig's were bullets. They had a smaller arc and hit their targets more rapidly. Gehrig had settled into a groove when Huggins interrupted.

"That's enough," he said.

Gehrig returned the bat to the back of

the cage, grabbed his glove, and ran to the outfield to shag fly balls.

Newspaper stories the next day made note of Gehrig's workout but revealed none of its details. Waite Hoyt, the team's best pitcher, recalled the day of Gehrig's first appearance with the Yankees in one interview. "We all knew that he was a big-league ballplayer in the making," Hoyt said. "Nobody could miss him." But he either wasn't asked or didn't comment on the batting practice story.

Huggins invited Gehrig to stick around for the game that afternoon. The young man sat in the shade of the dugout, kept to himself, and watched the Yankees lose, 4-3. Ruth walked four times in the game. The Indians never gave him any good pitches. They preferred to take their chances with the next batter in the lineup, Pipp, a capable hitter but not one who often launched balls over outfield walls. Pipp was only thirty years old. In 1922, he had hit .329 with nine home runs and ninety runs batted in. He hit nicely in the clutch and fielded his position as well as almost anyone in the game. Gehrig wasn't ready for a starting job. So for several days he sat on the bench, watching. Huggins wanted him to learn some of the game's finer points and to understand the intense level at which professional ball was played.

"Did you ever hear the story of the first time Pop and Mom came to see me play at the Stadium?" Gehrig once asked a journalist. "Neither had ever been to a ballgame before. I forgot to tell them to come early [for batting practice], as there was nothing for me to do after the regulars took their positions. Pop and Mom went in on the passes I procured for them; they saw a lot of ballplayers running around, but not their Louie. When I came home for dinner, they asked me, 'Well, where were you?' I had to reply, 'I was sitting on the bench.' 'What kind of bummer's game is that where they pay a young man good money to sit on a bench?' stormed my father."

In 1923, the Yankees were on their way to their first World Series triumph. Ruth hit forty-one homers and batted .393, still a record average for a Yankee. Pipp, batting behind Ruth, hit .304, with six home runs. Gehrig wasn't needed yet, but he did get a few chances to play that season. Four days after his batting practice performance, on June 15, he filled in for Pipp in the ninth inning of a game against the St. Louis Browns. He fielded an easy ground ball and stepped on first base for the final out of the game. He made another late-inning appearance two days later, as the Yankees trounced Detroit. The day after that, June 18, he got his first chance to hit. With the Yankees down by eight runs in the bottom of the ninth against the Tigers, Huggins sent Gehrig into the game as a pinch hitter for Aaron Ward. Facing Ken Holloway, a right-handed rookie, Gehrig struck out.

The Yankees were shredding their American League competition. Pipp, perhaps inspired by the presence of Gehrig on the bench, played some of the best ball of his life. Ruth, meanwhile, was both spectacular and spectacularly erratic. When he failed to show up for an exhibition game, he told Huggins that he'd been in a car accident. Then he changed his story and said he'd been stuck in traffic. Life with the Yankees was never dull. Gehrig must have been frustrated by his lack of action, but he was lucky to be along for the ride.

On July 7, in the ninth inning of a game against the St. Louis Browns, with the Yanks ahead by ten runs, Gehrig came in to pinch-hit for the pitcher. Facing Elam Vangilder, a pretty tough right-hander, Gehrig swung and smashed a long line drive that caromed off the fence in right field. The right fielder came up with the ball quickly and held Gehrig to a single, his first big-league hit.

Huggins expected almost nothing of the rookie. Even when the Yankees had huge leads against hapless opponents, the manager usually kept him on the bench. He wanted to give the young first baseman a small taste of the big leagues, just enough to whet his appetite. Gehrig paid attention and did what he was told. But he failed in one critical way during his first tour with the Yankees. He made little effort to get to know his teammates or the reporters who covered the team. When members of the Yankees teased him, he shrank. When members of the media lobbed questions, he froze. It was the start of a pattern he would follow for much of his career. He probably didn't intend to distance himself, but it happened anyway, mostly because he was too insecure to assert himself. Teammates decided he was a nice fellow but immature and dull, and newspaper reporters concluded he had nothing that would jazz up their columns.

On August 1, Huggins decided Gehrig had spent enough time on the bench. He sent him to Hartford, the scene of his collegiate indiscretion, to let him finish the season in the minor leagues. *The New York Times* noted that the young man "known as the Babe Ruth of the Eastern college circuit" would "probably be benefitted by some seasoning in the minors."

Paddy O'Connor, the new manager of

the Hartford Senators, was a small, wiry man. He was forty-four years old and kept himself in great shape. The hard lines on his face and his jutting jaw made him look as if he were always spoiling for a fight. By nature, though, O'Connor was a patient person. As a big-league catcher he hadn't amounted to much, but he had developed into a fine coach. "Paddy always took a fatherly interest in me," Gehrig once said, "and was always giving me good advice both about baseball and about the way a ballplayer should conduct himself off the field."

The Yankees instructed O'Connor to play Gehrig every day at first base, regardless of how he performed. He was considered an important prospect but also a raw one, and team officials wanted him to get as much experience as possible. Strictly because of his reputation and his stout frame, Gehrig was inserted as the fourth hitter in the Senators' batting order, the slot usually reserved for the team's top home-run hitter. (Babe Ruth was an exception to the rule, batting third, in large part because fans wanted to see him come to the plate in the first inning, and also because he hit for such a high average.)

Gehrig doubled in his first game with the Senators and homered over the left-field fence in his second. In his third game he committed two errors, but neither was costly, and he made up for them with a single and a long home run to center. After his tenth game, in which he went 4-for-4 with two home runs, a double, and a single, *The Hartford Courant* referred to him as "the stealer of Babe Ruth's thunder, the Eastern's Behemoth of Bing, Sultan of Swat and Kleagle of Klout."

The next day, though, the Behemoth began to blunder. From August 12 to August 21, he played in eleven games and managed only eight hits, none of them home runs. As his batting average fell, so did his spirit. "I couldn't hit, I couldn't field," Gehrig recalled. He grew homesick and considered quitting. While attending Columbia and warming the bench for the Yankees, he had lived with his parents. His mother had cooked and cleaned for him. Now, for the first time, he had no one to take care of him, no one to give his ego a boost. He had to adjust to living in a community of men — rough men who wrestled and cursed and idled in speakeasies. To make matters worse, he joined the team in mid-season, after most of the others had made friends and settled into their social habits.

"I've never seen anyone suffer so much," said Harry Hesse, an outfielder with the Senators that year. "He took everything to heart. He was a guy who needed friends but didn't know how to go about getting them. He'd get low and sit hunched over and miserable, and it was pretty tough to pull him out of it."

Gehrig had little money, another factor that might have kept him from socializing with his teammates. Whatever he earned each week went to his parents. Though he needed new clothes, he didn't buy any. Teammates, embarrassed by the sight of him, were relieved when he put on his uniform each day. "He looked like a tramp," said Hesse.

When Paul Krichell heard that Gehrig was slumping and depressed, he took the train to Hartford and invited Lou to join him for a steak dinner at the Bond Hotel. The scout could see the young man's confidence was shot. By some accounts, Gehrig, famously incapable of holding his liquor, had started drinking to relieve his pain. He had gone hitless in four at-bats in the game Krichell had watched, and he brooded over his poor performance all during dinner.

There's no telling why a batter slumps. One day the ball looks as big as a grapefruit as it zips toward the plate; the next day it's small as a pea. One day he's locked in; the next he lifts his eyes at the last second before he swings. One day his head is blissfully clear; the next it's cluttered with useless thoughts — keep your hands back, wrists locked, elbows up, bat high, knees bent — and he's too busy thinking to take a good swing. Hitting a baseball — the most difficult act in all of sports, some say — can be as much a mental exercise as a physical one.

Baseball players have to get accustomed to failing, Krichell told Gehrig that evening. The best hitters in the game, he said, fail to get hits six or seven times out of every ten tries. Even Ty Cobb suffered slumps. But good hitters eventually start hitting again, and Krichell assured Gehrig that he was a very good hitter. He recommended one of Cobb's tricks — concentrate on hitting the ball as hard as possible back to the pitcher, or past him, but always toward the middle of the field. After dinner, Gehrig walked Krichell to the train station and thanked him for coming.

On August 22, Gehrig started crushing the ball again. Perhaps it was something Krichell said. Perhaps it was a matter of luck, or the law of averages. Perhaps he needed time to adjust to a more talented crop of pitchers than he had faced in college. Whatever the reason, he came through with twenty-two hits, including six home runs, in the next eleven games. "I decided not to quit after all," he said.

" 'Lou' is already much the hero with Hartford's Young America," *The Hartford Times* reported, "and there is usually quite a delegation of youngsters parked outside Gehrig's favorite eating place." Even as his slump ended, though, Gehrig continued to experiment with alcohol, according to an interview he gave years later. He began consorting with some of the older, wilder men on the team.

O'Connor, worried, invited his young star home for dinner one night. "Lou," he said, according to Gehrig's recollection, "you have a great career ahead of you. Nothing can stop you, except Lou Gehrig. That gang you're traveling with is poison. You can be a rich man. Baseball is full of opportunities. Six months of work, six months of ease, all for two hours of hustle an afternoon in 154 games. Think it over."

"I did think it over," Gehrig said. "I quit that gang."

He finished the season with a .304 batting average and twenty-four home runs in fifty-nine games. On September 20, after the Senators had wrapped up the league title, O'Connor let Gehrig pitch against the New Haven Profs. He threw a complete game, striking out two, walking six, and giving up nine hits, in a 6-4 win. On offense, he had a single and a triple in four trips to the plate. Reported *The Hartford*

Courant: "He has shown no evidence of swell head and has proven one of the most popular players who ever performed here."

A few days after Gehrig's professional pitching debut, the Yankees invited him to finish the season in the big leagues. On September 26, with his team trailing Detroit in the eighth inning, Huggins decided to give Wally Pipp a rest, sending Gehrig to take his place at first base. In the second half of the inning, with the bases loaded and two outs, the rookie drilled a line drive over the head of Luzerne Atwell Blue at first base, driving in two runs and tying the game. Gehrig's heroics were quickly undone, though, when Joe Bush, the starting pitcher, gave up five runs in the tenth inning, losing the game for the Yanks.

Early the next morning, the players took the train to Boston for a game against the Red Sox. The Yankees had already clinched the pennant. Gehrig didn't expect to see more than a handful of at-bats in the season's four final contests, but he got a break. As Wally Pipp stepped off the train in Boston that morning, he wrenched his right ankle. By game time that afternoon, the ankle was stiff. Pipp was scratched, and Gehrig took his place in the starting lineup.

In the top half of the first inning, Babe Ruth smacked a deep drive and arrived, puffing for air, safely at third base. Gehrig stepped to the plate and stared out at the mound. One of the worst pitchers in the league, Wild Bill Piercy, stared back. The right-hander threw and Gehrig swung. He hit the ball solidly, dropped his bat, and hustled toward first base. As the white ball rose in an arc toward right field, he began to slow. He could see it was going to clear the fence. Ruth jogged home and waited at the plate to congratulate Gehrig on his first big-league homer.

While Pipp nursed his ankle, Gehrig kept killing the ball. The day after his home run, he banged three doubles off the left-field wall as the Yankees romped to a 24-4 win. In a doubleheader the next day, he had four more hits. Gehrig so impressed Huggins that the manager petitioned league officials for the right to add the rookie to his team's World Series roster. If the request had been granted, Huggins would have faced a difficult choice: Pipp's ankle had healed, but would Huggins dare take the red-hot Gehrig out of the lineup? Fortunately for Pipp, the league denied the Yankees' petition, saying the young first baseman had not been with the team long enough to qualify for post-season play. Some reports suggested that the league might have approved the request if not for the objections of John McGraw, whose Giants were meeting the Yankees in the World Series for the third straight time.

The Series opened on October 10. More than 55,000 fans packed Yankee Stadium. Just as he had on opening day, Jacob Ruppert turned away tens of thousands of fans. He looked out at his new stadium, considered the lost income represented by all those people pushing to get in, and announced that he would consider building an addition next year that would increase the capacity of his ballpark to 85,000. *The New York Times* printed a notice at the top of its front page asking readers not to telephone its offices for updates on the progress of the game because "to heed the overwhelming number of such inquiries would suspend other business."

Fortunately for telephone operators at *The Times*, the World Series was being broadcast by radio throughout much of the nation. KDKA in Pittsburgh had been first to broadcast a baseball game in 1921. The following year, New Yorkers who could afford a sixty-dollar Westinghouse radio were able to tune in to a regional broadcast of the World Series. Now, for the first time, the championship games were going out across much of the country. Fans heard the cries of vendors: "Cigars and cigarettes! Ice cold soda!" They heard the smack of horsehide on wood when a batter connected, and the collective gasp of the crowd as a well-struck ball took flight.

As in years past, a rotating group of newspaper writers had been hired to provide the play-by-play announcements. The men sat in box seats near the field, holding heavy microphones and offering the sparest possible description of events on the field. "Ruth hits a single to right field," Grantland Rice might say, followed by a long stretch of dead air. The sportswriters used radio the same way they used their pencils and scorecards, to record all the necessary details and none of the atmosphere. They saved their creative flourishes for their newspaper readers.

But in 1923, a former concert singer named Graham McNamee was hired to sit beside the sportswriters and liven up their broadcasts. McNamee had a deep, rich voice, and he loved to ramble. He didn't know much about baseball, but he had a terrific eye for detail, and he described what he saw in marvelous terms. When frustrated fans put their fists through their straw hats, when Gloria Swanson arrived at her seat wrapped in ermine, when John McGraw flashed all but invisible signals to his players, McNamee called it as he saw it. He was radio's first color commentator. "The crowd is ready, yowling, and howling," he said in one typically excited moment. "I never heard such a crowd in my life. . . . Strike one!"

McNamee gave baseball a common language. He took the game out of the ballpark and into homes and made it a part of the sound of American life, so much so that a New Yorker could walk down the street without missing a pitch as McNamee's voice boomed from window after window. In the process, he became a celebrity — bigger perhaps than all but Ruth. When he dropped a Thermos full of coffee and stained his suit while on the air, the incident made news the next day. Naturally, the sportswriters were jealous, and they tried, in vain, to point out that the broadcaster often seemed to mistake right-handed hitters for left-handed hitters, couldn't keep track of which man was at bat, and put runners on the bases when there were none. "I don't know which game to write about," Ring Lardner wrote after one World Series game, "the one I saw today or the one I heard Graham McNamee announce as I sat next to him at the Polo Grounds."

The 1923 World Series was a beauty. Casey Stengel hit two homers for the Giants, and Ruth hit three for the Yankees. After six games, the Yankees had their first championship. But it was McNamee, his voice full of exuberance and delight, his words traveling to corners of the nation that had never seen or heard a big-league game, who emerged as the most valuable player. He gave the nation one of its first shared experiences and made the game sound like fun — full of glamour, action, and bigger-than-life heroes.

In the coming seasons, local radio stations would begin broadcasting their teams' regular-season games. Before long, baseball and radio would become great and inseparable partners, like sausage and mustard. As a result, the men who played the game became national celebrities to a degree never before possible. Lou Gehrig arrived just in time to reap the rewards. Fans in the 1920s and 1930s got to know their favorite players as much through the radio as the newspaper, and Gehrig presented himself much better on the air than in print. Radio broadcasters for the most part didn't do post-game interviews. They didn't hang around the locker room to fish for colorful quotes. All they did was describe the action — and Gehrig was the ultimate man of action, in the game every day, playing hard, playing hurt, and hitting the ball with a piercing clap.

CHAPTER 5

GOODBYE, MR. PIPP

The sunshine and glory of summer faded fast for Gehrig. As the grass turned brown and autumn leaves grew stiff and fell, his mood darkened. He took a job in the fall of 1923 as an office clerk at the New York Edison Company — in part because his family needed the money, and in part because he feared the Yankees might lose interest in him at any moment.

He should have known better. He should have known that Jake Ruppert and Miller Huggins viewed him as one of their brightest young discoveries, and a bargain, too. If he'd made any close friends on the team, they probably would have told him as much. Yankee management fully intended to resign him, but they were hoping to do so at the lowest possible price. In the meantime, it didn't hurt to keep him guessing.

"The fall dragged along," Gehrig recalled in an interview eight years later, "and I didn't hear anything from the Yankees. I didn't know how baseball business was done or when contracts were sent out. Now and then I'd see in the papers that this club or that had signed some of its players and I began to wonder if the Yanks were going to sign me again. . . . I began to pay more attention to my work with the Edison Company and to hope for a raise."

As for baseball, he said, "I figured I'd had my fling."

Finally, at the end of January, the mail brought a new contract, offering him $2,750 for the 1924 season. Gehrig was so pleased that the thought of asking for more money never seriously occurred to him. "I signed it and sent it back in a hurry for fear they'd change their minds," he said. For the first time, though certainly not the last, the Yankees took advantage of Gehrig's timidity and his overarching desire to please. Ed Barrow, the team's general manager, knew that several big-league clubs had expressed interest in trading for Gehrig. If the first baseman had appreciated his value he might have negotiated a better deal. But he was not the sort to spy an opening and make a run for it. His approach was to tiptoe, taking care not to step too quickly and fall.

On the last day of February, Gehrig and six other Yankees boarded a railroad car for New Orleans. Paul Krichell caught the same train. Gehrig had twelve dollars in his pocket as he departed for his first spring training. The cash would have to last about a month, because the Yankees didn't pay their players until the start of the regular season.

Mardi Gras season was under way when they arrived, and rooms were in short supply at the Bienville Hotel, where the Yanks stayed. So the young first baseman was assigned a cot in a room occupied by two marginal members of the team — Benny Bengough and Hinkey Haines. None of them was in a position to complain. Bengough was a catcher of no great ability. He was five years older than Gehrig and couldn't afford to waste much more time kicking around in the minor leagues. But he was a sweet guy, chatty and full of laughs, and pitchers liked working with him. To break the tension in a tight game, he would sometimes take off his cap, shake his head, and run his fingers across his shiny, bald scalp, as if he were caressing a head full of glorious locks. That always cracked them up. If he had any chance to make the team, it was mostly on the force of his personality. Babe Ruth took an instant liking to Bengough, which meant his social calendar that spring would be packed solid, if nothing else. Haines, a twenty-five-year-old outfielder, had appeared in twenty-eight games for the Yankees the year before, batting .160. He was well liked, too, but he had even less chance than Bengough of gaining a spot in the club. To the twenty-year-old Gehrig, these two older men seemed like seasoned veterans. As they sat on their beds and talked about all the cities they'd seen, all the women they'd met, and all the gin they'd drunk, Gehrig listened, slack-jawed. "He was a fine boy," Bengough said of Gehrig. "He was very congenial to everyone. You never heard him pop off or get mad or anything."

During the first days of spring training, the Yankees practiced from eleven in the morning to one in the afternoon at Heinemann Park. Then they would break for lunch. The food was free, but players were expected to tip the waitstaff. When Gehrig found out, he began skipping the meal to avoid leaving the gratuity. Late in the afternoon, some Yankees would head to the track to gamble. Others played golf. At night, they would descend in force on the French Quarter. Some peeled off to movie theaters, others to dance halls, others still to the Tango Belt, where prostitutes had taken refuge since Storyville had been shut down a few years earlier. The beer flowed, the music roared, and just about anything could be arranged for a man who had money. Which Gehrig didn't, of course. Even if he had, he probably wouldn't have known what to do with it. He didn't drink much, and he continued to show no strong interest in women. So he left his hotel room each evening just to give teammates the impression he had plans. He would walk the city's crooked streets alone.

By some accounts, Gehrig went looking for a part-time job in New Orleans but couldn't find one. Sometimes he would head to the YMCA on St. Charles Avenue for a swim. On one occasion, a couple of the sportswriters invited themselves along. Gehrig welcomed them. But when he discovered that they intended to take a taxi to the Y, he excused himself, saying he had forgotten that he needed to write a letter to his mother. Taxis were not in his budget.

Most of his teammates paid no attention to the strange behavior, but George Pipgras, another one of the new Yankees, noticed that Gehrig seemed unhappy. He suggested they go out for a nice dinner. It isn't clear if Pipgras offered to treat or if he persuaded Gehrig to dip into his wallet. The latter seems unlikely. In any case, the men picked a restaurant in the French Quarter. But when they walked in, they spotted Joe Dugan and Whitey Witt, two Yankee veterans, seated at a corner table.

The younger men froze. "Lines were sharply drawn between the regulars and the rookies in those days," Gehrig later recalled. On the field, veterans let the rookies know their place, cursing and teasing and pushing them aside at batting practice. It was a friendly, boys-will-be-boys sort of teasing, but it had a rough edge to it. Gehrig perhaps took more abuse than most because he seemed somewhat slow-witted, unable to fire back when a wisecrack was shot his way, and he was a college boy, to boot. Given the environment, Gehrig and Pipgras didn't think it was wise to dine in the same restaurant as Dugan and Witt. They took off.

Gehrig did find at least one willing mentor that spring, a coach named Charley O'Leary, who agreed to come to the ballpark at ten in the morning to begin practicing with him before the veterans arrived. For all his doubts, Gehrig always believed in his ability to improve his skills by sheer repetition. O'Leary, a former shortstop, was a stocky man who got on well with everyone. He tutored Gehrig on the finer points of playing first base and threw him so many batting-practice pitches that Gehrig didn't care if he got edged out later in the day by more established players.

Wally Pipp worked with Gehrig, too, even though he knew he was helping the man who might eventually take his job. Both men were German-American, and both had gone to college. They might have become friends if not for the fact that neither of them talked much. Tutoring Gehrig was the decent thing to do, and Pipp was a decent man.

One day that spring, Fred Clarke, a future Hall of Famer, dropped by Heinemann Park. Clarke had played major-league ball for twenty-one years and had managed for nineteen, retiring from the game in 1915, before the advent of the long-distance home run. He received a hero's welcome at the practice field and then settled in to watch from the sidelines as the Yankees went through their drills. In batting practice that day, Gehrig rattled the wooden fence with a few line drives and then fielded grounders and caught throws at first base until his jersey was soaked through with sweat. "I like that big first baseman," Clarke said. "I certainly like him about as well as any boy I've seen come up in a long time. He can whack that ball."

When spring training ended, the Yankees set off for a series of small-town exhibition games. The team's traveling secretary, Mark Roth, handed out meal money to each of the players still with the team. At last, Gehrig had some cash in his pocket —

about sixty dollars. "My first thought was to step out and spend some of it just to have a good time," he said, "and then I thought of how hard it was to string out that twelve dollars. I haven't spent any money foolishly since."

As the team's train hissed out of New Orleans, Gehrig should have been thrilled. He was a Yankee. But he didn't feel like one yet. He still felt like a picked-on rookie whose time with the team could end at any moment. At Columbia, he had been too poor and too poorly dressed to mesh with the student body. Now, some of his teammates mistook his nervous silence as an air of superiority.

"When I started the 1924 season I thought I was still far from being a regular," he said in a 1935 interview. "I realized I was still clumsy and had lots to learn about playing first base."

Barrow wanted to send Gehrig back to the minors for more seasoning — in Hartford; Atlanta; or St. Paul, Minnesota — but the general manager ran into a problem. In order for a team to cut a player from the big leagues and assign him to a minor-league squad, the player had to clear waivers. In other words, every team in the league had to waive its right to offer that player a new contract. Owners usually colluded in such matters, because they all needed the same favor at one time or another. But when Barrow tried to secure waivers for Gehrig, at least five teams refused. They were hoping the Yankees might be willing to let the young first baseman go. Barrow had no such intention, and it appeared for a time that Huggins might have to keep Gehrig on the major-league roster all year as a backup to Wally Pipp. Huggins thought about using Gehrig as a reserve outfielder. In April, after a long series of negotiations, Gehrig finally cleared waivers and was ordered to return to Hartford. If he couldn't be with the Yankees, at least he'd be a short train ride from home and working again with Paddy O'Connor.

He had one other incentive: James Clarkin, the owner of the Hartford Senators, had promised him a $1,500 bonus, payable in two installments, if he returned to the team in 1924. He packed and went north. "Miller Huggins believes that with another year in the minors Gehrig will be ready for serious business in the majors," *The Times* wrote on the occasion of his assignment.

Gehrig tore through the Eastern League. The day before his twenty-first birthday, he homered with the bases loaded for the first time as a professional. On his birthday, he hit a double, a triple, and a two-run

111

homer, as Hartford beat the Worcester Panthers, 9-8. The homer, according to *The Hartford Courant*, was a huge blast straightaway to center field, "clearing the heads of the boys who see the games from atop trucks on the shady side of the wall." It was his seventh homer in seven days. The next day, with no game on the schedule, he took the train to New York and celebrated his birthday with his mother and father.

By mid-summer, Gehrig was Hartford's most beloved athlete. *The Courant* began mythologizing the young man, saying that he learned to swing as a two-year-old, knocking down towers made of blocks; that he broke three windows at his elementary school by batting balls across the playground; that his home run at Wrigley Field for Commerce High had been the game winner; that he liked steak and movies; and that while he loved to sing, he couldn't carry a tune to save his soul. He was beginning to enjoy some of the pleasures of a slugger's life. On July 5, he ordered his first customized Louisville Slugger baseball bat from the Hillerich & Bradsby Co. It was thirty-five and a half inches long and weighed forty ounces, and it was cut in the style favored by Rogers Hornsby, the great second baseman for the St. Louis Cardinals.

Gehrig played 134 games that year for Hartford, batting .369, with thirty-seven home runs, thirteen triples, and forty doubles. Only his defense was less than big-league. First basemen, as a rule, are not the most athletic men on the diamond. They don't have to run as far or fast as outfielders. They don't have to jump and spin as gracefully as shortstops and second basemen. But they've got to be reliable. After the pitcher and catcher, no fielder handles the ball more than the first baseman. Gehrig understood the basics of his position, but he was clumsy. Cutoff plays baffled him. On ground balls to his right, he pursued too eagerly, roaming so far from first base that he couldn't get back in time to cover the bag if the second baseman fielded the ball. The toughest play of all for most left-handed first basemen is the backhanded catch, and Gehrig had more trouble with it than most. When the ball is thrown to the left of a left-handed first baseman, he must put his left foot on the base, turn his back to the infield, stretch his body in the direction of home plate, extend his gloved (right) hand, and peek over his right shoulder to watch the flight of the ball. As the batter barrels toward him, the first baseman has to catch the ball and then get out of the way.

Even when he made a play properly,

Gehrig often looked inelegant doing it. He had no trouble hitting, however. Standing at home plate with a ninety-mile-an-hour fastball screaming at him left no time for thought. It was all about reaction. Plays in the infield unfolded more slowly, and it took years of practice before he learned to operate strictly from muscle memory.

He committed twenty-three errors that season with Hartford, and for a short time O'Connor toyed with the idea of moving him to the outfield. But O'Connor knew the Yankee outfield was set with Ruth, Bob Meusel, and the rookie Earle Combs. Gehrig had a far better chance to break in at first base. O'Connor also knew the young man was emotionally fragile. A move to the outfield might have damaged his confidence. The Yankees decided to wait and hope that he would get the hang of first base. Once again, Huggins invited Gehrig to join the big-league team for the final weeks of the season.

This time, the Yankees were locked in a close race for the pennant. On September 19, as the team arrived in Detroit for a three-game series with Ty Cobb's Tigers, they were tied with the Washington Senators for first place. The Tigers, stuck in third place with almost no chance at the pennant, were determined to wreck the New Yorkers' ambitions. Cobb seemed to hate all opposing teams, but he had a special enmity for the Yankees. Approaching his thirty-eighth birthday, the Tiger outfielder and manager still believed baseball games were won by slashing and slicing and sliding. He believed in tight defense, the sacrifice fly, the bunt, the drag bunt, the fake bunt, the squeeze play, the steal, the delayed steal, the double steal, the fake steal, and the spikes-high slide. He believed that spitting and cursing and sneering gave him a psychological edge and that all it took was the slightest glimmer of fear to make an opponent crumble.

The week of the series with the Yankees, the *Detroit Times* printed a big picture of Cobb, hands apart, holding the bat as if ready to slap and run. The headline read, "20 Years in Game, He's Still Setting Records." The Yankees, meanwhile, were winning games with an entirely different style of play. Who needed all that scratching and scraping when a couple of big home runs would do the trick? Cobb was a master swordsman who was suddenly star- ing down the barrel of a newfangled weapon called the cannon. He was approaching the end of his career when Gehrig came along, offering the older man convincing evidence that Ruth had been no fluke. There would be a whole line of beefy home-run hitters trailing the Babe.

The Tigers won the first two games in the series, dropping the Yanks one game behind Washington. Cobb was playing like a young man again, singling, stealing bases, and taunting his opponents. The Yanks did not respond well to the pressure. Wally Pipp made two errors in one inning. Huggins lost his temper and got ejected from the second game. Ruth seemed to walk or strike out almost every time up.

In game three, the Yanks looked as if they'd come undone. Meusel misjudged a fly ball and watched it fall for two bases. Fred Hofmann, the catcher, misplayed a bunt by Cobb, turning what would have been a foul ball into a hit. Cobb went to third on a single. The next batter bunted, and when Hoyt tried to throw Cobb out at the plate, Cobb slid hard and knocked the ball out of Hofmann's mitt, scoring the first run of the game. When Tigers pitcher Earl Whitehill came to bat, Hoyt threw behind him, perhaps trying to hit him. The crowd screamed. Two hundred police on hand to control the crowd stood at nervous attention.

The Yanks trailed 4-1 in the eighth but had the bases loaded when Huggins sent in Gehrig to pinch-hit for Everett Scott. The Tigers responded by replacing Whitehill with a new pitcher, Hooks Dauss. Gehrig got a good pitch and slammed it sharply to right field for a hit, scoring two. But then he made a mistake. He turned too far rounding first and got caught off the base. Gehrig dashed back and forth between first and second, trying to avoid the tag, but he had no place to go. It was Cobb, sprinting in from center field, who finally made the putout. As he tagged Gehrig, he added a sharp insult.

Gehrig was steamed. Though he had no one to blame but himself, he cursed at Cobb as he walked off the field. And he kept cursing as he reached the dugout. Umpire Bill Evans, who had been calling games for almost twenty years, turned to the bench and told Gehrig to pipe down. When the first suggestion failed, he walked from home plate to the dugout and gave Gehrig one more warning. Someone in the dugout should have told Gehrig that rookies were not supposed to act up. But by now he was out of control. The shouting continued and Evans ejected him from the game. The Yankees lost, 4-3.

It's not clear what happened next. Cobb wrote in his autobiography that Gehrig was still fuming after the game ended and came charging into the tunnel that led from the field to the clubhouse. Finding Whitehill there, Gehrig wrestled the Tiger pitcher to the ground. Ruth jumped in and grabbed Gehrig in a headlock, trying to calm the young man. Cobb said he came upon the commotion and tried to pull bodies off the pile. According to other accounts, Gehrig chased after Cobb, took a swing at him, and missed, landing on his skull and briefly losing consciousness. "Did I win?" he reportedly asked when he woke from the fight.

Newspaper accounts in New York and Detroit made no mention of the post-game brawl. Whatever happened, this much is certain: Gehrig overreacted. For the most part, he had performed well in his short stint with the Yankees, collecting six hits in twelve tries and playing without error at first base. But neither he nor the other Yankees had reason to celebrate. The Yanks finished the season two games behind the Senators. Cobb and the Tigers had spoiled their season.

For more than a year, Wally Pipp had been keeping a nervous eye on Gehrig. Everyone could see the kid had power, and everyone could see the Yankees had high hopes for the young man. In December of 1924, Gehrig worried that he might be traded to the St. Louis Browns for the thirty-two-year-old spitball pitcher Urban Shocker. He claimed years later that Huggins told him the trade was under consideration. In fact, however, the newspa-

118

pers that winter never mentioned Gehrig's name as trade bait. But the Yankees did want to acquire Shocker, and some reporters speculated that Pipp might be offered to the Browns, along with pitcher Joe Bush. Eventually, the Yanks gave up neither of their first basemen, trading away Bush and two other young pitchers, Milt Gaston and Joe Giard. While Huggins clearly had no intention of letting Gehrig go, the manager still was not prepared to insert his young slugger in the starting lineup. As long as the Yankees had a chance to win the pennant, he would play it safe and stick with Pipp.

Meanwhile, just as Pipp watched Gehrig, Gehrig watched Pipp. What he saw was a man ten years older than himself, tall and lean and tough, but built skinny as a fence post. If Gehrig felt the smallest surge of confidence, it was once again a result of his brawn.

When Pipp first joined the team in 1915, the Yankees were the American League bottom-feeders, finishing last or nearly last year after year. Although he'd been brought up in a religious family and had studied architecture at Catholic University, Pipp wasn't afraid to mix it up with the rougher Yanks. As a rookie, he had once challenged his entire infield to a fight. A few years later, in the middle of a game, he landed a roundhouse punch to Ruth's face.

When the Yanks signed Gehrig, it was not because Pipp had been slipping. He was only thirty. But he belonged to another baseball era, when even big men held the bat a few inches above the handle and lashed the ball to all corners of the park, swinging not for the fences but for the gaps between defenders. The Yankees had seen what Babe Ruth could do — both on the field and at the ticket booths — and they wanted more. Home runs were a narcotic, and management was hooked. Huggins and Ruppert had taken a look at Gehrig's massive shoulders and powerful thighs, they had watched him drive the balls into the right-field stands during batting practice, and they had recognized a potential star. He was Babe Ruth without the bad habits. The New Orleans *Times-Picayune* wrote, "He is rated by Yankee owners as well as many other major-league baseball men as the best batting prospect that has been turned up within the last two years in the way of long-distance hitting."

In 1925, virtually everything that could go wrong for the Yankees did. The team was built around Ruth, and so were its problems. The Babe's marriage was falling apart, suggesting that there might in fact be a limit to how much adultery one relationship can sustain. Ruth was juggling a paternity suit, a mistress who would eventually become his second wife, and who knows how many other women. He rarely drank before a game, but he made up for any temporary abstinence come dark, consuming more alcohol in one sitting than Gehrig had probably tasted in his lifetime. Before the start of the season, the Babe collapsed with what headline writers referred to as "the bellyache heard round the world." One journalist invented a story saying the illness had come from eating too many hot dogs. Others whispered that Ruth was suffering from a sexually transmitted disease. But in all probability, the problem was just what doctors said: an intestinal abscess, the result of heavy drinking and a poor diet.

Ruth returned too soon from his illness, gaunt and wobbly-legged, with a nasty scar across his belly. He was in no shape to help the team. Some writers predicted he was through, arguing that the Babe's thirty-year-old body had already absorbed fifty years or more of abuse. All around him, the Yankees were collapsing. Joe Dugan, the fine third baseman, had a bad knee. Shortstop Everett Scott seemed to have aged overnight. Some suggested that his record-setting streak of consecutive games played had sapped his strength. In May, the streak ended at 1,307 games when Huggins replaced him with Pee Wee Wanninger. Catcher Wally Schang was fading, too. The Yankees were sputtering. By June 2, the team was 15-26, thirteen and a half games out of first place. Attendance at Yankee Stadium was falling fast. The time for change had come.

The story of Lou Gehrig's emergence as a starting first baseman stands as one of America's great sporting legends. According to the tale, Wally Pipp showed up for work at Yankee Stadium on June 2 complaining of a headache and asked the team trainer for two aspirin. Huggins overheard this and said, "Wally, take the day off. We'll try that kid Gehrig at first today and get you back in there tomorrow." Pipp never got back in there at all. Gehrig played every game, in sickness and health, through streaks and slumps, with broken bones and high fevers, from Babe Ruth to Joe DiMaggio, for almost fourteen years.

It's a great story, a quintessentially American parable that squares with the nation's Protestant work ethic. Take a day off and you'll suffer for it. The boss will find someone better to do your job. Wally Pipp reminds us that we're all easily replaced, like old technology. He lives on today as a verb (don't get Pipped!), as an eponym, as a warning. And all because he complained of a headache.

But that's not what happened.

First, a technical matter: Gehrig's streak began the day before Pipp was benched. On June 1, against the Washington Senators, Huggins used Gehrig as a pinch hitter for Wanninger in the bottom half of the eighth inning. Walter Johnson threw him a fastball. Gehrig swung a little late and lofted a soft fly ball to left field, where it was easily caught. It was the last time he would ever serve as a pinch hitter. The Yankees were beaten, 5-3, their fifth loss in a row.

Huggins was frustrated. The season was only two months old, yet his team seemed to be giving up. Players had been missing curfew, practicing halfheartedly, mouthing off in the dugout, and drinking too much. Pipp wasn't giving him problems off the field, but on the field the first baseman was a disaster. Huggins had already dropped Pipp from the fourth spot in the batting order to the sixth, and Pipp had not responded. He was batting .244 with only three home runs and twenty-three runs batted in. During the last three weeks of May, his batting average was an anemic .181. After the loss to Walter Johnson, Huggins decided to try a new lineup. Maybe the veterans would respond to the threat of losing their jobs. He benched not only Pipp but also catcher Wally Schang and second baseman Aaron Ward.

In 1939, Wally Pipp told Dan Daniel of the *New York World-Telegram* that a childhood hockey accident had left him with a lifetime of headaches and blurry vision and that he was suffering from one of those headaches on the day he was benched. "Boy, was that a headache!" he said, joking about his misfortune. "It did not leave me for years." But two of his children, Thomas and Wally Jr., said in interviews that their father never complained of recurring headaches. If he did in fact feel poorly that day, Huggins might have used it as an excuse to juggle his lineup. But that seems unlikely. The writers covering the team made no mention of a headache.

"Huggins has arrived at the inevitable conclusion that he is carrying too many fading stars and that now is the time to lay a new foundation," a story in *The Sporting News* said at the time of the shakeup. Another writer noted that Pipp had been useless against left-handed pitchers all year and the Senators had lefty George Mogridge on the mound that day. John Kieran of the *New York Herald Tribune* reported that Huggins had simply lost patience with his veteran players: "The old order, as the late Lord Tennyson observed, yieldeth place to new, and the new sun rises, bringing in the new day."

The revamped Yankees snapped their losing streak that afternoon, beating the Senators 8-5. Gehrig had two singles and a double in five chances. He scored a run and played errorless defense.

Writers and athletes love to invent stories, as the Pipp tale shows. To sportswriters in the 1920s, an athlete's words and deeds were clay, waiting to be shaped and transformed. One more minor legend grew from the day of Gehrig's first start. It went like this: Running from first to second and trying to break up a double play, Gehrig was hit in the head with the ball and knocked unconscious. When he came to, someone asked if he wanted to rest on the bench for the remainder of the game. "Hell no!" he reportedly said. "It's going to take more than a crack on the head to get me out."

The words attributed to Gehrig were prophetic, but they were almost certainly not spoken. While accounts of the knockdown have appeared in numerous articles and books about baseball, all of them written long after the actual event, newspaper stories the day after the game mentioned no such incident. Gehrig's only baserunning adventure came in the fifth inning when he was caught once again taking too big a lead off first base. The pitcher threw to first base, and Gehrig, after a brief and unremarkable rundown, was tagged out. Perhaps the humiliation felt like a knock in the head.

Pipp had been the Yankee first baseman for ten years. Sitting on the bench was new to him, and he found the experience humiliating. But he didn't complain, and he continued to work with Gehrig before each game, helping him improve his technique around first base. He still held out hope that he might get back his job, but the hope diminished with every line drive off Gehrig's bat. It disappeared entirely on July 2, when Pipp was hit in the head by a pitch during batting practice. There were no batting helmets then. He spent a week in the hospital with a fractured skull and played little the rest of the season. That very real injury might explain how the headache fable got its start years later. Pipp, who dabbled as a sportswriter after his retirement, played a significant part in the invention of his own mythology. At banquets and in interviews he told the headache story over and over, making it sound as if he might still be in the starting lineup if not for those aspirin. He preferred to be remembered inaccurately rather than not at all.

The team finished the season with one of the worst records in franchise history —

sixty-nine wins and eighty-five losses — and attendance at Yankee Stadium fell by 34 percent from the prior season, to 697,000. Ruth and Huggins squabbled all year. The result at one point was a $5,000 fine and a nine-day suspension for the Babe. Huggins also informed Ruth that he was being stripped of his title of captain of the Yankees. "If you were even half my size, I'd punch the shit out of you," the Babe hollered at his manager. Huggins hollered back, "If I were half your size, I'd have punched you." Ruth finished with a .290 batting average and only twenty-five home runs. Gehrig played in 126 games, hit twenty home runs (fifth most in the league), and batted .295. The power numbers were encouraging, but his batting average was nothing special. The league average that year was .292. His most impressive statistic, though, was probably his total number of errors — thirteen — which was ten fewer than he'd made in Hartford the season before and about the same as Pipp's average for a full year. By the season's end, Pipp was expendable. The Yankees sold him to Cincinnati, where he played for three more years.

Lou Gehrig and Wally Pipp are forever linked, like the tortoise and the hare. But for all its mythical resonance, the legend does Gehrig a disservice. In truth, he didn't get Pipp's job because the older man had a headache or grew lazy. He got it because he was young and eager and hit the ball twice as hard as the player he replaced. He had an opportunity, and he seized it. In fact, Wally Pipp wasn't Wally Pipped at all — he was Lou Gehriged. He was replaced by a better man.

Gehrig was proud of his accomplishment. "That was the great kick of my career," he said, "the knowledge that I was the regular first baseman of my home town team. It wasn't that I'd beaten out Pipp, a really fine chap, who would play regularly on another club, but that I could go to my parents, who at first had looked at baseball with mild disapproval, and tell them that I had regular work at good pay so long as I could hit the ball and hustle."

Still, he couldn't stop worrying. The day after his first start, he clipped the box score from the newspaper — "Gehrig, 1B," the starting lineup read — folded it neatly and tucked it in his wallet. He carried it there for years as a reminder of what might happen if he ever stopped hustling.

CHAPTER 6
COMING OF AGE

Spring training was perhaps the best time of all to be a Yankee, a time for loose curfews and easy women, mornings full of baseball and afternoons full of fishing. In the spring of 1926, as the Yankees gathered in St. Petersburg, Florida, some players brought their wives to training camp. Others made a point of leaving them home. Gehrig was the only member of the team who arrived in the company of his mother. He rented her a room at the Del Prado Hotel.

Christina Gehrig was a housewife, forty-four years old and dowdily dressed. Never in her years of scrubbing floors and lugging pails of water could she have imagined that she would travel the length of the country in a Pullman car and bask in the sun for weeks without a single chore. She had come a long way from Yorkville, but some of the younger women who sat with her on the sands of Spa Beach nevertheless thought her crude. "Half a dozen writers' wives, including mine, would be there, three or four other writers, and Mom Gehrig," Fred Lieb, a writer for the *New York Post*, recalled in his memoirs. Lieb and his wife were among the minority who enjoyed Christina's company. Before the spring was out, the Liebs and the Gehrigs were dining together. Christina invited Fred and Mary to come to the Gehrig home for dinner when they all got back to New York. By befriending Christina, the Liebs earned the instant and lasting affection of her son. Fred and Mary would become two of Gehrig's closest friends.

"What struck me as odd for Americans in the late 1920s was that Mom and Lou would converse almost entirely in Mom's native tongue, German," wrote Lieb, who also spoke the language. If it struck him as odd that Heinrich was not in Florida with his wife and son, Lieb didn't mention it. Heinrich apparently had found work as the superintendent of the tenement house in which the family lived, and he remained in New York through the winter, taking care of the building.

In 1926, the Yankees bounced back from their poor performance the previous year. Ruth, fired up by the writers who said he was through, arrived at spring training in peak condition and taking the game seriously. As the season went on, he watched his weight, curbed his drinking somewhat, and played in almost every game. He batted .372, hit forty-seven home runs and drove in 146 runs, good enough to inspire a jaunty song, "Along Came Ruth," with music by Irving Berlin and words by Christy Walsh. It went like this:

> *He socks that old white apple*
> *To the bleachers far away*
> *He's the King of Swat*
> *He's the Yanks' big shot*
> *The idol of the day.*

Bob Meusel, the outfielder with the best throwing arm in all of baseball, was in his prime, hitting .315 for the season. Earle Combs, the speedy center fielder, was developing into a great leadoff man. Joe Dugan had recovered from his knee injury, and he was joined in the infield by two unpolished but talented new players. The first was shortstop Mark Koenig, twenty-one years old, a switch-hitter who played shaky defense but seemed loaded with potential. The other rookie was Tony Lazzeri, a second baseman who had hit sixty home runs the year before in the Pacific Coast League, where the schedule was 197 games long. Lazzeri, twenty-two years old, suffered from epilepsy, which explained why several big-league teams had been reluctant to sign him, but the Yankees were encouraged by the fact that his seizures seemed to occur almost exclusively in the morning. Mostly, though, they liked the way he hit. In San Francisco, he had acquired the nickname "Poosh 'em up Tony" for the way he "pooshed up" homers into the stands.

Lazzeri was the team's best addition in 1926. He was a tall, skinny kid, with big ears, a prominent nose, and cheekbones that looked as if they might poke through his flesh. He became an immediate sensation, especially among the city's Italian baseball fans, and the second most popular of the Yankees. He hit eighteen home runs in his first season (two more than Gehrig hit that year) and drove in 114 runs (also two more than Gehrig). If he suffered any epileptic seizures in his rookie year, they weren't reported. Huggins and Ruppert had been pursuing power hitters ever since the investment in Ruth had paid off so richly, and now the Yankees had one of the biggest and toughest lineups anyone had seen, with four home-run hitters — Ruth, Meusel, Gehrig, and Lazzeri — batting consecutively at the heart of the order.

Gehrig was fortunate to be surrounded by so many rookies and so many talented players. That relieved some of the pressure and reduced expectations. He was still immature, still shy. But his teammates were beginning to glimpse some of the characteristics that would emerge more strongly in years to come. Many of those traits were apparent in a letter he wrote before the start of the 1926 season to Kenesaw "Mountain" Landis, baseball's commissioner:

Dear Judge Landis,
In October, 1924, I filed a claim with you against Mr. James Clarkin, owner of the Hartford Ball Club for $877. Mr. Clarkin promised in September 1923 to give me a present of $1,500 provided I return to the Hartford Ball Club of the Eastern League for the season of 1924. He promised to pay in two payments of $750 to be given to me on May 1, 1924, and the remaining $750 to be given to me on May 15, 1924. I received the first $750 on July 1, 1924, and have not received the second payment to date. The other $127 is back pay which I did not receive. After referring the case to Mr. Farrell on your suggestion, Mr. Farrell did not seem to think I had much chance because I had no proof. Mr. Farrell must have communicated with Mr. Clarkin for at the meetings in December 1924, Mr. J. O'Hara, Secretary of the Hartford Ball Club, offered me $200 to settle the

case. I refused this sum at the time.

At the meetings in December 1925, Mr. Huggins, Manager of the New York Yankees, who knows about this whole affair from its beginning, advised me to see Mr. P. O'Connor, Manager of the Hartford Ball team in 1923, 1924 and 1925, to see if he would not be my proof and act as my witness. Mr. O'Connor said he would gladly verify the statements of Mr. Clarkin that Mr. Clarkin promised me a present of $1,500 for returning to Hartford for the season of 1924.

Mr. Huggins then advised me to write Mr. Clarkin and tell him I had a witness, and thereby try to make a settlement, which I did, and to date I have received no reply from Mr. Clarkin. Mr. Huggins then advised me to explain everything to you.

Mr. P. O'Connor's address is 191 Massasoit St., Springfield, Mass. He will be glad to verify and act as a witness to the above facts.

I hope you will grant me a little time to consider this case and advise me what to do.

Sincerely,
Louis Gehrig

The handwritten letter, with its impeccable penmanship, suggested that Gehrig could be stubborn, cheap, and trusting. His words carried a quiet sense of determination. At the same time, his approach to collecting on this debt was entirely civil. He made no threats. He sought no publicity. He did nothing to embarrass his former boss or the organization paying his salary.

Gehrig was still learning how to behave as an adult. He cried in the clubhouse when he thought he had disappointed his manager or hurt his team. He brought cookies and pickled eels for his teammates, courtesy of his mother, as an attempt to make friends. He was so earnest that his teammates found it amusing at times. Once, Gehrig confided in Ben Bengough and Koenig that he wanted to meet women but didn't know how. The men were hysterical. They told him he wouldn't know what to do with a woman if he ever got one. "He was just hopeless," recalled Mike Gazella, a backup infielder. "When a woman would ask him for an autograph, he would be absolutely paralyzed with embarrassment."

Though he wasn't ready to go out drinking or chasing women with Ruth, an approach that might have provided the quickest route to manhood, Gehrig was at least starting to get comfortable in his hero's presence. He invited the Babe home for dinner, and the Babe accepted the invitation. Ruth enjoyed walking in the door of the Gehrigs' little apartment and smelling a ham in the oven or cabbage on the stove and knowing that someone had set a place for him. He had rarely tasted his own mother's home cooking, and he came to adore Christina Gehrig and her elephantine portions. Ruth and his wife had recently separated, and while the Babe had many women and one serious girlfriend, Christina may well have been the only woman who cooked for him. Grateful, the Babe bought her a Chihuahua, which she named "Jidge," an approximate pronunciation of Ruth's real first name, George, and one of the Babe's many nicknames.

On the field, two dates in 1926 stood out for Gehrig. On August 13, facing Walter Johnson at the cavernous Griffith Stadium, he cracked two home runs. The Hall of Famer pitched more than eight hundred games over the course of twenty-one seasons, and in all that time he gave up only ninety-seven home runs. Jack Fournier once hit two inside-the-park homers off Johnson in a game, but Gehrig was the only man ever to take him over the fence twice in one afternoon.

Even bigger, though, was the game in Cleveland on September 19. The Yankees had been leading the American League all year, but in late August and early September they began to slump. The Indians had beaten the Yanks four games in a row and were only two and a half games out of first place when the teams met that Sunday afternoon. Trepidation like a chill autumn wind crept into the visitors' clubhouse in Cleveland's Dunn Field. Huggins looked more worried than usual.

With long shadows falling, more than 31,000 fans squeezed into a cozy park intended to hold 22,000. Roughly 8,000 of those spectators were standing shoulder to shoulder in front of the outfield fence, in fair territory. The scene probably reminded Gehrig of the old neighborhood ballpark in which the Highlanders had played. The umpires in Cleveland informed players of the ground rules: If a ball flew or rolled into the crowd standing on the field, the batter would be awarded a double. Runners would advance two bases. Meanwhile, outside the park, police on horseback held back fans trying to sneak or shove their way through the turnstiles.

The Yankees wore their gray road uniforms, with "NEW YORK" written in square black letters across the chest. In the first inning, with two men on and two out, Gehrig hit the ball just the way Ruth had been telling him to — hard down the right-field line. The fence was only 290 feet away, and with the fans standing on the edge of the grass, right field had shrunk to the size of a vegetable garden. Gehrig's shot disappeared into the mob for a double, driving in the game's first run. In the third inning, he hit one to almost the same spot for another run-scoring double. By the time he came to bat in the fifth inning, he had found his stroke. Another swing, another double into the crowd, giving the Yankees a 5-3 lead. Finally, in the seventh, he hit the ball over the heads of the standing throng for a home run, icing the win and the pennant. The Yankees went on to finish with a 91-63 record, three games ahead of the Indians.

As the World Series got under way, with the Yankees facing Rogers Hornsby and the St. Louis Cardinals, Gehrig was almost completely overlooked by the media. Babe Ruth predicted that the Yankees' pitching would make the difference. Herman Wecke, a sportswriter in St. Louis, comparing the teams by position, said the Cardinals were stronger than the Yankees at first base, thanks to the clutch hitting and smooth fielding of Jim Bottomley. Grover Cleveland Alexander, the Cardinals' veteran pitcher, said that the inexperienced Yankee infield would contribute to the team's undoing. And John McGraw of the Giants, considered the nation's sharpest baseball mind, submitted a long column to the *St. Louis Post-Dispatch* in which he evaluated almost every conceivable factor likely to affect the outcome of the Series, discussing such important players as "Hafer" (he meant Chick Hafey) and "Cooms" (he meant Combs) — but never mentioning Gehrig. Maybe he was still in denial about his failure to sign the first baseman to a contract.

Still, most objective observers thought the Yankees had the edge in the Series, not only because of Ruth but also because the Cardinals had never before played for the championship. If Gehrig felt any anxiety about appearing in his first Series, perhaps it was mitigated by low expectations.

On October 2, nearly 62,000 fans jammed Yankee Stadium for game one. U.S. Senate candidate Robert Wagner threw out the first pitch and took a seat beside Mayor Jimmy Walker, who was elegantly dressed in a trimly cut suit and a black derby. Former heavyweight champ Jack Dempsey watched from a box seat behind Commissioner Landis. Thousands of fans who couldn't get tickets went downtown to City Hall to watch the progress of the game charted on two giant scoreboards.

A light mist hung over the field. The grass was soggy, the sky gray. Pitching that day for St. Louis was a tough left-hander named Bill Sherdel who'd won sixteen games for the Cardinals during the season. In the bottom of the first inning, with the bases loaded and one out, Gehrig grounded the ball to the shortstop, who flipped it to second baseman Rogers Hornsby for the second out of the inning. When Hornsby looked toward first base, he saw Gehrig, head down, thick legs pumping like pistons, sprinting down the line with surprising speed for such a big man. Hornsby rushed his throw but couldn't get it there in time for the double play. Gehrig reached safely. The Yanks had their first run, and Gehrig had his first World Series RBI.

In the bottom half of the third, Babe Ruth singled and advanced to second on a bunt. While sliding into second, though, the Babe split his pants. "Babe is the color of a red brick house," Graham McNamee informed the nation. The team's trainer, Doc Woods, ran onto the field, sewed some stitches into Ruth's pinstriped pants, and jogged off to a smattering of applause and laughter. When the game resumed, Gehrig hit a soft fly ball to left field to end the inning.

The score remained tied 1-1 in the sixth

140

inning as a light rain began to fall. In the top of the sixth, Ruth singled past the third baseman. Meusel bunted the big man over to second. Then Gehrig knocked home the go-ahead run with a sharp single to right. Lazzeri batted next and lined a shot to left. Gehrig sprinted to second, then looked up and paused, trying to decide whether to go for third. He went, but his moment of hesitation cost him. He dove headfirst toward the bag, where Les Bell tagged him out. Somewhere, Ty Cobb was snickering.

Fortunately for Gehrig, Herb Pennock pitched beautifully and the Yankees held on, to win 2-1. The headline writers forgot all about the baserunning blunder. "Gehrig's Blow Decides It," *The Times* declared. In his first World Series game, he had driven in the winning run. Over the course of his career, he would accomplish this feat an astonishing eight times.

Alexander pitched game two for the Cardinals and allowed only four hits. He was thirty-nine years old and looked older. But when he stepped onto a pitcher's mound, he was ruthless, a hard-core con man. He did tricks with the ball that left hitters scratching their heads all the way back to the dugout. Ruth and Gehrig came up empty against the wily right-hander, and the Cards won, 6-2. After the game, both teams boarded trains for the trip west. The mayor of St. Louis ordered all work to stop at three the next afternoon so the city could properly welcome its team at Union Station. The Series was tied, 1-1, but the Cardinals were greeted like champions, with torrents of paper tossed from office windows and firecrackers lobbed from sidewalks. The streets were so crowded that cars attempting to pass through downtown looked as if they might disappear, swallowed by the surging sea of straw hats.

Hornsby, the team's star second baseman and manager, skipped his mother's funeral to prepare his team for the Series. When he and his players arrived back in St. Louis at about four in the afternoon on October 4, they were led to a podium just outside Union Station, where the mayor presented Hornsby with a new Lincoln sedan valued at $4,000 and paid for by some of the city's leading businessmen. Each of Hornsby's players got a new hat, a new pair of shoes, and an engraved white-gold watch "valued at $100, manufacturer's price," according to the *St. Louis Post-Dispatch*. Once the gifts were distributed, twenty cars full of ballplayers and city officials rolled through the city in a massive parade. Hornsby and his wife brought up the rear in their new Lincoln.

Some of the more savvy fans, however, skipped the parade to line up for tickets outside Sportsman's Park. They reclined on newspaper mattresses and sipped whiskey from flasks, in hopes of getting one of the last available unreserved tickets, which were priced at $3.30. Children brought soapboxes from home and rented them as temporary seating for the men standing in line, with prices ranging from twenty-five to fifty cents. "I ain't got no twenty-five dollars to pay a scalper for a reserved seat," said one man who intended to wait as long as necessary for an unreserved seat.

Game day broke cold and gray. But by early afternoon the clouds parted and the outfield grass at Sportsman's Park shimmered under a reddish autumn sun. Nearly 38,000 people jammed the ballpark, and the home team rewarded their enthusiastic supporters with a 4-0 win. Gehrig had two hits, but the rest of the Yankees together had only three.

The next day, Ruth slammed three home runs — the first time that had been done in a World Series contest and the first time Ruth had hit three in a single game. The third shot traveled more than 430 feet and cleared a 20-foot wall in center field; it was the longest homer ever hit in St. Louis, some said. Gehrig went 2-for-3, with a walk, a single, and a double. The Yankees won, 10-5, tying the Series at two games each.

In game five, the Yankees were trailing 2-1 in the ninth inning when Gehrig doubled, Lazzeri bunted him to third, and Ben Paschal singled to bring in the tying run. In the tenth inning, Lazzeri hit a sacrifice fly with the bases loaded to give the visitors the win. Herb Pennock pitched all ten innings for the Yankees.

The Series returned to New York for game six, the Yankees needing only one more win. But Alexander, once again, befuddled them. He pitched a complete game and gave the Cards a 10-2 win. Gehrig managed only an infield single. The Series — and the season — had come down to one game.

On Sunday morning, October 10, a woman named Lotty Schoemmell jumped into the Hudson River at Albany. Her plan was to swim all the way to New York City in four days, in pursuit of a record set six years earlier. In the giddy 1920s, everybody loved a stunt and everybody wanted to set a record, whether by sitting on a flagpole for days on end or hitting home runs. Icy temperatures and sharp winds kept Schoemmell from completing her swim, but she was still acclaimed for her courage.

Further south that day, in the Bronx, the cold winds and threatening skies kept a lot of fans away from Yankee Stadium, despite the fact that no more important game had ever been played in the park. Gehrig had a chance to get the Yankees going in the first inning, batting with two out and runners on first and third. After watching two pitches go by out of the strike zone, he swung hard at the third and smacked a sharp grounder to the right side of the infield. Hornsby stabbed at it, bobbled, then threw to first just in time, ending the threat.

In the fourth inning, Mark Koenig made his fourth error of the Series and Bob Meusel muffed an easy fly ball to left. Three runs scored. In the seventh, with St. Louis leading 3-2, the Yankees rallied. Combs singled and went to second on a sacrifice. Ruth was intentionally walked. Meusel, who had been miserably ineffective throughout the Series, hit a ground ball, forcing Ruth out at second base. Now there were two outs and runners at first and third — and a chance for Gehrig to be the hero. He took a strike, fouled off a pitch, and then calmly watched four pitches go by outside the strike zone. He jogged to first base, content at keeping the rally alive. Fans stood and screamed. A base hit now would break the game open.

Hornsby called time out, huddled with the rest of his infield, and signaled to the bullpen to send in a new pitcher. He wanted Alexander, even though the old man was a decade past his prime and had pitched nine innings the day before. Yankee fans watched in silence as the long-limbed pitcher made his way from the bullpen to the mound. He took the ball, rolled it around in the palm of his glove and stared toward home plate, as if contemplating his next sleight of hand, his next pitiless display of magic.

Lazzeri never had a chance. He went down on four pitches. It was such a dramatic moment that years later, when Alexander was out of baseball and out of money, an alcoholic reliant on strangers to buy a famous old man a drink, he would reenact the strikeout for freak-show customers in New York City. In those performances, he claimed to have been either drunk or hung over as he pitched. His intoxication made the story sound even better — and more believable.

The Yankees, now thoroughly mesmerized, were retired easily in the eighth inning. In the ninth, Combs and Koenig both grounded out. Then came the matchup everyone was waiting for: Alexander versus Ruth, one of the game's greatest pitchers against its greatest slugger. Long shadows fell over the loose dirt around home plate, a reminder that autumn had arrived. If Ruth looked down at the ground in front of home plate he would have seen the outline of his own cap and his big bat sweeping across the edge of the infield. The moment was packed with drama, but Alexander was too smart to take chances. A good gambler knows when to play a hand and when to fold. He walked the Babe and concentrated instead on Meusel.

The Yankees needed a double to tie the game or a home run to win it. In St. Louis, the streets were silent. At Yankee Stadium, 38,000 voices roared. Everyone stared at Alexander, looking for some sign that the old man was weakening. He betrayed nothing. Gehrig began swinging his bat in the on-deck circle, trying to stay loose.

Alexander wore the brim of his gray hat at a slant so that he seemed to be staring out with only one eye. His jaw worked violently on a gob of gum.

If Meusel felt anxious, he didn't show it. He never did. He was ornery and aloof, and the meanest man in the club now that Carl Mays, the beanball tosser, had moved on to the Reds. Meusel was a streaky hitter. When the Yankees signed him in 1920, management thought he would become one of the best to ever play the game. He was tall and powerfully built, he had a rifle for an arm, and his swing was one of the prettiest Huggins had ever seen.

But for some reason, he often fizzled under pressure. He tended to loaf in the outfield, making easy catches look difficult. All in all, he saw no reason to get his uniform dirty. "Hustling is rather overrated in baseball," he said in a 1926 interview. Though he had many fine years with the Yankees, fans sensed his indifference and never showed him much affection in return. If not for his critical error in the fourth inning, the Yankees probably would have been winning this game. Now Meusel had a chance to atone.

Gehrig stood in the dusty shadows, halfway between the dugout and home plate. He would get his chance only if Meusel reached base. But Alexander planned to pitch aggressively. He didn't want to face the big, eager first baseman.

Ruth took a few steps away from first base, clawing at the dirt with his cleats. Meusel stood tall at the plate, legs wide apart, bat back and pointed straight to the sky. As the pitch came, he shifted his weight forward and began to swing. That's when Ruth took off, trying to steal second.

From the dugouts to the grandstands, everyone in the stadium was caught by surprise. Even Meusel and Huggins had no idea Ruth planned to go. Meusel swung and missed. The catcher threw. Ruth reached for the base with his foot, and Rogers

Hornsby reached for the ball. Hornsby tagged Ruth out.

Later, Ruth explained that he had tried to steal because he thought the Cardinals wouldn't expect it. If he'd reached second, by his own logic, it would have been much easier to score on a single. He'd been stealing bases with reckless abandon all season, and all season Huggins had been warning him that he would one day cost his team an important game with his cavalier play. Now he had.

Gehrig, clutching his bat, returned to the dugout.

Ruth had committed a huge blunder, yet, astonishingly, it only seemed to enhance his popularity, reinforcing his image as a swashbuckler. Reporters pinned most of the blame for the loss on Meusel and Koenig, whose errors had permitted the winning runs to score. Ruth by now was so popular that few things short of a treason charge would have diminished his appeal.

Win or lose, he remained the center of attention. His publicist, Christy Walsh, helped make sure of that. After the Series, one of the most famous of all Babe Ruth legends began to surface in the press. The stories said that Ruth had visited a hospital before the Series and met an eleven-year-old boy named Johnny Sylvester. Little

Johnny was dying of blood poisoning, and the Babe promised to hit a home run on his behalf. When the Babe hit three in one game, the newspapers reported, the boy's condition miraculously began to improve. As with most baseball legends, this one contains a morsel of truth. Johnny was sick, but one reporter described the illness as a sinus condition; another said he had been injured falling off a horse. According to one of Ruth's biographers, a family friend visited the hospital before the World Series, presenting Johnny with two autographed baseballs and telling the boy Ruth had promised to hit him a home run. Other accounts suggest that the slugger delivered his promise via telegram. In any case, it's almost certainly true that Ruth didn't visit the boy until after the World Series, when the home runs had already been hit and the publicity coup assured.

The following spring, the boy's uncle met Ruth, thanked him for visiting the hospital, and informed him that Johnny had made a complete recovery. Ruth smiled and said he was glad to hear it. But when the boy's uncle stepped away, Ruth asked, "Now, who the hell is Johnny Sylvester?"

That fall, the Babe went on the vaudeville circuit, earning $8,333 a week — more than W. C. Fields, Fanny Brice, or Al Jolson had ever made. He jumped onto the stage through a tissue-paper hoop, tooted recklessly on a saxophone, tossed a baseball around, and attempted a few jokes. "It was boring as hell," Koenig said. Ticket sales were lackluster, and Walsh made a mental note that next season his client would have to incorporate more baseball in his off-season business ventures. Meanwhile, Ruth endorsed Chevrolets, Cadillacs, Packards, Studebakers, and Chryslers, as well as home appliances, boarding kennels, and housing developments. And when the vaudeville tour ended, he stayed on in Los Angeles to begin rehearsals for his starring role in the First National Pictures feature *The Babe Comes Home.*

For the moment, the Babe was a solo act, and the biggest in the land. But Lou Gehrig was swinging a bat in the on-deck circle.

CHAPTER 7

SINNER AND SAINT

On March 30, 1927, a warm Wednesday evening in St. Petersburg, Florida, the last wisps of orange clouds were disappearing over the Gulf of Mexico as the Yankees boarded a train going north. Gehrig was a few months shy of his twenty-fourth birthday. His neck had thickened like the trunk of a mighty tree. He had reached the height and weight — 6 feet 1 inch, 210 pounds — that he would maintain throughout most of his career. Down in Florida, his forearms had acquired a warm, dark tan, and his wavy brown hair had lightened several shades. When he flashed his dimpled smile, he still looked like a kid — a handsome, happy, healthy kid.

He'd worked hard in spring training. He knew he needed to stop making some of the mental errors that occasionally hurt his team. He had to learn to run the bases more carefully. Though his fielding percentage in 1926 had been about the same as the league average, he wanted badly to reduce the number of errors he made at first base. He still wasn't reacting automatically when balls were hit his way. Too often, he hesitated as he tried to make a play.

"Every time I think," he told one reporter, "the ball club suffers."

The winter and spring had been filled with uncertainty. It had begun in February, when the press picked up a rumor that the Yankees had considered trading Gehrig for a first baseman who hit from the right side of the plate. It's possible that Huggins, Barrow, and Ruppert had indeed toyed with the idea of swapping Gehrig, but it seems unlikely. They recognized his potential, as did everyone else in the game, and there was no right-hander in particular they coveted. In all likelihood, the trade rumor had been conceived of and fed to the newspapers to make Gehrig feel insecure about his future and thus more likely to accept whatever low salary the team offered him.

Ruth dominated the headlines throughout the off-season. He told the Yankees he had no intention of playing in 1927 for less than $80,000. When Ruppert balked at the unprecedented sum, the right fielder reminded the team's owner that he didn't need the Yankees as much as the Yankees needed him. By one estimate, Ruth had earned $20,000 playing exhibition games

that winter, $65,000 starring in his vaude-
ville show, $75,000 acting in movies, and
$10,000 selling ghostwritten columns to
newspapers. He may have inflated those
figures as a negotiating tactic, but there
was no arguing with the fact that he had
become a thriving enterprise, the greatest
celebrity the game had ever seen. Ruppert
was well acquainted with the value of
brand building. He had once tried to re-
name his team the Knickerbockers to pro-
mote one of his beers. Ruppert by now had
been the sole owner of the Yankees for
nearly four years. He knew that Ruth was
his greatest asset, but he also knew that
fans wanted more. They wanted to see a
championship team. So while Ruppert handled most of the high-level salary negotiations, he assigned the job of assembling the
team's roster to Barrow.

The pugnacious Barrow was powerfully
built, with a big, bald head and gargantuan
eyebrows, like the ones Groucho Marx
painted on. Born just after the Civil War,
Barrow played baseball as a boy, but he
lacked the talent to make a living at the
game. Instead, he began promoting and or-
ganizing semi-pro games in small towns
throughout the Midwest. In the 1890s,
while working as a promoter, he discovered
and signed Honus Wagner, the great shortstop, whom he sold to Louisville in 1897.

Barrow didn't know baseball strategy as well as Huggins (Barrow predicted in 1919 that Ruth would eventually give up trying to hit home runs and pattern his game after that of Cobb), and he didn't know the game's finances as well as Ruppert. But he knew enough in both departments to comport himself with supreme confidence. He scrunched those mighty eyebrows and wrinkled his brow and took no guff.

Throughout the major leagues, Barrow's peers tried to imitate his success by finding their own home-run hitters. In Chicago, the Cubs pinned their hopes on Hack Wilson, short and bull-necked, a tough guy who may have drunk more than Ruth, but homered less. In New York, the Giants were watching the progress of an eighteen-year-old outfielder from Gretna, Louisiana, named Mel Ott. In Philadelphia, management looked to a nineteen-year-old prospect named Jimmie Foxx.

But the Yankees had the prototype. Ruth was in his prime, and he knew he had leverage in his contract negotiations. But he knew, too, that it would not be wise to give up baseball and turn full-time to the stage. People weren't going to pay to see him sing, dance, or murder the saxophone if he didn't hit home runs. Nor would so many beautiful women undress for an overweight fellow who *used to play* ball. Ruth loved the game even more than he loved its fringe benefits. So, after a strenuous series of negotiations, he accepted a contract for $70,000 that made him far and away the game's best-paid player. Most men in the league earned less than $10,000. Even Commissioner Landis made only $65,000 a year.

Ruth's signing took place at Ruppert's brewery at the corner of 92nd Street and Third Avenue. The Babe wore a long, raccoon-skin coat and made time to talk to some of the fans and reporters who had gathered on the street. He adored the spectacle of his annual contract negotiations. For Ruth, hope bloomed in early spring. He dreamed of a season in which he stayed healthy, kept his wife away from his mistresses, avoided the ire of his bosses, hit home runs by the dozens, and helped his team win the Series.

Ruth was one of the nation's most beloved celebrities in large part because he was so human. Most of the nation's famous men were actors, which meant that fans rarely glimpsed their true personalities. On-screen, Douglas Fairbanks was a buccaneer and W. C. Fields a curmudgeon. Off-screen was anybody's guess. But Ruth was always the Babe — bigger than life and yet real as life. Sometimes he homered; sometimes he struck out. Sometimes he was witty; sometimes dense. Sometimes he visited kids in hospitals; sometimes he was wheeled in on a gurney. His fallibility made him more appealing.

"You can say for me that I'll earn every cent of my salary," he told the reporters outside Ruppert's office. "There'll be no more monkey business for me."

But with Ruth under contract, the Yankees still were not ready to play. Several of his teammates, including Herb Pennock, Earle Combs, and Bob Meusel, had followed their leader and told management that they wanted raises. Even the aging pitcher Urban Shocker, who lived with so much pain he couldn't sleep lying down, demanded more money. Once Ruppert gave in to Ruth's demands, he had little choice but to negotiate with the others. Herb Pennock, the team's best pitcher, became their highest-paid player after Ruth, getting about $20,000 a year for three years.

Sports fans debated whether their heroes were worth such money, but few begrudged the athletes getting all they could. The nation was enjoying one of its greatest periods of economic expansion, with new millionaires popping up every day. Greed had never been more in vogue. The mania didn't filter down to the piece-rate sweatshops of downtown Manhattan, where a girl had to sew for two weeks to make twenty dollars, but it did reach well into the middle and upper-middle class. Americans were working hard, their salaries were rising, and there seemed to be no end in sight to the prosperity. The number of automobiles sold in the United States hit twenty-three million in 1927, up from fewer than seven million a decade earlier. Radio sales hit $425 million, up from $60 million in 1922. The stock market, once the playing field for only the very rich, now attracted close to a million optimistic speculators. Cobb, his baseball career nearing an end, began trading stocks with much the same vigor he applied to running the bases. He turned out to be a shrewd investor, and if you happened to be among the people he could stand talking to, he'd tell you to buy shares of Coca-Cola.

In 1927, anything seemed possible. Motion pictures began talking. Charles Lindbergh soared across the Atlantic. Advertisers used airplanes to write slogans in the sky. To be sure, there were a handful of observers warning that the fun couldn't last, that the stock market couldn't soar forever, that there would be a price to pay for such excessive frivolity. "By 1927 a widespread neurosis began to be evident," wrote F. Scott Fitzgerald, "faintly signaled, like a nervous beating of the feet." But such warnings were easily ignored.

Gehrig never got caught up in the fashions of the day. He was too cheap to buy snappy clothes, too shy to be lured by the trappings of celebrity, too meek to demand a greater share of the wealth around him. Not yet a star, not yet rich, and not yet convinced he would have a long career in baseball, he was still living with his parents in an apartment in Morningside Heights at the start of the '27 season. When his contract arrived by mail — offering $8,000 for the year — he read, signed, and returned it without question or complaint. The money was more than enough to take care of his parents, and that's what mattered most. The newspapers were reporting that a couple of reserve players — catcher Benny Bengough and outfielder Bob Paschal — would also get $8,000 each. But Gehrig was not insulted. He was happy to have a job in baseball.

Huggins recognized that his team had talent but lacked discipline. If he could control them just enough, he thought they would win. After spring training, on the second day of the team's train ride north, he announced a few rules. Card games would have a twenty-five-cent limit. There would be no smoking in uniform, no golf on game days, and no staying out past midnight. The Yankees loved cards, especially pinochle and bridge. The games helped pass time on cross-country train rides, rainy afternoons, and long nights in small-town hotels. They usually gambled for no more than three or four dollars at a time — not so much that losing would break anyone, but enough to keep things interesting. When Ruth played, the betting sometimes went higher, because everyone knew that he bid recklessly and never remembered to call in his IOUs.

Huggins exerted enormous energy trying to keep his players focused on their jobs. The more he pushed, the heavier the bags under his eyes seemed to grow and the grayer his skin seemed to turn. The newspapers referred to him as an "unhappy little man." He seemed to exist in a constant state of worry — over his team, over the stock market, over his investments in real estate, over his health, over Ruth skipping curfew. Doctors told him the strain would kill him someday, but Huggins couldn't help it. Worrying was all he knew how to do. That and win baseball games.

Gehrig, at least, gave the manager little reason to lose sleep. He arrived at the ballpark on time, didn't drink, played hard, never missed curfew, smoked mostly in private, and spent his money cautiously. Huggins began offering Gehrig tips on the stock market and on Florida real estate investments. The market was booming, and Huggins urged all his young players to start planning for retirement. Gehrig never gave details of his investments, but he suggested on several occasions that he had followed his manager's advice.

Once, Huggins heard a rumor that Gehrig had blown almost a full year's salary on a new car. The more the manager thought about it, the angrier he got. Perhaps Huggins couldn't stand to think that Gehrig was falling under the sway of Ruth. In any case, Gehrig told an interviewer that when he walked into the clubhouse one day, Huggins sprang toward him.

"You big, stupid clown," the manager said.

Huggins jumped up and threw a punch at his first baseman's chin. It landed but without harm.

Gehrig stood and stared.

"Here I've been trying to teach you some sense and you go out and spend a year's salary on an automobile."

Gehrig told the manager that he had been misinformed. He had in fact bought a car, but it was a $700 Peerless Packard — used.

"Well, let that punch be a lesson to you," the manager said.

Most forecasters picked the Philadelphia

Athletics to win the pennant in 1927. After winning the World Series in 1914, the Athletics had sold off their best players. But Connie Mack, the team's careful, calculating manager, had set about rebuilding the club. Philadelphia fans were a testy bunch, and many had lost patience. But after thirteen years it appeared that Mack, one of the game's gentlest men, might finally have a shot at another championship. The Athletics had Lefty Grove, Rube Walberg, and Eddie Rommel, three of the toughest pitchers in the league. Mickey Cochrane was on the verge of becoming the best catcher in the game. In the outfield, they had Al Simmons, who had hit .347 over the first three seasons of his career, and Walt French, who had batted .312 over the same span. Jimmie Foxx, a powerful catcher-turned-first baseman, was almost ready to crack the starting lineup.

And in the off-season, Mack added a veteran to the mix, a player whose grit and hunger for victory had dimmed little with age. Athletics fans were well acquainted with the team's new right fielder. In fact, by the player's own estimate he had been the object of at least a dozen death threats by Philadelphians over the years while wearing the uniform of the Detroit Tigers.

"This is my year of vindication," Ty Cobb told fans in Philadelphia when he announced his new allegiance. "I regret that I am not ten years younger, but I promise you that I will give Mr. Mack the best I am physically able to do." Baseball's all-time toughest out and meanest cuss was forty years old and nagged by injuries, but he had still hit .378 in 1925 and .339 in 1926. Cobb was seen as the final piece in the puzzle for the Athletics. Mack was deemed a genius for getting him.

It was fitting then that the league's two heavyweights, the Athletics and the Yankees, should open the season in direct competition. James B. Harrison of *The Times* practically gushed in his opening-day dispatch from Yankee Stadium: "The weather was lovely, the peanuts and hot dogs were unusually tasty, Babe Ruth and Ty Cobb were there."

Opening day is almost always magical, but this one did indeed seem especially exhilarating. By game time, some 72,000 people had crowded the stadium's seats, aisles, and ramps. "No question, it was the greatest crowd that ever saw a game," said Ed Barrow, who consulted with police and fire department officials to make sure the park could handle such an extraordinary swarm.

Why were more people on hand for opening day than for the previous World

Series? Nice weather had something to do with it, but Ruth and Cobb had more. The Babe's off-season vaudeville tour and moviemaking, not to mention his contract dispute, had made him an even bigger star than before, and a long winter had left fans hungry to see him atone for the foolish play that had ended the previous year's World Series. The addition of Cobb to the Athletics had the feeling of a momentous event: The greatest hitter of all time, absent from the World Series since 1909, was making one last push at a championship.

The Yankees marched slowly onto the field in their elegant pinstriped uniforms. Though he was far from the center of attention, no one looked better than Gehrig. The thin blue stripes elongated his bulky frame while the baggy trousers hid his big rear end.

Ruppert's concerns about safety were unwarranted. Only Philadelphia's pitching corps got pushed around. The Yankees won the first game of the series, 8-3; took the next, 10-4; tied in the third game, 9-9 (the game was called on account of darkness); and won the following day by the score of 6-3. They went on to win their first six. Only briefly amid the hoopla did followers of the team pause to notice that young Lou Gehrig, not Babe Ruth, was leading the club.

"Huggins knew what he was doing when he benched the veteran Wally Pipp in favor of the former Columbia University player," wrote Joe Vila in *The New York Sun* on April 15, after Gehrig had banged four hits and driven in five runs in the season's first three games. "Gehrig today is first class in his position. He is faster on his feet and thinks quickly. As a hitter, he ought to lead all of the first basemen in the American League."

After two weeks, the team was in first place and Gehrig, batting .447, was tearing the seams out of the ball. The Yanks had scored eighty-six runs, and the first baseman had driven in or scored thirty-two of them. "This giant of a youth is heading fast for a prominent place among baseball's great players," wrote Arthur Mann in the *New York Evening World*. "No one on the team has more chance of playing all 154 games than Gehrig."

The sportswriters were finally beginning to take notice. They found in Gehrig a player who neither bragged nor fussed, a young man who clearly enjoyed making a living at play in a child's game, a shy fellow who treated everyone he met with respect. The journalists' only complaint was that Gehrig almost never said anything colorful. It was the one area in which he seemed not to make an effort.

By the end of May, for the first time, he earned a nickname based on his performance, not on his appearance or his background. In the past, the newspapers had called him "Columbia Lou," a reference to the fact that he was one of the only college men on the team, and his teammates had called him "Biscuit Pants," a reference to his big posterior. He had also been referred to at times in the press as "the Dutchman," or "the Big Dutchman," or "Herr Gehrig." But on May 24, *The New York Times* began its game story this way: "Babe Ruth and Buster Gehrig, the home run twins of the Yankees, put on their specialty act this afternoon."

"Buster" hung around awhile but didn't stick. Even so, it represented progress in the color department.

As the Yankees jumped to an early lead in the American League pennant race, the team began to enjoy the rhythms of a baseball season, on and off the field. With ball games beginning at three in the afternoon and ending before dark, there were long nights of leisure, particularly when the team was on the road, away from wives and families. On train trips, they would climb aboard carrying boxes of barbecued ribs and bottles of booze. As darkness fell, gnawed rib bones and empty bottles would fly from the train's windows, and the men would sing "The Beer Barrel Polka."

The Yankee roster included a former schoolteacher, several farmers, a seaman, a logger, a would-be priest, and a barkeep. They were diverse in their occupations yet fairly homogenous in their working-class backgrounds. They were anything but spoiled celebrities. Only Ruth enjoyed nationwide celebrity, although Tony Lazzeri was fast becoming a big star in Italian communities across the country. Six players from the club would eventually gain election to the Hall of Fame — Ruth, Gehrig, Lazzeri, Combs, Pennock, and Hoyt. But there were more mortals than deities on the squad.

Among pitchers, Hoyt was the ace. Pennock, with a wicked curve and fine control, was the staff's best lefty. Dutch Ruether was considered too old and too inebriated by most other teams, but Huggins liked him and Ruether consistently rewarded his manager's confidence. Shocker, a silent, brooding man who threw a baffling assortment of slow curves, rounded out the rotation, winning game after game even as he scuffed along in nearly constant pain. George Pipgras, after knocking around the minor leagues for three years, became a starter in the middle of the season and finished with a 10-3 record. Wilcy Moore, an Oklahoma dirt farmer, was a rookie with a beguiling sinker who often worked out of the bullpen.

It wasn't just the pitching that proved better than anyone expected in 1927. Gehrig was playing better-than-average defense at first base and hitting the ball with more power than ever. Lazzeri, a slashing hitter, played a nearly flawless second base. Koenig still made too many errors at shortstop, but he had nice range and a strong arm and Huggins believed he would cut down the errors with time. Third baseman Joe Dugan was nearing the end of his career and no longer hitting for either power or average. But the Yankees had enough pop in the lineup that they could live without his bat. His experience helped steady the infield. The only weakness in the lineup was at catcher. Joe Collins, Benny Bengough, and Johnny Grabowski were all fine on defense but fairly useless at the plate. As the season stretched on, none of them would ever get hot enough to solidify his place as the starter. Collins would get the greatest share of the playing time, but he never hit well enough (.275, 7 HRs, 36 RBIs) to prove he deserved it.

The outfield was superb. Bob Meusel, a Yankee since 1920, was one of the league's most graceful athletes. He drank heavily and enjoyed chasing women with Ruth, but while the Babe pursued these activities with a childish joy and an endless fascination with all that the world had to offer him, Meusel behaved churlishly, as if he were owed something. A scowl seemed his natural expression, a grunt his favorite means of communication. He loped around the outfield, turning easy catches into hard ones and hard catches into hits, his pinstripes perpetually unstained. He seemed not to care for his fans, his teammates, or his coaches. But when he felt like playing ball, he was one of the best in the league, his arm a cannon, his swing simply gorgeous. Fortunately for the Yankees in 1927, Meusel felt like playing most of the time.

In center field, the Yanks had Earle Combs, a smooth fielder, a swift sprinter, and perhaps the finest leadoff hitter the game had ever seen. Born to a big family from the mountains of Kentucky, Combs could never understand the lazy work habits of men like Meusel. Combs knew he was lucky to be making money at baseball. Huggins gave him a job — get on base and wait for Ruth and Gehrig to drive you in — and Combs performed it brilliantly. He hit for high average — that season he would bat .356 — drew a lot of walks, and ran the bases with a perfect balance of caution and zeal. Along with Gehrig, Combs was one of the manager's favorites. "If you had nine Combses on your ball club, you could go to bed every night and sleep like a baby," the manager once said.

Ruth, of course, was the right fielder. He not only led the Yankees in the pennant race, he led them in fun. He hit, fielded, joked, drank, strutted, and cackled. And no matter how selfishly he behaved at times, teammates couldn't help adoring him. In 1927, Ruth made a running gag out of Wilcy Moore's horrendous hitting. He bet the pitcher fifteen dollars at twenty-to-one odds that Moore would get no more than three hits all year. Moore's season-long pursuit of those three hits became a terrific source of entertainment for the Yankees. On August 26 in Detroit, Moore topped a feeble ground ball that rolled to a stop in the grass for hit number three. After the game, he bragged: "This is just an easy park to hit in." When he won the bet, Moore used Ruth's $300 payoff to buy two mules for his farm back in Oklahoma. He said he named one ass Babe and the other Ruth.

Even without the Babe, the Yankees might have been good enough to win it all in 1927. Of course, trying to imagine the '27 Yankees without Ruth is like trying to imagine the American Revolution without

George Washington. Today, the '27 Yankees are the standard against which all great teams are judged. Other clubs have won more games. As batters have gotten bigger and stronger, other players have hit more home runs than Ruth and Gehrig. Yet no club has ever displayed anything near their sparkle or swagger. No team has been so exalted. No team has ever been such a gas.

"When we got to the ballpark," Pipgras told a writer once, "we knew we were going to win. That's all there was to it. We weren't cocky. I wouldn't call it confidence, either. We just *knew*. Like when you go to sleep you know the sun is going to come up in the morning."

It didn't take long for the Yankees to leave behind the competition. Philadelphia started slowly and never recovered. The White Sox, led by pitcher Ted Lyons, got off to a strong start, and for a short time it appeared they might give the Yankees a run for the pennant. The Sox came to New York on June 7 for a four-game series trailing the Yankees by only a game and a half in the standings. Ruth and Gehrig (referred to by the *New York Post* as the Babe's "little boy friend") hit back-to-back homers in the first game, a 4-1 Yankee win. In the next game — a 12-11 Yankee win — Lazzeri became the first Yankee to hit three home runs in a regular-season contest. By the time the Yankees won the third game on a three-run homer in the seventh inning by the little-known Ray Morehart (filling in at second for Lazzeri), the pennant race was effectively over. Lyons salvaged the final game of the series for the Sox, but by then the Yankees had made their point.

The team's nickname, "Murderers' Row," dated to 1921, when every member of the starting lineup had hit at least four home runs, but it was never more apt than in 1927. The White Sox as a team would hit thirty-six home runs in 1927. The Athletics, the second most powerful team in the league after the Yankees, would hit fifty-six. The Yankees would finish with 158. The team won so many games with dramatic, late-inning blasts that writers began to refer to the phenomenon as "five o'clock lightning." The nicknames piled up as fast as the wins.

The players would sing in the shower after a victory. Then the celebration would often move to a speakeasy or to one of the city's better restaurants. Prohibition, no obstacle to revelry, had succeeded mostly in glamorizing the consumption of alcohol. By some estimates, the city offered more than a hundred thousand places to get a drink. The *New York Telegram* reported that alcohol was available in

dancing academies, drug stores, delicatessens, cigar stores, confectionaries, soda fountains, behind partitions of shoe shine parlors, back rooms of barber shops, from hotel bellhops, from hotel headwaiters, from hotel day clerks, night clerks, in express offices, in motorcycle delivery agencies, paint stores, malt shops, cider *stubes*, fruit stands, vegetable markets, groceries, smoke shops, athletic clubs, grill rooms, taverns, chop houses, importing firms, tea rooms, moving van companies, spaghetti houses, boarding houses, Republican clubs, Democratic clubs, laundries, social clubs, newspapermen's associations.

And, the report might have mentioned, anywhere Babe Ruth went.

"With only a few exceptions, centered around Lou Gehrig, we were night owls," Waite Hoyt once wrote. Babe Ruth liked to rent a hotel suite, put on a red robe and a pair of Moroccan slippers, and hold court for anyone interested in a good time. He had plenty of company. There were always women in the Ruth suite, and they were not the sort who required seduction. According to one famous story, the Babe stood atop the piano at one of his parties and announced that the time had come for all women not interested in having sex to leave. Bill Werber, who joined the Yankees in the middle of the 1927 season, remembers looking through the transom in Ruth's suite as the Babe simultaneously enjoyed a woman and a cigar.

The men who didn't go for sex and alcohol were referred to in the clubhouse as "the movie set," those who would set out after most road games to see a motion picture. The movie set included Gehrig, Combs, Koenig, Ben Paschal, Cedric Durst, and Wilcy Moore. Gehrig was easily the most handsome and eligible bachelor in the movie set — and perhaps in all of major-league baseball. But he had little apparent interest in women. His teammates assumed that he was a virgin. When the Yankees were in New York, he would spend most nights at home with his parents. On days off, he might go fishing, alone or with his father. He sometimes traveled by himself to Rye Beach, where he would ride the roller coaster alone for hours. Only rarely would he accept an invitation to socialize after hours with his teammates.

"He used to come up to the apartment Benny Bengough and I shared and sit around waiting for us to introduce him to girls," Koenig once said. "He would wear a nice new suit, perfectly pressed by his mother, and would sit on the sofa with his hands in his lap. When a woman was introduced, he usually found it too difficult to speak."

He took some teasing for his shyness, but he never let on if it bothered him. The more he hit, the more his teammates accepted his idiosyncrasies. No one on the team took the game more seriously or worked harder to improve. He loved baseball so much that he sometimes went home after a game, rounded up a few of the kids from the neighborhood, and played in the street until dark.

On June 13, when New York City hosted a huge parade for Charles Lindbergh, celebrating his successful flight to Paris, only about 20,000 fans showed up at Yankee Stadium to see the Yankees play the Indians. The Lindbergh parade was the biggest celebration in the history of the city. New Yorkers who lined the city streets to cheer must have felt as if they were standing on the threshold of a new world, a suddenly smaller and more manageable one. Soon, they marveled, everyone would be flying, and not just for thrills. Fred Lieb of the *New York Post*, one of the brightest men in the press box, wrote a few days after the parade that it wouldn't be long before the Yankees started flying cross-country to play the San Francisco Seals and the Los Angeles Angels. "The development of commercial aviation within the next ten years should bring New York and Los Angeles as close together as New York and St. Louis are today, probably closer," he wrote. "And only the fact that Los Angeles and San Francisco have been too far removed from other major league cities has prevented them from getting big league franchises."

By the time of Lindbergh's appearance in New York, the Yankees were four games ahead of the Chicago White Sox in the standings. Gehrig was hitting .394 with fourteen home runs and sixty runs batted in. "Gehrig has everything in his favor — power, youth, perfect physical coordination, an ideal stance, and splendid coordination," wrote Dan Daniel in the *New York Telegram*, the day after Gehrig hit two homers, one of them a grand slam, against the Senators. "If Gehrig could master the trick of pulling his drives into dead right, there would be no real contest with the Babe. Lou would hit at least sixty-five homers this season."

Unwilling to let his teammate upstage him, the Babe played every day and stayed out of hot water with Huggins. He also began to get better pitches to hit than he'd seen in years. Pitchers who once would have worked the corners of the plate were more likely now to throw down the middle, or at least close to the middle. They didn't want to walk Ruth only to have Gehrig come up with a man on base.

On June 22, the Babe smashed two home runs in the opening game of a doubleheader against the Red Sox, putting him slightly ahead of his 1921 pace, with twenty-four for the season. With each homer, Ruth would put another small notch in the barrel of his bat. The day after Ruth's two homers, Gehrig hit three in one game for the first time in his career; that gave him twenty-one for the season. He didn't notch his bat, or engage in any other form of braggadocio, so Ruth did it for him: "There's only one man who will ever have a chance of breaking my record," the Babe said in one interview, "and that's Lou Gehrig. He's a great kid." And Gehrig returned the compliment. "There'll never be another guy like the Babe," he said. "I get more kick out of seeing him hit one than I do from hitting one myself."

A great contest was shaping up. By July 1, Ruth and Gehrig were tied with twenty-five homers each. When Ruth hit a homer, Gehrig would wait at home plate to greet him before taking his turn at bat. If Ruth happened to be on base when Gehrig belted one, the Babe would wait to greet Lou and the two men would laugh their way back to the dugout as the fans stood and cheered and waved their straw hats. They cheered for the two sluggers, reported the *New York World*, "and other happenings meant nothing."

As Gehrig began to gain fame, Ruth's ambitious business manager, Christy Walsh, spotted an opportunity for his client. Ruth was in no danger of being eclipsed by Gehrig as a celebrity. The kid didn't have the personality for it. But he was handsome and wholesome, clean-shaven and polite — attributes that played nicely in contrast to Ruth's boorish image. Walsh thought he could sell the sluggers as a pair — Babe and Buster, the legend and the kid, the rascal and the choirboy. He encouraged photographers to shoot the men side by side and pushed writers to play up the theme of a friendly competition. He invited Ruth and Gehrig on fishing trips to create the impression that the men socialized together. "Every day brings this chronicler a dozen queries regarding the social state of affairs existing between the Babe and the Buster," a *Times* writer dutifully told readers. "The answer is that they're pals."

In truth, there was no great friendship. Not yet, anyway. For one thing, Ruth and Gehrig were sharply divided on the subject of Huggins. Gehrig, naturally inclined to obey authority, saw in Huggins yet another father figure, a man of iron will and great determination, a mentor. Ruth saw a worthless little squirt. If not for Walsh's prompting, it seems unlikely that a Ruth-Gehrig relationship beyond the playing field, locker room, and Pullman car would have developed. Ruth's social calendar was such that he did not spend a lot of time nurturing new friendships.

As summer heated up, the Yankees kept winning. Combs seemed to be on base every inning. Lazzeri was driving in almost as many runs as Gehrig or Ruth. Meusel was playing with surprising tenacity. The pitching staff, to almost everyone's surprise, had emerged as the league's best. By July, the Yankees — "the frolicking, rollicking, walloping Yankees," as Richards Vidmer of *The Times* wrote — were running away with the pennant. Rumors circulated that Huggins was spotted wearing a smile.

Bigger crowds than ever greeted the Yankees when they traveled. And while these throngs had once been satisfied when Ruth stepped outside the train to wave and utter a few words, now they wanted something new: Gehrig, the wunderkind. Ruth had to cajole his young teammate to come outside. Sometimes the crowds gathered long after midnight, when Ruth and Gehrig thought their train would pass unnoticed. Still, the men would rarely disappoint. They would put down their cards or get up from their narrow berths to put on some clothes and smile and shake hands. Even when roused from his sleep, Ruth was energized by an audience. Gehrig, no matter the hour, never seemed to enjoy the attention. He would stand with his hands in his pockets, glancing nervously at Ruth, as if waiting to be told what to do. Then, looking like the child who wished not to be called on by his teacher, he would mumble a few words into his chest.

On days off, the Yankees often scheduled exhibition games in minor-league cities like St. Paul, Dayton, Buffalo, and Indianapolis. Requests came even from big-league cities like Cincinnati and Pittsburgh, where the Yankees rarely played because there were no American League teams. As a result, players seldom had a day off. And Ruth and Gehrig could scarcely ask to sit out the exhibitions. Customers didn't pay to see Bengough and Gazella take their swings. Still, Ruth did manage to rest his legs a bit during some of these exhibition games by switching from the outfield to first base. That meant Gehrig had to stumble around in right field, but he was younger and not one to gripe.

In 1927, audiences at Yankee Stadium were so large that the team had to hire a second announcer — a big-voiced man with a megaphone — to stand on the field and shout the names of the pitchers and batters. As a result of the overflow audiences, increasing numbers of radio stations began broadcasting games. At first, owners of major-league teams protested, concerned that fans would no longer pay to come to the park if they could hear baseball at home for free. But their fears quickly dissipated. Radio, it turned out, was the best advertising the game had ever had, carrying the sport to countless people who otherwise might never have fallen under its spell.

Nineteen twenty-seven was a critical year in the development of baseball. Seven years after the "Black Sox" scandal, fans finally began to embrace the game again. The emergence of Lou Gehrig — this sweet, dimpled child with seemingly superhuman strength — played a big part in the revival. Suddenly, baseball had more than a big star — it had a big star and a dramatic narrative. It had a home-run race, referred to by writers as "The Great Home Run

Derby." It had a notorious character and a squeaky-clean one battling for supremacy, a sinner and a saint.

Homers were flying so fast that fans began bringing baseball gloves to games, hoping to grab souvenirs. Die-hards complained that the integrity of the sport had been dealt a blow by all these "circuit blasts," that fans no longer appreciated the subtlety of the sport, that they went away disappointed even by terrific games if these famous sluggers failed to hit at least one ball out of the park. Similar cries are heard today. But then, as now, the majority of fans were thrilled by the display of power and lusted for more. America's love of the home run said something about the nation's expectations in 1927, about the population's delight in muscle and spectacle. Across the country, highways were sprouting from cornfields. Industrial output was soaring. Stock prices were rising and rising. Once, thrift had been a virtue. Now Americans wanted more, more, more. More toasters, irons, and vacuum cleaners. More refrigerators. More radios. More cars. More airplanes. More home runs.

By mid-summer some newspapers were predicting that Gehrig would not only win the home-run derby but go on to shatter all the Babe's records. His youth and superior conditioning, they said, would carry him long after Ruth tired. The pressure of these expectations must have been enormous, but Gehrig handled it well. He never tried to convert his celebrity status into a more prominent position in the team's social order. He never tried to cash in on endorsements. He never made demands of management. When each game ended, he sat on a stool in front of his locker and dressed as quickly as he could, while Ruth held court before the media a few feet away.

All his life, Gehrig wrestled with his ego. He was built to conquer, yet programmed for failure. He had a subtle and active mind, yet he lived and worked in an environment in which the expression of deep thoughts often incited teasing. Now, in only his third year with the Yankees, things were going better than he could have hoped. Babe Ruth, his hero, had become his friend. He was batting fourth and starting at first base for a winning team. He had the complete trust of his manager and the respect of the fans. Still, Gehrig did not so much set aside his self-doubt as manage it. He learned once again that he could always count on his body, that his brawny legs, wide chest, and enormous shoulders could be trained to do almost anything. The young man who once wanted to be an engineer now treated baseball as a mechanical affair. See the ball; hit the ball. He developed a smooth, simple swing — one much more compact than Ruth's — until he became almost frighteningly consistent. It was inside the straight white lines of the batter's box that he seemed most comfortable.

Most of the force generated in the swing of a bat comes from the thighs and torso, and Gehrig was built hugely around the middle. He lowered his center of gravity when he swung so that his left knee almost scraped the ground. He didn't need to flail. Ruth, with his wild, up-from-the-heels swing, hit soaring rockets that disappeared high in the air and then fell to earth, often in the bleachers. Gehrig swung from the shoulder, as if wielding an ax. His home runs seemed to zip just over the second baseman's head and continue rising until they banged off a seat in the right-field bleachers. His shots almost seemed to whistle.

"I have as much respect for a home run as anybody," Gehrig told *Baseball Magazine* in the summer of 1927, "but I like straightaway hitting. I believe it's the proper way to hit. If a fellow has met the ball just right, on the nose, he's done what he set out to do. A lot of home runs are lucky. I've seen more than one ball carried into the stand by the wind. But there's nothing lucky about a solid smash, straight out over the diamond. It means only one thing — that the batter has connected just right."

On August 8, the Yankees left New York for their longest road trip of the year. They would travel to Philadelphia, Washington, D.C., Chicago, Cleveland, Detroit, and St. Louis. Then, after just one game back home in New York on August 31, they would take off again for Philadelphia and Boston. For more than a month they lived in hotels and railroad cars. Sometimes a player would forget where he was. Even more difficult was remembering where he had been. The pretty blonde waitress in the tight, white uniform — was that Cleveland or Detroit? Everything blurred but the baseball.

Ruth seemed to have every advantage in the home-run competition as it entered its final stage. First, he adored the attention. But more important, in a practical sense, he had the good fortune of batting before Gehrig in the team's lineup. "I'd rather see Ruth than Gehrig in a tight place," said Dan Howley, manager of the St. Louis Browns. "Sometimes you can figure what the Babe is going to do, but you can never tell about Gehrig. He is likely to hit any kind of ball to any field."

Gehrig enjoyed his success, but he never seemed to believe that he could be Babe Ruth's equal, much less his superior. "The only real home run hitter that has ever lived," he said in reference to Ruth. "I'm fortunate to be even close to him."

On September 3, in the first inning of another game at Shibe Park in Philadelphia, Ruth hit a towering shot into the right-center field stands for his forty-fourth homer, taking a lead of three on Gehrig. But on the next pitch, Gehrig smacked one over the rooftops of the neighboring cottages. One inning later, Gehrig hit another, bringing his total to forty-three.

The men were neck-and-neck heading into the final turn. On September 5 in Boston, more than 70,000 fans showed up outside Fenway Park, hoping to get in to see the Yankees. Almost half of them were turned away. When the seats in the stadium filled, fans began sitting atop the outfield fence and along the foul lines in the outfield, which inspired the umpires to declare that any fair ball that rolled into foul territory and hit a fan would be declared a double. Those fans not lucky enough to get in watched from beneath the grandstand or from rooftops in the surrounding neighborhood.

In the third inning of the first game, Gehrig saw a pitch from Charlie Ruffing that he liked. He swung and hit it squarely. The ball carried into the right-field bleachers for a long home run. The Boston crowd, usually hostile toward the Yankees, screamed in delight. Gehrig and Ruth were tied at forty-four with twenty-three games to go. For either man to break the Babe's record of fifty-nine, he would have to hit homers at a terrific pace — more than one for every two games. And yet the question gripping fans wasn't whether the record would be broken, but who would break it.

"The most astonishing thing that has ever happened in organized baseball is the home run race between George Herman Ruth and Henry Louis Gehrig," wrote Paul Gallico. "Gehrig, of course, cannot approach Ruth as a showman and an eccentric, but there is still time for that. Lou is only a kid. Wait until he develops a little more and runs up against the temptations that beset a popular hero. Ruth without temptations might be a pretty ordinary fellow. Part of his charm lies in the manner with which he succumbs to every temptation which comes his way. That doesn't mean Henry Louis must take up sin to become a box office attraction. Rather one waits to see his reactions to life, which same reactions make a man interesting or not. Right now he seems devoted to fishing, devouring pickled eels, and hitting home runs, of which three things the last alone is of interest to the baseball public. For this reason it is a little more difficult to write about Henry Louis than George Herman. Ruth is either planning to cut loose, is cutting loose, or is repenting the last time he cut loose. He is a news story on legs going about looking for a place to happen. He has not lived a model life, while Henry Louis has, and if Ruth wins the home run race it will come as a great blow to the pure."

It wouldn't be the first time, or the last, that the Babe had dealt purity a blow. On September 6, Ruth hit three home runs in a doubleheader. He had the lead again. Then, the next day, he hit two more — numbers 48 and 49.

Gehrig entered the game on September 7 batting .389, with 45 home runs and 161 runs batted in (he was driving in an astonishing 1.2 runs per game). Ruth had the slight edge in home runs, but Gehrig was putting together the most productive season the game had ever seen. He could have stopped on that date, nearly a month early, and still have had one of the greatest seasons any baseball player had ever enjoyed. If he had continued at the same pace, he would have finished with 52 home runs and 186 runs batted in to go along with his .389 average. No one, not even

Ruth, had ever hit for such a high average and so much power.

His slump began not long after the Yankees returned from their long road trip. It was not uncommon for young men to get worn down over the course of 154 games, what with the cramped and stuffy train cars, the strange beds, the frequent double-headers, the numerous exhibition games, and the inescapable heat. Was Gehrig tired? Did his nerves get the best of him? It's possible. But Fred Lieb said Gehrig struggled because he was worried about his mother, who had developed a goiter (an inflammation of the thyroid) and needed surgery. "I'm so worried about Mom, that I can't see straight," Gehrig said.

Over the last twenty-two games of the season, he hit only .275, with two home runs, two triples, and five doubles. He committed four errors and drove in only fourteen runs.

On September 29, with three games remaining in the regular season, Ruth hit two more home runs — numbers 58 and 59 — to tie his record. The next afternoon, in the eighth inning of a game against the Washington Senators, he sent one arcing into the right-field bleachers for his sixtieth. The Babe waddled around the bases, waving his cap to the delirious crowd. Gehrig greeted his teammate with an energetic handshake and a pat on the back.

The final game of the year was meaningless. Only 20,000 turned out at Yankee Stadium. Gehrig could have sat it out and rested for the start of the World Series. But he knew he had played every game that season, same as the year before, and he was proud of it. Perhaps, too, he was hoping a few more swings would help him break out of his slump in time for the World Series. So he trotted out to first base again. Even Ruth declined to take the day off. The two men had been having fun. Their home-run challenge had never become burdensome. They had never griped about the media attention or the unrealistic expectations or the fact that some pitchers threw them few good pitches to hit. On the last day of the regular season, Gehrig hit his forty-seventh home run. The fans cheered, but without enthusiasm. Franklin Pierce Adams, a columnist for the *Herald Tribune*, wrote that Gehrig would be remembered as "the guy who hit all those home runs the year Ruth broke the record."

It was just Gehrig's luck to have his accomplishments overshadowed. Even with his slump, he set a major-league record with 175 runs batted in for the season and he hit .373. Ruth drove in 164 runs and hit .356. Gehrig won the most valuable player award, referred to at the time as the League Award, but even that honor came with an asterisk: Ruth was ineligible because he had already won it once.

Most of the talk around baseball revolved around what Ruth would do for an encore. Would he hit sixty-five in 1928? Why not seventy? If the stock market could keep going up, up, up, why couldn't Ruth? The Babe had this to say: "Will I ever break this again? I don't know and don't care. But if I don't, I know who will. Wait 'til that bozo over there" — he pointed across the locker room to Gehrig — "gets waded into them again and they may forget that a guy named Ruth ever lived."

The World Series in 1927 seemed a mere tip of the cap, so confident were the Yankees that they would beat the Pirates, whose biggest stars were the sibling outfielders Paul and Lloyd Waner. Compared with Ruth and Gehrig, they looked like stick figures.

For a time, though, Gehrig wasn't certain he would travel with the team for the start of the Series in Pittsburgh. His mother was in the hospital to have her goiter removed, a fairly risky operation. Gehrig told Ruppert and Huggins that he wanted to stay by her side. But when the train left for Pittsburgh on October 3,

Gehrig was on board. The next day, doctors operated on his mother and declared the result a success.

The players checked into the Roosevelt Hotel and then taxied to Forbes Field for a brief warm-up. Gehrig hit two batting-practice home runs; Ruth hit another. Gehrig spent much of his time working out at first base. He was getting better on defense all the time. Just now he was inspecting the infield grass to get a sense of how quickly ground balls would come toward him and measuring the distance between first base and a new set of box seats that had been installed in foul territory. He practiced catching pop-ups near the seats until he finally felt comfortable, until he knew automatically how many steps he could take before hitting the wall. He quit when a light rain began to fall.

Some say the Yankees had the Pirates beaten, at least psychologically, before the first game began. According to the legend, their batting-practice home runs were so impressive that the Pirates, who had managed only fifty-four homers all year, lost hope before they lost a game. In truth, the Pirates were simply overmatched.

In the first inning of the first game, Gehrig drove in the first run of the Series with a sharply struck triple that scooted under Paul Waner's glove. Gehrig might yet have been worried about his mother, but if so, the World Series (not to mention the train ride out of town) offered a nice distraction. His mother survived her surgery, and now his slump was over. In the fifth inning, he hit a long sacrifice fly to drive in the decisive run, as the Yankees held on for a 5-4 win. When a reporter contacted his mother at the hospital to tell her about the triple, Christina supplied a quote that sounds as if it received some doctoring of its own: "I am so happy to hear the good news. I am sure he will contribute several more and his team will win."

In game two, Gehrig walked, doubled to right-center, and had a sacrifice fly as the Yankees won again, 6-2. In both games, Gehrig's fielding was as impressive as his hitting. He was scooping bad throws from the dirt, knocking down line drives, and gobbling up even the trickiest ground balls.

The Series moved to New York for game three, where Charlie Chaplin and Harold Lloyd showed up to watch. Gehrig drove in two runs in the first inning with a long triple to the deepest part of center field. He was thrown out trying to stretch it to a home run — yet another baserunning mistake — but it hardly mattered, as the Yanks romped to an 8-1 victory.

Only game four had any real drama.

With the score tied, 3-3, in the ninth inning, Gehrig came to the plate with the bases loaded and nobody out. Here was the situation he must have dreamed about as a boy — and probably as an adult, too — the chance to win the World Series for his team with a single at-bat. A soft ground ball, a looping base hit, a medium-range fly ball — any one of these would have scored the run and sealed the championship.

John Miljus, a Pittsburgh native, was on the mound for the Pirates. The right-hander had been kicking around in the bush leagues for six years. He had a pretty good curve ball and not much else. He'd gotten his team into the mess. Now he would try to get them out.

With a count of two balls and two strikes on Gehrig, Miljus went into his motion and threw a beautiful pitch that seemed to curl from the outer edge of the plate to the inner. Gehrig squeezed the handle of his bat, stepped into the pitch, and swung.

The ball dropped harmlessly into the catcher's mitt for strike three. There was one out.

Next came Meusel, who had done nothing in the Series. He did nothing again, striking out on five pitches. Two outs.

As Tony Lazzeri stepped to the plate, New York fans remembered his poor showing against Grover Alexander a year earlier. Suddenly, it seemed to many in the crowd that Miljus was on the verge of performing something truly spectacular. As much as they wanted the Yankees to win, they were not quite ready to see such a wonderful season end. They were rooting for Miljus to get the out so that the game would go on. Lazzeri crouched in the batter's box, ready to go.

He swung at the first pitch and fouled it off.

"Go on, you Miljus," a man in the mezzanine shouted.

Miljus threw the next one high and outside — so far high and outside that his catcher couldn't get a glove on it. The ball rolled all the way to the backstop. Combs sprinted in from third base. With a fizzle, not a bang, the World Series was over. The greatest team in the game's history had its crown.

That Gehrig failed to drive in the winning run would eat at him for weeks. It was the first time all season, he told one reporter, that he had failed to knock in a run with the bases loaded and fewer than two outs. Nevertheless, the rest of his performance had been superb. He had played the best defense of his career, and he had hit .308, with two doubles, two triples, and five runs driven in.

In one fantastic season, everything had

changed for the young first baseman. How much so? When the Yankees traveled to Pittsburgh for the Series, the local chapter of his old fraternity, Phi Delta Theta, invited him to be the guest of honor at a smoker on the campus of the University of Pittsburgh. At Columbia University, he'd been an outcast even among his fraternity brothers. But the invitation itself was not as remarkable as the fact that Gehrig accepted.

CHAPTER 8
BARNSTORMING DAYS

Early on the morning of October 11, a small crowd gathered in the great hall of New York's Pennsylvania Station. At the center were Babe Ruth, the two call girls with whom he had spent the previous night, Lou Gehrig, Gehrig's mother, and the Babe's business manager, Christy Walsh.

Ruth tipped the call girls and sent them on their way. Gehrig kissed his mother goodbye. The Babe, puffing a black cigar, hugged Mrs. Gehrig and said he would see to it that Lou wrote her every day. Reporters on the scene made no record of whether he said it with a straight face.

Walsh, always focused on the business at hand, urged the ballplayers to break from the cluster of autograph seekers and get aboard the train. They were going on the road, barnstorming, bringing baseball's biggest stars to remote corners of the country that had never witnessed the big-league game. In two weeks they would travel 8,000 miles and stop in sixteen cities, visiting places that Gehrig had seen only on maps.

Barnstorming was born in the earliest years of the twentieth century. Two or three players from each of the World Series teams would travel the rails, visiting small cities and big towns, replaying the pivotal events of the Series in games that were part sporting contest and part theater. Local amateurs sometimes were hired to fill out the teams. But in 1911, fearing that the not-so-instant replays were somehow hurting the game, baseball officials banned the entertainment. In 1921, after Ruth and some of his teammates had violated the ban for the third consecutive year, the commissioner handed down a stiff punishment: Ruth, Bob Meusel, and Bill Piercy were fined the sum of their World Series shares ($3,362 each) and suspended for six weeks the following season. But by 1927, the ban had been lifted.

Gehrig and Ruth had no intention of recreating the events of the World Series. No one wanted to see a repetition of such a trouncing. Fans wanted to see the long ball. They wanted to see line drives and moon shots. They wanted to see if everything they'd read was true — that these two men, the Babe and Buster, were bashing baseballs farther than they'd ever been bashed. Ruth and Gehrig could have charged admission for batting practice, and thousands would have paid.

As their train left the station at nine in the morning, the two athletes and the business manager sat down to breakfast. Gehrig was always amazed to see how much Ruth could eat, and how much he tipped the men who brought his feasts. Three hours later, they were met in Trenton, where they were greeted by the governor, A. Harry Moore, who stood at a podium and welcomed them to New Jersey.

"Meet Lou Gehrig, Gov," the Babe said. "The kid don't say much."

Gehrig mumbled something the reporters standing nearby couldn't hear. Earlier in the day, he had learned about his selection as the league's most valuable player. Still, he slipped quietly into the role of Ruth's subordinate.

The players were driven from the train station to the local ballpark for a two o'clock game. They joined a semi-pro team from Trenton and played against a Negro Leagues squad called the Royal Giants, who had driven from Brooklyn in their team bus. Negro Leagues baseball was a popular enterprise in the 1920s, but teams like the Royal Giants usually struggled to make money. Negro Leagues fans tended to be poorer than big-league fans and didn't attend as many games. Sunday games often sold out, but crowds thinned during the rest of the week. Some teams were only loosely connected to their home cities, barnstorming all summer in search of new audiences. Even teams that stayed put would often test the patience of their fans because their rosters changed as players came and went.

Some Negro Leagues owners, however, found they could attract big crowds by scheduling games against white players. The games were only scrimmages. No one kept track of whether the Negro Leagues teams won more often than they lost against white opponents. Still, these contests played an important role in preparing Americans for the integration of the game in 1947. Owners of big-league teams often defended the game's segregation with the argument that black players were inferior. But when black and white teams met — either in barnstorming games or in winter leagues in the Caribbean — the Negro Leaguers routinely exposed the lie. There were plenty of hard-core racists in baseball in the 1920s (Earle Combs of the Yankees was said to be one of them), but many white players were impressed by the caliber of play in the Negro Leagues. Gehrig, who played in more interracial games than most, was one of the few white ballplayers of his era to go on record in support of integration. "There is no room in baseball for discrimination," he said once. "It is our national pastime and a game for all."

The Royal Giants, in truth, were neither royal nor giants. They had joined the Eastern Colored League in 1923. By 1927, their play had become sloppy and attendance at their home games had plummeted. Their best player was an outfielder named Chino Smith, a short, speedy runner who hit with good power. Teammates called him Chino because his almond-shaped eyes gave him a vaguely Asian look. Statistics from the Negro Leagues are not reliable, but Smith's were impressive. He reportedly hit .482 in 1927 and had a career batting average of .428. In games against major leaguers, when he had something extra to prove, he reportedly hit .458. But Christy Walsh hired the Giants not for the skills of Chino Smith or anyone else. He hired them because they were cheap.

Fans didn't care about the competition. They wanted home runs and autographs. In Trenton, they got what they came for. Ruth homered to right field in the first inning. As soon as the ball cleared the fence, he was mobbed by screaming children who burst from the stands. The Babe waddled around the bases with children wrapped around his legs and clawing at his arms. In the third inning, he homered again. Again, he was mobbed. Finally, when he hit his third home run in the seventh inning, the fans stormed the field and refused to return to their seats. Walsh ushered his men to the train. Gehrig had a single and a double to show for the afternoon.

The next day, at Dexter Park in Brooklyn, Ruth and Gehrig faced the Bushwicks, a semi-pro team of white players that sometimes competed against Negro Leagues squads. The Bushwicks would play anybody if fans would pay to watch. "Who cares about winning ballgames?" the team's owner, Max Rosner, once said. Rosner was a genius for marketing. But at baseball he was something less than whip-smart. He told the story, perhaps apocryphal, of a day in the early 1920s when a young man with his glove and spiked shoes in a "bathing bag" showed up before a doubleheader and asked for a tryout. "We don't need any lifeguards here," Rosner told the young man, sending Lou Gehrig on his way. Now, with Gehrig appearing at Dexter Park in grand fashion, the Brooklyn crowd went wild. Boys didn't wait for home runs; they sprinted on and off the field at random, stealing bats, balls, and gloves. By the fifth inning, all the bases had disappeared. By the ninth, the forty-five baseballs supplied by Walsh were gone and police had to escort Gehrig and Ruth from the field.

They boarded a train the next day for Asbury Park, New Jersey, for another game against the Royal Giants. More than 7,000 fans packed High School Field. The game was delayed an hour because William Truby, the promoter, failed to produce the $2,500 cashier's check that he had promised. Walsh always demanded money upfront, with paydays ranging from $1,000 to $2,500, depending on the size of the town and the expected crowd. If receipts from ticket sales went beyond a predetermined level, he and his players would also receive a percentage of the gate. When a local politician offered to write a personal check for the $2,500 so that the game might begin, Walsh rejected it, saying only a cashier's check would do. He and Gehrig and Ruth went to the Berkeley-Carteret Hotel to wait. When the cashier's check finally arrived, Gehrig pulled a cardigan sweater over his baseball jersey, tucked his mitt under his left arm, and walked out of the hotel into the afternoon sun. Outside, cars were waiting to drive the men to the ballpark.

The entire Asbury Park police force guarded the stadium, but they were useless once the game began. Early in the contest, with Ruth on first, a bad pitch squirted past the catcher. Ruth took off for second, but as the catcher scrambled to retrieve the ball, a boy jumped out of the stands and got to it first. Ruth jogged safely into second as the catcher chased after the boy with the ball. The thieves eventually grew bolder, not only stealing balls but also approaching Ruth and Gehrig for autographs as the men were trying to field their positions. It became clear as the game went on that Walsh's supply of baseballs (he had brought thirty-six this time) wasn't going to last. In the sixth inning, he was down to his last ball when Gehrig blasted a home run that cleared the right-field fence and landed in Deal Lake. It was time to take the show out west.

The train traveled under a canopy of red and yellow leaves, past bubbling streams, cemeteries, and freshly cut cornfields. The scenery began to blur as the engine gathered speed. For Gehrig, the trip promised all sorts of new experiences. For the first time in years he was removed from the support system that had propped him up. Gone were his mother, his manager, and his coaches. Gone too were some of his more easygoing teammates. He was on his own now, more or less, and he was expected to step into the role of a star.

Ruth already knew the drill. The trip to him was a delightful venture — delightful not only because of the terrific income it produced but also because it liberated him from his wife, from at least a portion of the media swirl that followed the team, and from his Yankee bosses. When the train stopped in some small town, he would send a porter to get half a dozen hot dogs and Cokes from the nearest diner. He handed out the key to his hotel room not just to women but to anyone he thought might be able to arrange for women to meet him. Gehrig would not have been his first choice for a traveling companion. He would have preferred a good drinking buddy, a partner with whom to prowl. But Walsh had left him no choice. The purpose of the trip was to make money, and Gehrig was the best man to help sell tickets.

Walsh, an Irish-American, was born in St. Louis in 1891. He was tall and handsome, with deep-set eyes, a high forehead, and a magnificent head of slicked-back, jet-black hair. He was the sort of fellow who always looked as if he were about to say something smart. He'd been an unemployed advertising man in 1921 when he met Ruth. According to the legend — one that must be taken with a grain of salt, since Walsh made his living in the generation of mythology — he bribed a grocer five dollars for the chance to deliver beer to Ruth's apartment. Once inside, he made his pitch.

Walsh knew that newspapers would pay good money for a series of syndicated columns under the Babe Ruth byline. Ruth knew it, too. He had been approached by would-be ghostwriters before, but he had never wanted to be bothered. The Yankees were already paying him a relative fortune. Walsh, however, knew how to get Ruth's attention. He promised him $1,000 — on the spot — just for agreeing to the deal, followed by a percentage of all sales from his columns. It was money for nothing, Walsh said, since Ruth would never have to touch a typewriter or a pencil.

That did the trick. Walsh wrote a check. Then, so that the check wouldn't bounce, he went directly to his bank and borrowed $1,000 at 6 percent interest.

For the promoter, it marked the start of a long career running a stable of ghostwriters. He employed dozens of ghosts — including Damon Runyon, Gene Fowler, and Ford Frick — to pen columns for a roster of celebrities that included Knute Rockne, Amos Alonzo Stagg, John McGraw, Dizzy Dean, Bill Tilden, Schoolboy Rowe, Rogers Hornsby, Ty Cobb, and Walter Johnson. Walsh's writers dominated American newspaper pages, simultaneously creating and feeding the nation's appetite for news and gossip about its sports stars. Thanks in no small part to Walsh, players began speaking more directly to the fans, boosting the game's popularity. Most readers knew that ghostwriters were involved, just as they knew that stuntmen were involved in Douglas Fairbanks's movies. They didn't really care.

The athletes and writers were happy. The readers were happy. Objective journalism was the only casualty. By making the jocks and reporters partners, Walsh compromised a lot of solid reporters, turning them into fawning propagandists. As baseball soared in popularity, thanks largely to Ruth, Gehrig, and the new media, baseball writers were in demand. Newspapers, magazines, and even motion picture producers were clamoring for baseball stories. And the men who covered the Yankees recognized that the demand would continue to grow so long as they continued to romanticize and mythologize the players. It wasn't sexy to characterize Gehrig as thoughtful, shy, and prone to self-doubt. So Frank Graham of the *New York Sun* described him this way in 1927: "He's burly, broad shouldered, deep chested, long waisted, stout legged, and muscled like a wrestler. He walks with a rolling gait, chews tobacco, reads the funny papers, and plays pinochle. He would rather play ball than eat, though he has a tremendous appetite, and he thinks he's lucky to be permitted to play every day."

Gehrig had no need for an agent. He had few endorsement deals and no vaudeville ambitions. Walsh, in turn, had no great interest in Gehrig, except as he added value to Ruth's various enterprises. In years past, Ruth had barnstormed with half a dozen big leaguers. But Gehrig's drawing power made a more economical tour possible. Gehrig would never have the personality to charm the public or the media the way Ruth did. Their respective roles were clear every time they autographed a baseball: Ruth signed on the sweet spot, Gehrig on the side. But Walsh was smart enough to know that Ruth would not always command life's sweet spot. His skills would fade, his belly would bulge, and many of his crude but lovable characteristics would become merely crude. When that happened, Gehrig might well become baseball's top star. And Walsh probably figured that in that event he would find a way to imbue the young man with a dash of color.

Walsh and Gehrig had at least one thing in common: Both were tight with their money. Gehrig rarely opened his wallet on the barnstorming tour, except to buy stamps to send letters home to his mother. This drove Ruth crazy. But Gehrig was happy to have time alone with Ruth, and he was eager to strengthen their friendship. He still was awed by the grandeur of the man, much the same way he must have been awed by his first glimpse of the Great Plains of Montana. Their relationship was a complicated one. Perhaps what Gehrig loved in Ruth was his free spirit, his charisma, and his casual way of dealing with authority figures.

"It was an education to travel around with the Big Bam," Gehrig said, reflecting on their barnstorming days. "Not a book education, I mean, but for a boy like me getting his first long-distance close-up of these United States it was an education in meeting people and seeing things."

But the education only went so far. Gehrig mentioned that the Babe taught him how to act in a parade. But if his mentor offered instruction in more private acts, Gehrig didn't say. He remained the straightest of straight shooters. "This sturdy and serious lad takes copybook maxims as his guides in life and lives up to them," wrote John Kieran, the *Times* columnist. " 'Strive and succeed.' 'Early to bed, and early to rise.' 'If at first you don't succeed, try, try again.' 'Labor conquers everything.' " Gehrig knew he was no Ruth. He knew he could never let loose. Even alcohol didn't help. One or two drinks left him plastered, ending his evening before it could begin. He had little interest in gambling (though he enjoyed card games for the competition), and he remained too nervous to attempt intimacy with women. If he had had any desire to shed his shyness and violate some of those copybook maxims, though, the barnstorming trip would have been an ideal time to try.

On the morning of October 14, in Lima, Ohio, the barnstormers were met by a brass band, a gaggle of local bigwigs, and a thousand or so fans. Gehrig received a bronze statuette in the image of a right-handed hitting baseball player. He had a message engraved on the base ("Hello, Mother — with my Lima friends today") and sent it home.

For the rest of the tour, Gehrig and Ruth would play on opposite squads. Walsh gave the teams names, the Bustin' Babes and the Larrupin' Lous, perhaps intended to appeal to the rodeo-loving crowds they would meet out west. And he had special uniforms made for his two stars. Ruth wore a black jersey, black pants, white socks, and a white cap with "BB" above the brim. Gehrig wore a white jersey, white pants, black socks, and a black cap with "LL" on it. Each man would play surrounded by a team full of local amateurs.

In Kansas City, Missouri, Gehrig and Ruth visited children in a hospital. The next day, the men played to a crowd of 4,500 at Omaha's League Park. Before the game, they were introduced to a champion hen named Lady Norfolk that had laid an egg every day for 171 days in a row. It was precisely the sort of accomplishment that appealed to Gehrig, who swelled with pride over the fact that he hadn't missed a game in the first three years of his career. But no one made the connection between Gehrig and Lady Norfolk. In fact, the hen was referred to, predictably enough, as the Babe Ruth of egg laying.

Ruth hit two homers, Gehrig tripled, and when the fans screamed for more, Ruth pitched a few to Gehrig until Gehrig banged one over the right-field fence. During the game, Ruth approached one of the promoters, Johnny Dennison, and handed him the key to his room at the Fontenelle Hotel. "He spotted a couple of good-looking girls in the grandstand," Dennison recalled years later in a newspaper interview. "He said I should tell them to leave in the seventh inning and that he would meet them later."

It would appear, however, that the girls failed to accept the Babe's offer, because Ruth, Gehrig, and a reporter named John B. Kennedy were in the Babe's hotel room that evening when the phone rang.

"This isn't Babe Ruth," Ruth lied to the caller. "I'll get you his secretary."

The caller complained that she had already spoken to his secretary.

"But this other one's his social secretary," he said, handing the phone to Gehrig.

Gehrig disposed of the call.

"See, Lou, you've got to be careful who you talk to and what you say," Ruth said. "A guy sued me for damages in New York because he said I slapped him for crowding me as I came out of the baseball park. I don't even remember shaking hands with him. And another fellow threatened to sue me for damages because he was walking down the street when something flew out of the air and hit him on the head. Said I'd smacked a ball out of the park and beaned him. What hit him was an L rivet. You've got to be careful about some of these birds."

From Omaha, it was on to Des Moines, where they attended to more sick children and more city officials. Then they were off to Sioux City, Iowa, where Ruth rode a pony as Gehrig watched, refusing to saddle up. By the time they reached Denver, they had played nine games in nine cities in nine days. They got their first break as the train crossed the Rocky Mountains.

In San Francisco, Tony Lazzeri and a Yankee farmhand named Jimmie Reese stopped by Recreation Park to say hello. Before the first game, Gehrig was asked to present a $1,000 check to Lefty O'Doul, the most valuable player of the Pacific Coast League in 1927. Gehrig read from a note card as he introduced O'Doul. He seemed nervous, according to one observer. Maybe he was uncomfortable being on stage without Ruth. Or maybe he was upset that O'Doul got all that cash. Gehrig had received nothing but a trophy and handshake for winning his most valuable player award.

From San Francisco the tour moved on to Marysville, California, where ticket sales were soft; then Stockton, where Ruth became the first man ever to hit a ball out of the stadium; San Jose, where the Babe was carried off the diamond by fans after a ninth-inning home run; Fresno, where the Larrupin' Lous were made up, in part, of Japanese immigrants; and San Diego, where a local amateur named Pete Grijalva lined a single to center and arrived at first base with a huge grin on his face. He had been thrilled merely to be in the same stadium as Gehrig and Ruth. Now, having managed a hit, he could barely contain his joy.

"Geez, kid, did you hit that on your

thumb?" Gehrig asked as Grijalva reached first base.

Grijalva thought it had been a pretty solid hit. Gehrig's comment wiped the smile from his face.

The first baseman laughed and tapped the young man on the head with his mitt to let him know he was teasing.

"You hit the hell out of that ball!" he said.

Ruth and Gehrig were not always so jovial. As might be expected, they sometimes grew tired of their two-ring circus and the sycophants it attracted. In one California hotel room, Ruth sat in a throne-like armchair, Gehrig on a divan, as local celebrities and reporters filed in and out for hours.

"You guys gave those Pirates a terrible beating in the World Series," one of the visitors said.

"Yeah," said Ruth.

"Four straight games, a terrible beating."

"Yeah."

"How does it feel to hit a home run, Babe?"

"Ask the pitchers."

Gehrig and Ruth developed a signal. When one of them grew tired of a visitor's company, he would make stropping motions with his right hand on his left sleeve.

That indicated that the guest had become a "barber" — a tiresome conversationalist who wouldn't shut up until the interviewee wriggled away. Sometimes, when Ruth gave the signal, Gehrig would try to create a diversion. He might go into the next room, phone the hotel operator, and ask her to ring back in a few minutes. The incoming call would provide an excuse to break up the gathering.

The tour concluded in Los Angeles on a cloudless day, before a crowd of 25,000. Charley Root of the Chicago Cubs pitched for the Larrupin' Lous. Gehrig hit two homers and Ruth none. Ruth would remain in Los Angeles to make a movie and indulge some of his more cosmopolitan cravings. Gehrig would head straight home, where he would sell life insurance in the winter to bring in extra money. His first customer was Ruth, who reportedly bought a pricey policy.

By Walsh's accounting — and he was a very careful accountant — Ruth and Gehrig had played before 200,000 fans and signed close to 10,000 autographs. Ruth batted .616 and hit twenty home runs. Gehrig hit .618 with thirteen home runs. Ruth had earned about $30,000; Gehrig's take was $10,000, all of which he intended to turn over to his mother.

When asked at a press conference how he

planned to spend the winter, Ruth said, "I ain't doin' a thing, except you know what!"

The reporters knew what, but they couldn't print it.

Gehrig said, "I plan to play a lot of basketball."

CHAPTER 9

A CHARMED LIFE

When their barnstorming days were done, Ruth left Gehrig with a final piece of advice: Don't accept the first contract Ruppert offers you this winter. No matter what offer the colonel puts on the table, said the Babe, insist on $10,000 more, and when the negotiations are over, make sure you don't settle for a penny less than $30,000. If Gehrig did not yet appreciate his value as a ballplayer, Ruth had a pretty good idea.

Late in December, Ruppert mailed contracts to his players. Each contract came with a letter explaining that, regrettably, the club's operating and maintenance costs had been greater than expected in 1927 and profit margins had been surprisingly slim. In other words, Ruppert said, the enclosed contracts represented management's best offer.

The Gehrigs that winter had been shopping for a new house, and Lou was hoping for a big raise to propel his family northward to Westchester County. No one knows the amount of Ruppert's initial offer, only that Gehrig initially followed Ruth's advice. He decided not to sign the contract that came in the mail. On January 4, when a harsh cold snap broke, he traveled across town to Ruppert's brewery to discuss things face to face. Since the start of Prohibition, the Ruppert brewery had been making nonalcoholic beer and other malt beverages, earning enough to stay afloat but hardly as much as it had earned before. Fortunately for the colonel, he had one of New York's most impressive portfolios of real estate to supplement his income. Gehrig walked into the boss's paneled office — past framed photos of some of Ruppert's grandest buildings along Central Park — and greeted his boss with a handshake.

The deal was done within minutes. According to information leaked to the press, Gehrig signed a three-year contract for about $25,000 a year (the equivalent of about $275,000 in 2004).

The salary was nothing to be ashamed of, despite Ruth's assertion that Gehrig was selling himself short. But the length of the contract surprised many. "Baseball men were at a loss to understand why the ex-Columbian should want such a long-term contract," *The Times* reported. Gehrig was twenty-four years old and had just won the most-valuable-player award. There was no telling what he might do next, the thinking went, no telling how high baseball salaries might soar, and no telling how much he might be worth to Ruppert in another year or two. If he'd been willing to gamble, he might have doubled or tripled his salary.

Ruth had played plenty of games of cards with Gehrig. He should have recognized that the young man had little appetite for risk. Bill Werber, who traveled with the team in 1927, recalls watching them play contract bridge on train rides and in hotels. Ruth and Gehrig were often partners. Ruth would sip from a glass of Seagram's and ice, not so much to get drunk but to stay loose. By Werber's estimate, he consumed about six ounces of scotch an hour. The more he drank, the more outrageous his bets became. "Phonky" was the word Ruth used for his wild style of play. Gehrig wouldn't drink at all when he played.

"Ruth would start making bad bids just to aggravate Gehrig," Werber said. The Babe thought it was fun. But the outcome was always the same: Gehrig would throw his cards on the table and storm out. "The game's over. Add up the score," he'd say.

Ruth could never understand Gehrig's cautiousness. What Gehrig wanted more than anything was stability, an alien concept to Ruth. Gehrig wasn't tricked into accepting the three-year contract. He wanted it. In fact, he initially asked Ruppert for a five-year deal.

In Gehrig's defense, players had little leverage in negotiating with management. Contracts at the time included a "reserve clause," upheld by the Supreme Court in 1922, that said a player had no choice but to remain with his team so long as the team's owner chose to re-sign him for the coming season. If a player didn't like what management offered, he could refuse to play. But he had no other recourse. Owners, acting in collusion, would not hire a disgruntled player who'd quit another team. There had been two attempts to unionize players between 1903 and World War I, but both were halfhearted, at best. Many players, it seems, were as averse to risk as Gehrig was. Baseball had taken them out of the coal mines and off the factory floors, and they were not eager to go back. There were a mere four hundred men in the United States fortunate enough to play big-league baseball. Hundreds more stood ready to fill openings. Even the most poorly paid major leaguer was probably making two or three times what most of his friends back home earned, and the ballplayer worked only seven or eight months of the year.

In 1913, a group of wealthy investors had founded the Federal League and attempted to raid National and American League rosters. Some players won raises by threatening to jump to the new league. But few actually took the leap, and when the Federal League collapsed two years later, owners retaliated by freezing salaries. After that, players were almost powerless in their negotiations. They had no way to liberate themselves from the team that owned their contracts, no right to appeal decisions made by league officials, and no pension plans. Even at the end of his career, when Gehrig might have felt he had more clout, he was hesitant to pick a fight and doubtful that meaningful change would ever occur. Asked if he thought baseball players might eventually form a union, he answered: "I don't see how it could possibly work, because . . . a ballplayer's union would put everybody in the same class. It would put the inferior ballplayer, the boy who has a tendency to loaf, in the same class as far as salary is concerned with the fellow who hustles and has great ability and takes advantage of his ability. I can't see it, no." Hard work and strong results would pay off in the long run, he believed. Rebellion was not an option.

With his new contract set, Gehrig bought

a white, Colonial-style house in New Rochelle, roughly fifteen miles to the north of the family's apartment on Eighth Avenue. The day that he took his parents to see the place for the first time, he said, was "the proudest day of my life." The house, at 9 Meadow Lane, sat on a corner lot atop a gentle slope of grass. Pines and magnolias shaded the front yard, and shrubs surrounded the porch. The land amounted to only about half an acre. But to the Gehrigs, accustomed as they were to matchbox apartments with paper-thin walls, creaky floors, and little or no sunlight, this place was a slice of rural paradise.

Guests entered through a small vestibule, a good place to knock the dirt from one's shoes, and walked down a short, parquet-floored hall. To the left they saw a large study with a bay window and a handsome fireplace, where Heinrich liked to sit and smoke his pipe. To the right they looked in on a formal dining room with exposed wooden ceiling beams. Christina favored the kitchen, not surprisingly, which was bigger than some of the family's early apartments, with seemingly endless reserves of cabinet space. A door from the kitchen opened to the backyard, where apple and cherry trees blossomed throughout much of the year. Upstairs were four bedrooms and a bathroom. The master bedroom, where Christina and Heinrich slept, had a lovely, screened-in porch that faced the backyard. Lou slept in one of the smaller bedrooms across the hall, the view from his window obscured by trees. He had his own bathroom, probably for the first time, with a pedestal sink and a tub.

That winter, a nationwide poll rated Gehrig the fourth most popular athlete in the country, after Jack Dempsey, Ruth, and boxer Gene Tunney. Yet Gehrig was still living the sheltered life of a child in many ways. When baseball fields sat idle, he spent most of his time in search of another game, another chance to flex his muscles and win. He put together a basketball team stocked with some of the city's best players and took on all challengers, including professional teams like New York's Original Celtics. Gehrig was a talented enough basketball player — and a popular enough attraction — that the Philadelphia Warriors of the American Basketball League recruited him in the winter of 1927 to play professionally.

Gehrig never did try professional basketball, but he always found plenty of athletic endeavors to fill the winter months. During one off-season he showed up in street clothes for the Columbia baseball team's first indoor practice and volunteered to serve as Coach Coakley's assistant. Another time he agreed, for $250, to participate in a bizarre competition against a professional golfer, a top fly fisherman, and an accomplished archer. Each man used his talents to navigate a golf course at the Belleclair Country Club in Bayside, New York. Gehrig, throwing a baseball, completed the nine-hole course in thirty-two throws. The golfer used thirty-three strokes, the archer thirty-three flings, and the fly fisherman forty-five casts. Gehrig's accurate approach shots, according to newspaper accounts, were the key to victory.

When he wasn't shooting baskets or throwing baseballs down fairways, he liked to get up early and play with his dogs. (In addition to Jidge, the Chihuahua that had been a gift from Ruth to Christina, Gehrig also owned a black, pure-breed German shepherd named Afra of Cosalta that he sometimes entered in kennel competitions.) Afterward, he might go to work with a hammer or a saw, fixing up the house. When the weather was mild enough, he liked to take his boat out on Long Island Sound. Even in the off-season, he went to bed early. In the morning, he would come down the stairs, floors creaking beneath his feet, and find his father reading the paper and his mother in the kitchen. Life was as warm and sweet as a batch of Christina's raisin cookies.

On February 24, Gehrig boarded a Pullman car, along with Ruth, Paul Krichell, the young infielder Leo Durocher, and a couple of up-and-coming catchers, Johnny Grabowski and Bill Eiseman. It was not unusual for hungry young players such as Durocher, Grabowski, and Eiseman to report early to camp. Gehrig and Ruth, it would appear, joined them for the best of all reasons: They were eager for sunshine and baseball. They were coming off the most exciting year two ballplayers had ever had, full of fame and fortune, wine and women (at least for Ruth), homers and heroics, and all they wanted now was more of the same.

The train stopped in Charleston, South Carolina, where a heavy rain hummed against the roof of their Pullman car. Ruth and Gehrig paused from a game of pinochle to talk to reporters.

"I hope to crack out sixty-one homers this season," Ruth said. "With Gehrig following me at the bat, most of the intentional pass stuff is eliminated, and as long as pitchers will pitch to me I see no reason why I shouldn't break my record."

"I'm just learning what it's all about," Gehrig said. "I'm still young, and I ought to improve steadily for the next three or four years at least. If the Jedge [Ruth] hits sixty-one this year I'll be right up there close behind him, and we'll breeze in by almost as big a margin as we did last year, too."

At the start of the season, the Yankees looked as solid as the year before. The biggest concern facing Huggins was how to motivate a bunch of high-priced veterans who had won seemingly without effort in 1927. The last thing he wanted was a clubhouse full of Meusels, men who considered hustling overrated.

Huggins, as obsessed with the booming stock market as any American, decided to apply principles of capitalism in his preseason pep talks, reminding his men that hard work on the baseball field was the smartest investment they could make. By March of 1928, the stock market was growing not slowly and steadily, as it had through most of its history, but by huge leaps. People were borrowing money from banks to buy stocks, so eager were they not to miss out on the great bull market. Some of the Yankees invested in real estate, others in service stations, and others in clothing stores. Ruth, on the advice of Walsh, reportedly spent $65,000 on waterfront property in St. Petersburg. He put much of the rest of his money in bonds.

Gehrig never bought a restaurant, never set up a business, and never purchased real estate, other than his home in Westchester. He did play the market, on the advice of Huggins, but he never publicly discussed the details of his investment portfolio.

In 1927, each member of the championship team had received a World Series bonus of $5,592.17. Huggins urged his players to think about what another paycheck like that one would do for their families. The stock market offered no guarantees — "If you're in the market, get out," he supposedly said — but a World Series victory paid off every time — enough to double some players' annual incomes.

Once again in 1928, the Athletics posed the greatest threat to the Yankees. Philadelphia had had a good team the year before. Now they were even better. Jimmie Foxx was getting more playing time at first base. Connie Mack experimented with an outfield that included 41-year-old Ty Cobb and 40-year-old Tris Speaker, along with 26-year-old Al Simmons. Eventually, Speaker was replaced by Mule Haas in center. As the season wore on and Cobb's legs grew creakier, Bing Miller began to get more playing time in the outfield. Age was giving way to youth.

By mid-June, the Yankees opened a big

lead over Philadelphia. Gehrig made it clear right away that his performance in 1927 had been no fluke. Once again, he was among the league leaders in every offensive category. On June 12, against the White Sox, he put on an awesome show, hitting two home runs (his fourteenth and fifteenth of the season) and two triples while driving in six runs. The Yanks won, 15-7. The *Chicago Tribune*, which retired the last of its horses that day and began delivering all its newspapers by motorized coaches, offered this comment after Gehrig's performance: "You'll be sorry twenty years from now if you're not able to turn to your companion in the cabin of the transcontinental airship and say: 'I remember way back when I watched Babe Ruth and Lou Gehrig knock home runs over the bleachers at Comiskey Park. That was a great team — those Yanks of 1928.' "

By the first of July, the Yankees had run their record to 50-16, putting them eleven and a half games in front of the Athletics. Ruth, with thirty home runs, was far ahead of his record-setting 1927 pace. Gehrig was hitting .363, which ranked him among the league's leaders. But he had only sixteen homers. In all likelihood, pitchers were approaching him with more caution. Gehrig resisted the temptation to swing at bad pitches or to try to loft every ball into the bleachers. He settled for line-drive singles and doubles. With the whole team hitting so well (Lazzeri and Koenig were both batting .347, and Combs and Meusel were over .300), there was no reason for Gehrig to press.

Still, a few dents were beginning to appear in the team's armor. Urban Shocker had gradually turned to a willow of a man. Doctors said the catcher-turned-pitcher had heart-valve trouble. He pitched only two innings in 1928 before announcing his retirement. Herb Pennock missed time with a strained arm. Lazzeri hurt his shoulder.

Huggins had always been a worrier, but now he worried even more than usual. Meanwhile, the Athletics got stronger as the season stretched on, closing the gap in July and nipping at the Yankees' heels in August. On September 8, Philadelphia took over first place.

The next day, the Athletics arrived in New York for a crucial series. More than 85,000 fans packed the ballpark's seats and aisles for a doubleheader. George Pipgras shut down the visitors in the first game, and Meusel came through with an eighth-inning grand slam to give the New Yorkers a 7-3 win in the second. As the Yankees came off the field, ready to celebrate their return to first place, Mark Roth, the team's secretary, gathered the players in the clubhouse and delivered the news that Shocker had died at his home in Denver. His death, at thirty-six, was attributed to pneumonia and heart disease.

Two days later, the Yankees beat Philadelphia again, thanks to an eighth-inning home run by Ruth. Cobb appeared as a pinch hitter in the ninth inning and popped out to short. It would be his last appearance as a batter in the big leagues. He retired with more hits, more runs scored, more stolen bases, and a higher lifetime batting average than anyone else who had ever played the game. In most of those categories, the runners-up weren't even close.

The Yankees hung on to win the pennant by two and a half games. Once again, Gehrig insisted on playing the season finale, even though the game was meaningless. Ruth started the game, too, but after hitting a home run in the fifth inning — his fifty-fourth of the year — he benched himself. He finished the year with a .323 average and 142 runs batted in. Gehrig hit a homer in the top of the seventh — his twenty-seventh — and still decided to stay in the game. It was an unfortunate decision. In the bottom half of the seventh inning, a hard ground ball scooted past his mitt and hit him in the face. He collapsed, dust rising all around his motionless body. When he regained consciousness, Huggins sent in a replacement. Gehrig finished the season with a .374 average. He tied Ruth for the league lead in runs batted in with 142.

When the World Series started, Gehrig's face was still sore, but, as *The Times* noted, "the face plays a very small part in batting."

In the first inning of game one, Gehrig drilled a double to right field, driving in Ruth. It was a sign of things to come, as Gehrig and Ruth destroyed the St. Louis Cardinals almost entirely on their own. In the first inning of game two, with Grover Alexander on the mound, Gehrig came to bat with two men on. He swung at a screwball and watched it fly. It landed almost at the base of the scoreboard in right-center field. Gehrig chuckled as he rounded the bases. The Yankees went on to win, 9-3.

"The ball Gehrig hit was the same kind I fed him all through the 1926 Series, when he never hit a hard one off me," Alexander said after the game. "This time I gave him a screwball on the outside, and look what he did to me."

Leading the Series two games to none, the Yankees left for St. Louis. Most players traveled alone or with their wives. Gehrig brought his mother. In game three, leading off the second inning, he hit a ball high and deep to right field. Fans sitting in the pavilion craned their necks and stared into the sun as the ball came their way. The Yankees climbed to the dugout steps and tried to follow the arc of the shrinking sphere. The ball bounced off the pavilion roof and bounded onto Grand Avenue for another home run. In the fourth inning, with the Yanks trailing 2-1, Gehrig cracked a sharp line drive to center field. Taylor Douthit dashed toward the ball and tried to scoop it off his shoestrings. It skidded beneath his glove and rolled all the way to the flagpole in center field. Ruth scored all the way from first. Gehrig, arms pumping, came in right behind him. He had tied a World Series record with eight runs driven in — and he had done it in only three games.

The Cardinals had seen enough of Gehrig. In game four, they walked him three times. When he came up in the seventh inning, they should have walked him again. Gehrig got a pitch he liked and parked it on the roof in right field, giving the Yanks a 3-2 lead. With that shot, he tied Ruth's record by hitting four home runs in a World Series and set a new record for runs batted in, with nine. His accomplishment was overshadowed, as usual, by the Babe, who hit three homers in the final game and finished with a .625 batting average. Gehrig hit .545.

But there was another, less obvious statistic that told the most important story of the Series. Ruth, who had been walked twelve times in the 1926 Series, drew only one free pass this time around. Gehrig walked six times. Ruth and Gehrig both tore the Cardinals apart. But Gehrig was the most feared hitter in the Yankee lineup.

On a cool, clear day in the fall of 1928, after the World Series, Gehrig drove to the Bronx to visit a friend who worked year-round at Yankee Stadium, as a groundskeeper. Gehrig and the groundskeeper were chatting in the locker room when Sam Dana approached. Dana, one of Gehrig's former teammates on Columbia's football squad, was playing that winter for the New York Yankees of the National Football League.

Gehrig was a big star now, a World Series hero, and Dana wondered if he'd taken on airs. He wondered if Gehrig would remember him. He said hello, and Gehrig greeted him warmly.

"He hadn't changed a bit," Dana recalled. "I introduced him to all the fellas, and he greeted them all in his own shy way."

Dana waited until Gehrig had shaken hands with each member of the football team and then started to say goodbye. But Gehrig was in no rush to get home.

"I'll beat you at punting," he said, picking up a football from the locker room and challenging his old teammate to a kicking contest.

Dana and Gehrig walked onto the field. Dana was in his uniform. Gehrig wore a sport coat, slacks, and a pair of oxfords.

Dana was no punter, but he thought he had a chance, given that Gehrig probably hadn't kicked in a while.

"Oh, he won," Dana said. "There was no comparison. Lou kicked it fifty or sixty yards in his street clothes."

CHAPTER 10

THE CRASH

Jacob Ruppert was a collector of many things, including monkeys, trotting horses, Saint Bernard show dogs, yachts, doves, jades, rare books, dress shoes, fine suits, Chinese porcelains, Indian relics, and skyscrapers. Now, he also owned the finest menagerie of baseball players the world had ever seen. And to many, in particular those not inclined to root for the Bronx Bombers, it didn't seem fair that the colonel had cornered this particular market. "Break up the Yankees," became the cry of sportswriters before the start of the 1929 season. Teams in smaller cities such as Detroit and Cleveland would never compete with the mighty army of Ruth, Gehrig, Meusel, and Lazzeri. At least one of the sluggers ought to be traded, the writers suggested. Gehrig seemed to be their choice.

It was true that Ruppert's team had the highest annual payroll in the league, at about $350,000. But his organization also made the most money. The Yankees had the biggest stadium, sold the most tickets, and attracted the largest crowds on the road (visiting teams received 25 percent of the revenue from ticket sales). What's more, no owner leveraged his assets more shrewdly than Ruppert. If the team had a day off between games in New York and Washington, he'd have the train stop in Norfolk, where thousands would pay to see Ruth and Gehrig compete against minor leaguers. If the schedule included a day off during a home stand, the Yankees would arrange an exhibition in Binghamton, New York, or Brooklyn or even at Sing Sing prison up in Westchester County. The players didn't like it, but they had no say in the matter.

The success of the Yankees was built not only upon Ruppert's personal wealth but also upon smart decisions by the men he'd hired to run the team, namely Ed Barrow and Miller Huggins. Furthermore, Gehrig wasn't a Yankee because Ruppert was rich; he was a Yankee because Ruppert employed Krichell as a scout. Still, the sportswriters were not about to let common sense get in the way of a good story. Having Ruth and Gehrig on the same team was superfluous, like having Charles Lindbergh and Amelia Earhart in the cockpit of the same plane.

If Ruth had been the one nominated for

extradition, he probably would have let the writers have their fun. He would have filled reporters' notebooks with thousands of words on just how much he would be worth to the Yankees in a sale or swap. He would have laughed, delighted at the thought of hitting home runs against Yankee pitching, and he would have bragged that his pal the colonel would be crying in his alcohol-free malt beverage when Ruth led his new team to the World Series. The Babe would have recognized the story as the journalistic sham that it was. But Gehrig had no gift for dissembling, which might help explain why the local newspapermen felt they could live without him in the first place. Gehrig took things seriously — too seriously, sometimes. As the headlines blared, he remained silent.

At last, Ruppert released a statement in an attempt to hush the controversy: "I have no intention of selling Gehrig or any of my players who, in the judgment of Miller Huggins, can help the team to win another pennant, if possible, in 1929," he wrote. "I not only have no thoughts of breaking up the Yankees, but Ed Barrow, Huggins, and myself will exert our best efforts to strengthen them. . . . Baseball is a sport as well as a business. In every sport the object should be to win on your own merits and not ask the other fellow to weaken himself deliberately to aid your cause."

Huggins, meanwhile, didn't believe that the Yankees were a lock to win another pennant. He'd won eight straight World Series games, yet no matter how high his team seemed to fly, he focused on its rusted and rattling parts. Huggins believed he had been lucky to escape with the championship in 1928. The pitching staff had shown signs of age, the left side of the infield had been sloppy, and the catching corps had once again produced almost no offense. He also knew that the Athletics were too good to be taken lightly.

"It won't be necessary to break up the Yankees," the manager said that winter. "No matter what we do, the law of averages will take care of us. We can go on, trying to improve the team to the best of our ability. But the time will come when we will crash."

The Yankees and the Indians tried something new at the start of the 1929 season: They wore numbers on the backs of their uniforms. John McGraw, the hidebound manager of the Giants, didn't care for such a break from tradition. Baseball was a team game, and he feared that numbers would put too much emphasis on individuality. McGraw believed that a ballplayer ought to compete for what's on the front of his uniform — his team's name — and nothing more. Numbers were one more sign that the game had grown. A game born in small-town pastures belonged to the big city now. It wasn't enough anymore to recognize a player by his smile or by the length of his stride or the style of his swing. Baseball was a business, the ballplayers were commodities, and it paid to label the products. For the Yankees, perhaps more than any team, the innovation made sense. A lot of tourists and newcomers to the game came out to see the Bronx Bombers. The novice fans might have known Ruth and Gehrig by their distinctive shapes, but they wouldn't know Bengough from Burns or Pennock from Pipgras, and certainly not from way out in the fifty-cent bleachers. At the start of the 1929 season, there were still no public address systems in major-league parks (the Giants would install the first set of amplified speakers at the Polo Grounds a few months later).

The Yankees were numbered, for the most part, in the order in which they were expected to bat that year. But Huggins wasn't sure, even on opening day, which one of the three catchers would win the job, so numbers 8, 9, and 10 all went to catchers.

1. Combs
2. Koenig
3. Ruth
4. Gehrig
5. Meusel
6. Lazzeri
7. Durocher
8. Grabowski
9. Bengough
10. Dickey

After two rainouts, the season began on April 18, a cold, colorless day in the Bronx. In the first inning, Ruth hit a long home run to left field. As he jogged around the bases in his famous pigeon-toed style, he doffed his cap and blew kisses to his new wife, Claire Hodgson, seated in box 173, who smiled from under a full-length fur coat. Ruth's estranged first wife, Helen, had died in a house fire three months earlier. Gehrig matched Ruth with a sixth-inning home run to right field, and the Yankees beat the Red Sox, 7 to 3. The home-run derby of 1929 had begun, the newspapers declared.

The season started nicely. Gehrig hit three home runs in one game against the White Sox on May 4, giving him a league-leading total of six for the season. The Yankees, too, jumped to an early lead in the standings. By the middle of May, the rookie Bill Dickey, twenty-one years old, began to establish himself as the Yankees' best catcher, a position he would hold for more than a dozen years. He also established himself as Gehrig's new best friend.

William Malcolm Dickey was four years younger than Gehrig. Born in Louisiana and raised in Little Rock, Arkansas, he was one of seven children. He was a quietly elegant man, long-legged and strong. Yet his face was that of a boy, with ears that stuck out like handles on a jug, and a sweet, wide grin. He looked like a lazy old horse when he walked, as if each section of each limb required a separate call to action. For such a young and lean athlete, though, he was a terribly slow runner. Everything about him seemed to operate in slow motion, most of all his speech. He didn't talk much, but when he did, his smooth Southern drawl made even the most urgent plea sound calm.

"I signaled for a fast ball and you threw me a curve," Dickey complained once to the pitcher Lefty Gomez, in his most furious tone.

"How are your bird dogs?" Gomez replied.

It was nearly impossible to feel threatened by Dickey. Even Gehrig approached without fear.

"Listen, Bill, I've been watching you and I think I know what is wrong with your batting," Gehrig said to him one day by the batting cage in 1929. "Maybe I can help you correct it."

Dickey was flattered to be offered help from a big star.

"You're trying to hit up at the ball," Gehrig said. Ruth could get away with taking an uppercut, but the Babe was the exception to the rule, Gehrig explained. Most hitters need a quick, compact swing to catch up with big-league fastballs. "These pitchers have too much stuff on the ball," Gehrig explained.

They worked together for an hour that day and for at least a few minutes every afternoon for days after. Gehrig's patience was never exhausted. He loved to talk about hitting, and with a soft-spoken rookie like Dickey he could exert a small measure of authority. It was one of his first steps toward becoming a team leader. "I guess he was the best batting coach that ever lived," Dickey said.

The Yankees got hot at the start of May, winning eight in a row, then stumbled, and by the middle of the month Philadelphia moved into first place. Foxx was firmly entrenched now as a starter, and he responded to the promotion by punishing almost every pitcher in the league. In 1929, he, not Gehrig, was the best first baseman in the game. The rest of Philadelphia's infield didn't provide much pop, but Max Bishop (second base), Joe Boley (shortstop), and Sammy Hale (third base) were good enough. And the hard-hitting outfield of Al Simmons, Bing Miller, and Mule Haas drove in plenty of runs to support the team's stingy pitching staff, which included Lefty Grove and George Earnshaw.

It looked as if the Yankees and Athletics would probably battle all year long for first place. On May 19, a Sunday, the Yankees were only a game and a half behind. It felt like the first real day of summer. More than 50,000 New Yorkers packed Yankee Stadium for a doubleheader with the last-place Red Sox. In the bottom of the fifth inning, skies over the Bronx suddenly turned gray, then purple. A violent storm erupted, sending fans rushing for the stadium's exits. In the bleachers, two people were killed and about seventy-five were hurt in the stampede. After the disaster, the Yanks lost seven of their next eleven games and dropped to third place. The A's, meanwhile, rumbled on. Simmons and Foxx were hitting every bit as well as Ruth and Gehrig. Grove and Earnshaw were better than any of the pitchers on the Yankee staff.

Huggins juggled his lineup in an effort to jumpstart his team. He had Gehrig bat third and Ruth fourth (Ruth still wore number three on his jersey, and Gehrig still wore number four, as they would throughout their careers). He moved Koenig from shortstop to third, tried Durocher at shortstop, then put Koenig back at short and inserted Lyn Lary at third. None of it helped. In June, Ruth caught a bad cold and missed more than two weeks of action. Gehrig handed out rabbit feet to his teammates — a gift sent by a fan from Pennsylvania — to bring the team luck. That didn't work either.

In the summer of 1929, on a scouting trip to Massachusetts, Paul Krichell discovered a player that he felt certain would become the next Lou Gehrig.

The young man's name was Henry Benjamin Greenberg, and he had just graduated from DeWitt Clinton High School in New York City. He was playing first base that summer for the Schuster Mills team in the Blackstone Valley League. Already, Greenberg was several inches taller than Gehrig (though not as thick across the rear or the chest) and was hitting the ball with big-league power. Krichell knew the Yankees didn't need another first baseman, but he couldn't afford to pass up such a promising prospect. Greenberg was Jewish, too, which Krichell knew would please his bosses, who for some time had been looking for a player to appeal to Jewish fans. Greenberg was offered $10,000 to sign with the Yanks.

"I had a look at Lou Gehrig, and said no thank you," Hank Greenberg recalled years later. It was a smart move. Over the years, a lot of men joined the Yankees hoping they might fill in from time to time at first base and perhaps win the starting job when Gehrig slowed down. But Gehrig showed no signs of slowing down. Most years, the Yankees didn't even carry a backup at first base. So Greenberg signed with the Detroit Tigers for $9,000. When the first installment on his salary arrived in September, he gave it to his father. David Greenberg, enthralled with the rapid rise in stock prices, invested the first $6,000 installment of his son's money in one of the market's hottest equities, the American Tobacco Company, which was trading that summer for about $200 a share.

As the season wore on and the train trips and hotels began to melt into one long blur, the Yankees grew weary and uninspired. Ruth recovered from his cold and began hitting the ball well, but not well enough to make up for the team's creaky pitching. Gehrig slumped, his average dipping below .300 at times, and was dropped from fourth place in the order to sixth, behind Lazzeri and Dickey. He was trying too hard to hit home runs, according to some of the writers who followed the team. It's a common affliction for hitters. The more they struggle, the harder they try. The harder they try, the more they struggle. And when their batting averages start to slide, they often attempt to make up for it by swinging for the fences. When that happens, they forget all the good habits that helped make them good hitters in the first place. Gehrig's great powers of discipline, instilled from youth by his mother, abandoned him for the first time in his professional career.

He may also have been trying to live up to his own press clippings. On August 10, *The New Yorker* published a long profile of the Yankee star, under a less than glamorous headline: "The Little Heinie." The piece, written before the start of the slump, began:

Lou Gehrig has accidentally got himself into a class with Babe Ruth and Dempsey and other beetle-browed sluggers who are the heroes of our nation. This is ridiculous — he is not fitted in any way to have a public. I don't think he is either stimulated or discouraged by the reactions of the crowds that watch his ponderous antics at first base for the Yankees, or cheer the hits he knocks out with startling regularity and almost legendary power. He enjoys playing ball and indicates his enjoyment by grinning at everyone he sees and occasionally running around bases on a diamond-shaped field, his calves pumping methodically under his baggy pants, bulging in an outer as well as an inside curve like those of football players in old drawings. Aside from baseball his principal amusement is fishing, and his principal associates are his mother and Babe Ruth.

Though the article went on for four pages, and though Gehrig appeared to have welcomed the writer to his home, there were almost no quotes from the story's principal subject. Gehrig's father, who refused to disclose the name of the family's German shepherd, was more cooperative than his son.

"It was recently rumored," the writer, Niven Busch Jr., was forced to continue, "that he had been seen at a movie theatre with a red-cheeked German girl who wore a bunch of flowers in her hair, but this could not be verified." Gehrig's only comment to the writer came when asked if he thought he would ever get married. "My mother makes a home comfortable enough for me," he said.

One evening, after a road game, Huggins sat in a rocking chair on the porch of the team's hotel and lit an old briar pipe. The orange glow of the match revealed a face full of deep creases. He was tired, he told the writer sitting next to him. He talked about getting out of baseball and opening a roller rink. Roller skating was extremely popular at the time. Wherever he traveled, he inspected the local rinks, he said, scrutinizing the construction, the music, the architecture, the seasonal ebbs and flows of the business. He'd invested in a rink once. He lost money on the deal. But he'd learned from his mistakes and would know what to do next time. He wasn't serious about quitting the Yankees, at least not just yet, but the roller rink seemed to tug harder whenever his job gave him migraines.

Late in August, the team lost four straight games to the St. Louis Browns. In three of those games the Yankees failed to score a run. Sensing his men had given up, Huggins called a meeting. He reminded his players that they had only a month left to catch the Athletics, and he tried to explain what it would take to turn things around. The players didn't seem impressed. Maybe they could see their manager's fatigue. Even so, Huggins was not ready to let them give up. He summoned the strength one more time to exhort his charges, using the same motivational tool he had tried in years past. Think of what it means to win the World Series, he told them. Think of the money. Think of the things the money can buy. His bloodshot eyes took in their faces. He could see in their expressions the same sense of defeat that pulled at his own conscience. When it became clear that he wasn't getting through, he sent everyone home.

As the locker room emptied, Huggins bowed his head and lit his pipe. He went upstairs to the executive offices, which were located between the lower deck and the mezzanine at Yankee Stadium. Ruppert and Barrow waited. Outside, darkness enveloped the playing field.

"They're through, Colonel," Huggins told his bosses, according to one writer's account.

"But we still have a month," Ruppert said.

"Forget about it," Huggins said. "Start getting ready for next year."

"But why?"

"I guess they're just tired, Colonel."

Huggins hauled himself up from his

chair and walked to the door.

"I'm tired myself," he said. "I'm tired out and I can't sleep."

During the next two weeks, the manager's appetite eluded him. His right leg shook involuntarily. Sleep, a long-lost friend, stretched further out of reach. The languid rhythms of a baseball game did nothing to calm his nerves. Neither did the stock charts in his newspaper. The Dow Jones industrial average had doubled the past two years — from 191 in early 1928 to 381 in September of 1929 — as speculators drove prices higher and higher. When someone dared suggest that the economy could not sustain such lofty prices, *The Wall Street Journal* fired a shot at the messenger: "Why is it that any ignoramus can talk about Wall Street?" But in September, stock prices fell sharply, and this time there was no rebound — only a slow, steady slide.

Huggins seemed to take each blow personally. He had already witnessed the implosion of the Florida real estate market. He had learned the hard way that prices stayed high only as long as speculators believed they would. People hadn't bought swampland to build resorts; they had bought so they could sell later at higher prices. But in 1926, after a pair of hurricanes tore through the state, a lot of people stopped believing. The market collapsed and investors got creamed. Now the storm clouds were gathering over Wall Street. The two things Huggins most loved and nurtured — his team and his portfolio — were falling apart at the same time. On September 19, a bitterly cold day, before a crowd of only a thousand fans, the Yankees barely roused themselves. They scratched a mere four hits in a 7-0 loss to the White Sox. The pennant race was over. Huggins, shrunken beneath his heavy, blue warm-up jacket, felt feverish and weak on the dugout bench. He had an ugly red blotch under his right eye.

The next morning, his whole body ached and the sore under his eye pulsed with heat. When the game that afternoon was cancelled on account of the frigid temperatures, Huggins checked into St. Vincent's Hospital, where doctors said he had a bad case of the flu and an infection under his eye. His condition had probably been made worse, they said, by his shattered nerves and deep exhaustion. They treated him with fluids and blood transfusions, but he only grew sicker. His fever ticked higher. The infection spread.

The Yankees left New York with coaches Art Fletcher and Charley O'Leary in charge. It had been a trying season, and now, with eight meaningless games left to play, the Yankees wanted nothing more than to be finished with it. A few days earlier, Gehrig had been concerned with getting his batting average back up above .300. Ruth had hoped to get to fifty home runs. Such matters seemed trivial now. All thoughts were on Huggins.

On Wednesday, September 25, the Yankees were leading the Red Sox, 5-2, in the fifth inning when the umpires called time-out. Players from both teams were asked to gather at home plate. The Yankees must have suspected at once what had happened. The dugouts emptied. Players from every position jogged to home plate. A telegram had just arrived, one of the umpires said. Huggins was dead. Within seconds, a man with a megaphone ran from one section to another spreading the word through Fenway Park. Bill McGowan, the home plate umpire, looked at his watch and asked for one minute of silence. The crowd rose as the flag in center field was lowered to half-staff. The players stared at their feet and kicked at the dirt. The flag remained at half-staff as the game continued. It took eleven innings for the Yankees to win, 11-10.

A brief funeral service was held the next afternoon at the Little Church Around the Corner, on East 29th Street in New York.

Gehrig and Ruth were among the eight pallbearers. About two thousand fans and friends filed past the coffin.

"I guess I'll miss him more than anyone else," Gehrig told a reporter. "Next to my mother and father, he was the best friend a boy could have. When I first came up he told me I was the rawest, most awkward rookie he'd ever seen or come across in baseball. He taught me everything I know. He gave me my job and advised me on salary matters. He taught me how to invest my money. Because of him I had everything a man could ask for in a material way. There was never a more patient or pleasant man to work for. I can't believe he'll never join us again."

The Yankees had crashed, just as Huggins predicted, finishing eighteen games behind the Athletics. Gehrig wound up with a .300 average (down 74 points from the previous season), thirty-five home runs, and 126 runs batted in. The Athletics clobbered the Cubs in the World Series, winning it four games to one.

Then, a few weeks after the season's last game, came the biggest crash of all. On October 29, 1929, the wobbling stock market buckled. An unprecedented 16.4 million shares changed hands, and about $26 billion in market value was lost. Most of the Americans who had leapt into the market late in the 1920s on the assumption that it would go only up were devastated. Hank Greenberg, for one, saw much of his investment in the American Tobacco Company disappear.

The nation's economy was falling apart. Auto sales, construction activity, employment, consumer purchasing — these were all sinking fast. Gehrig, eager as always to earn extra money in the off-season, chose an unfortunate occupation: He became a stockbroker with the New York firm of Appenzellar, Allen & Hill. He worked with Walter Koppisch, the All-American football player who had been his partner in the backfield at Columbia in 1922. The men shared an office in the St. Regis Hotel. Koppisch was one of the few Columbia students with whom Gehrig had stayed in touch. Sam Dana, another of their classmates, says Gehrig had lent Koppisch thousands of dollars to open his brokerage office in 1927.

Gehrig never spoke in detail to reporters about his finances or his interest in the market. Nor did he say whether he planned to make a career as a broker when his playing days were done. Ballplayers were often granted soft off-season jobs by insurance agents, brokers, and retailers who wished mostly to be associated with the famous athletes. Gehrig had no way to know when he accepted the job that within weeks brokers would be some of the most reviled people in the country. Many investors were convinced that the same men who had urged them to buy stocks throughout the market's bubble had made off with the money when the bubble burst.

Investors had been buying on margin throughout the late 1920s. With $1,000 in cash, someone might buy $10,000 worth of stock on a 90 percent margin. This worked nicely so long as stock prices went up. If they dropped, though, the borrower's collateral lost value and he was required to put up more money. If he failed to do so, the lender would cancel the loan and take all the stock. Beginning in October and stretching on into the winter, the system began to melt down as prices fell. People borrowed money from relatives, emptied their bank accounts, and pawned their jewelry and furniture to meet margin calls and keep lenders from seizing their assets. In November, a New York City police officer reportedly found an abandoned parrot that cried, "More margin! More margin!"

Bankers faced a run on cash, and brokers were left with little business. In 1929, brokers nationwide earned $227 million in commissions. By 1930, many of them couldn't pay the rent on their offices. The Great

Depression had begun. Stock prices would continue to fall, record numbers of men and women would lose their jobs, and the nation would find itself mired in the longest and deepest crisis since the Civil War.

For Koppisch, hiring Gehrig may have been an act of desperation. He probably hoped that customers would visit his office just to meet the Yankee slugger and shake his hand. He called a few photographers and had them come take pictures of Gehrig wearing a three-piece suit and reading tickertape stock prices. In the end, of course, it didn't matter. All the celebrity stockbrokers in the world couldn't restore investor confidence. Before long, Gehrig, delighted now with his three-year contract, went back to baseball. Koppisch went out of business.

While everything else seemed to fall apart during the Depression, baseball carried on, led by some of the greatest heroes the game would ever see, providing welcome entertainment to a nation soaked in gloom. The 1930s would be remembered for rising stars such as Greenberg, Joe DiMaggio, Bob Feller, and Dizzy Dean. But no one would play better baseball in the thirties than Lou Gehrig. If Babe Ruth was the perfect hero for the glorious days of prosperity, Gehrig — durable, dependable, and dignified — was the man for hard times.

CHAPTER 11

IRON HORSE

One day in Florida in the spring of 1930, Ruth, Gehrig, Ruppert, and the Yankees' new manager, Bob Shawkey, hammed it up for a movie-reel photographer.

"Well, Ruth, what have you got to say?" asked Ruppert, dressed in an impeccable gray suit, holding his fedora in his left hand and dangling it at his hip. "Gonna make more home runs than you did last year?"

"Well, I hope so," Ruth answered. He frowned, as if he didn't feel like talking to the boss.

Hoping for a warmer response, the colonel turned to his left, to his faithful first baseman. "How about you, Gehrig?" he asked.

"I can tell you better in September," Gehrig said. He spoke so quickly, in that high-pitched New York accent, that the words were momentarily difficult to discern. Gehrig never showed disrespect for management, and even this remark was far from nasty. Still, it would have been difficult to imagine him attempting a wisecrack in front of Miller Huggins.

Under Shawkey, the Yankees, and even Gehrig, were loosening up. Curfews were routinely ignored. Card games had no limits. The Yankees were behaving like a bunch of sixth-graders with a substitute teacher. Shawkey, who had pitched for the team from 1915 to 1927, was only thirty-seven years old. As a player, he had been one of Ruth's wilder cohorts, lapping up the Babe's leftovers. Now he hoped to make people forget all that drinking and all those blown curfews. He was trying to re-cast his image and establish himself as a disciplinarian, but no one was buying it.

Ruth had lobbied aggressively for the manager's job in the off-season. He'd wanted it for years. Every time he'd feuded with Huggins, he'd wished for the chance to prove his superior knowledge of the game. Speaker, Cobb, and Hornsby had all served as player-managers. When Huggins died, Ruth had thought his time had finally come. He was wrong. Ruppert passed him over, not once but four times. The owner offered the job first to Donie Bush, who had managed Pittsburgh to second place before resigning in August 1929; then to Eddie Collins, who had managed the White Sox in 1925 and 1926; then to Art

Fletcher, the Yankee coach; and finally — after three surprising rejections — to Shawkey. If it had been written on the Yankee Stadium scoreboard in big white letters, the message to Ruth could not have been clearer. He would never manage the team.

Some teammates spoke publicly on Ruth's behalf when the job came open. But Gehrig, a man of the establishment, kept his mouth shut. Privately, he might have offered Ruth words of encouragement, but he made no official endorsement.

Gehrig was a veteran now, with five years of experience, and he was beginning to appreciate the subtle dynamics of the clubhouse. He had earned the respect of his teammates, if not their adoration. They could all see that he was a company man, and that he cared as much for the approval of his bosses as he did for the camaraderie of his mates. Such behavior might have aggravated some of the players, but Gehrig made up for it with hard work. No one prepared better for a game, no one stayed in better condition, and no one hustled harder on the field. It was a great comfort to be on Gehrig's team. He flung his body over railings to catch foul balls, used his bare hand to scoop bad throws out of the dirt at first base, and scampered all over the infield to back up his teammates.

"There is no excuse for a player not hustling," he once said. "I believe every player owes it to himself, his club and to the public to hustle every minute he is on the ball field." He didn't have to say it, though. He proved it every day.

"He's got the old-time playing spirit," said Eddie Collins, the Columbia alum and future Hall of Famer. "He works hard all the time. . . . You can see it in every move he makes. He's all baseball."

It was the hustle that initially earned Gehrig admiration, but over time, despite his standoffishness, teammates began to more fully understand and appreciate his personality. "He wasn't as outgoing as Ruth or Lazzeri or Combs," Bill Werber recalled. "He didn't make a great effort to be friendly. It wasn't the nature of the man. I wouldn't say he was timid. He had the heart of a lion. But he was aloof." At the card table, Gehrig spoke only of cards. At the ballpark, he spoke only of baseball. In social settings, he spoke hardly at all. But most of his teammates were respectful of his silence and seriousness. In his own peculiar ways, Gehrig showed them that he cared. He remembered the birthday of pitcher George Pipgras's mother every year and usually bought her a box of candy to mark the occasion. When players were sick, he would invite them to come stay at his house for a night or two and let his mother take care of them.

Simple routines were a source of comfort to Gehrig. Each spring, he would hand two dollars to Doc Painter, the team's trainer, and Painter would buy him forty packs of chewing gum. Each morning, when Painter arrived in the clubhouse, he would remove one piece of gum from a pack — two if the Yankees had a doubleheader that day — and place the gum atop Gehrig's locker.

Gehrig liked to smooth the dirt around first base with his toe cleats before each pitch. He liked to spit on the palms of his hands between swings. When he drew a walk, he didn't drop his bat at home plate but tossed it gently in the direction of the dugout to make it easier for the batboy to retrieve. He believed in eating a big breakfast and getting a lot of fiber in his diet. He took a laxative called Agarol every night before bed. He seldom drank but smoked more than he cared to admit. He put himself through no elaborate pre-game rituals and required no long post-game rubdowns. Only the gum was an obsession. He wouldn't chew more than one stick a game, wouldn't accept a stick from anyone but Painter, and insisted on paying for it himself.

"If all ballplayers were like Gehrig there wouldn't be any job for trainers like me on

261

ball clubs," Painter said. "I've been with the team for five years now and during that time I don't think I have been asked to give Lou . . . more than five rubdowns. When he does ask for attention it is almost apologetically as if he were imposing on me."

At the start of the 1930 season, Joe Sewell of the Cleveland Indians owned the major league's longest-running streak of consecutive games played. But on May 2, Sewell developed a 102-degree fever and missed a start against the Red Sox, ending his run at 1,103 games, only 204 games short of the all-time record set by Everett "Deacon" Scott, the former Yankee. After hitting better than .315 in seven straight seasons, Sewell saw his average slip to .289 in 1930. He lasted only three more years, batting .282 across those seasons, and was finished at the age of thirty-four. Some players blamed the sudden deterioration of Sewell's skills on his stubborn insistence on playing without rest all those years.

With Sewell's streak done, it took reporters little time to recognize that Gehrig now held the longest string of consecutive games, at 744. But Gehrig's streak almost ended the same week Sewell's did. Before a game against the Indians on May 7, reporters noticed that Gehrig seemed to be limping. He started the game that day, hobbled his way to first on a single, and kept playing for six innings. But in the top of the seventh, with the Yankees leading the Indians by five runs, he took a seat on the bench. The Yankees had no backup to Gehrig, so Lazzeri filled in for him at first base. One newspaper said Gehrig had hurt his foot, another said it was his hip, and yet another said it was "a charley horse in one of his limbs." No one ever said what caused the injury, but Will Wedge of the *Sun* assured readers that it was not serious: "That is, not serious in the eyes of Herr Louie Henry, who has a physique that a professional wrestler might envy, and a plucky disposition that makes light of the buffets and bruises that come his way on the ball field." Gehrig, still limping, was back in the lineup the next day.

It was Wedge, a year later, who appears to have first referred to Gehrig by the nickname that would fit him best and stick the longest. "Gehrig certainly is one of the Yanks' prize locomotives — a veritable Iron Horse to pull the team along over the grades," he wrote. "And certainly he has an important run on the main line; he is steaming along with throttle open wide after the 1,307-game mark set by Deacon Scott."

Shawkey had more serious concerns than

the condition of his stoic first baseman. On offense, the Yankees were terrific. But all too often, the slugging wasn't enough to make up for shoddy pitching. The Yankees weren't the only team with pitching problems. All year long, teams were racking up double-digit scores. John McGraw, still pining for the dead-ball era, complained that A. G. Spalding & Bros., manufacturers of the rubber-and-cork-centered balls used since 1910, had manipulated their product to make it more bouncy. "It is lively," McGraw said, "and every sensible baseball man knows it." Some fans began to wonder if the circuit clouts had finally become too easy to hit. That concern, however, did not stop them from buying tickets. In fact, teams around the league were shattering attendance records.

Somehow, the baseball business seemed immune to the effects of the Great Depression, at least for the moment. The nation's total income fell to about $68 billion in 1930, down from almost $83 billion the year before. Industrial production was sliding, and unemployment was rising. Banks were beginning to fail. Mickey Cochrane, the catcher for the Athletics, reportedly lost $80,000 in a Philadelphia bank failure. Cochrane's broker phoned him in the clubhouse during games, begging him to come up with more money to meet his margin calls. Lazzeri had his savings wiped out when his bank in San Francisco collapsed. Al Simmons of Philadelphia said he was spared a huge loss because he forgot one day to deposit two checks for $3,000 each. Before he could get around to making the deposit, his bank had collapsed.

The Yankees sold tickets at a record-breaking pace in 1930, even as the team faded from the pennant race. The more the team lost, the more Shawkey seemed to relinquish control. The Yankees finished the season in third place, sixteen games out, with an 86-68 record, despite a team batting average of .309 and a record-breaking total of 1,062 runs scored. Gehrig had another phenomenal year: a .379 batting average, 41 home runs, and 174 runs batted in. Ruth compiled impressive numbers, too (.359, 49, 153), as did Simmons (.381, 36, 165) and Foxx (.335, 37, 156) of the Athletics. But it was Gehrig, in a year of awesome slugging, who emerged as the game's biggest hitter. If he hadn't played the last three weeks of the season with a broken pinky finger on his right hand, an ailment that he never mentioned, he might have led the league in all three of the most important batting categories.

As soon as the Yankees played their last game, he checked into St. Vincent's Hospital to have the finger fixed. Doctors also found bone chips in his left elbow. Both injuries required surgery. Gehrig spent more than a week in the hospital, dressed in pajamas and a long robe.

The Yanks were the first team built on the home run. They were the Ford Motor Company of baseball — bigger, stronger, and better, at least until the competition caught up and improved on the original design. By the early 1930s, though, almost every team had at least one accomplished home-run hitter. Philadelphia had two. If the Yankees hoped to win again, they would have to be better, instead of merely stronger.

After the 1930 season, Ruppert dumped Shawkey and brought in Joe McCarthy, who had recently been fired by the Cubs. McCarthy, stout and surly, was a disciplinarian. "Marse Joe," the players called him, for he established almost immediately that there would be no other master in the clubhouse. Marse Joe expected his players to stay in shape, get plenty of sleep, and dress in a coat and tie every day. "He insisted that they look like professionals and act like professionals," Werber recalled. Even shaving in the locker room was banned; players were to be properly groomed before they came to work. McCarthy believed the Yankees would win not by hitting the most home runs, but by preparing and executing better than their opponents.

When he managed the Louisville Colonels in the early 1920s, McCarthy developed his "Ten Commandments of Baseball." Now the Yankees would be expected to obey his orders:

1. Nobody ever became a ballplayer by walking after a ball.
2. You will never become a .300 hitter unless you take the bat off your shoulder.
3. An outfielder who throws in back of a runner is locking the barn after the horse is stolen.
4. Keep your head up and you may not have to keep it down.
5. When you start to slide, slide. He who changes his mind may have to change a good leg for a bad one.
6. Do not alibi on bad hops. Anybody can field the good ones.
7. Always run them out. You never can tell.
8. Do not quit.
9. Do not fight too much with the umpires. You cannot expect them to be as perfect as you are.
10. A pitcher who hasn't control hasn't anything.

One day during McCarthy's first spring with the team, the Yankees battered a minor-league team from Milwaukee by a score of 19-1. When Jimmie Reese, a reserve infielder, celebrated a bit too loudly, McCarthy shouted at him, letting the whole team hear it, suggesting that a team as great as the Yankees shouldn't gloat about beating a bunch of minor leaguers.

"You know, Bill," Gehrig told Dickey, "I like this McCarthy."

Gehrig was the perfect player for McCarthy's system. The manager didn't care for Gehrig's pipe and cigarette smoking. But in every other way, they were seemingly made for each other. Gehrig loved rules. When his manager or his mother didn't provide them, he constructed and enforced his own. He played each game as if it were the most important of his life. Even now, six years into his career with the Yanks, he sulked when he lost, brooded when he slumped, and turned a cold shoulder to teammates who didn't play as hard as he thought they could. He quickly became his manager's favorite player.

When Gehrig's contract expired at the end of the 1930 season, he told a few friends that he planned to demand a two-year deal for $35,000 a year. Instead, he settled for one year at $25,000, the same as he had made the year before. He was hitting at least as well as Ruth, and playing more games each year, but he was earning $55,000 less. Yet again, sportswriters gently criticized the first baseman's negotiating skills. Gehrig, *The Times* said, "emerged not even a fair second in his brief financial skirmish with the Yankee officials." Gehrig had no comment.

On January 25, 1931, another writer for *The Times*, columnist John Kieran, offered Yankee management some unsolicited advice concerning Gehrig's career: "It might pay Joe McCarthy to yank Lou Gehrig out of the line-up for one day this coming Spring. Lou hasn't missed a Yankee game in the past five seasons. McCarthy should snap this string before it becomes a worry to Lou."

But Gehrig played every game in 1931, and he was even better than the year before. He finished with a .341 average and forty-six home runs, led the league in hits with 211, and broke his own American League record for runs batted in with 184. His forty-six homers tied Ruth's for the league lead. If not for a freakish play early in the season, he would have had one more home run than Ruth — winning his first home run crown — and the American League RBI record would have been 186.

It happened on April 26, a wet and windy day at Griffith Stadium in Washington. After a walk to Lyn Lary in the top half of the first inning, Gehrig smashed a ball to deep center field. He ran hard toward first base, not sure yet if he had hit it hard enough to clear the fence. The ball crashed into the stands and then bounced back onto the field and into the hands of center fielder Harry Rice. Gehrig eased into his home-run trot, head down, eyes a few feet in front. Lary, meanwhile, looked out, saw Rice holding the ball, and assumed the outfielder had made the catch for the final out of the inning. He stepped on third base and jogged into the dugout without crossing home plate. He ran within a few feet of McCarthy, who was coaching third base for the Yanks at the time, but somehow McCarthy didn't notice.

Neither did Gehrig. Still running with his head down, he assumed his teammate had scored. When Gehrig crossed the plate, the Senators ran toward the umpire and complained that Gehrig should be called out for passing the runner ahead of him. The umpire agreed. Gehrig was out. The home run, as far as baseball records were concerned, never happened. The Yankees lost the game by two runs.

The Yankees were much improved in 1931, winning ninety-four games and losing fifty-nine. The team hit for a higher average and scored more runs than Philadelphia. But they still couldn't match the Athletics' pitching. Lefty Grove won thirty-one games and lost only four, while George Earnshaw won twenty-one and lost seven. In the World Series, Grove and Earnshaw pitched an incredible fifty of their team's sixty-one innings. And then they ran out of gas. The Athletics lost to the Cardinals, four games to three.

In October, Christy Walsh invited Gehrig and Ruth to join him on another barnstorming tour through the nation's heartland. Walsh was pleased that the men had tied for the home-run crown. It supplied him with a surefire promotional strategy: *Come see the two great sluggers settle it once and for all.* But this time Ruth and Gehrig had a competing offer. Fred Lieb invited the men on a barnstorming tour of Japan.

It was not the first Asian expedition for American ballplayers. In 1922, a promoter named Herb Hunter had led a goodwill tour across the Pacific, bringing along Cobb, Waite Hoyt, Casey Stengel, and others. But Commissioner Landis had accused Hunter of deliberately letting his American team lose a game in Korea. Normally, no one would have cared, but with the Black Sox scandal still fresh,

Landis was determined to clean up the sport's image. By 1931, Hunter thought Landis would forgive, or at least forget, and would grant him permission to make another trip to the Far East. He was mistaken. Only after Lieb paid the commissioner a visit did Landis change his mind, and then only on the condition that Lieb handle the finances and manage the players. Hunter and Lieb agreed to split the profits.

Gehrig decided to join Lieb on the trip to Japan, while Ruth remained loyal to Walsh and confined his barnstorming to the United States. Gehrig had always enjoyed Lieb's company. Lieb was a small, thin man who wore a Gatsby hat to cover his bald head. His mustache and eyebrows were so fair they were almost invisible. Lieb spoke fluent German, and his thoughts and conversations were not confined entirely to baseball. He lived with his wife and daughter in Greenwich Village. He read philosophy. While most of the other sportswriters thought of themselves as minor celebrities, entitled to at least a share of the booze and sex enjoyed by the athletes they covered, Lieb was more humble. He liked baseball and enjoyed writing about the game, but he didn't let the job consume him.

Gehrig also enjoyed the company of

Lieb's wife, Mary, and was pleased to hear that she too would be making the trip to Japan. Mary was modest, both in her manners and in her appearance. She was a delicate woman, with a long, narrow jaw and welcoming eyes. A person could get lost staring into those eyes. Some people did. Strangers tended to confide in Mary Lieb. Married men shared secrets with her that they didn't tell their wives.

Mary read the Bible almost daily yet studied all brands of religion. She was particularly attracted to Eastern mysticism. She practiced yoga and spoke of telepathic powers and, along with her husband, became expert in the use of a Ouija board. Sometimes when she meditated, she said, she felt as if another person, a Hindu perhaps, was telling her what to say. Jacob Ruppert would ask her to read his palm each spring and forecast whether the Yankees would win the pennant. "Mary, look again!" he would say, when the outlook was not good.

The trip by steamer to Japan took two weeks. Joining Gehrig and the Liebs were some of the game's top players, including Mickey Cochrane, Lefty Grove, George Kelly, Rabbit Maranville, Frank Frisch, Lefty O'Doul and Al Simmons. Gehrig enjoyed being with the athletes, especially Grove and Maranville. But once again the other men found his behavior somewhat strange. He seemed to disappear from the ship for hours at a time, just as he often seemed to disappear from team parties and group photographs during the baseball season. He wasn't in his cabin. He wasn't on deck. How does a man disappear from a ship at sea?

"Have you seen Lou?" O'Doul asked Fred Lieb one day.

"I've looked all over and I can't find him," Maranville said.

Lieb knew where he'd gone, but he didn't tell.

Gehrig and Mary Lieb were sneaking off and hiding in a lifeboat on the ship's top deck. Lieb didn't say anything because he thought the players and their wives would gossip.

"But I knew Mary was as safe with Lou as with Billy Graham or the Pope," Lieb wrote in his memoirs. Lieb said it was Gehrig who suggested the lifeboat as a meeting place. It would seem a strange arrangement. Was Gehrig so ashamed of what he had to say to Mary that only complete seclusion would suffice? Gehrig and Mary met again and again, swaying to the beat of the ocean in their private hideout. With each visit, Gehrig became more comfortable. He began to open up to Mary in a way he had rarely, if ever, done before. He talked about his fears and frustrations, his sorrows and sacrifices. Most of all, he talked about his loneliness.

He liked women, he told Mary, and he wanted to marry someday. But it was complicated. His mother had already suffered so much. She had lost three children and had worked herself to exhaustion to take care of the family, and without much help from her husband. Gehrig could never repay her, and he could never stand to disappoint her. He loved his mother with a great passion, he said, but he wondered sometimes if that devotion would keep him from ever loving anyone else.

At least twice he had brought women to the house to meet his mother — women he liked, women he might have married — and both times they had failed to win Christina's approval. Once, Christina had traveled to a young woman's hometown and started asking questions. Returning from her trip, she pronounced the woman unfit for her son.

About a year before the cruise, Gehrig had met a beautiful young woman from the College of New Rochelle. Alice Barrett was dark-haired, slender, and smart. She could have been a movie star with those big eyes and that tantalizing smile. In a college production of Shakespeare's *Twelfth Night*, she had played the part of Olivia. Gehrig had met Barrett in 1930, when she was a freshman. They had dated on and off for several years. Once, he took her ice skating at an indoor rink. He dressed like a college professor, in dark slacks, a white shirt, a bow tie, and a cardigan sweater. She looked like an angel, in a long, dark coat with white lapels that flapped like downy wings as she skated. In a picture taken that day at the rink, they're holding hands and smiling, looking every bit like a young couple in love. They were still together in the spring of 1931, it would seem, when Alice attended the season opener at Yankee Stadium. She showed up for another game five days later. But Gehrig's mother eventually wrecked the relationship with Alice, just as she wrecked the others. Gehrig wasn't happy about this, but he apparently felt so beholden that he wouldn't challenge his mother's judgment.

Mary Lieb knew Christina Gehrig and knew she could be a bully. She knew also that Christina might never meet a woman she deemed good enough for her son. Lou was the most important man in Christina's life, and she was not prepared to give him up, or even share him. Mary decided that Gehrig needed prodding.

"Lou, you know I'm fond of your mother and wouldn't do anything to hurt her," she said. But she reminded Gehrig that he was twenty-eight years old. "If you wait around for a girl that will suit Mom, you'll still be unmarried at fifty."

She advised him to stand firm the next time he met a woman he liked. Once you and your wife have children, she said, your mother will forget her objections.

When he wasn't huddling with Mary in the lifeboat, Gehrig spent time on the ship with an attractive young divorcee, who was apparently traveling to Japan for reasons unrelated to the baseball tour. When the ship docked in Tokyo, the woman phoned Gehrig at the Imperial Hotel and asked if she might drop by his room. Here he was, some 6,700 miles from his mother, with what appeared to be the perfect opportunity to enjoy the company of a beautiful woman. At first, he invited the woman to come to his room. Then he had second thoughts. He quickly phoned Fred Lieb and asked him if he would come up to the room and sit with him for a few hours.

"You know the game some of these girls try to pull off," he said. "If you can spare this time I'd like you to stay in the room until she leaves. I want you as a witness that nothing happens."

Nothing happened.

As the tour of Japan got under way, Gehrig bought jade jewelry, rolls of silk, ivory statues, and brightly colored kimonos for his mother, spending a good chunk of the $5,000 he earned for the trip. Seven games into the tour, he was struck by a pitch and broke two bones in his right hand. He continued to travel with the team, but he was finished for the tour as a player.

The barnstorming split did no apparent damage to the friendship between Gehrig and Ruth. While it was clearer than ever that Gehrig was not cut out to be one of Ruth's closest chums, Gehrig still admired Ruth and Ruth still enjoyed being admired. The Babe had calmed down a good deal since his second marriage, drinking less and staying home more. He tended to socialize with his assorted business associates as often as his teammates. On the field, he was growing fatter and slowing down. Bending for balls seemed an effort. He tottered around the outfield where he used to sprint. Still, sportswriters were beginning to sound silly with their annual pre-season predictions that he would soon break down. He continued to hit the ball a mile and flashed some speed on the bases when he needed it. Gehrig was bigger, stronger, and more reliable, but Ruth remained the team's star.

"I could never be another Ruth if I lived

to be 500 years old," Lou said in 1932. When asked if he thought he'd get better pitches and hit more home runs after Ruth retired, Gehrig became upset. "Say," he shot back, "don't be talking like that."

The effects of the Depression were finally beginning to hit the game. Ruth took a cut in salary in 1932, dropping to $75,000 from $80,000. "Never again will any player get that much money for a year's pay," Ruppert said. Gehrig's income was reduced to $23,000 from $25,000. One month into the season, attendance was down 45 percent. It didn't help that the cash-strapped federal government had added a 10 percent amusements tax on every ticket. Team owners, looking to save money, voted to reduce their rosters to twenty-three players from twenty-five and to lay off a couple of umpires. At one point, they proposed forcing fans to return baseballs hit into the stands. They dropped the idea, however, fearing a backlash.

McCarthy and Barrow put together a good team in 1932, and the players were beginning to accept their new manager's militant style. The mood of the country had changed. With so many men unemployed, most professional athletes knew better than to whine about their work conditions. The Yankees were also helped by the addition of several new faces in the early 1930s. Frankie Crosetti, a rookie from the Pacific Coast League, won the starting job at shortstop. Joe Sewell, dropped by Cleveland not long after his streak ended, took over at third base. Ben Chapman, one of the game's best base stealers, replaced Bob Meusel in the outfield. Lefty Gomez, Charlie "Red" Ruffing, and Johnny Allen joined the fading Herb Pennock on the pitching staff. But for all the fresh talent, Gehrig and Ruth yet again carried the team.

By now, Gehrig's streak of consecutively played games had begun making headlines. He started the season having played in more than a thousand straight. On May 9, with the Yankees scheduled to play the St. Louis Browns, Christina Gehrig was called to court to testify in a lawsuit filed by Anna Stelzle, who was seeking $40,000 in damages for injuries allegedly suffered in 1927 while riding in a car driven by Christina. Gehrig accompanied his mother to the courthouse that afternoon. Though little rain fell, the ballgame that day was canceled. Some writers have speculated that Jacob Ruppert called off the contest purely to preserve Gehrig's streak, but that seems unlikely. Ruppert probably thought, given the crummy weather, that he would make more money rescheduling the game as part of a Sunday doubleheader in July.

Gehrig was not called upon to testify that day, so he could have left the courtroom and made it to the ballpark in time for the game, had it not been postponed.

Three weeks later, on June 3, the Yankees were in Philadelphia for a game against their principal rival, the Athletics. Gehrig loved hitting in Shibe Park. The fence in right field stood only 331 feet away. In left, the distance was 334 feet. But the left-field and right-field fences converged out by the flagpole at something close to a right angle, which made for a vast canyon in straightaway center field. Over the course of his career, only Yankee Stadium and Sportsman's Park in St. Louis were the scene of more Gehrig homers. George "Moose" Earnshaw pitched that day for the Athletics. He had won sixty-seven regular-season games and four World Series games the past three years, establishing himself as one of the best right-handers in the game. But even the best pitchers come out flat occasionally. In the first inning, Gehrig hit a long, two-run homer to left-center field. In the fourth inning, he drove another one over the wall in right. In the bottom half of the same inning, when the Athletics came to bat, he dropped a foul pop. "It was a fairly hard chance, but I should have caught it," he said. The error contributed to a big inning, and Philadelphia took an 8-7 lead.

In the fifth, Gehrig faced Earnshaw for the third time. "I was still boiling over that error," Gehrig recalled a few years later. He took out his anger on Earnshaw, cracking yet another homer to left-center. For the fourth time in his career he had hit three home runs in a game. No one else had ever done it more than three times. And the game was only five innings old.

After Gehrig's third home run, Connie Mack stretched his long legs, climbed out of the dugout, and walked to the mound. He took the ball from Earnshaw and handed it to Leroy Mahaffey, another righty. But Mahaffey had no better luck. In the seventh inning, Gehrig turned on a fastball and thumped it over the left-field fence for his fourth straight homer. Not since the dead-ball era, when home runs were usually inside-the-park affairs, had anyone hit four in a game. Bob Lowe of the Boston Nationals had done it in 1894, and Ed Delahanty of the Phillies in 1896. No one had ever hit five. (Two days later, when the Yankees were in Boston, Lowe, age sixty-three, would put on his old uniform, grab his skimpy glove, and head down to the ballpark. Gehrig put his beefy left arm on the skinny old man's shoulder and smiled for a photographer.)

When Gehrig came to bat in the eighth

inning, he had a chance to hit his fifth homer. The small crowd of Philadelphians got on its feet to encourage him. He swung hard but a bit too high, grounding into an easy out.

The Yankees got six runs in the ninth, bringing their total for the afternoon to twenty, and finally putting the game out of reach. Thanks to the rally, Gehrig got one more turn to hit. Eddie Rommel was on the mound now. Gehrig saw a pitch he liked. He stepped into it, swung, and hit the ball on the thick part of his bat. It felt solid — better than any ball he'd hit all day. At the sound of the crack the fans stood to watch the ball fly. It rose and rose. Gehrig took off running. The ball rocketed toward straightaway center field, into the deepest corner of the park.

Al Simmons, who'd been switched from left field to center earlier in the game, started sprinting. He could see that the ball wasn't going to clear the fence, but he wasn't sure if he would get to it in time. If it landed and hit the wall, it might bounce around awhile. Gehrig would have at least a triple, maybe an inside-the-park home run. Simmons leapt. As he raised his glove and stretched his left arm high above his head, the ball disappeared into the soft leather of his mitt. Gehrig, approaching second base, must have had a good view of the catch. He lowered his head and jogged back to the dugout.

"You know," he said after the game, "I think that last one was the hardest ball I hit all day. Gosh, it felt good. . . . I wonder what Mom and Pop up at New Rochelle thought of it. Too bad Mom didn't see it."

Even without Mom on hand and without the fifth home run, it was one of the greatest days he'd ever had on a baseball diamond. Yet, once again, he found his accomplishment partially obscured. Back in New York, John McGraw, fifty-nine years old, tired, and disappointed with the performance of his team, decided the time had come to announce his resignation. After thirty-one years, ten National League pennants, and one missed opportunity to sign Lou Gehrig, he'd seen enough. In newspapers the next day, the bigger headlines by far were for McGraw.

Gehrig must have been used to it by then. Somehow, the spotlight always seemed to miss him. He had all the talent in the world but little of the luck. Yet he never grumbled and never cried for attention. He seemed happy with his middling level of celebrity and the handful of endorsements that came his way. Life was zipping along neatly, like a double-play ball from Tinker to Evers to Chance, and he had few complaints.

As the air grew crisp and the shadows long, the Yankees found themselves back in the World Series, this time against the Chicago Cubs, a solid team but far from a powerhouse. Hack Wilson was gone, playing out the last years of his beer-stained career in Brooklyn. The Cubs counted on good pitching now to win, with Lon Warneke and Guy Bush their best starters.

The Yankees had extra incentives to beat the Cubs. For Joe McCarthy, it was a chance to get back at the organization that had fired him. For Gehrig, Ruth, and some of the others, it was a chance to defend the honor of a former teammate. Mark Koenig, their old shortstop, had signed with the Cubs in August after kicking around in the Pacific Coast League earlier in the season. He had played only thirty-three games with Chicago, but he hit .353 and fielded splendidly. Some said the Cubs would not have won the pennant without him. Yet his Cubs teammates had voted to pay him only a partial share of World Series income, which was expected to be about $4,000 or $5,000 for each player. It was common practice to award fractions of shares, depending on a player's length of service, but the Yankees didn't care about common practice. Koenig had been well liked in

New York. Now, rallying to his cause, they blasted their opponents as cheapskates.

"They're chiselers and I tell 'em so," Ruth said.

It was raining so hard in New Rochelle on the morning of the first game that Gehrig delayed his departure for the ballpark, counting on a rainout. When the clouds finally broke, shortly before noon, Gehrig got in his car and hurried to the Bronx. He was the last Yankee to reach the clubhouse. The field was soggy, but playable. The Cubs scratched a couple of runs in the early innings. In the bottom of the fourth, with Ruth on first and the Yankees trailing, 2-1, Gehrig walked to the plate. He hacked at a pitch and drove it deep into the right-field bleachers, out in the direction of the Canada Dry billboard. The Yankees went on to win, 12-6. In game two, Gehrig hit three singles, drove in one run, and scored two more as the Yanks won again, 5-2.

The defining moment of the Series — the moment no one would ever forget even if no one ever seemed exactly sure of what happened — came in game three, as the Series moved from New York to Chicago. It was a moment that would in many ways epitomize the careers of both Gehrig and Ruth. By now, the Yankees were getting cocky, and this time McCarthy didn't seem to mind a bit of gloating. Fans at Wrigley Field threw lemons on the field before the game, and the Yankees lobbed them back into the stands. In the fifth inning, with the score tied, 4-4, the crowd screamed vulgarities as Ruth stepped to the plate. Charlie Root stared down at the Babe from atop the pitcher's mound. Root threw a strike. The Cubs and their fans hollered. Ruth let two balls go by. Then Root threw another strike. By now the shouting was so loud, the abuse so terrific, that the outcome of the game seemed secondary. It was all about the Babe.

What happened next has been debated and discussed for years. Most agree that Ruth held up two fingers, indicating in the style of an umpire that there were only two strikes. Old newsreel footage shows that Ruth often made the same gesture when batting in exhibition games. It was his playful way of reminding the pitcher and the audience that two strikes didn't mean anything; it took only one pitch to hit a home run. According to some accounts, though, the Babe not only signaled that there were two strikes but also pointed to the spot in center field where he intended to hit the next pitch. If he did in fact point, it would have been a gaudy hunk of showmanship, even by Ruth's standards. Never before, not even on the barnstorming circuit, had he pulled such a stunt.

On the next pitch, a curve, Ruth smashed one of the deepest home runs ever hit at Wrigley Field. It landed just to the right of the scoreboard in center field, more or less in the spot he had supposedly indicated. He roared with laughter and shouted at the Cubs as he rounded the bases. In a box seat near home plate, Franklin D. Roosevelt, running for president against Herbert Hoover, leaned back and laughed as he watched the Babe romp around the bases.

Did Ruth call his shot? Probably not. Most of the newspaper accounts from the game make it clear that he held up two fingers. A few stories, like the one by columnist Westbrook Pegler in *The Chicago Tribune*, interpreted Ruth's gesture as a prediction that he would hit a home run to center. But film footage of the game, discovered in recent decades, shows that Ruth made some sort of pointing gesture.

As days, weeks, and years went by, more and more reporters gravitated toward Pegler's version of events. Ruth would never say whether he'd forecast the homer. "It's all right there in the papers," he coyly said. Gehrig at first told reporters that he didn't see Ruth call the shot. Later, he waffled, suggesting that it might have happened the way the myth-making writers said. But in the great swirl of discussion about what did or did not happen that afternoon, hardly anyone remembers what happened after Ruth's home run. On the next pitch, Gehrig hit another homer, giving the Yankees a 6-4 lead and effectively icing the Series.

In the fourth and final game, the Cubs jumped to an early lead. In the sixth inning, with the Yankees trailing by a run, Gehrig came to bat with runners on second and third and two outs. As he dug into the batter's box, he was distracted by the presence of umpire Bill Klem, who was standing near second base, directly in Gehrig's line of sight. Ordinarily, when a batter asks an umpire to move, the umpire takes a few small steps one way or the other and the game resumes. It's a routine courtesy. But Klem shook his head and held his ground. Gehrig asked him again to move. Klem refused. When Jakie May threw his pitch, Gehrig swung and lined a rocket aimed almost perfectly at Klem's head. The umpire jumped — "old Klem has never moved faster," one writer noted — and the ball scooted into center field. Both runners scored. When the inning was over, Gehrig ran past Klem and told him what he thought of his behavior.

The Yankees went on to win the game,

13-6. After a three-year drought, they were champions again. Gehrig finished the Series with a .529 average, three home runs, eight runs batted in, and nine runs scored.

In the showers after the game, the Yankees threw towels and hugged and sang:

> East Side, West Side,
>   all around the town
> The kids sang "ring around Rosie,"
> "London Bridge is falling down."

During the off-season, *Liberty* magazine asked Gehrig to write an article addressing the question of whether playing in the shadow of Ruth had made him jealous. It's not clear whether he employed a ghost-writer, though the subdued tone of the piece and the absence of the usual sporting clichés suggest that he might have handled the assignment himself. Gehrig wrote that he had "no trace of the inferiority complex toward Ruth that the reporters love to talk about." He made it clear that he viewed Ruth as a competitor, as well as a friend. He didn't mind finishing second to Ruth in home runs each year, he said, but he was determined to drive in more runs than his teammate. Referring to the RBI category, he said, "that's my baby."

Gehrig admitted in the article that he was shy.

But I have a pretty definite idea of my value and I know I can hit a baseball very hard and very far. The point is that I do this in a pretty matter-of-fact way, whereas Ruth hits them with a flourish of drama that is instinctive, natural, and all his own. In other words, there is only one Babe Ruth, so why argue with facts?

Off the ball grounds I'm just a plain comfort-loving citizen who likes to go to bed early and take life at a slow pace. I smoke a little, drink a little beer, like fishing and ice skating, and just recently I've begun to go for golf.

I'm no Good-Time Charley, in other words.

Finally, he said he was happy to have a good job and a good salary, given the Depression. While retirement was a long way off, he would probably become a manager when he could no longer play. Until then, he said, his life might sound "a little dull for some tastes," but he and his parents were happy.

Maybe we're missing something, but I can't help thinking that people who see life through a train window must be missing something too. They're going too fast to get anything but a fleeting glimpse of what it's all about.

I'm not rich in the accepted sense of the word, but what millionaire can buy my serenity? What king can live exactly as he wishes, with an obligation to nothing except his conscience? In fact, I have yet to meet the man who can look backward over his shoulder as he passes his thirtieth birthday and say, as I do:

It's all been worth the while.

CHAPTER 12
COURTSHIP

Eleanor Grace Twitchell lived with her mother and her younger brother on Chicago's South Side, in a working-class neighborhood of brick bungalows and two-story apartment buildings. She had a decent job, making about forty dollars a week as a secretary, but the work left her unsatisfied. Her social life had once been dazzling, even dangerous, like pages torn from a Fitzgerald novel. Now it wasn't.

The Depression had hit her like a blow to the gut, taking her wind away. Her father's business had collapsed. Her girlfriends, one after another, sought shelter in marriage. Her boyfriends seemed much less attractive stripped of their financial security and bluster. Eleanor was twenty-eight years old, no kid anymore, and her prospects were dimming.

But on the night before the third game of the 1932 World Series, Kitty McHie, one of her old poker-playing pals, was tossing a party in Chicago. Kitty had recently married Emory Perry, a man who had made a small fortune by manufacturing bathroom fixtures. Emory was a friend of Babe Ruth's, and Kitty promised that there would be some handsome young Yankees at her party. That night, Eleanor would meet her future husband, Lou Gehrig.

Eleanor was a fashionable woman. She had her hair cut just below the ears and dressed in long, narrowly tailored dresses. She drank hard liquor and smoked cigarettes in public at a time when doing so was considered daring. But her full cheeks, upturned nose, and small smile undermined her careful attempts at glamour. Her slender figure lacked dramatic curves. No matter how she tried, she always looked like someone's kid sister.

There were few things sadder than an aging flapper still trying to dance the Charleston after the music had stopped, and Eleanor didn't want to play that part. She was trying to do the responsible things that women her age were supposed to do. That's why she had taken a course in shorthand and gone to work. She was receptive to marriage, perhaps even eager to wed, but the men she met seemed too ordinary, too poor, or too dull. Or they were already married.

Stability did not run in the family. Eleanor had spent the first few years of her childhood on the road, bounding across the country in dusty coaches, cradled firmly in her mother's arms. Her father, Frank Bradford Twitchell, worked as a price-maker, calculating the odds for horse races. The Twitchells were always on the move, chasing the warm weather, hurtling from track to track, staying in one cheap boardinghouse after another, without a featherbed or frying pan of their own. While Frank Twitchell studied the horses, his wife, Nell, took care of their daughter. Eleanor had only one memory of her "gypsy days," as she referred to them. She remembered hanging around a candy store near Fort Sam Houston in San Antonio, Texas, cajoling spare change from soldiers and officers. All through her life she would have little difficulty getting what she wanted from men.

When Eleanor was five, her mother became pregnant. The family quit the road and settled in Chicago, where Frank found a job managing Heidelberg Gardens, a South Side restaurant popular among local politicians. He had a knack for remembering faces and names. He had movie-star good looks, with black hair that he slicked back like Tyrone Power. Men enjoyed his company. Women enjoyed it, too.

In 1910, Nell gave birth to a boy. The

Twitchells named him Frank Jr. The family was putting down roots, albeit shallow ones. They lived on Calumet Avenue in an apartment they shared with a couple of boarders. But Frank Twitchell was too ambitious and too amiable to continue living so humbly. After a few years of shaking hands and rewarding influential guests with good tables, he began to recognize opportunities for advancement. In 1916, he founded the F. B. Twitchell Co., and named himself president. His new company was immediately awarded a city contract to manage the concession business at Jackson Park, a 543-acre expanse that lined the lakefront south of downtown Chicago. It was a big job for someone with so little experience. He took control of all the park's food businesses, which included a tea room, a golf course lunch counter, and several snack stands. But the prize holding in Twitchell's empire was the restaurant housed within the German Building. The German Building was one of the few structures kept intact after the World's Fair of 1893, and it remained one of the city's most popular destinations in the first decades of the twentieth century. A spire shaped like a teardrop topped the two-story building. Like a Teutonic lighthouse on the shores of Lake Michigan, it could be seen for miles around. When the weather was warm, thousands of people came to Jackson Park every day to swim, play golf, or picnic. There were many places in the park to buy refreshments, but there was only one full-service restaurant, and that was in the German Building. Though its glory had faded a good deal by the time Twitchell took over, it was still a terrific source of revenue.

How a man with no experience in running a business received such a plum contract is anyone's guess. As manager of the concession business, Twitchell had the power to hire and fire. He decided whether to buy his sausage from Oscar Mayer, Ogden Armour, or one of Chicago's other meatpackers. Public records show that he paid $5,000 a year for the right to run the concession business. It looked like a sweet deal. The business had gross sales of more than $100,000 a year. Twitchell kept a lot of cash around his home, thousands of dollars sometimes, and Eleanor routinely supplemented her allowance by snatching bills from her father's dresser drawer. He always claimed to have won the money at the racetrack.

The family's fortunes improved dramatically after Twitchell got the concession contract, and they settled down to what appeared to be a stable, middle-class existence on the thriving South Side. Twitchell bought a Stearns Knight, an automobile not quite as regal as a Cadillac but showier than a Model T. Eleanor was enrolled in riding lessons, and when she fell in love with a horse named Black Cloud, her father bought it for her. The family moved to a home of its own at 6242 Ellis Avenue. Eleanor and Frank Jr. used Jackson Park as if their father owned it, strolling along the lakefront, learning to play golf, and riding horses along its endlessly winding paths.

As she entered adolescence, Eleanor lost interest in school. She was bright and sharp-tongued, with a gift for writing, but school had too many rules — and too many children. She considered herself more sophisticated than her classmates. One picture, probably taken early in her adolescence, shows her stretched out on a beach blanket wearing a dark beret, a striped, short-sleeve dress shirt buttoned all the way to the collar, pleated dress pants, and a pair of pointy-toed, high-heeled shoes. Her fingernails are painted a dark shade, and there's a cigarette in her right hand. She's the ideal of adolescent sophistication, and she's smiling at the photographer as if she couldn't be happier.

The perfect image shattered with stunning suddenness when Eleanor was fifteen years old. "It happened one Sunday at breakfast when my father picked up the *Tribune*, glanced at it and turned pale," she wrote in her memoirs. "He stacked the paper under his arm and literally ran out of the house." An hour later, a messenger arrived holding a large manila envelope. Nell opened it. Inside was a note from Twitchell and a copy of the Sunday *Tribune*. Nell spread the paper across the dining room table and opened it to page 12.

Her mother was still shaking as Eleanor squeezed in beside her and read the headline: "Marine Returns to Charge Wife Loves Another." Frank Twitchell had been having an affair with the wife of a Marine who had just returned from action in World War I. At the end of the war, it was not uncommon for soldiers to return home and find that their wives and girlfriends had moved on. But rarely did the breakups make the newspaper. Eleanor, in her memoirs, remembered the story's headline almost precisely.

Nell and Frank stayed together for a few years after the revelation that he'd been cheating. At times they struggled to repair the damage to their marriage, and at times they simply ignored each other. Census records show they were still living together in 1920, but in 1930 Nell was named in the census as the head of household. Her husband was nowhere to be found.

But Nell wasn't finished with Frank. Like an amateur detective, she followed him around town. Sometimes Eleanor would drive so her mother could watch more closely. Once, the women followed Twitchell to a stranger's apartment. They waited until he had time to settle in. Then Nell instructed her daughter to climb the fire escape to prevent him from getting out the back. Nell went to the front door and knocked. As she suspected, Frank tried to get out in the other direction. "My father opened the bedroom window to beat a diplomatic retreat — only to stare into the wide-open eyes of his daughter," she wrote. "I was devastated and amazed. The Other Woman was . . . just a skinny tart in a negligee and nowhere near my mother in sheer looks. She was the front-runner of a whole series of disillusions that crowded me over the next few years. My father, my well-loved father — was just another guy with other flaws."

Eleanor was shaken. She began skipping school to play golf, treating herself to expensive clothes, and traveling with an older crowd. Rebellion had its pleasures, she quickly learned, especially for a teenager with cash and well-connected friends. Chicago was sexy and dangerous, with a soundtrack played by Louis Armstrong, booze supplied by Al Capone, and the law enforced, more or less, by Mayor Big Bill Thompson. The South Side was the hub of the action. "I was young and rather innocent," she recalled, "but I smoked, played poker, drank bathtub gin along with everyone else, collected $5 a week in allowance from my father, spent $100 a week."

Eleanor's poker-playing partners included some of her well-connected neighbors: Kitty McHie was the daughter of a well-known newspaper editor; Anna Torrio was the wife of Johnny Torrio, one of the city's most powerful mobsters; Mary Grabiner was the wife of Joe Grabiner, a gambler; and Mary's sister, Dot, was married to Joe Grabiner's brother, Harry, an executive for the Chicago White Sox. The women and their husbands frequently supplied Eleanor with dates. Many of her dates were older, married men. "By then, I was well-known in speakeasy society," she wrote.

While Eleanor danced and drank and spent freely, the source of her financial support was crumbling. The German Building, never meant to last beyond the World's Fair, was falling apart. Profits sagged. In 1921, Twitchell asked the park commissioners for "not less than $4,000 or $5,000" to make repairs. When they refused, he asked to be excused from his contract. In 1925, the restaurant was destroyed in a fire. Arson was suspected but never proved. Soon after, the commission stopped doing business with the F. B. Twitchell Co.

By the time the Great Depression hit, Twitchell didn't have far to fall. His concession business had collapsed, and a big investment in Florida real estate had gone bust. Eleanor's poker winnings were hardly enough to support her in the fashion to which she'd become accustomed, and at least some of the married men who had treated her to pricey dinners were unemployed and no longer interested in expensive dates.

The party at Kitty McHie's house was extravagant. For Eleanor, it must have felt as if she were stepping back to the days when she and her friends had so much time and so much to celebrate. Of course, the Yankees attended lavish parties wherever they went. Few Americans enjoyed more immunity from the effects of the Depression than major-league players, and among those players, none were better off than the Yankees. Traveling with the Yankees in 1932 was like traveling in a time machine with the dial stuck on "Good Old Days." The Yankees went from train station to train station, hotel to hotel, ballpark

302

to ballpark. They rarely, if ever, caught sight of a breadline, a shantytown, a migrant camp, a union rally, a Communist Party meeting, or a stockbroker poised on an office ledge. A professional baseball player often earned more money than his entire extended family.

"I never heard of the Depression," Bill Werber said, exaggerating only slightly. He signed with the Yankees as a shortstop in 1927 and was traded to the Red Sox in 1933. "All the ballplayers were making good money. The first and fifteenth of every month, after the game you'd find a check on your stool in the clubhouse. Hell, Ruth was making $80,000, and Gehrig was making about $35,000. That was more money than a bank president or the president of a university. We stayed in the very best hotels in every city — the Cadillac Hotel in Detroit, the Hotel Cleveland — and the ball clubs paid for all the meals you ate."

Werber's numbers may have been rough estimates, but his point was exactly right. The Yankees led charmed lives. And they were thrilled to find themselves in Chicago for the World Series, because Chicago was still the most raucous stop on the tour. The jazz blew more hotly in Chicago, the booze flowed more freely, and women, under the influence of both intoxicants, presented themselves more wantonly.

Gehrig was one of the few men on the team who looked as glamorous in a jacket and tie as he did in Yankee pinstripes. That wavy brown hair, those bright blue eyes, that chiseled smile, those gargantuan muscles. Women stared and sighed. Then, when they tried to talk to him, they saw the fear in his eyes, the look of a little boy lost in a big man's frame. There was a sweetness about him, but most women didn't see past the naïveté. Gehrig tended to stand alone at these parties, back to a wall, watching his teammates eat, drink, and seduce. When his curfew neared, he would slip away and return to his hotel room.

He did his usual wallflower act for most of the evening at the McHie party, but this time Eleanor Twitchell caught his eye. She could see she was being watched. Gehrig had met Eleanor at least once before, at a party a few years earlier in Chicago. But he always claimed not to remember the earlier encounter. Ken Sobol, one of Ruth's biographers, interviewed many of the players, coaches, and sportswriters who knew Gehrig best, including Fred Lieb. He says Lieb and some of the others told him Eleanor had been a regular on the team's party circuit. Such regulars were referred to by some of the ballplayers as "circuit girls."

By 1932, it would appear that Eleanor and Gehrig were both ready to settle down. For Eleanor, that meant abandoning much of her social life. For Gehrig, it meant beginning one. He summoned the courage to approach her at the party, offering to fetch a drink. Eleanor accepted. They began to chat. Eleanor's voice was loud and strong, like a trumpet. Gehrig, for all his reticence, spoke loudly, too, but his voice tended to jump an octave whenever he got excited. Eventually, Gehrig volunteered to walk Eleanor home. But when they reached her address, he lost his courage. Without offering so much as a handshake he said a quick good night, turned around, and disappeared down the block under the cover of darkness.

When the World Series ended, the Yankees returned to New York. Eleanor assumed that she'd heard the last of her escort. Then, a week after their encounter, she received a package containing a diamond-cut crystal necklace and a note from Gehrig explaining that he had purchased it the year before in Japan. Most likely he had bought the gift with his mother in mind, but he was smart enough not to mention that. A week earlier he'd been too frightened to ease in for a peck on the cheek; now he was sending jewels that probably cost a fortune. This was new terrain to him, and he was moving across it awkwardly, unsure of each step.

They began exchanging letters. "The notes were fairly noncommittal," Eleanor wrote. "We hadn't begun to confide in each other, at least not yet." The pen pal act continued through the winter and into the spring. Eleanor, comparing her new acquaintance to her old horse, said she couldn't figure out whether he would respond to a loose rein or a taut one. Afraid he would bolt if she pulled too hard, she ultimately chose the gentle approach.

Finally, on May 8, 1933, the Yankees returned to Chicago for a three-game series at Comiskey Park. The Yankees won the first game, 7-3, on a Monday afternoon. Gehrig went two-for-four with a double and a run batted in. After the game, he and Eleanor at last had their reunion.

But they were not alone. They went for dinner at the Shoreland Hotel — "a family hotel, at that," said Eleanor, hinting at frustration — with a big group of friends. If the location and the company bothered her, her date's behavior only made things worse. When Gehrig's curfew neared, he excused himself from the group and walked out. Alone.

Eleanor remained at the table. But later in the evening, after the dinner had broken up, she summoned her courage and phoned Gehrig at his hotel.

"I just wanted to say good night, dear," she said.

"For Chrissake," he said, sleep coating his voice, "do you know what time it is?"

He hung up.

Eleanor was shattered. The next morning, she woke up and went to work. "So this was it," she told herself, according to her memoirs, as she trudged up the wide marble stairs to her office on Chicago's lakefront. Her hopes for romance appeared to have been dashed. All she could look forward to now, she wrote, was a lifetime of "spinsterhood and alarm clocks."

Outside, the sky was gray, with a wicked wind tipping the sailboats on Lake Michigan. She was at her desk when a visitor interrupted. Gehrig never said what compelled him to leave his hotel and show up at Eleanor's office that morning. Perhaps he recognized that another opportunity for happiness was about to slip away — and that this time he had only himself to blame. Perhaps his concerns were more mundane: The weather was so lousy that the game was almost certain to be a rainout, which would have left him with a lot of free time. But whatever his rationale, the result was the same. He swung and connected. That morning he told Eleanor he loved her and wanted to marry her.

They hugged and kissed. Then they went to the Drake Hotel for breakfast and began planning for the future. It was the first time they had ever spent more than a few minutes alone together.

The game that day was indeed rained out. Eleanor took Gehrig to the South Side to share the news of their engagement with her mother and brother. Gehrig joined the Twitchells for dinner. But he didn't stay late, and he returned unaccompanied to his hotel.

"That old curfew again," Eleanor wrote.

Curfews, Eleanor soon discovered, would be the least of her frustrations. She had yet to meet her future mother-in-law. Gehrig warned Eleanor about Christina. He told her that she could be stubborn and jealous. He told her that his mother might not be happy about the news of their engagement. Ever hopeful, he suggested that matters might be helped if Eleanor were to invite Christina to Chicago so that the women could get acquainted. Eleanor agreed, telling Christina she was welcome to stay at her mother's home on the South Side. Christina accepted. So far, so good.

But the trouble began almost as soon as these strong-willed women met. Christina was fifty years old and had constructed much of her identity around being the mother of the great Lou Gehrig. She had given him life, had raised him out of poverty, and continued to provide the food and support that fueled his home runs. She viewed herself as the nurturer of his legend. Everyone — even the newspapermen — referred to her as "Mom Gehrig." When Christina met Eleanor's mother, she was aghast. Nell was in her late forties, separated from her husband, and she behaved more like Eleanor's sister than her mother. "Call me Nell," she instructed most of the people she met, including her daughter's friends. Christina considered such familiarity inappropriate. She was also offended that her first meal in Chicago was served at a supper club rather than in Nell's home. She soon discovered, to her further horror, that her future daughter-in-law was a culinary illiterate, scarcely able to boil a pot of water.

Christina spent more than two weeks in Chicago. She arrived in early June and stayed until the Yankees came to town for another series of games against the White Sox, beginning June 17. Before the start of the first game at Comiskey Park, Gehrig sat atop the dugouts, holding a six-inch piece of animal bone in his right hand and rubbing it firmly against the barrel of his bat, trying to harden the surface of the wood. A reporter from the *Chicago Tribune* approached and asked if he would confirm the rumors that he had gotten engaged to a Chicago girl. Gehrig smiled and shook his head. No, he said, he wasn't going to comment. But Marshall Hunt of the New York *Daily News* somehow got the scoop, filing this paragraph from Chicago: "Henri [*sic*] Lou Gehrig, robust first baseman of the Yankee baseball team, is preparing to make a home run in the matrimonial league." Gehrig went four-for-five that afternoon, with two singles, a double and, yes, a home run.

Two days later, a photographer caught the couple flirting near the Yankee dugout. Gehrig smiled like a kid showing off his new bike. Eleanor, wearing a white hat curved rakishly across her face and a billowy white blouse, offered a more subdued grin. Once again, Gehrig was asked to confirm the rumors that he was engaged. Once again he refused. "They are shown in Comiskey Park just before yesterday's game," said the caption in New York's *Evening Post*, "after Columbia Lou finally had admitted that the young lady's constant attendance at Yankee games had some significance."

Gehrig's teammates were surprised. They thought he was too much in love with his mother to ever take a girl. "I couldn't believe my ears when I heard about it," Mark

Koenig said. In all the stories filed that week from Chicago, Christina Gehrig was never quoted. It may be that she couldn't think of anything nice to say.

The domestic tumult had no effect on Gehrig's play. All season he remained among the league leaders in batting average, home runs, and runs driven in. With Ruth in and out of the lineup, nagged by a string of injuries, Gehrig lifted the team on his shoulders. He did everything but pitch, which is probably what the Yankees most needed him to do. Through early August, the Yanks stayed in the pennant race, but the Washington Senators were the surprise leaders. The Senators, led by Joe Kuhel and Heinie Manush, were winning the old-fashioned way, with lots of base hits, gutsy baserunning, and thrifty pitching. The team didn't hit a lot of home runs, but they kept piling up the victories. As August rolled around, they were in first place, leading the Yankees by two games.

It was about that time that a few reporters began to note that Gehrig would soon play in his 1,300th consecutive game. The all-time mark, set by Everett Scott, was 1,307. But Gehrig felt compelled to correct some of the stories about his pursuit of the record. "The published dope on my consecutive games record is incorrect," he told reporters on August 1. "I have played in 1,294 straight contests since June 1, 1925. The generally accepted total is short by one." Now that he was getting close to the mark, he wanted to set the record straight. So much for the myth that he gave the streak no thought.

"The baseball writers have overlooked the fact that I was a pinch hitter the day before I broke in as a regular on the Yankees," he said. "Walter Johnson was pitching and we were getting our fifth straight defeat. . . . I'm sorry to say that I flied out to Goose Goslin."

Gehrig reached into his wallet and showed the press corps that he still carried the box score from June 2, 1925, his first game as a starter.

On August 17, Gehrig quietly broke Scott's record, playing in consecutive game number 1,308. He had a single and a triple, but the Yankees lost in ten innings to the St. Louis Browns, the worst team in either league.

By September, the Yankees were playing out the remainder of a lost season. The Senators had built a big lead, too big to overcome. As the Yanks settled in for a long stretch of home games, Eleanor arrived in New Rochelle and moved in with the Gehrigs. The home was lovely, set on a small hillside and swaddled in trees. A silk painting from Japan hung over the fireplace. Sweet smells from the oven filled the air most days. With Heinrich and Christina sleeping in the master bedroom, Lou and Eleanor probably slept in the two rooms across the hall. Eleanor made it clear that she didn't like the arrangement and planned to stay only until she could find an apartment of her own. Her search took on added urgency with each evening she spent at the Gehrig home. If their two weeks in Chicago had been unpleasant, this new, more permanent arrangement on Meadow Lane was turning out worse than Eleanor had imagined possible.

"Formidable, built something like a lady wrestler, with yellowish gray hair snatched back in a bun," she wrote in describing her soon-to-be mother-in-law.

No hairdresser for her, certainly no makeup. Not that it would have mattered anyway, since she was in a state of perpetual motion, no idle hands, chores around the clock. A huge breakfast to be prepared for her husband and son, then an attack on the sinkful of dishes, then an almost compulsive session with the vegetables and meat for the night's dinner.

Finally, she would jam a hat on her

head and leave for Yankee Stadium *with* Lou, in time for batting practice. Afterwards, back in the kitchen while Pop walked the dogs again and the parrot kept shouting baseball lingo until he was covered for the night. And at last the evening meal, starting with caviar on toast, thick soup, a Caesar salad, meat, potatoes, the vegetables, oversized dessert, the whole works. In the backwash of this way of life, several maids came and went as members of the cast; they simply got in the way of the steamroller.

After dinner and the dishes, we would settle in the living room. Mom would grab either the crochet or the knitting bag and get her fingers flying, uttering sage little philosophies like "what goes up must come down," and Pop would invariably nod in agreement. Sometimes a glint would creep into her steel-blue eyes, and I'd swear she was trying to figure out how to "acquire" me as a part-time maid and full-time playmate for her son.

Three square meals, a house full of pets, a doting mother, and a go-along, get-along father would have struck some people as a reasonably happy family. No doubt Christina could be overbearing, but there appears to have been an especially explosive chemistry between these two women. They were battling for control, and almost everything Christina said and did irritated Eleanor. Her dessert portions were too big. Her vegetable soup was too thick. Her knitting was too frantic. Even Heinrich got on her nerves, apparently for nodding.

One night after dinner, Eleanor rose from her seat near the fireplace and asked her fiancé to join her in the kitchen. She said she intended to pack her things and leave as soon as Christina and Heinrich were asleep. She would go to Long Island and stay with her uncle and aunt while she contemplated her next move. Gehrig said he understood. That night he helped Eleanor load her bags in the car. Gehrig backed out of the driveway, passing beneath his parents' window. As the Packard puttered down the road, past rows of sleeping houses, they talked about calling off the engagement. They both cried. By the time they crossed Long Island Sound by ferry and drove the rest of the way to the home of Gene and Blanche Austin, they had agreed not to give up on marriage. Things would be better once they found their own place to live, they decided. But Gehrig agreed that Eleanor should stay away from his parents until the wedding.

"Mom is the most wonderful woman in

the world," Gehrig told Lieb during this tumultuous week. "She broke up some of my earlier romances and she isn't going to break up this one."

The couple soon found a two-bedroom apartment in a seven-story brick building at 5 Circuit Road in New Rochelle. Their perch was on the fourth floor, high enough to offer a view of Long Island Sound. Gehrig kept a small fishing boat there — *The Water Wagon*, he named it, with characteristic directness — and he was pleased to find a place within walking distance of his dock. The new apartment was also less than half a mile from his old home. In all likelihood, Gehrig's German shepherd, Afra, stayed behind at the house. Clearly, Gehrig was ready to move out, but he was not prepared to move away.

On September 27, at Shibe Park in Philadelphia, Gehrig told a reporter that he'd be getting married any day now. Maybe Saturday, after the game, he said, or maybe Tuesday, once the season had ended. A picture of the happy couple — the same one taken earlier that summer in Chicago — made the front page of the *Daily News* along with the ambiguous announcement.

The day the picture appeared in the paper, fans at Yankee Stadium were treated to an even more surprising sight: Gehrig riding the bench. He started at first base, but after he walked and scored a run in the first inning and singled in the third, he removed himself from the game. Babe Ruth, hobbling on a creaky leg, filled in at first base. By now, Gehrig had played through nine seasons and four World Series, and he hadn't missed a start. One writer (apparently forgetting the missed games on the Japanese tour) calculated that he had probably played at least 1,600 consecutive games, if exhibitions, World Series games, and spring training contests were included. The streak provided him with some of the biggest headlines he'd ever received. Writers marveled about all the pain he'd endured, all the times he'd dived over railings in pursuit of foul balls, all the beanings, all the broken bones, bent fingers, and bruises. Now, with only a few games left in the season, he wasn't about to skip a game. Still, he never bothered explaining to reporters whether he was tired, whether he had wedding arrangements to attend to, or whether he had some other excuse.

"Lou played in his 1,348th consecutive game yesterday and was entitled to a rest," James P. Dawson of *The Times* wrote. The *Daily News* reported: "Gehrig retired at the end of the third, possibly for no other reason than that Ruth had a hankering to clown at the position." The *Herald-Tribune* didn't shed any more light: "Lou Gehrig, whose wedding takes place today, quit early yesterday afternoon."

But Gehrig's wedding didn't take place after the game. It waited one more day. The morning after, on September 29, he and Eleanor were in their new apartment, surrounded by painters and carpenters. Christina had dropped by earlier, and she and Eleanor had argued. This time, apparently, it was about the drapes. Eleanor threatened yet again to call off the engagement.

Gehrig had had enough. He told Eleanor he wanted to get married right away. He phoned the mayor of New Rochelle, Walter Otto, and asked if he was available to perform the ceremony. The mayor agreed. Some accounts say the couple were married at City Hall; others, that Mayor Otto came to their apartment. Their certificate of marriage doesn't say where the ceremony took place.

As she filled out the wedding application, Eleanor fudged the date of her birth. Though she was six months shy of her thirtieth birthday, she gave her age as twenty-seven. Blanche Austin, Eleanor's aunt, served as a witness. Gehrig's abrupt decision to marry might have been a spontaneous expression of love, or frustration, or both. But it also appears to have been an effort to defuse a crisis: If a proper wedding with a fixed date had been announced, that would only have created another conflict. Given that he probably hadn't planned to invite more than one or two friends, and given that Eleanor knew almost no one in New York, they had nothing to lose with a municipal wedding. If Christina was angry at having missed the ceremony, it hardly mattered. She was already angry.

After the ceremony, bride and groom hustled to the ballpark for a game against the Senators. Gehrig announced his marriage to teammates and reporters before the first pitch. He told Dickey that Eleanor's aunt and uncle were hosting a party Saturday night on Long Island. Most of his teammates were not invited.

The Yankees lost that day, 8-5. Gehrig played all nine innings and went hitless (though he did manage to drive in two runs with sacrifice flies). Even as he played, his joy was apparently tempered by guilt. He wondered if his wife and mother would ever get along. Already, Christina was vowing to stay away from the reception on Long Island.

Gehrig had made his commitment to Eleanor. He had broken at last from his mother's powerful arms and struck a blow for independence, but he still loved his mother and yearned for her approval. He must have recognized that his wife and his mother were not destined to be pals, but he held out hope that they would at least learn to tolerate each other. At one point during the game, he called out to one of the clubhouse attendants and asked him to take a message to Lieb in the press box. In the message, Gehrig asked Lieb to talk to his mother and see if she might be persuaded to come to the party. Lieb abandoned his work and walked down to the grandstand. He sat down next to Christina. Heinrich wasn't at the game that day.

"Lou asked me to pick you up this evening and bring you to the reception," he said.

"Freddy, I won't go," Christina answered. "If I went there I would only raise hell."

Lieb somehow changed her mind. When he pulled up in front of her house at 5:40 that evening, she was standing on the porch wearing her best dress and a pair of shiny earrings. Again, Heinrich wasn't with her. The bash was small but ritzy. Lieb was the only reporter on hand. The only Yankee in attendance was Dickey, who was accompanied by his wife. Dickey by now was well accustomed to Gehrig's aloof nature. Days would go by when the roommates wouldn't speak. Then Gehrig would apologize, saying he'd been preoccupied and hadn't meant any offense. One bad game might leave him brooding for the better part of a week. Dickey didn't mind. Nothing ever rattled him. Now Eleanor would have to learn to cope with Gehrig's mood turns.

An enormous, dome-shaped wedding cake held down the center of the buffet table. There were flowers everywhere. Champagne corks popped all night. Eleanor wore a black, V-neck dress and no jewelry except her wedding ring. Gehrig, his hair freshly cut, wore a smartly tailored suit with a white carnation in his lapel. Before the cake was sliced, everyone gathered in the dining room for a photograph. The groom held his bride gently by the elbow. Their smiles beamed. Lieb glanced nervously in the direction of Christina. But Christina was doing fine. She stood slightly behind Eleanor, mouth wide open in a laugh as the flashbulb popped.

Christina still didn't care for her daughter-in-law. She never would. But she behaved herself at the party. On the way home, Lieb fell asleep as they rode the ferry across the Long Island Sound. Christina woke him when she leaned over and whispered in his ear: "Freddy, wasn't I a good girl? I kept my Dutch mouth shut."

CHAPTER 13
OUT OF THE SHADOWS

In the autumn of his first year of marriage, Gehrig got up from the dinner table one evening and announced to his wife that he was going downtown to see a Western — and he was going alone. He had always enjoyed solitude, especially in the off-season. But since his wedding day, he and Eleanor had been together almost constantly. When he walked out the door that evening, he was interested in more than a motion picture. Gehrig, Eleanor wrote in her memoirs, "wanted to establish the point, in a small boy's way, that he was his own man."

Eleanor never says whether Gehrig had a particular reason to feel like something less than his own man. But the weeks and months following their wedding must have been trying. The tension between Christina and Eleanor showed no signs of easing. And while a honeymoon might have helped the marriage start sweetly, Gehrig had decided that they couldn't afford one. On the occasion of his marriage he had turned over most of his savings, plus the house and car, to his parents. The payoff may have helped assuage his guilt, but it also left him feeling poor. So they stayed in their new apartment, making occasional trips to Manhattan to shop at Macy's or to take in a show. Only now, as they spent their first long stretch of time together, did Eleanor begin to realize how sensitive and uncommunicative her husband could be. He was an Iron Horse, but his ego dented as easily as aluminum foil. He brooded when his feelings were hurt, or when he perceived that he had somehow disappointed his wife. He didn't shout. He didn't complain. But the same strong silence that defined his courageous image on the field did nothing to help his marriage.

So he set out down Circuit Road that evening toward downtown New Rochelle, walking in the direction of the sunset. But he never reached the theater. Thirty minutes after his departure, he walked back through the door of the apartment with a sheepish look on his face, as if he expected to be punished for his silent uprising.

Eleanor was pleased that her husband's first rebellion had been so feeble, and so brief. "I'm no psychologist . . . but I knew enough about human nature not to lord it over him," she wrote. "I just broke the short silence by asking why he hadn't brought back the evening paper. He took the opening like a flash, shooting out the door and hustling back in a few minutes with the evening paper. Relaxed, happy, reprieved."

Eleanor had a habit of making her husband sound like a puppy: lovable and energetic, but helpless without the firm hand of his master. Her first task had been breaking the chain that tethered him to his mother. Eleanor referred to it as a divorce. With that out of the way, she began working on his public image. Lou Gehrig, thirty years old, was a national hero and superstar athlete who enjoyed few of fame's rewards. He exemplified the nation's most cherished virtues. He had worked hard, climbed from poverty, and been kind to his mother. He was handsome, strong, and well behaved. Yet he had made no effort to capitalize on the Horatio Alger story that was his life. He was content to play the game he loved, play it hard, and go home to a nice, quiet dinner. He made few attempts to charm newspaper writers or local nightclub owners. Ruth would make more money endorsing breakfast cereal than most players earned over the course of their entire careers. Gehrig had few endorsement contracts. Ruth was the subject of enough songs to fill a Broadway show, including "Oh! You 'Babe' Ruth"; "Babe

Ruth, He Is a Home Run Guy"; and "Babe Ruth! Babe Ruth! (We Know What He Can Do)." No one was singing about Lou Gehrig. Ruth had already been the subject of several biographies, but no one wrote books about Gehrig.

Eleanor was more cunning and sophisticated than her husband. She knew the value of a handshake and a slap on the back. She'd seen how far her father had gone on little more than good looks and charm, at least until his little kingdom on Lake Michigan collapsed. She knew that it took only a drop of talent for most men to succeed. And yet she'd married a man with seemingly limitless talent and not a clue about how to exploit it.

Eleanor took her husband to Abercrombie & Fitch and had him order a new wardrobe. She told him he ought to hold out for a raise when his two-year contract expired at the end of the 1934 season. Gehrig usually parked his car two blocks away from Yankee Stadium, coming and going through a gate under the bleachers, because he didn't like to cause a commotion and didn't care to sign autographs before a game. Eleanor persuaded him to use the main entrance and to greet his fans. She also hired Christy Walsh to perform some of the marketing magic that he had performed for Ruth. In 1934, Gehrig became the first athlete to appear on a box of Wheaties cereal. He also did ads for Camel cigarettes and Aqua Velva aftershave. "He knew I wasn't leading him into a madcap life; he also knew I didn't want a dilettante on my hands," Eleanor wrote. "I just wanted him to develop his capacity for enjoying life and for identifying with some of the better things in it. We were partners, it was that simple."

Life with Eleanor, however, was anything but simple. She played the role of housewife solely for photographers. If Gehrig wanted his meat and potatoes and mulled wine for dinner, he would have to walk down the block to his mother's. Eleanor envisioned her role as that of manager, agent, and promoter. She didn't care for the baseball wives who applauded politely from the box seats and then faded into the background. She considered them naïve. And the baseball wives didn't care much for the new Mrs. Gehrig, who may have suffered for having been several decades ahead of her time. Some of the wives thought Eleanor seemed too eager to cash in on her husband's good name. She introduced herself not as Eleanor or Eleanor Gehrig but as Mrs. Lou Gehrig, a habit that irked some of the other women.

"She was difficult, I would say," said Frances Metheny, wife of the Yankee outfielder Arthur "Bud" Metheny, who met Eleanor in the years just after Gehrig's retirement. "She was quiet, in a way, but she was outgoing in what she wanted to accomplish. He accomplished what he did just by being himself, being quiet and going about his way. But she sort of pushed her way through whatever she wanted."

Eleanor probably would not have argued with that assessment. She had a vision for how Gehrig's career — and their lives — would proceed, and she did not intend to achieve it by wearing an apron.

Sometimes, however, her ideas conflicted with her husband's. "We had planned on his retiring from baseball when he reached thirty-five," she wrote. "I swore that I would never live through the spectacle or the ordeal of a fading athlete who was traded from one team to another, his price tag declining, sale merchandise on aching legs and muscles."

Gehrig, however, had no intention of quitting at thirty-five. He wanted to play as long as he could. He had become increasingly concerned with his statistical legacy and intended to leave his name on as many pages of the record book as possible. He was fueled by ambition, but it was a different sort of ambition from Eleanor's. Money had never been his guiding force.

He wanted to be remembered for greatness, for having hit the ball harder, driven in more runs, and won more championships than anyone. He took better care of his body than almost any player in the game and got lots of sleep. Men ten years his junior were awed by his stamina and strength. If Ruth in his sorry condition was still playing at thirty-nine, Gehrig couldn't imagine quitting any sooner than that. Gehrig told friends he might try coaching when his playing days were done. Neither he nor Eleanor discussed publicly whether they intended to raise a family.

On May 10, 1934, Gehrig awoke with a nasty cold. He'd played through worse. That afternoon against the White Sox, he hit two home runs (including a grand slam) and a pair of doubles, tying a record with four extra-base hits. And he did it all in only five innings. In the fifth, after smashing a ball into the right-field bleachers and putting the Yankees ahead 11-3, he benched himself. "Fans wondered what Larruping Lou would have done at bat if he had been in perfect health," wrote *The Times*. Though the story contained no comment from Gehrig, the writer noted — correctly — that the Iron Horse would surely play the next day, "cold or no cold." The *Daily News* published a cartoon that pictured Gehrig joyfully stepping out of Babe Ruth's shadow.

The Yankees started strongly that season. But Gehrig found himself surrounded by an unfamiliar cast that included some less than legendary names. Tony Lazzeri was still at second base, though his production had started slipping. Frank Crosetti had taken over at shortstop and Jack Saltzgaver at third. The outfield was a revolving door: Ruth and Combs were on the way out, Ben Chapman, Myril Hoag, and Sammy Byrd were on their way in. Chapman, who hit .308 that year and led the league in triples, was the best of the bunch in 1934. Ruth still showed glimmers of greatness and continued to hit the ball higher and farther than almost anyone, but he was slowing down. For years, his massive chest had helped disguise his swollen gut. Now there was no hiding the flab. After every swing, he hitched his pants back up around his waist. He huffed and puffed on the base paths, and he fielded his position at times like a beer-addled softball player. His average slipped below .300, and he frequently needed days off to rest.

All year long opposing pitchers were going after Ruth and avoiding Gehrig. It was clear who presented the greater danger. Gehrig was leading the team in almost every offensive category, including walks. The Detroit Tigers were stacked with good hitters — including Hank Greenberg, Charlie Gehringer, Goose Goslin, and Mickey Cochrane — and threatening to overtake the Yankees. But at least through the early part of the season, Gehrig kept the Yankees in the race. At times, he seemed like a one-man wrecking crew.

"He's the guy that swiped me," said Billy Rogell, who played shortstop for the Tigers in 1934, batting .296 and driving in 100 runs. "I hold no grudge. I was standing on second base, and he slid in there for no reason at all and knocked the hell out of me. So I stuffed his nose in the dirt. Sometimes you get a little confused and everything happens so fast. Did he say anything? What the hell could he say? He was taking the dirt out of his nose." Rogell needed seven stitches above his knee as a result of the encounter, but he waited until after the game to get patched up. Like Gehrig, he prided himself on playing every day. "I don't know why he slid," said Rogell, still clearly upset about it at the age of ninety-seven. "There was no play."

Mel Harder of the Indians, one of the American League's best pitchers in 1934, said Gehrig was the toughest batter he ever faced. "He was great," Harder recalled almost seventy years later. "He would hit it hard no matter where I threw it. When you were pitching to him, you'd try to pitch around instead of right at him. Make him work."

William "Dutch" Fehring played only two and a half innings in the big leagues. His moment of glory arrived in 1934 as a catcher for the White Sox, and he came away from the experience with a vivid memory of Gehrig's strength and determination. Fehring was behind the plate in the seventh inning of a game played on June 25 at Yankee Stadium. As Gehrig stepped up to bat, the rookie was in awe. The pinstriped legend looked like a giant, Fehring recalled. The Yankees were ahead by eight runs, the game all but over, which is the only reason Fehring was getting a chance to play. Gehrig had already hit a homer, a double, and a single in the game. He was playing with a chipped bone on the big toe of his right foot — the result of a foul ball from his own bat. He probably should have taken a seat on the bench and rested. Instead, he dug in and whacked a deep drive to right field. Fehring rose from his crouch and followed its arc.

"It was out there a mile," Fehring said.

But the ball hooked just right of the foul pole. Gehrig was already in his home-run trot and approaching second base when the umpire, George Moriarty, waved his arms and shouted "Foul ball!" Gehrig returned to the plate, picked up his bat, and hissed at Moriarty.

"You're taking food off my table," he said.

On the next pitch, Gehrig hit the ball hard again, beyond the reach of center fielder Mule Haas. As Haas took off after the ball, Gehrig lowered his head and steamed around the bases. Even with his injured foot, he still moved pretty quickly. Fehring watched Gehrig touch second base and sensed that he had no intention of stopping, that he wanted to reclaim the homer he felt the ump had taken away. The relay went from Haas to Al Simmons to Joe Chamberlin to Fehring. Fehring, in his first inning of big-league ball, was determined not to blow it. He clutched the ball with both hands, turned to face the freight train chugging down the tracks, and braced himself for a collision. Gehrig could have tried to knock the rookie on his rump and jar the ball loose, but he didn't. He didn't even slide. He could see he had no chance, and he accepted his fate gracefully. Fehring applied the tag. Gehrig jogged back to the dugout.

Fehring, who never played another game in the big leagues, would brag about the putout for the rest of his life. But he wasn't aware — even at the age of ninety — that by tagging Gehrig, he made a small but important mark in the baseball record book. When a batter is thrown out at the plate trying for a home run, he still gets credit for a triple. Gehrig's triple meant that he had hit for the cycle that day — with a single, double, triple, and home run. It was the first time he had ever accomplished that feat.

The Yankees were playing their best baseball of the year, even as Ruth sat out more frequently to rest his aching body. On June 28, the team won its sixth in a row and clung to a one-game lead over Detroit. But the men were tired. They had played eight straight days without a break, and when the schedule finally did provide for a rest, management scheduled an exhibition in Virginia against the Norfolk Tars, the Yankees' minor-league club from the Piedmont League. It was bad enough that he'd been deprived of his day off, but Gehrig was also told he'd have to play right field during the exhibition so that Ruth could avoid strain on his legs. Gehrig didn't moan about it. He did, however, inform his bosses that he intended to skip the pre-game autograph session at Blair Junior High School in Norfolk.

For the Yankees, the exhibition was an

annoyance, but in Norfolk it was the summer's biggest event. Thousands lined up for tickets outside Bain Field on a dry, hot Friday afternoon. For members of the Tars, the game marked an opportunity. The minor leaguers hoped to impress Joe McCarthy and boost their chances of making it to the big leagues. Whenever a major-league team played in Norfolk, the minor leaguers made an extra effort. "Five big-league teams came through Norfolk, and we beat four of them," said Robert Stevens, who played shortstop for the Tars that year. But the players gave their greatest effort against the Yankees.

Ray White, the starting pitcher for Norfolk, was one of the Piedmont League's finest. He had long arms and a wicked fastball. Like Gehrig, he had attended Columbia University and had dominated his Ivy League competition. The Yankees signed him after he'd won eight of nine games in his senior year. According to some reports, Gehrig and White had been introduced a few years earlier by Columbia's baseball coach, Andy Coakley. But when the two met subsequently to that introduction, Gehrig behaved as if he didn't know his fellow alumnus. White, normally a gregarious man, took it as an insult.

"They didn't like each other," said Bud Metheny, a longtime friend of White's.

Now White was determined to impress Gehrig and the rest of the Yankee organization. His manager had rested the pitcher for five days to help him stay sharp. But he got off to a very shaky start, giving up a home run to Myril Hoag with his first pitch of the game. Ruth followed with a single; then Gehrig belted another homer over the short fence in right. That fast, the Yankees led, 3-0. The temperature was about 90 degrees and climbing. White, rugged and handsome, stood on the mound and fumed. He was being humiliated — in front of the Yankee stars, in front of the team's top management, and in front of the biggest and most animated baseball crowd in Norfolk history.

The Tars rallied for four runs in the bottom of the first. White trotted out to the mound to start the second inning with a chance to redeem himself. When Gehrig came to bat in the second, White threw him another fastball. But there was no way the Yankee slugger would hit this one. It was high and inside, and zipping straight at his head. In the split second that it takes to react, Gehrig tried to get out of the way, but he didn't make it. The ball struck him about two inches above the right eye. It bounced up in the air and carried almost to the grandstand. Gehrig collapsed like a rag doll.

"I swear to God, you would have thought he was dead," said Stevens, who watched from his position at shortstop.

The Yankees rushed from the dugout and gathered around Gehrig's fallen body. He was out cold. Doc Painter, the team's trainer, sponged Gehrig's face with a wet towel and unbuttoned his gray flannel shirt. For five minutes, he lay motionless. The fans, stunned, sat in silence, waving their hats to circulate the muggy air. Finally, Gehrig's feet began to paw at the dirt. He opened his eyes and squinted at a sea of worried faces. Slowly, he climbed to his feet. Hair tussled, a vacant look in his eye, he threw his arm over Bill Dickey's shoulder and wobbled toward the dugout.

Joe McCarthy escorted his star first baseman to Sara Leigh Hospital, where an X-ray showed no sign of a fracture. Dr. S. B. Whitlock announced to reporters that "Gehrig sustained a moderate concussion of the brain. However, it is a common result of blows to the head and I had no fear in permitting him to go back to Washington with the club. He probably will be out of the lineup tomorrow. It was a painful lick, but not serious."

Gehrig had an enormous welt on his head, but he was fortunate that the ball struck just above his eye. His vision was unimpaired. He took a bath in his hotel room, got dressed, and went downstairs to the hotel bar for a beer. "A little thing like that can't stop us Dutchmen," he told a reporter.

White, meanwhile, made no apologies for his knockout pitch. He was still peeved. He gave up five runs on ten hits and two walks in four innings. And if that were not enough to damage his chances of making the Yankees, he'd also caused injury to the team's most precious commodity. After the game, the Tars showered, dressed, and went out for a few drinks.

"I guess the streak's over now," White said, bragging about what he'd done. "I didn't throw at him, but somebody had to end that streak."

After the game, the Yankees traveled by boat from Norfolk to Washington. The next morning, Gehrig woke with a splitting headache. The bump on his head was enormous. He went for another set of X-rays, and once again the doctors said there were no signs of a fracture. Gehrig told McCarthy he wanted to play, and McCarthy wasn't going to stop him. For all his resolve, Gehrig nonetheless must have been hoping for a rainout. The air was thick and the sky gray. Winds were whipping the flags atop Griffith Stadium. But at game time, no rain was falling. Gehrig decided to play. "The big problem," he later recalled, "was to find me a cap." The lump on his head made it impossible for Gehrig to wear his own, which was size $7^1/_8$. Someone fetched one of the Babe's caps and loosened the seams until it fit.

In the top of the first inning, after a single by Crosetti and a walk to Ruth, Gehrig stepped in, determined to show no fear. If a pitcher sensed that a hitter was nervous about being struck in the head, he would throw inside, exploiting that fear. Once a batter starts leaning away from inside pitches, he has almost no chance of hitting balls thrown on the outside portion of the plate. Gehrig knew it. So he dug his feet in the dirt of the batter's box, stared out at the mound and took a couple of practice swings. When the pitch came, he didn't shrink. He swung hard, lined it to left field, and took off running. The ball scooted past the outstretched glove of Heinie Manush in left. Two runs scored, and Gehrig landed at third with a triple. His head must have been pounding. In the third inning, he smashed another triple, this time to center field. And in the fifth he hit yet another, this one to right. Three at-bats, three triples.

But after the triple in the fifth, the skies opened and a thumping rain fell, turning the infield to mush. The game was called off. Gehrig's 1,415th consecutive appearance — along with his three triples and three runs batted in — were washed from the record book.

When news reached the Norfolk Tars that Gehrig had not been forced from the lineup by his injury, some of White's teammates teased him about his failure to end the Iron Horse's streak. "Must not have been much of a fastball," Stevens told him.

Two weeks later, the Yankees visited Navin Field for a critical series of games with Detroit. The Yankees led the Tigers by only half a game in the standings. Fans and players buzzed. But after the first game, a 4-2 Tiger win, Gehrig began complaining of a backache. In the second game of the series, on July 13, he led off the second inning with a single. But when he reached first base he could no longer stand up straight. Head down, left hand clutching the shoulder of the team's trainer, Gehrig hobbled off the field. In all probability, he was already resting in the clubhouse in the top of the third inning when Ruth blasted a 480-foot home run to right, the 700th of his career. *The New York Times* referred to it as a "record that promises to endure for all time." The second leading home-run hitter at that moment was Lou Gehrig, with 314. Gehrig would have to last ten more years and hit forty home runs a year to catch up, the writer noted. The Yankees went on to win the game, moving back into first place.

Gehrig woke the next day feeling no better. The throbbing in his spine seemed to radiate through his entire body. He couldn't draw a deep breath. The pain, according to *The Times*, made "breathing difficult and swinging a baseball bat torture." He knew he was in no condition to play, knew he couldn't help his team win. Still, he couldn't bear to give up the streak. It wasn't that he feared being "Pipped." The Yankees had no backup first baseman on the bench. It was simply that he had become attached to his streak. Sometimes newspaper reporters made it sound as if Gehrig were not aware of his feat, especially in the early years of his career. That wasn't true. He had nurtured it and watched it grow since his rookie year, and the bigger it got the more he cherished it. Like his mother, who had established her family's place in America by lugging pails of water and cleaning up other people's messes, Gehrig had built a legacy on determination and grit. It was something Babe Ruth never could have dreamed of doing.

Gehrig's back was knotted in pain, but it wasn't a broken leg, or a crushed skull, or a ruptured internal organ. It wasn't the sort of thing that would require weeks or months to heal. It seemed a shame to lose the streak for an injury that might be gone in a day.

He went to the ballpark and slowly dressed. When Joe McCarthy filled out his lineup that day, he inserted Gehrig as the leadoff hitter, playing shortstop. He planned to let Gehrig make one appearance at the plate and then take him out of the game. Technically, his streak would remain intact. It's not clear whether Gehrig or McCarthy came up with the idea. In an interview two years later, Gehrig said that his manager insisted that he play. "He wouldn't let me end the record," Gehrig said. "He helped dress me, had me carried to a taxi and hauled out to the park where fellow players aided me in putting on the uniform." But one reporter who covered the game that day said it was Gehrig who "insisted" on getting in the game.

In any case, Gehrig limped to home plate, batted leadoff for the first time in his career, and slapped a single to right field in the top of the first inning. He winced all the way to first base and was replaced by a pinch runner, Red Rolfe. Though the box score the next day listed him as a shortstop, it was Rolfe who went out to play shortstop in the bottom of the first. Jack Saltzgaver, a utility infielder, played first. It was a cheap way to keep the streak alive, but it worked. The Yanks lost the game, however, 12-11.

The next day, Gehrig was back at first base for the entire game. Though he was still moving gingerly, he banged three doubles and a single against Detroit's outstanding young pitcher Schoolboy Rowe. The rest of the team didn't have as much luck. The Yankees lost, 8-3, dropping a game and a half behind the Tigers.

McCarthy was convinced that Gehrig's bad back was the result of sleeping in air-conditioned Pullman cars. Players loved the new cooling devices, which eliminated not only the midsummer's heat but also the coal dust that flew in through open windows. Nevertheless, McCarthy gave the order, and for the rest of the season the Yankees went without air conditioning.

The ache in his back eased day by day. But while Gehrig grew stronger, Ruth continued to fade. One day in Cleveland, after the Babe singled, Gehrig whistled a line drive between first base and second. Ruth, too slow to react, was struck in the right leg by the ball. He collapsed as if felled by a sniper's bullet. "I'm getting out of this game before I'm carried out," Ruth said, while waiting for an ambulance. "I'm getting banged up more now than I ever have been before."

Gehrig was breaking free of Ruth, and the sportswriters, perhaps realizing that the quiet first baseman, like it or not, would soon be the team's biggest star, finally showed some appreciation. They commented on his strength, his endurance, his uncanny ability to come through with the timely hit. On July 5, when Gehrig hit an inside-the-park grand slam, the seventeenth bases-loaded homer of his career, the writers noted that Gehrig had already surpassed Ruth's total. On August 3, when Gehrig hit his thirty-fourth and thirty-fifth homers, the Associated Press reported that he was ahead of the Babe's record-setting 1927 pace.

But while Gehrig continued to hit all through the summer, the Yankees wilted. The pitching staff grew tired, and the holes in the day-to-day lineup became more glaring. Through most of August and September, the Yankees trailed the Tigers by four or five games. They finished seven back. Gehrig wound up leading the league in homers (49); total bases (409); runs batted in (165); batting average (.363); slugging average (.706); and, though no one kept track of the statistic at the time, on-base percentage (.465). He finished second in the league in hits (210); third in runs scored (128); and second in walks (109). He struck out only thirty-one times.

On defense, he was better than ever, making only eight errors.

He was fully in his prime. Despite the most serious bunch of injuries he'd ever suffered, the streak remained intact. By 1934, the rules — and the name — for the Most Valuable Player award had changed. Players were no longer prohibited from receiving it more than once. Still, sportswriters that year voted to give the honor to Mickey Cochrane, the catcher for the Detroit Tigers, who hit .320, with seventy-six runs batted in and two home runs. The voters liked the fact that Cochrane, who played and managed the Tigers, had led his team to the pennant. Gehrig was only the fourth player in American League history to win the so-called Triple Crown — leading the league in batting average, homers, and runs batted in. Yet he finished fifth in the voting for Most Valuable Player, trailing not only Cochrane but also Charlie Gehringer, Lefty Gomez, and Schoolboy Rowe.

As their roles changed, the relationship between Gehrig and Ruth worsened. The chill had been there for years, on and off. Gehrig hadn't liked Ruth's criticism of Miller Huggins. Ruth, who barely spoke to McCarthy, resented Gehrig's adoration of the new manager. Gehrig didn't care for

Ruth's philandering. Ruth thought Gehrig a prude. They were still looked upon as a duo: numbers three and four in the lineup, the Babe and the Iron Horse, the greatest one-two punch in the history of the game. But the relationship had always depended to some extent on Gehrig's willingness to play second fiddle, and by 1934 that was becoming increasingly difficult. The women in their lives presented an additional complicating factor.

Ruth had always been fond of Gehrig's mother. When he visited the Gehrigs in New Rochelle, he often brought his daughter Dorothy along. But when the Babe married Claire, the reception in New Rochelle grew chilly. Christina didn't care much for the new Mrs. Ruth. Once, Claire and the girls showed up at the Gehrigs' without the Babe. Dorothy, a tomboy, was about twelve years old at the time. Julia Ruth, Claire's daughter from an earlier marriage, was seventeen, and she dressed with much more style and feminine grace than her stepsister. Later, Christina Gehrig told someone that she thought it shameful that Claire didn't dress Dorothy as well as Julia. The remark got back to Claire. She complained to Ruth, and Ruth complained to Gehrig. Gehrig didn't take it well. He was already getting enough criticism of his mother from Eleanor. He didn't need more. According to some accounts, it was this altercation that ruptured their friendship, leaving it beyond repair. But there may have been another, more dramatic reason behind the split.

After the 1934 season, Gehrig and Ruth joined manager Connie Mack for a tour of Japan. There were a dozen other players along: pitchers Lefty Gomez, Earl Whitehill, Clint Brown, and Joe Cascarella; catchers Moe Berg and Charlie Berry; infielders Jimmie Foxx, Charlie Gehringer, Rabbit Warstler, and Eric McNair; and outfielders Earl Averill and Bing Miller. Ruth brought Claire and Julia along. Gehrig brought Eleanor. They departed Vancouver, Canada, on October 28 and stopped at Honolulu before beginning the long voyage to the Far East.

Ruppert had asked Gehrig not to go. He had been furious in 1931 when Gehrig hurt his hand playing in Japan, and now he worried about another injury. Gehrig was torn. He respected Ruppert and almost always obeyed the boss, but he had promised Eleanor that the trip to Japan would be their honeymoon — albeit a working honeymoon and albeit a year late. When they finished in Japan, the couple planned to travel on their own through the Middle East and Europe. Only when Gehrig explained to Ruppert the romantic component of the trip did the colonel offer reluctant blessings.

They sailed on the *Empress of Japan*, under cold, gray skies. One day during the journey, Eleanor was taking a walk when she saw Claire Ruth sitting on a deck chair. She knew that the Ruths and Gehrigs were not on speaking terms, but she nevertheless decided to say hello, according to her memoirs. Claire returned the greeting. When Eleanor passed by again later, the women spoke, apparently agreeing that they found the feud between their husbands silly. Claire invited Eleanor to drop by her cabin to talk to the Babe. As Eleanor entered, she wrote, she saw "the resplendent Babe, sitting like a Buddha figure, cross-legged and surrounded by an empire of caviar and champagne. It was an extraordinary picnic, especially since I'd never been able to get my fill of caviar, and suddenly I was looking up at mounds of it."

Eleanor stayed in the cabin with Ruth and his wife for two hours, according to her own account. Meanwhile, her husband was searching frantically, afraid that his wife had fallen overboard. When he found her in Ruth's cabin, he was furious. Eleanor, who always enjoyed alcohol more than her husband, admits in her book that she was drunk. For a long time after the incident, rumors circulated that Eleanor and Ruth had indulged in more than champagne and caviar. Eleanor denied having had sex with the Babe. Years later, Dickey, Gehrig's best friend, would steadfastly refuse to broach the subject. "It just is unpleasant to think about even now," he told one interviewer. "When I went up there [to the Yankees] they were good friends and they kidded each other a lot and they got along fine. Then something happened. I don't want to tell you about it." Whatever happened, it completely ruined the relationship between Gehrig and Ruth, and it didn't do much for the Gehrigs' honeymoon.

"The result was a long siege of no-speaking, one of Lou's spells of speechlessness," Eleanor wrote, "and we were silently dressing for dinner later when there was a muscular banging on the door. Babe Ruth burst in — jovial, arms both stretched out in a let's-be-pals gesture. But my unforgiving man turned his back . . . and the Babe retreated. They never did become reconciled, and I just dropped the subject forever."

CHAPTER *14*

A NIGHT AT
THE OPERA

"Singapore, Penang, Ceylon, Bombay, Suez, Cairo, Alexandria, Naples, Rome, Munich, Paris, London. . . ." Gehrig was gushing as he stepped down the gangplank of the *Berengaria* on February 13, 1935, oblivious to the winter's wind in his face. "And then the good old United States!" he said. "Best place in the world!"

He couldn't wait to tell all about his trip, about how he and Eleanor had watched a mongoose kill a snake in Bombay, rented camels in front of the pyramids of Egypt, sat in the seventeenth row for a performance of *La Traviata* in Rome, and strolled along the Place de la Concorde in Paris. If his wife's run-in with Ruth was still on his mind, he wasn't letting on. He and Eleanor had eaten in fine restaurants and stayed in fancy hotels. Gehrig had even splurged on taxis. Eleanor was teaching her husband to relax somewhat, especially when it came to money. But he was not entirely reformed just yet. By traveling home aboard the *Berengaria* — or "the Bargain-area" as some travelers called it — he had chosen one of the least expensive and least glamorous ships in the Cunard line.

Back in New York, the reporters scratching notes in their pads must have been surprised to find Gehrig in so chatty a mood. After listening to his travelogue, they called his attention to the matter in which they were most interested: his new contract. When talk turned to money, Eleanor became more attentive. She looked up at her husband from under an elegant black hat and crowded in close to hear his every word. Now she would see if her coaching had really made a difference. One reporter asked if Gehrig was satisfied with Ruppert's initial offer.

"How do I know?" he said, grinning. "I haven't seen the contract, so I don't know whether I'll like the figures or not. Suppose it calls for fifty or sixty grand?" He was joking. He knew he wouldn't get that much. He was hoping for something between $30,000 and $35,000.

"You know, I've got a new manager now," he continued, referring to Eleanor. "We feel that I've earned something on the record that's behind me and the one that's yet to be made. I had a big year in 1934 —

batting title, most runs driven in and forty-nine homers. I won't be thirty-two until June and I figure I've still my best years ahead of me. The Babe was thirty-three when he set his home-run record of sixty in 1927. Am I going after that record? Why not? I know I can hit more homers than I have."

Roscoe McGowen, *The Times*'s man on hand, wrote that he detected in Gehrig a "new mental attitude." He was speaking more boldly, as if he recognized at last that his time had come. In the past, reporters had seen him behave confidently only with his eyes hidden beneath the brim of a blue cap. Eleanor was helping him to emerge. She had done more work on his wardrobe, too, buying him a new collection of suits during their stay in London.

Gehrig was eager to see what kind of offer Ruppert had made, but the post office had been holding his mail for the three months that he was away. So when he and Eleanor got back to their apartment, Gehrig picked up the telephone and called the colonel's office. He got no answer.

A little while later, the phone rang. It was McGowen from *The Times* with a few more questions. He wanted to know exactly how much Gehrig wanted to be paid. Gehrig dodged the question. McGowen tossed out some numbers. Gehrig wouldn't bite. He wasn't going to negotiate in the media. He was hungrier, yes, but he wasn't prepared to behave in a manner that seemed ungentlemanly. The two men dodged and parried until McGowen felt he had enough to work with: "He didn't say outright that he would demand a salary of $35,000," he wrote, "but neither did he deny that such a figure would be asked by him."

Gehrig asked another writer: "If I don't get the big dough now, when am I going to get it? For years I was content to sit back and let Ruth take all the money and all the spotlight, as well, because he deserved it. But now the time has come for me to step out."

This newly emboldened negotiator didn't know it, but Ruppert needed to close the deal with his first baseman in a hurry. The colonel had an even bigger piece of business to attend to, one that would profoundly alter the shape of his team, and he needed to make sure his best slugger was already under contract before he made his move. The men met on February 19, at the colonel's office. Gehrig told the boss he wanted about $35,000, which would have represented a $12,000 raise. Ruppert countered with $27,000. They settled quickly on $31,000, though they never announced the precise figure to the media. Then Ruppert's office phoned reporters and told them to drop by for an announcement.

"We had no trouble signing Gehrig," the colonel said, as the two men sat behind a desk, pretending to examine the contract's fine print as flashbulbs popped. "He merited a raise in salary on the strength of his wonderful record last year. He is satisfied and so is the club." In the history of the game, only six other players had earned $30,000 or more: Ruth, Cobb, Hornsby, Tris Speaker, Hack Wilson, and Al Simmons. Salaries had dropped during the Depression as attendance fell and teams struggled to make profits.

Ruppert, however, had increased his fortune during the darkest years of the Depression. The bulk of his money had always been in real estate, not the stock market, and his baseball team and brewery provided a steady supply of cash. So the colonel took advantage of the poor economy to snatch up some of the best bargains in the history of Manhattan real estate. In 1931, he paid $7 million for the thirty-six-story Bank of United States Building at Fifth Avenue and 44th Street. Then, for about $3.2 million, he bought the thirty-five-story Commerce Building at Third Avenue and 44th. By 1935, as the economy began to show signs of recovery, he estimated that he owned more than $35 million in property, most of it in Manhattan. Meanwhile, Franklin Roosevelt's New Deal programs were putting people back to work, though often at reduced hours. The combination of increased income and a shortened work-week gave people more money and time to spend on baseball games. Attendance at Yankee games had risen about 17 percent in the previous year. Ruppert could certainly afford to give Gehrig his raise. But the colonel had another reason to keep his star first baseman happy. He still wasn't ready to announce it yet, though.

"Gehrig," said the colonel, "it is a pleasure to do this. You are one of the few players who always does his work without a murmur. Since you have been with this club you never have given us a moment of worry. We always know where you are and what you will do. You run out every play, hustle every minute and always are on the job. No pains, no aches, no complaints. Gehrig, I like you. I hope you work for this club a long time."

Ruppert told one writer: "That Gehrig is getting to be a real man."

It was an extraordinary bit of fanfare — extraordinary not only for Ruppert's grand praise but also for its obvious signal to Babe Ruth. Ruppert's remarks highlighted the contrast between Gehrig and Ruth, the

Iron Horse and the rusted old battleship, the mama's boy and the rascal, the man of the future and the man of the past.

For much of the winter, Ruppert had been conducting talks to unload the game's all-time greatest slugger. In fact, the Yankees had already completed a deal that would move Ruth from the Yankees to the Boston Braves. The Babe returned to New York one day later than Gehrig. Though he now weighed about 240 pounds by some reports, he told reporters that he hoped to play at least one more year before becoming a manager. He said he was looking forward to talking to Ruppert and settling on a new contract.

But Ruppert had no intention of settling anything. Ruth had been valuable to him, despite his faults, so long as he'd been able to hit home runs and bring in fans. Now the Babe played neither well nor often enough to justify his price tag. During the off-season, Ruppert had worked out a complex deal. In effect, he let the Boston Braves have Ruth for nothing. The Braves did their best to make their new star feel welcome, saying he could play as much or as little as he liked. They named him an assistant manager and suggested that he would probably become the team's top manager in 1936. Ruth was surprised to be tossed aside so quickly but professed at least in public to be pleased.

The Yankees belonged to Gehrig now. On April 12, as the team arrived in New York to start the season, McCarthy announced that his first baseman would become the team's captain. The designation conferred no rights or privileges. But it was an honor, to be sure. The last Yankee captain had been Ruth, but he'd been stripped of the title ten years earlier in one of Miller Huggins's frustrated attempts at discipline. Gehrig promised to lead the team back to the top.

"The Yankees, for various and good reasons, are a greatly improved ball club," he said, serious as usual. "We figure to regain the American League pennant. . . . We will have more speed, plenty of power and we will get better pitching than Detroit. It looks like a good race, probably a close one, but we will have the best team in the league, all things considered." The Associated Press added: "That was one of the longest non-stop statements Gehrig had ever issued, in addition to being the most dramatic."

On the same day that McCarthy announced Gehrig's new role with the team, the Yankee first baseman agreed to take part in a publicity stunt at Artie McGovern's downtown gymnasium, where

Ruth, Gehrig, and other famous athletes sometimes liked to work out. Reporters and a few fans turned out to watch an exercise session with Gehrig and Jack Dempsey, the former heavyweight champ.

Gehrig wore a pair of skintight shorts and a gray sweatshirt. For those accustomed to seeing the man attired elegantly in pinstripes, the outfit was revelatory: Gehrig wasn't just big; he was immense. His muscles had muscles. Each of his thighs was roughly the size of McGovern's torso. Even Dempsey, a savage fighter who won the heavyweight crown in 1919 and retired in 1927, looked small next to Gehrig. As the two athletes playfully sparred, it was clear that Dempsey moved more smoothly, but Gehrig looked more dangerous, even if he couldn't keep a straight face. The men dropped to the floor for some sit-ups. While McGovern held his legs, Gehrig rocked his shoulders up and back, up and back, smiling as if he might go on all day. Dempsey sat beside him and tried to keep pace, but after only three or four sit-ups he began losing ground.

Gehrig gazed into the movie camera and tried to make a smart remark. "Baseball's got fighting skinned by a mile," he said. Or something like that. As often happened when he became excited, he spoke too quickly, the sharp edges of his New York accent chopping up syllables and rendering them indecipherable.

The men stood and shook hands for the camera.

"I certainly wanna congratulate you on the wonderful shape you've kept in," the former champ said, "and I wish this year that you won't only hit 75 home runs, I wish you'd hit 175."

"Well, I might if I eat a couple of more steaks down at your restaurant," Gehrig said. He was really turning on the charm now, pitching not only for McGovern but for Dempsey's steakhouse, too.

McGovern stepped in to break up the love affair: "They're both supermen," the trainer said, "especially Lou here."

That night, more than a thousand people attended a testimonial dinner in Gehrig's honor at the Biltmore Hotel. The event was a fundraiser for the New York City Baseball Federation, which sponsored sandlot ball games throughout the city. Robert Ripley of *Ripley's Believe It or Not* had drawn Gehrig's portrait for the program's cover. The back of the program featured a stunning, Hollywood-style portrait of Gehrig, shirtless, arms folded, his bare shoulders stretching endlessly. Among the celebrities paying tribute were former Notre Dame halfback Jim Crowley; heavyweight fighter James J. Braddock; and baseball players Red Ruffing, Don Heffner, Lefty Gomez, Dixie Walker, Joe Glenn, Earle Combs, Joe Sewell, and Walter Brown. If Gehrig spoke at the dinner, the papers didn't quote him, but he smiled, shook a lot of hands, and signed a lot of autographs. In one long day he had received more adulation than he usually did in a year.

It was a season of change. On May 24, a cold and cloudy night, more than 20,000 fans crowded Crosley Field in Cincinnati to see the Reds and Phillies play the first big-league night game. When President Roosevelt pushed a button in the White House, 614 bulbs were lit, each shining 1,500 watts onto the field. It would take some time for night games to catch on. Most players were reluctant to accept the innovation, saying they couldn't see the ball well at night, or that the night games would ruin their daytime vision. Gehrig never played a night game, but that didn't stop him from offering an opinion. "Well, night baseball is strictly a show and is strictly advantageous to the owners' pocketbook," he said. "But as far as being a true exhibition of baseball, I don't think I can say it is. It's very hard and very difficult on the ballplayers themselves. Of course we realize that the men who work in

359

the daytime like to get out at night and they really see a spectacle and we do all in our power to give them their money's worth. But after all, it's not real baseball. Real baseball should be played in the daytime, in the sunshine."

Gehrig was right about one thing: Night baseball did prove advantageous to owners. In Cincinnati, an average of 18,600 people turned out to see the team's seven night games in 1935; the team's day games were watched by an average of fewer than 3,000 fans.

With Ruth gone, it quickly became clear that Gehrig was the only batter in the Yankee lineup capable of rattling outfield fences and bouncing balls off the bleacher seats. Dickey slumped. Tony Lazzeri battled injuries and inconsistency. Ruth's replacement, George Selkirk, played reasonably well, but not well enough to make anyone forget the national monument he'd replaced. Jesse Hill, Red Rolfe, and Ben Chapman struck little fear in the hearts of opposing pitchers.

The Babe might have laughed as he watched the Yankees stumble, if not for the fact that he had bigger problems of his own in Boston. At the outset of the season the Braves didn't know where to play the aging legend. He was too slow for the outfield and too clumsy at first base. On opening day, he singled to drive in a run in the first inning and hit a two-run homer in the fifth. But after that, nothing went right. He lasted only twenty-eight games with the Braves, batting .181 with six home runs. Late in May, he hurt his knee chasing a fly ball and left the game. He never played again, and he never got the managing job that he coveted.

Even with their gimpy offense, the Yankees managed to hold on to first place for half the season. Gehrig was hitting the ball hard, but the men batting before him — Hill, Rolfe, and Chapman — weren't getting on base nearly as often as Combs, Koenig, and Ruth once did. The Yankees scored an average of only 5.5 runs per game, their lowest total since 1925.

Yet again in 1935, Gehrig played every game. This time, he had only two serious threats to his streak. On June 8, in the first inning of a game against the Red Sox, Bill Dickey made a wild throw to first base after fielding a ball off the bat of Carl Reynolds. When Gehrig stepped across the bag to try to catch the toss, Reynolds, a big man with surprising speed, flattened him. The force of the blow knocked Gehrig unconscious. But when he came to, he insisted on staying in the game. He homered, singled twice, and stole a base before giving way in the eighth inning to a replacement. The only reason he rested at all, probably, was that the Yankees had a big lead and there was another game to be played that afternoon. He played all nine innings in the second half of the doubleheader, collecting one hit.

His second close call of the season came two months later, on August 5, when he complained of a backache before the game began. He played four innings in the rain against the Red Sox, singling, driving in a run, and scoring two. But by the fifth, the pain was too intense. Myril Hoag was sent in to pinch-hit. Gehrig was back in the lineup the next day, playing all eighteen innings of a doubleheader.

"I guess I have been very lucky," he said in an interview that year with Fred Lieb. "I must have been, to have dodged serious accidents and illnesses all of these years. Any player, no matter how sturdy he may be, must thank his lucky stars if he can play through ten seasons without any real mishap. Then I suppose I can thank my sturdy German ancestry for this iron constitution. Both my father and mother weigh over 200 pounds. We are a big-boned family. It has been my observation that it is usually the small-boned player who is most liable to suffer injury."

The Yankees won seven games in a row

in the season's final week, bringing their record to 89-60, but it wasn't enough to catch Detroit. Hank Greenberg led the Tigers with a .328 average, thirty-six homers, and 170 runs batted in. The Tigers also got fine hitting from Goose Goslin, Charlie Gehringer, and Mickey Cochrane, and terrific pitching by Elden Auker, Schoolboy Rowe, Alvin Crowder, and Tommy Bridges. They went on to beat the Cubs, four games to two, in the World Series.

Gehrig finished the season with a .329 average, thirty home runs, and 119 runs batted in, tops on the Yankees in every category. In fact, his home-run total was more than twice that of any of his teammates. Yet it was Gehrig whom some writers blamed for the team's disappointing finish. "The players on the team looked to Lou for leadership and he gave them disappointment," sportswriter Dan Daniel wrote. Daniel contended that Gehrig had tried too hard to fill Babe Ruth's shoes. He seemed determined to hit home runs every time up, the columnist wrote, and the more he pressed the more he struggled. Ruppert had a different theory for Gehrig's struggles. He blamed the slugger's long trip through Asia and Europe, saying it deprived him of his proper off-season rest.

It was true that Gehrig hadn't been a fiery captain. Still, he was hardly responsible for the team's failure. Not including Gehrig's contributions, the Yankees hit only seventy-four home runs and batted .275. Pitchers were working around Gehrig because they knew the rest of the lineup wouldn't hurt them. Gehrig walked 132 times in 1935, more than in any other season in his career. That's the sign of a patient hitter, not one who's desperate to hit home runs. Despite whatever frustrations he may have experienced, he still managed to lead the league in on-base percentage (.466) and runs scored (125). He finished third in the league in home runs and second in RBIs.

The song was called "I Can't Get to First Base with You." It was composed by Eleanor Gehrig and the noted songwriter Fred Fisher. Gehrig's photo appeared on the cover of the sheet music. He wore his gray Yankee road uniform, held a cigarette in his right hand, and smiled at the camera like an All-American Madison Avenue pitchman. A separate photo of Eleanor graced the bottom right-hand corner of the page. She still wore her hair like a flapper, short and wavy. She posed with her head turned in dramatic profile, a strange half smile on her lips.

More than ever, baseball was becoming entertainment, and Eleanor recognized this long before many others. Three baseball movies premiered in 1935: *Alibi Ike*, based on the Ring Lardner story; *Dizzy and Daffy*, which starred the Dean brothers, along with Shemp Howard of the Three Stooges; and *Swellhead*, starring Wallace Ford, whose character got beaned by a pitch and nearly went blind. Eleanor recognized the power of the media. She knew that movies and music could help spread her husband's name far beyond the nation's ballparks. But there was something odd about her attempt to immortalize her husband in song.

"I've sacrificed and bunted my heart," her lyrics began.

I laughed with tears in my eyes;
After each ending you want a new start,
Lover you can't realize.

Then comes the chorus: "The game is over, there's nothing else we can do/I can't get to first base with you."

Putting aside the creative license that permitted Eleanor and Fisher to borrow heavily from Bing Crosby's big hit of 1932 "I Don't Stand a Ghost of a Chance with You," the tune had other problems. For one thing, it never mentioned her husband's name. For another, it was dismal. It sounded like a dirge compared to that humdinger of 1928 "Babe Ruth! Babe Ruth! (We Know What He Can Do)." It was certainly not the sort of thing that Dizzy Dean, Ducky Medwick, or any of the game's other manly men would have cared to be associated with. It seemed to emphasize the part of Gehrig's personality — his emotional distance — that least needed emphasis.

The marketing of Lou Gehrig was not always easy. General Foods paid him to drop his affiliation with Wheaties and endorse its Huskies brand cereal. All he had to do was pose for some pictures and mention the Huskies brand on a few radio broadcasts. One day, Gehrig appeared on Robert Ripley's *Believe It or Not*, a General Foods network radio program with an enormous national audience. Ripley went into his windup. How did Gehrig get so strong? What did he eat? Did he enjoy any special breakfast food? The celebrity endorser never hesitated: "Wheaties!" he blurted.

Gehrig's flub became a national news story. Humiliated, he wrote to officials at General Foods and offered to return their money. The company refused. The amusing incident earned Huskies more publicity than its manufacturer could have hoped for. Ripley was delighted as well — so delighted in fact that he invited the slugger back on his program and threw him the same pitch. This time, Gehrig hit it right on the button: "My favorite is Huskies," he said, "and I've tried them all."

Gehrig was so earnest that he at times seemed two-dimensional. Even Eleanor needed some time to discover that her husband was "no automaton, no unfeeling giant." She introduced him to literature and opera and saw that he was a "sensitive and even soft man." He suspected that some people doubted his intelligence, and that suspicion made him all the more eager to prove himself, Eleanor wrote:

So he wasn't simply the strong, silent type; he was vulnerable, easily hurt, quickly cut. So much so that when he thought he had treated me brusquely he'd go around the house and refuse to talk to me for what seemed like hours . . . exiling himself and not me, sulking at his own moodiness. . . .

What he badly needed was confidence, building up; he was absolutely anemic for kindness and warmth. He had never known closeness or close love before, and when he found it, he grew frightened to death that he might lose it. . . . This was my man, maybe my man-child, my Luke.

One winter, Eleanor and her Luke saw every performance of Wagner's *Tristan und Isolde* at the Metropolitan Opera in New York City. *Tristan* — with Lauritz Melchior and Kirstin Flagstad in the title roles — was the biggest opera to hit New York since *Pagliacci*, featuring Enrico Caruso, had opened more than twenty years earlier. For many members of the audience, being seen at the opera was no less important than seeing the opera. The men in the lobby wore dapper suits with high-waisted pants and long wool coats. The women were draped in furs, with pearls and diamonds cool against their skin.

In his stylish, sharply cut evening wear, Gehrig looked not so much like a baseball player as a movie star. But the fancy clothing did nothing to disguise his brawn. When he moved, crowds gave way. As the lights dimmed, he and Eleanor took their seats. Chilling dissonances flowed from the orchestra pit and flooded the audience. The curtain rose to reveal a richly decorated room on the foredeck of a warship as it sailed from Ireland to Cornwall. The knight Tristan was transporting Isolde, an Irish princess, to Cornwall, where she was to marry King Marke. Isolde, built like a battleship, and rapturous in her long red braids and shimmering gown, prayed the vessel would sink rather than carry her to the forced marriage.

"Hark to my bidding, fluttering breezes!" she sang in German. "Arise and storm in boisterous strife!"

Gehrig's ability to understand German no doubt added to his rapture. He listened to the soaring voices and the majestic orchestra filling the cavernous hall with raging passion and omens of doom. As the opera unfolds, Isolde tries to poison Tristan, but her servant replaces the poison with a love potion. The potion fills them with a love so great they can barely contain themselves. The music grows delirious — buoyant, swirling, and swelling — but the delight is too intense to last. Such great love can end only in tragedy.

"Mild and softly he is smiling," Isolde sang, as Tristan fell into her arms and died. "How his eyelids sweetly open!"

By this point, Gehrig was sobbing in the dark. Eleanor looked at her husband and wondered what had upset him so. She wondered, as she wrote years later, whether Gehrig had experienced a premonition. She wondered if he had a sense that his own love "couldn't last, that it was a tantalizing trick of some kind, never really meant to be."

In the opera's final moments, Isolde fell atop her beloved's body and joined him in death. The curtain fell.

CHAPTER 15

THE NEXT BIG THING

Gehrig spent one year as the team's big star, but the sportswriters who followed the Yankees were not satisfied with his performance as a leading man. Between the foul lines, he was terrific, but outside them, he almost never said or did anything interesting enough to satisfy the men who pointed notebooks in his face. He didn't hang out after hours in hotel lounges or nightclubs, didn't consort with celebrities, didn't turn his head just so when the flashbulbs popped. He didn't do much of anything, really, but smash baseballs.

Gehrig's greatest attributes were his steadiness and his all-around decency — fine stuff for a Boy Scout manual, but not much good for filling newspaper columns. He wasn't as two-dimensional as he seemed, and some of the smarter writers who followed the Yankees recognized as much. They could see that he was still nagged by insecurity, even after all his years as one of the game's giants. They could see he remained uncomfortable with his fame — sometimes painfully so. But most sportswriters had neither the tools nor the talent to handle such subtle matters. They were billboard painters, not fine artists.

So, even before the start of the 1936 season, the writers made up their minds that the team should have a new star: a rookie from the West Coast named Joseph Paul DiMaggio. In 1933, while playing for the San Francisco Seals in the Pacific Coast League, DiMaggio had become the most famous minor-league player in the country. During one stretch that summer, he had at least one hit in sixty-one consecutive games, the second longest streak in the history of professional baseball. The following summer, he badly injured his knee, prompting some big-league teams to lose interest in purchasing his services. But when the Yankees decided to take a chance, DiMaggio proved that the injury hadn't damaged his confidence. He sent back the first two contract offers without signing them, holding out until the third contained a fantastic figure for a first-year player: $7,500.

DiMaggio was the next big thing, the sportswriters promised, warming up their portable typewriters and their hyperbole for a new season. To help ensure that the

DiMaggio prophecy was fulfilled, *The Times* published a note on the proper pronunciation of his name.

He was twenty-one years old, a lanky kid with a long face and a gap-toothed smile, when he showed up for his first spring training. He had driven across the country with a couple of Yankee veterans and fellow Italian-Americans — Tony Lazzeri and Frankie Crosetti — in Lazzeri's new Ford. The San Franciscans had timed their trip to arrive in St. Petersburg by night and avoid the crush of reporters. But when DiMaggio appeared the next morning in the clubhouse, the pencil pushers rushed him.

"Hey, Joe, give us a quote, will ya?"

"Don't have any," he answered.

Even before he'd earned a job with the big-league team, DiMaggio carried himself with the elegant confidence of a prince. He sauntered through the clubhouse and glided across the outfield. Everything had gone so well all his life that it no longer occurred to him to worry. Would he be good enough to hit against big-league pitchers? Would his teammates like him? Would the media treat him kindly? Would McCarthy find a spot for him in the team's overpopulated outfield? There is no evidence that such questions concerned him in the least. He was smooth. Reporters fawned, followed him around, gobbling up his meager utterances the way starving men gobble crumbs. The crumbs only made them hungrier.

DiMaggio and Gehrig had a lot in common. Both were shy. Both were second-generation Americans earning fame and fortune beyond their wildest imagination. But the same characteristics that made Gehrig seem colorless somehow made DiMaggio mysterious, even sexy. DiMaggio had flair. He had charisma. He had style. He was Fred Astaire in pinstripes. He came along at a time when the public was becoming infatuated with new and improved designs. It was no longer enough for products to be useful. Now they had to be sleek and modern, too. Americans were entranced by *Flash Gordon*, Chrysler's streamlined Airflow automobile, the rocking rhythms of Count Basie's band, and Jean Harlow's sensual, satin-covered curves. DiMaggio, his body as smoothly aerodynamic as the brand new DC-3 commercial passenger plane, was the perfect athlete for the times. Before the newcomer played his first game, Dan Daniel of the *World-Telegram* stated as fact what every writer must have hoped would be true: "Here is the replacement for Babe Ruth." Gehrig, after getting his first look at the rookie in spring training, seemed inclined to agree. "DiMaggio will develop into one of the greatest right-handed hitters of all time within the next three years," he said. "He has an amazing calmness, a thorough preparedness at the plate. . . . We are indeed fortunate to have so great a prospect."

The Yankees were eager to make DiMaggio a featured attraction at Yankee Stadium. The economy was improving, with attendance at ballparks climbing steadily from its low point in 1933. Formerly jobless men and women were at work building airports, schools, post offices, and hiking trails, thanks in large part to President Roosevelt's New Deal policies. They were playing in orchestras and painting murals in public schools. By 1936, the Works Progress Administration provided jobs for more than three million previously unemployed Americans. Ruppert, anticipating the economic recovery, decided to reinvest in Yankee Stadium. He finally installed electronic loudspeakers, and he ordered work crews to remove the old wooden bleachers in the outfield and replace them with concrete. He also ordered Barrow to find a player who would attract more of the Jewish fans who lived near the ballpark in the Bronx. Barrow tried, reportedly offering more than $100,000 to the Senators for Buddy Myer, a second baseman who had led the league in hitting with a .349 average the year before. The Senators wouldn't go for it.

But the Yanks had DiMaggio, and that would be enough to attract fans of every faith. DiMaggio's coronation continued almost without pause throughout the spring. "Rookie Outfielder Blasts Three Homers in Debut," said the *Herald Tribune* headline after DiMaggio's first day of spring training. The headline writer seemed not to care that the homers had been hit in batting practice, not during a game. Gehrig usually hit eight or nine in batting practice, but no one rushed that news to print. DiMaggio missed the first weeks of the season with an injured foot, but the writers gushed even in his absence. The *World-Telegram* ran an eight-part series purporting to be DiMaggio's autobiography. The ghostwriter did a lousy job of hiding his handiwork, though. "My full name is Joseph Peter DiMaggio Jr.," he wrote, flubbing his subject's middle name. Even so, the most remarkable thing about this piece of journalism was its mere being — an eight-part series on a man who had yet to play his first official big-league game.

When DiMaggio finally recovered from his injury and began to play, he dominated almost every game story, even when Gehrig dominated the game. "DIMAGGIO'S 3

HITS HELP YANKS SCORE," read *The Times* headline on May 4. Gehrig that day had four hits and scored five runs.

Later that month, DiMaggio needed a police escort to protect him from his fans as he left the stadium. Gehrig, presumably, slipped out quietly, same as ever. A week later, in a game against the Browns, DiMaggio had a homer, a triple, and a single. Gehrig had a homer, a double, and a single in the same game. The headline in *The Times* was by now predictable: "YANKS SCORE, 12-3, AS DIMAGGIO STARS." The rookie played left field for the first few months of the season, before McCarthy switched him to center. In the left-field bleachers, fans waved huge Italian flags to show their pride. Given the recent behavior of Benito Mussolini, whose troops had invaded Ethiopia the previous fall, Italian-Americans in New York had not been in much of a flag-waving mood prior to DiMaggio's arrival. By the All-Star break, the rookie had established himself as a wonderful player (.358, 10 HR, 60 RBIs), fully justifying the acclaim. But Gehrig was even better (.399, 20 HR, 61 RBIs). He was leading the league in nearly every category, including invisibility.

"Joe became the team's biggest star almost from the moment he hit the Yanks," pitcher Lefty Gomez said. "It just seemed a terrible shame for Lou. He didn't seem to care, but maybe he did. Sure, the relationship between Joe and Lou seemed pretty good; they never had a cross word that I heard of. They got along, but how could you ever know how Lou really felt?"

The Yankee captain was more outgoing than he used to be. He was the first on the team to own a portable, battery-powered radio, which allowed him to listen to classical music on the team bus. And instead of tuning out his teammates, he passed the radio around. But he wasn't always so friendly. He barked at teammates who didn't hustle and shot icy looks at those who didn't dress properly on road trips. He wasn't trying to be cruel; he was trying to teach the younger ballplayers some lessons. "Lou was the perfect team man," Tommy Henrich once wrote. "He did what he was told, and in so doing, he set an example for the rest of us. If this towering star was willing to obey his manager and approach the sport with the same deadly seriousness that McCarthy did, then who were we to do any less?" Once, when DiMaggio turned to argue with an umpire after a called strike, Gehrig called out from the on-deck circle, interrupting the rookie's complaint with his own attack on the ump. By diverting the ump's attention, Gehrig was protecting DiMaggio and also reminding him that rookies were expected to show respect for the men behind the plate.

DiMaggio recalled another bit of tutelage he received from Gehrig that spring. "We opened my first Western swing with the club in St. Louis," he wrote in *Lucky to Be a Yankee*, his 1946 autobiography, "and the morning before the game I was sitting in the lobby of the Chase Hotel with Gehrig. He was reading the morning paper and I asked him if it mentioned who would pitch for the Browns that day.

" 'Never worry about that, Joe,' advised Lou. 'No matter whether it's St. Louis or Philly or any place else, just remember they always save the best for the Yankees.' "

The All-Star Game was in just its fourth season in 1936, and players took the contest almost as seriously as they did the World Series. Gehrig, elected by the managers to start for the fourth consecutive year as the American League's first baseman, played the whole game and contributed a mammoth home run in the seventh inning against the Cubs' pitcher Curt Davis. But DiMaggio, who appeared on the cover of *Time* magazine in advance of the contest, helped lose it for the American League when he misplayed a ball in right field, leading to two runs.

A few days later, Gehrig sat down for dinner with Sid C. Keener, the sports editor of the *St. Louis Star-Times*, for a rare extended interview. Keener treated the strapping first baseman as if he were a national treasure, like Old Faithful, a living relic of another era. "Henry Louis Gehrig, baseball's most remarkable iron-man performer, has just completed his 1,744th consecutive game for the New York Yankees," he wrote. "He entered the lobby of the Chase Hotel with a hop, skip and a jump, showing the vigor of a frisky juvenile." Keener found his subject in excellent spirits, whistling and humming and eager to tell his whole life story.

"Why, this game is a continuous vacation for me," Gehrig said. "Look what it has done for me. I'm fixed for life financially, and I've been playing only a trifle more than ten years. How many big business men in other professions are able to retire with their nest egg after working ten years? Not many, I tell you."

"But wouldn't you like to take an afternoon off and get away from the ball park and the uniform?" Keener asked.

"I should say not," Gehrig answered. "I don't know how much longer I can keep adding to my record, but I hope to add at least seven more seasons to my career.

"I'm thirty-three, and — let's see —

seven more years will make me forty years old. Gee, I hope Mr. Ruppert is still owner of the Yanks when I roll around to forty and he wants me to keep on playing for these Yankees."

Keener asked whether the athlete enjoyed any hobbies as much as he enjoyed baseball. In his reply, Gehrig overlooked the fact that he was an avid fisherman in order to give a short lecture on discipline.

"That's the trouble with many ballplayers," he said. "They earn their salary out on the diamond, yet they give too much attention to other affairs — like the ones you mentioned; fishing and other things like that.

"See this finger," he said, holding up the little finger on his left hand, which Keener described as resembling a "piece of granger twist tobacco," with heavy knots on the knuckles and a badly bent tip. "This finger has been fractured four times."

"And you continue to play?" the writer asked.

"What's a broken finger when you're with a ball club that is fighting for a pennant? Since I have been with the Yanks we have won four championships, finished second in five seasons, came home third once, and the only bad year we had was my first one in 1925, when we were seventh.

"The finger isn't the only scar I have. I've had a couple of busted toes, sprained an ankle half a dozen times and let me tell you about two other great moments in my life. They almost finished me a couple of years ago in Raleigh, N.C. We were playing an exhibition game and I was hit in the head with a fastball. I was knocked out. Wow, that was a close call. It almost finished me, but I was back at first base the next day in a game against the Washingtons."

Gehrig appeared to be confusing Raleigh with Norfolk, a mistake perhaps attributable to the concussion, or else to the team's monotonous schedule of exhibitions. He ordered two scoops of ice cream for dessert and continued.

"I almost had to give up my record two years ago in Detroit. I caught a severe cold on the train and lumbago put me in bed. I realized that it was impossible for me to get out on the ball field that day.

"I had sent word to McCarthy that I was down for good this time, and Joe comes a-running up to my room. He wouldn't let me end the record. He helped dress me, had me carried to a taxi and hauled out to the park where fellow players aided me in putting on the uniform. Joe insisted on me making an official appearance at the plate, so they put me as the leadoff batter and announced my name as the shortstop in our lineup. I took one turn at bat and retired from the game. Incidentally that was the only time I have failed to complete a full game since I have gone on the record. I shook off the attack of lumbago in a hurry, and here I am still going."

Now Gehrig appeared to be exaggerating. It's always possible that Keener embellished the story, of course. Reporters didn't use tape recorders in those days, and athletes understood that their remarks would be polished, sometimes beyond recognition. But it's more likely that Gehrig was enjoying himself in the interview and decided to give his image a little boost. In any case, he was playing loosely with the facts. He had failed to complete plenty of games over the years, either because of injuries or simply because he needed a rest. In fact, there had been only one season — 1931 — in which he had played every inning of every game.

Gehrig reached for the check and told Keener he was eager to get back to the hotel so he could finish reading a book. Before departing, though, he made a short speech.

"I have been very fortunate as a ball player," he said. "I have played with the greatest batter of all time — none other than Babe Ruth. My home runs are fouls in comparison with the Babe's drives. And here's something, too: I have played for two of the game's greatest managers — Miller Huggins and Joe McCarthy. I can't overlook my big boss, either, Mr. Jake Ruppert, owner of this club. For myself, Little Lou hopes to keep plugging on and on."

In the summer's hottest months, the Yankees blazed. They were running away with the American League pennant. In the National League, the race was shaping up to be a beauty, with the Giants, Cardinals, Cubs, and Pirates all in the chase. Even so, the sports pages were dominated by events in Berlin, where U.S. Olympic athletes were putting on an astonishing show. Jesse Owens, the Buckeye Bullet, or the Brown Streak, as reporters called him, won four gold medals in Berlin, soundly drubbing Adolf Hitler and his pronouncements of Aryan supremacy. White Americans embraced Owens as they had no other African American athlete, and his celebrity prompted some to question the segregation that kept black athletes from competing against whites in so many sports.

On August 29, *The Times* published a letter from one of its Brooklyn readers, Laurence Helffrich, that read:

The Olympic Games exploded very effectively the myth of Aryan superiority. Although snubbed by Hitler, the Negro Athletes of the United States made possible our winning the track and field competition. The achievements of Negro track and field stars are generally recognized, but in other sports we find discrimination against the Negro race. In this country Negroes are among our best baseball players, but there isn't a single Negro player in the big leagues. In the interest of fair play and sportsmanship we must wipe out this jimcrowism and allow Negro ball players of ability on big-league teams. This "freedom" should be carried further and there should be no discrimination against Negroes in other sports, such as tennis, swimming and golf. There is no place for racial discrimination in the American plan of fair play and sportsmanship.

There were no formal rules keeping African American athletes from playing in the big leagues, but Commissioner Landis wasn't ready to let that happen. Sometimes he offered the patently absurd argument that there were no black players talented enough to compete. At other times he said their presence on big-league teams would be "detrimental" to the game, but he never said why. Perhaps he was afraid that fights would break out among players and riots among fans. He may have also feared that an infusion of new players would change the economics of the game and put a lot of white men out of work. Maybe his personal prejudices came into play. Mr. Helffrich of Brooklyn and the Negro Leaguers would have to wait.

Gehrig plugged on beautifully as the summer days grew long, crushing homer after homer into the unfinished concrete bleachers at Yankee Stadium, where construction workers paused from their work to collect the balls. "In the past, I played ball without thinking," he said, "without wondering why things happened. . . . Now I am giving the pitchers a mental tussle and I personally feel that I was never as good as I am today." His swing was steady and strong, his body holding up nicely. He felt as rugged and powerful as ever. When the Yankees installed seat cushions on the dugout bench, Gehrig scoffed, refusing to use them. "What's the matter with you, anyway?" McCarthy asked when he saw Gehrig pull off a cushion and take a seat on the hardwood bench. "Nothing," Gehrig said, "only I get tired of sitting on cushions. Cushions in my car, cushions on the chairs at home — every place I go they have cushions."

Meanwhile, his teammates suffered their usual roster of injuries: DiMaggio missed action with a damaged foot; Dickey and Lazzeri with sprained fingers; Hoag with a head injury; Red Rolfe with a wrenched back (ending his 275-game streak, second longest on the team); Crosetti with a spike slash to the left wrist; and Monte Pearson with a sore back. Gehrig watched them fall, same as he did every year, and soldiered on. On August 2, as a game against the Indians stretched drearily into the thirteenth inning, the first baseman swung at a pitch and missed it badly. He felt a twinge run down his spine. He watched the rest of the contest from the bench, as the Yankees and Indians settled for a sixteen-inning tie, called on account of darkness. But Gehrig was back for the next game, and the next, and he was still playing on September 19, when New York's diminutive mayor, Fiorello H. La Guardia, presented him with a scroll in honor of his 1,800th consecutive performance. His teammates gathered around him in loose formation and removed their caps, squinting in the sun and chuckling among themselves. Gehrig, one reporter said, seemed embarrassed by the attention.

These Yankees were built differently from the teams that had been constructed around Ruth. McCarthy and Gehrig were its leaders now, and they inspired a quiet brand of professionalism. The ballpark was their office, not their playground. They were in the business of producing hits, runs, and wins, and they performed their work with studied efficiency. They still banged a lot of home runs, same as they did with Ruth in the lineup, but now they did more of the little things that helped a team win. They sacrificed, hit the cutoff man, and slid hard to break up double plays. Dickey had become one of the game's premier catchers, and his intelligence and calming influence made the talented corps of pitchers — Pearson, Gomez, Ruffing, and Johnny Broaca, to name the best of them — that much better. When they won, they reacted calmly, as if they had expected nothing else. When they lost, they stewed. Gehrig as much as anyone set the tone.

"I had watched Lou Gehrig hit down in St. Petersburg and I couldn't see how there ever could have been a more powerful batter, including Babe Ruth, whom I had never seen," DiMaggio once recalled. "And I couldn't understand how so great a hitter could be taken so matter of factly by the rest of the squad and by the sports writers."

Down the stretch, Gehrig played every

inning of every game, even after the Yankees had clinched the pennant on September 9, with three weeks to play. Only in the last two games of the season, against the Senators, did he rest, telling reporters that his back hurt. After singling to center in the second inning on September 26, he spent the remainder of the game on the bench. The next day, he played five innings, changed into his civilian clothes, and watched the last four innings from the seats behind the Senators' dugout. He finished the regular season with a .354 average, forty-nine homers, and 152 runs batted in, good enough for his second Most Valuable Player award.

Asked how he had managed to stay in the lineup every day through so many seasons, he answered bluntly: "Damned if I know."

Then he paused and asked himself the next question. "How will it be when I can't bend for the ball or do the team any good at the plate? They'll have to take me out, won't they?"

Before the start of the World Series, with the Yankees set to meet their neighbors the Giants, Gehrig appeared with Giants' pitcher Carl Hubbell on the cover of *Time* magazine. Ruth and DiMaggio had already been on the magazine's cover, but for

Gehrig this was a first, and there was no shame in sharing the honor with Hubbell, who was the game's best pitcher in 1936. A couple of years earlier, in the All-Star Game of 1934, Hubbell had struck out Ruth, Gehrig, and Jimmie Foxx in order and then mowed down Al Simmons and Joe Cronin to start the next inning. Good as he had been in 1934, Hubbell was better in 1936, with a 26-6 record and a 2.31 earned run average. Coming into the Series, he hadn't lost a game since June 16. Though the Giants were not well stocked with sluggers, they felt as if they couldn't lose when Hubbell took the mound.

In the first game of the Series, the slender pitcher's fastball was buzzing, his curveball dropping as if on a string, his screwball moving in directions that made no sense at all to the men trying to hit it. Gehrig grounded out in his first at-bat, tapped one back to Hubbell the next time, and struck out the time after that, before getting hit by a pitch on his final turn. It was a feeble effort, and the rest of the Yankee lineup didn't manage much better. "We were swinging at headlines," Gehrig said. "We had read so much about Hubbell's screwball that we were all but mentally whipped before we took up our bats." The Giants won easily, 6-1.

In the next game, happy to see Hal Schumacher on the mound, the Yankee offense erupted for eighteen runs. Gehrig drove in one run with a sacrifice fly in the first inning. Then, with the bases loaded in the third inning, he slashed a single down the right-field line, knocking in two more. It was the longest World Series game in history to that point, at 2 hours 49 minutes, but President Roosevelt, seated behind the Giants' dugout, stayed until the last out as the Yankees tied the Series.

The competition moved to Yankee Stadium for game three, on a cool, beautiful Saturday afternoon. The biggest crowd in Series history — 64,842 fans — wedged into the ballpark. Outside, thousands more stood on nearby rooftops and fire escapes, paying up to a dollar for partial views of the field. Freddie Fitzsimmons, otherwise known as "Fat Freddie," took the mound for the Giants. He was thirty-five years old and past his prime, the newsmen said. But this time out he threw one of the finest games of his career, giving up only four hits. Unfortunately for Fat Freddie, he made a bad pitch to Gehrig and Gehrig knocked it more than 400 feet into the sun-drenched bleachers in center field.

"There it goes," shouted Tom Manning in his radio broadcast, "a long smash deep into center field, way up, going, going,

going . . . A home run! A home run! Lou Gehrig!"

Gehrig smiled and waved his cap to the crowd as he rounded the bases and crossed the plate. The Yankees won the game, 2-1.

The next day, Hubbell pitched again. He had to win, or else his team would be all but finished. In the third inning, with the Yankees leading, 1-0, Crosetti opened with a double and scored on a single by Rolfe. After DiMaggio fouled out, Gehrig stepped in. With the count at two balls and a strike, Hubbell threw a curve that bounced short and scooted away from the catcher, allowing Rolfe to go all the way from first to third. Now the count, at three balls and a strike, favored Gehrig. At three-and-one, a batter can afford to look for a pitch he likes — a fastball up and in, for example — and make up his mind not to swing unless he gets precisely what he's looking for. At three-and-one, a good hitter becomes a great hitter and a great hitter becomes a superman.

Bill Terry, the Giants first baseman and manager, called time out and walked to the mound. With first base open, Terry and Hubbell probably discussed whether to give Gehrig an intentional walk. Walking Gehrig and pitching instead to the slow-footed Dickey would give the Giants a fair chance of ending the inning with a double play.

When the conference on the mound ended, Hubbell stared in at Gehrig. He went into his windup and threw a pitch he thought Gehrig couldn't possibly hit — a curve ball so high and so far inside that it might have shaved the batter's whiskers had he leaned the wrong way. In Hubbell's view, it was practically an intentional walk. Gehrig probably wouldn't swing. And if he did, he would almost certainly miss, or swing awkwardly and hit the ball weakly. Then Hubbell would come back on the next pitch and try for the strikeout. But Gehrig surprised everyone. He pretzeled his body and took a vicious hack. And somehow he got the meat of his Louisville Slugger on the ball. By the time Hubbell turned around to track the ball, it had already landed in the right-field bleachers. This was the only time all year the pitcher had allowed a homer with a man on base. The Yanks went on to win, 5-2.

Years later, Hubbell and several other members of the Giants would mutter in dismay about Gehrig and that seemingly untouchable pitch. Gehrig had too much admiration for Hubbell to gloat, but he surely swelled silently with pride. He'd hit a hugely important home run against the toughest pitcher in baseball on the game's biggest stage. Later, he would recall this as the greatest moment of his career.

In the next game, the hero became the goat, at least temporarily. Gehrig singled in his first at-bat and went to third as Mel Ott misplayed the ball in right field. But when Dickey topped a grounder to first base, Gehrig hesitated before dashing toward home. The hesitation cost him. He slid with a grunt and was tagged out. "Not overly bright," said *The Times.* One batter later, George Selkirk hit a solo home run. Going into the ninth inning, the score was 4-4. If Gehrig had been on base for Selkirk's homer, the Yankees would have been ahead.

In the bottom of the ninth, Gehrig dug into the batter's box with two men on and two out, facing Hal Schumacher. A base hit would have been the sweetest atonement, winning the game and the championship for the Yankees. Anyone who's ever swung a bat — whether in a sandlot game or in the big leagues — dreams of a chance like this one: the chance to win a championship with one swing. At this stage in his career, Gehrig's reputation as a clutch hitter was secure. He had more grand slams and more World Series game-winning runs batted in than anyone in baseball's history. But somehow his big hits usually came in the early or middle innings, when there were no smothering celebrations to be enjoyed. Over the course of his career, he hit only three game-ending home runs, and all three came in relatively meaningless games. His homer against Hubbell in game four was the closest he had ever come to towering drama. But even that couldn't compare to Grover Alexander's strikeout of Lazzeri in 1926, or Ruth's called-shot in 1932. Would this be Gehrig's moment at last?

Schumacher threw, Gehrig swung . . . and the ball rolled weakly to second base, sending the game to extra innings. In the top of the tenth, the Giants scored a run on a sacrifice fly and held on to win. The Series returned to the Polo Grounds with the Yankees leading, three games to two.

The Giants needed one more victory to set up a decisive seventh game, in which they no doubt would have sent Hubbell to the mound. But in the ninth inning of game six, with the Yankees clinging to a one-run lead, DiMaggio led off with a single and Gehrig sent him to third with another base hit. The Yanks went on to score seven runs, turning a great game into a romp. Gehrig fielded an easy ground ball for the final out in the bottom of the ninth and dashed toward the clubhouse. He celebrated briefly with his teammates; then he cleaned out his locker and left. He didn't show his emotions very well, but he was as sentimental as anyone. Though most people in the park hadn't noticed, he'd stuffed the ball in his pocket after the last out of the game. He took it home as a souvenir.

CHAPTER 16

LORD OF THE JUNGLE

Two weeks after the final game of the World Series, Gehrig made an announcement: He wanted to be Tarzan. The role had recently been vacated by Johnny Weissmuller, the Olympic swimming champion, and if the studio executives in Hollywood would give him a chance, Gehrig intended to audition. "I guess the public's entitled to a look at my body," he said, sounding somewhat less than bold for a man aspiring to play the lord of the jungle.

The plan had been hatched by Christy Walsh. Gehrig was one of his biggest and most important clients now, and the agent was more determined than ever to see him succeed. The Tarzan part had certainly been good to Weissmuller. He was a lousy actor with a squeaky voice and a frustrating inability to remember his lines, but he had long, rippling limbs, massive shoulders, and a chest as wide as the grille on a Chevrolet. That and a good roar had been enough to earn him a fortune. But Weissmuller's studio, MGM, had lost the rights to the Tarzan series in 1936, and a low-budget producer named Sol Lesser had purchased them. With Weissmuller under contract at MGM, Lesser needed a new star for his upcoming features, tentatively titled *Tarzan's Prisoner*, *Tarzan's Folly*, *Tarzan's Secret*, *Tarzan's Revenge*, and *Tarzan's Last Call*. Enter Gehrig. Like Weissmuller, he had an instantly recognizable name, great looks, and no particular talent as an actor. Walsh suggested a tryout. Lesser agreed. But first, he said, he wanted to see how Gehrig looked out of his baggy, flannel uniform.

Quickly, while the buzz was strong, Walsh leaked the news to reporters — "GEHRIG SEEKS ROLE AS TARZAN" — and hired a photographer to take some publicity shots. Within days, the pictures began appearing in newspapers and magazines nationwide. In one, Gehrig wore a leopard-skin loincloth only slightly bigger than a jock strap and swung a papier-mâché war club, as if batting against a coconut-hurling ape. In another, he wore a caveman-style outfit that covered one shoulder and came down barely low enough to cover his crotch and rear end. These were the most revealing portraits of Gehrig's body ever taken, and they must have prompted some of the pitchers Gehrig had bludgeoned to marvel (after they stopped snickering at the wardrobe, that is). His torso formed a perfect V. His shoulders and forearms were as taut as rope. His chest looked like a hunk of marble. His stomach revealed not an ounce of fat. Yet while his upper body looked like something out of an anatomy textbook, his lower body appeared to belong to another species, neither man nor ape. Each thigh was bigger than many a man's waist, each calf the size of a Christmas ham. Here was the hidden source of his tremendous power and durability.

No one doubted that Gehrig had the good looks for Hollywood. His skin had weathered somewhat from more than a dozen summers in the sun. He had a few creases on his forehead now, and deep lines framed his mouth like a pair of parentheses. But the years had made him more handsome, if anything. He was a big man with a rock-solid jaw and a sweet, dimpled smile. The question now was whether he had the charm and grace to turn those God-given assets into a Hollywood career.

Edgar Rice Burroughs, creator of the Tarzan character, sent the baseball star a telegram expressing his certain opinion: "Having seen several pictures of you as Tarzan and paid about $50 for newspaper clippings on the subject, I want to congratulate you on being a swell first baseman."

Undeterred, Gehrig tried to flash a bit of Hollywood-style wit in an interview with the Associated Press. "Afraid of animals?" he asked. "No! At least, I'm not afraid of Tigers — I've faced many of 'em in twelve years of baseball — but those lions, well, we'll have to wait and see." Asked to name the leading lady with whom he would most like to appear, he chose Irene Dunne, who was more of a screwball than a siren. But even that choice wasn't safe enough for Gehrig, who wished to make it perfectly clear that he had no intention of abandoning his Boy Scout image to become a louche Hollywood star. "I could act much better with my wife in my arms," he said.

B. R. Crisler, a columnist for *The Times*, wrote that he was eager to see Gehrig's dimples on the big screen — "a place where, it seems to us, they have always belonged — home runs or no home runs."

Then, a few weeks later, came the announcement from Lesser. Gehrig was not cut out to be Tarzan after all, he said. The problem was those legs, which Lesser described as "more functional than decorative" and one writer called "a trifle too ample." The role went to Glen Morris, winner of the decathlon at the 1936 Olympics. Gehrig's star turn would have to wait.

On January 30, 1937, a peculiar piece of news appeared near the bottom of Roscoe McGowen's baseball story in *The Times*. The bulk of McGowen's article concerned Joe DiMaggio's contract negotiations, which were not going well. But before closing his report, McGowen mentioned that Lou Gehrig was also engaged in contract talks. Ruppert was reportedly offering about $33,000, while Gehrig wanted something in the neighborhood of $40,000. The Yankee captain, who had spent the previous afternoon signing autographs for children at a school in Greenwich, Connecticut, planned to negotiate directly with Ruppert, the story noted, as was his habit. Then came the peculiar part: "Gehrig will entertain the press at a 'tea party' at the Commodore Hotel," McGowen wrote. Gehrig would use the occasion to make his case for a raise, cajoling the media to put some pressure on his boss. And to make sure the reporters showed up and treated him kindly, he even agreed to supply food and drinks. The man was finally playing hardball.

He might have been motivated by his wife, or by Christy Walsh, or simply by the sense that he'd been too nice for too long. But there's another possible explanation. Gehrig was almost certainly motivated by anger at remarks made earlier in the week by his former friend and teammate, Babe Ruth.

"I think Lou's making one of the worst mistakes a ballplayer can make by trying to keep up that 'iron man' stuff," Ruth had told a reporter. "He's already cut three years off his baseball life with it. . . . He oughta learn to sit on the bench and rest. . . . They're not gonna pay off on how many games he's played in a row."

Ruth was a loudmouth, and his remarks reeked of sour grapes. He was out of baseball and not at all happy about it. But he was right, at least in part, about Gehrig. The Yankees paid their first baseman to knock in runs and hit homers. Management didn't care whether he played in every game, so long as he played in most, and played well. Gehrig was thirty-three, a bit past prime for most baseball players. The occasional day off might have done him good. Did he need to play both halves of doubleheaders in August, when perspiration could add several pounds to the weight of a woolen uniform?

"The next two years will tell Gehrig's fate," the Babe went on. "When his legs go, they'll go in a hurry. The average ball fan doesn't realize the effect a single charley horse can have on your legs. If Lou stays out there every day and never rests his legs, one bad charley horse may start him downhill."

Gehrig was furious. He knew his body and what it could do. And Gehrig, unlike Ruth, took good care of himself. He didn't suffer the chronic charley horses (not to mention the chronic hangovers and chronic bellyaches) that had afflicted the Babe. Gehrig did get backaches, and doctors said there was some trouble with his gallbladder, but those things didn't bother him much. He felt as strong as ever. He looked it, too. Even in the dead of winter he appeared to be taking good care of himself. He knew he'd been lucky to play all those consecutive games without an injury, and he wasn't so naïve as to think that the streak couldn't end with one freak twist of the ankle or beanball to the skull. But as long as he felt strong enough to play every day, he intended to do just that. After the 1936 season, the streak stood at 1,808 games. Two thousand would be a breeze, he figured. But Gehrig had another round number in mind, and he announced his goal at the press conference. Twenty-five hundred, he said, seemed like a reasonable target. He was only thirty-three years old, he reminded the reporters, and playing baseball every day never seemed like much of a strain. "If it develops that I am hurting the team by trying to stay in, why,

I'll get out and the record will end right there."

He said that A. F. Lorenzen, an advertising executive and friend of his parents, had encouraged him to stick around as long as possible. Gehrig thought it sounded like solid advice. To play in 2,500 straight would require another four and a half years. Lorenzen had pointed out that some of baseball's most impressive records might belong to Gehrig if he continued to play well for that long a stretch. Gehrig said he might not match Ruth's home-run record, but he thought he had a good chance to come out tops for runs scored, runs driven in, and walks. *The Times* presented a chart showing where Gehrig stood in his pursuit of some of the game's records:

Most years with 200 or more hits in a season: Cobb 9; Gehrig 7

Most runs scored in a career: Cobb 2,244; Gehrig 1,633

Most years with 100 or more runs scored: Ruth 12; Gehrig 11

Runs batted in during a career: Ruth 2,209; Gehrig 1,702

Most years with 100 or more runs batted in: Ruth 13; Gehrig 11

Most years with 150 or more runs batted in: Ruth 6; Gehrig 6

Most consecutive years with 100 or

more runs batted in: Simmons 12;
Gehrig 11

Most home runs during a career: Ruth
714; Gehrig 428

Most extra base hits during a career:
Ruth 1,356; Gehrig 1,033

Gehrig was a modest man, but he had clearly given some thought to his legacy. He knew he would be remembered chiefly for his accomplishments on the ballfield. And those accomplishments were measured in cold, hard numbers. It was an aspect of the game that he'd always liked. He knew that Ruth, Cobb, and Hornsby had all played at least until they were forty.

If Gehrig had played on until the age of forty-two, he quite possibly could have rewritten the game's record books, according to Bill James, the baseball statistician and writer. James calculates that Gehrig would have finished his career with 689 home runs (more than anyone but Babe Ruth, Hank Aaron, and Barry Bonds); 3,928 hits (third after Pete Rose and Cobb); 2,879 runs batted in (almost 600 more than today's record, held by Aaron); 2,475 walks (a number no one has ever reached, though Barry Bonds is fast approaching); and a lifetime batting average of .330.

He could have been slowed by nagging injuries. His legs could have gone soft. He could have lost his batting eye. He could have slumped and been replaced by a rookie. He could have enlisted in the military after the Japanese bombed Pearl Harbor. To be sure, James's projections are based on a lot of speculation. "But these are not unreasonable numbers," says James. "They just look unreasonable because they are so extraordinary."

Gehrig never mentioned Ruth during his press conference, but at least some of the reporters on hand realized that the first baseman's boasts were intended at least in part as rebuttal. A few weeks later, it would appear that he was still fuming. Sitting at home in his living room and chatting with reporter Dan Daniel, Gehrig was asked to name the greatest player he'd ever seen: "Honus Wagner," he said, referring to the Pittsburgh shortstop, and ignoring the obvious choice. "There was a marvelous player who went along doing a grand job without any thought of himself." Daniel may have been reading between the lines, but it's also possible that Gehrig made some off-the-record swipes at Ruth. In any case, the writer drew this conclusion from his interview: "War between Lou Gehrig and Babe Ruth? Well, we should say!"

In March, Walsh had his client fly to

Hollywood for a screen test. Lesser, while not interested in seeing more of Gehrig in a loincloth, was willing to consider him in roles that included long pants. Lesser's studio was brand new. He needed all the stars he could get, even if they were baseball stars rather than actors.

But it became apparent as soon as Gehrig touched down in tinsel town that he was no Clark Gable. He was not even the sort of person who yearned to meet Clark Gable. He had no interest in making a splash, in getting his name in the gossip sheets, in being seen at the right hotel lobbies and cocktail lounges, or in having his name linked to the latest young starlets. The mere act of putting on makeup for his screen test made him uncomfortable.

"I have to make you beautiful," said the pretty young woman who powdered his nose, as she reached for a tube of lipstick to darken the color of his lips.

"Hey, hey," Gehrig said, smiling nervously in the direction of a movie-reel camera. "This stuff's all right, but no lipstick."

Even without lipstick, Gehrig passed his audition. It's difficult to imagine how he could have failed it. He didn't command a high salary, and he wouldn't be expected to carry a film on his own. In all likelihood, he'd play the part of a sidekick, with just enough lines to justify putting his famous name on movie posters. After the screen test, at a luncheon at the California Club, Gehrig, Walsh and Lesser announced to reporters that they had agreed on a one-picture contract, the terms of which were not disclosed.

"And I won't go for that Tarzan stuff, either," Gehrig said, as if it had been his choice. Lesser said his new star would probably play a "hardy American pioneer of frontier days" in a film to be called "The Trail Blazers." Richard Arlen would play the lead, Lesser promised, and Gehrig would have a prominent supporting role. They planned to start shooting after the 1937 baseball season.

"I know I'm no actor now," Gehrig said at the luncheon, "but I'm going to give 'em my best and try to learn how. If I have a screen flop, it won't be because I haven't tried my best."

Hollywood had done nothing to rob him of his virtue.

"And if there are any love sequences, I hope they'll be with Shirley Temple, which would please my wife."

A few days after his return from California, Gehrig and Ruppert met at the colonel's office to talk about his contract.

Gehrig assured reporters that he had no intention of leaving baseball for a career in acting. When Jack Miley of the *Daily News* took a shot at Gehrig's Hollywood ambitions, Gehrig might not have liked it, but he was probably smart enough to recognize that the columnist was right.

"Strangers in town used to go to Yankee Stadium to see Ruth," Miley wrote in his assessment of Gehrig's star power. "He was one of the city sights, like the Empire State tower and the Statue of Liberty. Today they go to see the Yankees, not Gehrig. Young Joe DiMaggio, a first-year rookie, has more color than Gehrig. . . . When it comes to that personal magnetism, you've either got it or you don't. Roosevelt has it; Hoover hasn't. Dempsey has it, but not Tunney. DiMaggio, like Ruth, has; but not Gehrig. This is a shame, for Lou is a great athlete. He's probably worth more to the Yanks than DiMag, but it is Joe, through no efforts of his own, who captures the imagination of the fans."

By mid-March, long after most of his teammates had signed contracts and three weeks after he ordinarily would have reported to spring training, Gehrig still hadn't agreed to terms with the Yankees. It was by far his longest holdout, forcing him for the first time to miss several spring training games. He appeared not to be happy about it. "I can't say," he told reporters when asked what might happen if he and Ruppert failed to make a deal. "I don't know," he answered, when asked about future movie-making opportunities. It was too cold for fishing, so he puttered around his apartment in New Rochelle with not much to do. He had purchased a new Packard convertible for $2,000 a few weeks after the World Series had ended, so he probably went for some leisurely drives when the roads were clear of snow. Maybe he passed some time at the Elks Club, where he occasionally played hearts in the off-season with the local bankers, dentists, and politicians. He also liked to walk to Dunkel's on South Division Street to get a haircut, or to Singer pharmacy for a coffee malted. But Gehrig traveled New Rochelle like a tourist, never staying long in one place and never making deep connections. He was on the road so much every year that he never acquired a lot of friends back home. Among citizens of New Rochelle he had developed a reputation as a nice fellow, but not an overly warm one. Among shopkeepers and delivery boys, he was known as a tightwad.

Dom Bruzzese earned twenty-five cents an hour in 1937 as a delivery boy for Dillon's pharmacy in New Rochelle. He remembered taking a package to Gehrig's fourth-floor apartment one day. Gehrig patted his empty pockets to indicate that he had no money for the teenager. Bruzzese waited. "Eleanor," Gehrig yelled, "do we have any change for the boy?" Then he went back into the apartment. When he returned, he handed the delivery boy five pennies. Bruzzese said he had the impression Gehrig went digging into his piggy bank. Even by 1937 standards, five cents was a lousy tip. "He was cheap," he said. "As cheap as they come."

But Gehrig was generous in other ways. When the ice broke on Long Island Sound, he would walk from his house to the boathouse. On the way, he would pass Isaac Young High School, and if there were boys out playing ball in the schoolyard, he would sometimes stop to join their games. Down at the boathouse, he would help the staff move the heavy wooden swim floats out of storage. Only when he was done with the work would he climb aboard *The Water Wagon*, paddle out from the dock, and cast a line. Some people around town used to joke that Gehrig was too tightfisted to buy a motor for his little fishing boat. They were probably right. But Bruzzese, who watched Gehrig row on several occasions, had a different opinion: "He would row hard," he recalled. "He did it for the exercise."

Gehrig also may have visited his parents'

house on Meadow Lane when he was in the mood to work his muscles. The house today stands almost exactly as the Gehrigs left it. Eleanore Jonas, who moved in with her husband, Hans, in the 1950s, says she found a stationary bicycle in the basement that probably had belonged to Gehrig.

On the morning of March 18, Joe McCarthy phoned Gehrig at home and asked if he was ready to join the team in Florida. Gehrig said he wanted very much to head south, but he was determined not to give in yet again to Ruppert. Their negotiations had been unusually acrimonious. Ruppert had offered $31,000 — the same as Gehrig made in 1936 — and Gehrig had insisted on $50,000. Ruppert called it an unreasonable demand. Gehrig called it payback for the Depression-era pay cuts. Now, Gehrig told McCarthy he would settle for $45,000 a year for two years, or $40,000 for one year, with a $10,000 bonus to be paid if he played more than 100 games. Why would a man who hadn't missed a day at work in a dozen years need a $10,000 incentive for playing 100 games? And why would the Yankees offer one? It seemed an odd demand, to say the least. Gehrig probably floated the idea because he thought he deserved a reward for his incredible fortitude — and perhaps to show Ruth that he was

411

wrong, that the Yankees did value his everyday performance. McCarthy must have recognized that even the first part of Gehrig's request, the $40,000 in straight salary, was not likely to be met. Still, the manager promised to telephone the colonel and see what he could do.

Ruppert, McCarthy, and Gehrig spent the morning swapping long-distance calls. Finally, Ruppert spoke directly to his star first baseman and said he would pay $36,000 — a $5,000 raise from the previous season. Gehrig said he'd take $37,500. Ruppert held the line at $36,000, but he offered to throw in a $750 bonus. Ruppert understood that Gehrig had decided to make a stand. At the same time, he knew that Gehrig hated to disappoint the authority figures in his life. By tossing him a small bonus, he permitted his faithful employee to end his rebellion and claim a small victory. Gehrig signed on the dotted line.

DiMaggio was the team's rising star now, but Gehrig remained its most important player. He was a permanent fixture at Yankee Stadium, like the handsome white trim that haloed the grandstand. Yankee fans saw their favorites come and go through the Roaring Twenties, the Great Depression and, now, into the uneasy years of international tension. Ruth gave way to DiMaggio. Koenig gave way to Crosetti. Pennock gave way to Ruffing. Huggins gave way to McCarthy. Gehrig remained.

"Lou is the perennial youth of the game," wrote *The Sporting News* that winter. But Ruppert, Barrow, and McCarthy were not sentimentalists. They recognized that the perennial youth had sprouted a few gray hairs, and although he was still strong and swinging the bat well, he wouldn't last forever. While Gehrig held out for his raise, McCarthy tried Babe Dahlgren at first base during spring training. Dahlgren, not yet twenty-five years old, had played two years with the Red Sox, fielding his position smoothly but hitting poorly. Dahlgren, who had seen Gehrig play the previous year, must have had the impression that the big man wasn't going soft just yet. When he signed his contract with the Yankees he went out and bought an infielder's glove and began taking grounders at second base, shortstop, and third.

The Yankees made one more move to prepare for a future without Gehrig. In April, Commissioner Landis ruled that the Cleveland Indians had held Tommy Henrich too long in the minor leagues, ostensibly to keep him from being claimed by another major-league club. Henrich, a lanky power hitter who played outfield and some first base, was declared a free agent. After a heated bidding war, the Yanks signed him for $25,000. The price tag alone suggested high expectations.

"If Gehrig ever knocks off," one writer said to Joe McCarthy, "you've got a fellow to take his place."

"That's what I was thinking," said Mc-Carthy.

But Henrich wasn't. He wanted to play the outfield. It looked to him as if Gehrig had a lot of good years left.

Two days after forging his deal with Ruppert, Gehrig arrived in St. Petersburg, eager to take his first swings. He went directly from the train station to Huggins Field, where he stepped into his uniform and jogged onto the field. In his first game, he hit two long fly balls for outs and connected for a single to drive in a run. He showed little if any rust.

The spring training exhibition schedule took the Yankees to Mobile, Alabama; Houston, Texas; Galveston, Texas; Oklahoma City, Oklahoma; Knoxville, Tennessee; and Spartanburg, South Carolina. They played a lot of long games in a lot of hot weather against a lot of lousy competition, but Gehrig felt great. The balls were pinging off his bat. He seemed to drive in a run every time he swung. In Spartanburg, he suffered a bruise on the middle finger of his left hand. He didn't tell anyone at first, so it's not clear how the injury happened. But a few days later in Norfolk, Virginia, after going hitless in two at-bats, the finger was causing him so much pain he had to take himself out of the game. Enter Dahlgren, who hit a three-run homer and a single in two chances. That got Gehrig's attention. Five days later when the Yankees opened the season at home against the Senators, Gehrig's finger was still throbbing, but he played, banging two doubles and a single.

He was streaky through the first weeks of the season. He revealed at the end of April that he had a broken finger, but he downplayed the injury. "I just hold it above my other fingers when I grip the bat," he said. "Naturally, it takes some power away, but I've been getting my hits."

He didn't hit his first homer until May 2. Two weeks later, after going hitless in twenty straight tries, he was dropped from fourth to fifth in the batting order. He responded that day with a resounding double to right field. A week later, he was back in the clean-up spot and hammering the ball. In fact, as the weather warmed, Gehrig went on one of the greatest hitting tears of his career, dealing a serious blow to

Tommy Henrich, Babe Dahlgren, and anyone else who might have been waiting for him to give way. Suddenly, it was 1927 again and Gehrig was the toughest out in baseball. Fastballs, curves, and sliders: He pounded them all. Fifty games into the season, he was hitting .394 with ten home runs and thirty-nine runs batted in. In the All-Star Game on July 7, he provided a memorable moment. With a runner on first and Dizzy Dean on the mound, Gehrig hit a towering fly. A pulse of energy moved through the crowd as the ball rose higher and higher — then hooked foul and sailed over the roof of Griffith Stadium. A few pitches later, he got hold of another one. Fans and players stood to watch it go. Gehrig, who had never cared much for Dean, would remember it as one of his favorite home runs.

"Ha! Shucks!" said Cy Perkins, who managed the Detroit Tigers for part of the season. "What difference does it make what you throw to that Gehrig? He hits everything. You just try to make it not too good for him — and then duck! That's all."

The Yankee clubhouse looked like a hospital ward for much of the season. Di-Maggio missed two weeks after having his tonsils removed. Jake Powell lost playing time after an appendectomy. Dickey,

Broaca, Selkirk, and Crosetti all had arm problems. Bump Hadley wrenched his back. Spud Chandler missed action with shoulder pain. But the injuries didn't keep the team from winning. On August 1, the Yanks collected seventeen hits in a 14-5 win against the Browns. For the second time in his career, Gehrig hit for the cycle.

The next morning, with no game on the schedule, Gehrig and Dickey drove from New York to Ocean City, Maryland, for a deep-sea fishing expedition. Gehrig preferred a light line when he went after big fish, saying he thought the fish deserved a fair fight. He liked to feel the tug of the line run all the way up his arms and into his shoulders as he wrestled to bring in the catch. "Why not make it harder for yourself?" he said. "It really challenges your endurance and skill." This time, the fish didn't have a chance. Dickey caught a 90-pound marlin that measured 7 feet 3 inches, with a 22-inch sword. Then Gehrig got one that was only slightly smaller.

A few weeks later, Gehrig collected the 2,500th hit of his career. "The first 2,500 are the hardest," he joked.

The Yankees had a comfortable hold on first place, and would maintain it all season long. He had everything in the world going his way.

How sweet was Gehrig's life in the summer of 1937? Even his mother received an endorsement deal. Christina appeared in a full-page ad for Royal Baking Powder:

Lou Gehrig's Mother Says — "You Should See Lou Go for my BAKED GRAPEFRUIT PUDDING"

The ad included a copy of the recipe and a picture of the white-haired Christina preparing to take a bite of pudding. Suddenly, even Gehrig's diet was a matter of public knowledge.

"I eat a light breakfast, no lunch and a big dinner," he told one interviewer.

I eat a lot of fruit and go light on bread and potatoes. I don't avoid bread and potatoes. I just don't take that extra slice or that extra potato. I don't eat sweets very often — but I eat them as often as I want them. The other night I saw some pie that looked good to me, and I ate a piece of it. The next night I had another piece. I hadn't eaten pie in a long while and probably won't eat any more for a long while to come. But I might. I might eat a piece tonight if I happen to feel like it. It is my notion that the most important part of my diet is the fruit and fruit juices that I eat or drink morning and night. I have roast or broiled meat every night for dinner, and I eat a lot of green vegetables and salads, but in the matter of fruit I am practically an addict.

First the tea party, now this detailed discussion of his feelings toward pie. Eleanor had finally gotten through to her husband, it would seem. He was loosening up and learning to enjoy his celebrity. Reporters in turn were starting to treat him like a big shot. One day in September, a photographer for *The Sporting News* stopped him and asked if he would agree to let readers see what he carried in his pockets. Sure, he said, he'd do it. Gehrig, wearing a dark sport coat, pleated trousers, and polka-dot bow tie, smiled as he began pawing at his pockets. From his jacket he pulled an envelope addressed to "Mrs. Lou Gehrig, 5 Circuit Road, New Rochelle, NY." From his pants pockets he removed a handkerchief, a pack of Camels, and some matches. He brought forth no keys and no wallet. When the photographer asked why he had no money, Gehrig said he often carried no cash, depending instead on credit for incidental expenses like gas and groceries. In any case, the photographer must have been disappointed that Gehrig had failed to come up with anything more exciting.

"That's all there is," said Gehrig. "There isn't any more."

Gehrig faded slightly late in the season, his average falling more than twenty points from the start of August until the end of September. Early in the year a few flecks of gray hair had begun to appear around his temples. Now the flecks had turned to solid streaks. The wrinkles in his brow had deepened, too. His body was still rock-solid, but for the first time his cheeks and jaw had begun to soften. It was possible to imagine how he might look as an old man.

Despite slumping at the start and finish, he had one of his finest years, finishing third in the league in homers (37), third in runs batted in (159), second in batting average (.351), first in walks (127), and first in on-base percentage (.473). No hitter in either league created more runs for his team. Second baseman Charlie Gehringer of Detroit (.371, 14 home runs, 96 runs batted in) won the Most Valuable Player award. Given that the Yankees finished thirteen games ahead of the Tigers in the standings that year, and given the obvious inferiority of his numbers, Gehringer would seem a questionable choice. DiMaggio came in second in the voting, (.346, 46, 167), followed by Hank Greenberg (.337, 40, 183), and then Gehrig.

Even so, with Gehrig hitting as well as ever and DiMaggio entering his prime, the Yankees were in the process of establishing a new dynasty, one that would draw inevitable comparisons to the teams that dominated the game in 1927 and 1928. They faced the Giants again in the World Series, and once again the competition wasn't close.

The Giants tried to avoid pitching to Gehrig, walking him five times. He still managed five hits in seventeen chances (for a .294 average), but the performance left him unsatisfied. "I don't seem to be timing the ball right," he said. Though he didn't make excuses, one of his teammates noted that Gehrig looked as if his strength had been sapped by a cold that had hit him during the last week of the regular season. In the final game, with the Yanks leading 3-2, Gehrig lashed a double against pitcher Cliff Melton for the last run of the Series. It was the thirty-fifth World Series RBI of his career — and it would be his last. Only Mickey Mantle and Yogi Berra have ever knocked in more World Series runs, but Gehrig worked much more efficiently than Mantle or Berra. He needed only thirty-four games to drive in thirty-five; Mantle needed sixty-five games to drive in forty, while Berra needed seventy-five games to drive home thirty-nine. When the games counted most, no one came up bigger than Gehrig.

In the clubhouse, as his teammates celebrated and sang "The Beer Barrel Polka," he lit a cigarette and sat in front of his locker, the expression on his face more appropriate for a member of the losing team. When a radio reporter approached and asked for an interview, Gehrig kept his remarks brief, saying simply that he felt lucky to be a Yankee.

CHAPTER 17
STRANGE TIMES

Amyotrophic lateral sclerosis struck Lou Gehrig in 1938. It might have hit him as early as January, when he went to Hollywood to act in a Western called *Rawhide*. It might have happened a couple of months later, when he reported to spring training in St. Petersburg and developed bruises and blisters on his hands. It might have been around the time of his thirty-fifth birthday, when his wife noticed he was having trouble with his balance. Or it might have been a bit deeper into the summer, when his manager detected a change in the way his star slugger was swinging the bat. But it was almost certainly no later than that. As the baseball season ran its course, Gehrig's strength and skill seemed to slip away like a ground ball through the legs. If he sensed that something wasn't quite right, he certainly had no way to know he was dying.

Since its discovery more than a century and a half ago, no one has been known to survive ALS. In a healthy person, messages travel in an instant from the brain to the fingers or toes. But the messages travel a long way — through motor nerves running from the base of the skull down the spine. In a person with ALS, these motor nerves begin to die, with no warning and for no apparent reason. Messages can't get through. The disease begins shutting down the body's functions one by one, like a night watchman switching off the factory-floor lights. Muscles waste away.

The first symptoms are small and easy to miss — some weakness or cramping in the hands or feet, typically. Most people ignore the signs for a year or more. Soon, they start stumbling and dropping things. They have trouble buttoning their shirt or turning the key in the ignition of their car. Then walking becomes difficult. The disease moves up and down the spinal cord, killing more and more nerve cells. Within a few years, in most cases, the patient will be unable to walk, unable to sit up straight, unable to talk, unable to swallow and, finally, unable to breathe. Through it all, the patient remains awake, alert, and fully aware of what is happening. While ALS leaves the victim's brain in perfect order, few diseases can so thoroughly bulldoze a person's spirit.

Before it became known as Lou Gehrig's disease, ALS was associated primarily with the French doctor who identified it in 1874: Jean-Martin Charcot. In much of Europe, it is still known as Charcot's disease. When Charcot went to medical school in the 1840s, Paris was the scene of the world's most progressive scientific community. Doctors were beginning to understand the body as a complex tangle of tissues and organs. They were beginning to identify diseases and, in some cases, learning to treat them before they killed. Charcot began his career as an intern at the Salpêtrière Hospital, one of the largest in the Paris system, a massive compound on Paris's Left Bank. There was no such thing as a neurologist when he started out. The first textbook on neurology was not published until 1871. But more useful than any book were the thousands of patients who passed through the Salpêtrière Hospital each year. In the 1850s and 1860s, Charcot treated all kinds of patients, but he took special interest in those suffering from nervous system and psychiatric disorders. He had learned in medical school to observe patients carefully, taking detailed notes and making sketches. When his patients died, he would perform autopsies to see if he could find within their corpses a cause for the symptoms and injuries he had observed while they were alive. Throughout years of work, Charcot became curious about patients who reported weakness or paralysis yet suffered no pain, no numbness, and no cognitive problems. Sometimes the patients experienced weakness in one limb and not the others. Sometimes the first symptom was slurred speech. Sometimes the weakness progressed slowly, other times quickly. When Charcot performed autopsies, he found hardening of certain portions of the spinal cord in all of them. That was the signal to Charcot that these patients had all died of the same disease. A practical man, Charcot gave the malady a clumsy but perfectly descriptive name: "Amyotrophic" refers to muscle atrophy; "lateral" refers to the location of the dying nerve cells, in the lateral spinal cord; and "sclerosis" refers to the hardening of those dead cells.

Although Charcot identified the disease, he didn't discover its cause. Neither did he find a cure. By the time Lou Gehrig became sick, not much had been added to Charcot's work. The disease was so rare, and the central nervous system still such a mystery, that many doctors in the United States had never heard of ALS. Only nine scientific papers on the disease were published in 1938 in medical journals. Some were mere case studies in which a physician documented a single occurrence or a small series of cases. Simply to have encountered a patient with ALS was remarkable enough that witnesses felt compelled to record the experience.

Dr. Israel S. Wechsler, a neurologist at Mount Sinai Hospital in New York, was one of the few men in the United States who had seen more than one or two patients with ALS. Wechsler was a brilliant and supremely confident doctor. He was a small and slender man with a touch of gray hair at the temples. He wore a more generous sprinkle of white in his thick mustache. His high forehead and wide, deep-set eyes gave him the appearance of a man who had spent much of his life bent over books, as he had. But Wechsler was no stuffy academic. His eyes opened wide and his voice popped with energy when he spoke about medicine, or Torah study, or American democracy, or classical music, or his favorite baseball team, the New York Yankees. He seemed to marvel at times at the capacity of his own brain to absorb and enjoy such diverse pleasures. And he was not shy about his intelligence. He counted Sigmund Freud and Albert Einstein among his friends and loved to drop their names in conversation. When he straightened himself from his desk and stepped across the room to greet a patient, hand outstretched, he seemed to assume the stature of a giant. He was so certain of his abilities and so passionate about his work that patients believed in him utterly. His personality was one of the most powerful drugs at his disposal. Patients wanted to get better just so they wouldn't disappoint him.

In 1927, Wechsler wrote a textbook on neurology that would remain the authoritative source on the subject for decades. With each reprinting, he updated the chapter on ALS according to his most recent observations. The ailment seemed to fascinate him, perhaps because so few men in his field knew what to make of it. The 1939 edition of the book included three pages on ALS. Within those pages Wechsler presented a theory that patients who reported weakness in the hands in the earliest phase of the disease tended to live longer than those complaining of slurred speech. It was a good observation, but not a hopeful one. The difference was slight, he noted, and even the most fortunate patients usually died within two or three years.

On the subject of treatment, Wechsler was blunt: There was none. "The treatment is palliative," he wrote. "Exertion and stimulating medication should be avoided. Nursing care, especially in feeding, is ultimately necessary."

By the time Lou Gehrig entered his office in 1940, Dr. Wechsler would come to change his mind. He would come to be-

lieve that he had discovered a treatment —
and possibly a cure — for ALS. He would
begin to think he had found a way to save
the world's most famous victim of this
mysterious disease and give hope to thousands of others who had received the same
sentence of death. And, for a time, he
would make Gehrig a believer, too.

Gehrig began the year in California,
where Christy Walsh continued his campaign to make the ballplayer a Hollywood
star. But Walsh had an ambivalent client
on his hands, one who refused to pose for
publicity photos with Hollywood's sexy female stars. After more than four years of
marriage, he was still sweet on his wife. He
loved her with all the innocent excitement
of a schoolboy. He called her "Pal." She
called him "Luke." It wasn't that he
thought Eleanor would get angry if he
posed for a photograph. She was shrewd
enough to understand the purpose of a
publicity shot. Gehrig avoided the photos
anyway.

So, while Gehrig was working on the set
of *Rawhide*, Walsh borrowed one of Gehrig's nightshirts and got the actresses Jean
Harlow, Joan Crawford, and Jeanette Mac-
Donald to autograph it. Then the agent
mailed it to Eleanor back in New Rochelle
and alerted the media. As publicity stunts

go, this one was halfhearted, at best. Even so, at least one newspaper photographer made the trip from Manhattan to New Rochelle and persuaded Eleanor to pose with a rolling pin in her hand, waving it around like an angry housewife who intended to give her husband a knock on the head when he came through the door.

Eleanor planned to join her husband in Hollywood as the filming neared its end. In the meantime, she had little reason to worry that Gehrig might misbehave. She had seen his performance as a single man, in the early 1930s, when he would stand with his back against the wall at parties, ignoring numerous women who would have been willing to do anything for such a handsome and well-paid athlete. Still, she might have been impressed at how often her husband got out of his hotel room. On January 22, he was listed among the guests scheduled to appear at a glitzy benefit for the widow of actor Ted Healy. If Gehrig actually attended (the event was scheduled for midnight on a Saturday, well past his usual bedtime), he might have met James Cagney, Martha Raye, Judy Garland, George Jessel, Jack Benny, Al Jolson, Spencer Tracy, Mickey Rooney, Rudy Vallee, Fanny Brice, and Eddie Cantor. He almost certainly bumped into Brice a few days later when the two appeared on Robert

Taylor's *Good News* radio program. Gehrig, no doubt with help from Walsh, sent telegrams to sportswriters nationwide asking them to plug his radio appearance. He wrote: "The sponsor — I'm not going to forget that this time — is Maxwell House Coffee. Hope you'll be listening."

But Gehrig most enjoyed the part of Hollywood that brought out the wide-eyed little boy in him — the horseback riding, the phony saloon fights, the whiskey bottles that shattered harmlessly, the guns that shot blanks. "Boy, I never had so much fun in my life as I'm having on this picture," he told one reporter in California. "You ought to see me in my boots and saddle and ten-gallon hat. . . . I'd sure like to get all dolled up in my movie togs and ride a horse into Yankee Stadium on opening day."

Sol Lesser, perhaps recognizing that his new star had somewhat limited range as an actor, assigned Lou Gehrig to play the part of Lou Gehrig, a famous baseball player for the New York Yankees. The movie was produced in about six weeks. Director Ray Taylor was a busy man. That year he also directed *Scouts to the Rescue*, *Flaming Frontiers*, *Frontier Town*, *The Painted Stallion*, *Panamint's Bad Man*, *The Spider's Web*, and *Hawaiian Buckaroo*. No one on the set of *Rawhide* had any illusions about the task at hand; they were out to make money, not art.

The script had Gehrig going west to visit his sister (played by Evalyn Knapp) on the family ranch. Gehrig arrived in time to discover that his sister was being terrorized by one of the town's greedy businessmen because she refused to join the businessman's association and pay jacked-up prices for hay. To fight the bad guys, Gehrig and his sister hired a singing, gun-slinging lawyer played by Smith Ballew. Ballew got most of the best lines and all the movie's romantic scenes. For Gehrig, there was not even the hint of an on-screen love. His faithful horse, Snookie, was his closest companion.

In one scene, Gehrig, riding up front in a stagecoach, opened his mouth and appeared to sing a verse from a song called "A Cowboy's Life."

I've played the major leagues for years
with a versatility
I've seldom missed a fly I chased
But now the flies chase me

But the voice on film was clearly not Gehrig's. He was lip-synching. A singer named Buddy Clark did the dubbing.

Still, Gehrig acquitted himself nicely in his big-screen debut. He looked comfortable on a horse, given that he'd never ridden before. He cut a dashing figure in tight blue jeans, a Western shirt, and a ten-gallon hat. And though his New York-streaked accent sounded harsh at times, he delivered his lines smoothly and with conviction. He was never so nervous that he failed to smile.

"Take it or leave it, I'm through with baseball," he said in his first scene, as a cluster of newsmen surrounded him at Grand Central Terminal. "My sister and I bought a swell ranch in a peaceful valley a hundred miles from a railroad. . . . I'm gonna wallow in peace and quiet for the first time in my life. I'm gonna hang up my spikes for a swell ol' pair of carpet slippers." His voice rose as he bid the boys an excited farewell and stepped on the train headed west: "So long, gang!"

To the untrained eye, the film captured no evidence that he might have been suffering the early stages of a neurological disease. When he signed an autograph in the movie's opening scene, the camera zoomed in close on his right hand. It was steady, his penmanship perfect. In another scene — a brawl in a saloon — Gehrig picked up an average-sized man, lifted him completely overhead, and hurled him across the room. The distance traveled by the man appeared to be enhanced by a splice in the

433

film, but there was no trick involved in the heavy lifting. A frame-by-frame view shows Gehrig did it all by himself.

In 1989, more than fifty years after the release of *Rawhide*, Dr. Edward J. Kasarskis, a professor of neurology at the University of Kentucky, published a paper in the journal *Neurology* claiming to have detected in the film evidence of Gehrig's first symptoms. He described two scenes in which Gehrig appears to rely on his hands to get up from the ground. Kasarskis writes that the movement — known as a partial Gower's maneuver — is common among people suffering weakness in the legs. In another scene, when Gehrig sits near a campfire and listens to Ballew sing, Kasarskis writes that he sees atrophy of the first dorsal interossei, or the small muscles between the thumbs and forefingers. Other neurologists who have closely watched the movie say they spotted nothing out of the ordinary. Even completely healthy people sometimes use a partial Gower's movement to lift themselves from the floor, especially if they're unaccustomed to wearing cowboy boots. And while the campfire scene does permit a good view of Gehrig's hands, these doctors say they spotted no atrophy. If Gehrig had been playing Tarzan or some other role that required fewer clothes, it might have been easier to spot shrinkage in the large muscles of his shoulders or thighs. But in his Western duds he looked just fine. In fact, he looked great.

Gehrig brought home a souvenir from his trip out west: a Colt .38-caliber revolver. Though he had no plans to use the gun, he promptly applied for a permit in New York, listing Barrow, the Yankees' general manager, as his reference. A few days after his return, he sat down for coffee with the writer Dan Daniel at Jack Dempsey's restaurant in Manhattan. He told Daniel he'd enjoyed moviemaking so much that he planned to act in two more films the following winter, and he might make another two the year after that. He said he had no intention of giving up baseball to become a full-time film star — he hoped to continue playing ball for a long time — but he backed off some of the bold pronouncements he had made a year ago about how long he intended to continue with the Yankees.

"I am a slave to baseball," he said, "and only because I really love the game, hate to think of taking even one day away when we are playing, hate to think of the inevitable time when I will have to hang up the spikes and put the uniform away in camphor. I may have had some idea of a five-year plan, as some of the boys have put it.

But just now I am willing to go along from year to year, and let Destiny make my plans for me. We are living through strange times. The man who says what he intends to do in three or five years is a super-optimist. So let's forget all that and stick to the things that face me today."

The first thing facing Gehrig upon his return from Hollywood was the matter of his contract. He wanted $41,400 — a 15 percent raise from his previous salary of $36,000. Ruppert initially offered Gehrig no raise at all. The men did their usual waltz and, over the course of several weeks, arrived at a compromise. Gehrig got $39,000, which made him one of the best-paid players in the history of the game. Cobb had made more when he doubled as a player and coach. Ruth, of course, had earned much more. But in 1938, no one in the game came close to matching Gehrig's salary.

In interviews leading up to spring training, Gehrig predicted that the Yankees would once again dominate the league. Lazzeri was gone, released by the team at the end of the previous season and replaced at second base by Joe Gordon. With Crosetti at short and Red Rolfe at third, the Yankees had a great infield. And the outfield wasn't bad, either, with DiMaggio, Selkirk, and Henrich. Gehrig said Henrich "looks like the real thing," and he predicted that DiMaggio, good as he was in 1937, would only get better. The Yankees had a nice mix of veterans and kids. They had good speed and great power. And their pitching staff, led by Red Ruffing and Lefty Gomez, looked to be the best in the league. Once, Gehrig would have been content to shine the light on his teammates and ignore his own contributions. No more. His wife, his manager, and his days under the bright lights of Hollywood had helped him emerge. He was willing to brag — a little.

"Irrespective of any other players on our club," he said, "I am the man to whom the team looks as a pacesetter. Every year I am told I am the hitter who must lead the Yankees to the pennant. That suits me fine. I want it to go on that way for many years to come."

In other interviews before the start of training camp, Gehrig admitted to reporters that he hadn't worked much on conditioning that winter, saying, "a man is entitled to a little rest." He added, "Besides, I'm never very far out of shape anyhow."

Gehrig planned to join Ruppert on a train bound for St. Petersburg in mid-March. He had already missed the first few games of spring training. But when

Ruppert's train departed, Gehrig wasn't on it. He needed one more day in New York. He and Eleanor were moving from their apartment in New Rochelle to one in Larchmont, also in Westchester County. The new building, at 21 N. Chatsworth Avenue, was swankier than the old one, on a shady street near the train station. He certainly could have afforded a house — and if he and his wife planned to have children, it would have made sense to look for something bigger. Instead, they rented another small apartment. Eleanor told at least one friend that she and her husband had been unable to have children. She told another acquaintance that they had simply never got around to it. In any case, the relocation put Gehrig out of walking distance from his two favorite destinations in New Rochelle: his mother's house and the harbor where he docked *The Water Wagon*.

When he reached St. Petersburg on March 15, a brutally hot day, Gehrig went straight to the practice field and grabbed a bat. To get in shape, players wore rubber shirts and refrained from drinking water, hoping to sweat off some of their winter blubber. Gehrig stepped on a scale in the clubhouse and weighed himself. He came in at 212 pounds, which was just about right. He was the first man to hit the field that Tuesday morning — and the first to retire. The heat was too much for him.

But the heat wasn't his only problem. In batting practice, he felt lousy. Only a couple of swings produced solid knocks. On most of his cuts, he either popped the ball high in the air or grounded it weakly into the dirt. Before long, his hands began to ache.

"I'll get into the feel of this thing in a hurry," he said.

But it took longer than he'd hoped. In a game on March 20 against the Cardinals, he drove in the winning run with a single, but he tripped rounding first base — "his cleats stuck," noted *The Times* — and was thrown out as he tried to get back to the bag. One week into the spring and he still wasn't hitting the ball with any thump. Two weeks and he had a bone bruise on his left hand and blisters on some of his fingers. "He has a couple of sore lunch hooks," wrote James M. Kahn of *The Sun*.

Never before had Gehrig shown signs of wobbly legs or blisters or bruises on his hands, not even in spring training, when he might have been a bit soft from the leisure of winter. The hands play a relatively small part in generating a batter's power. They function mainly as a pivot, taking the energy generated by the legs, hips, and shoulders and transferring it to the bat. But if ALS had already begun to drain strength from Gehrig's shoulders and legs, he might have squeezed harder with his hands to compensate, causing the blisters and bruises. He was still seeing the ball well and felt as if he were reacting to it with the same speed and power he always had. But the pain in his hands indicated otherwise. He tried taping a piece of foam rubber around the handle of the bat to absorb some of the force, but it didn't help.

On March 25, in a game against the Newark Bears, he flied out, struck out, and rolled out. Then he sat out. He took a spot on the bench and watched Babe Dahlgren fill in for him. He didn't play at all in the next three exhibition games.

It was about this time that *Rawhide* premiered in St. Petersburg. The city, not accustomed to cinematic celebrations, arranged for a parade down Main Street, fireworks, and a marching band. Ruppert, McCarthy, and most of the Yankee players were there. When Gehrig and his wife appeared, police and ushers had to hold back the surging crowd.

For the most part, the critics were kind. "Of all the movie-struck athletes, Lou Gehrig is my favorite," wrote Wanda Hale of the *Daily News*. "Why, he's no more afraid of the camera than he is of one of Carl Hubbell's screw balls. The big, amiable first baseman walks through a scene and tosses off his lines as naturally as he walks to the plate and clouts one of those home runs. . . . He looks as though he's having such a good time at his playacting, and what's more, it's fun watching him."

On March 29, the day Gehrig finally returned to the Yankee lineup, John B. Foster, the editor of *Spalding's Baseball Guide*, released his list of baseball's All-Time All-Stars. His lineup read as follows: at first base, Gehrig; at second, Nap Lajoie; at third, Jimmy Collins; at shortstop, Honus Wagner; at catcher, a platoon of Gabby Hartnett and Mickey Cochrane; and in the outfield, Ruth, Cobb, and Speaker. "You know," Gehrig said, "I've got clippings at home where [John] McGraw picked me as the all-time first baseman, and Connie Mack did, too. Now, it pleases me to see an old-timer like John B. Foster give me the same rating. There would have to be something the matter with a fellow if he didn't say he liked things like that."

Yet Gehrig still wasn't playing like an All-Star, much less the finest first baseman of all time. In five chances at the plate that day against the minor-league Kansas City Blues, he walked three times, flied out to center, and reached first on a slow roller to third. His hands were still sore. Over the course of the next week, when he did manage to get a hit, it was usually a soft single. Against bush-league competition that included the New Orleans Pelicans, the Dallas Steers, and Houston Buffaloes, he couldn't hit a home run. In a game against the Little Rock Travelers on April 9, he lobbed a soft double in the first inning but went without another hit the rest of the day. In the fifth inning, he swung so hard at a third strike that he spun around and landed, like a drunkard, on his rear end.

At last, on April 12, in a game with the Knoxville Smokies, Gehrig hit a homer over the fence in left center field. The ball traveled 360 feet. Given the poor quality of the competition (Knoxville allowed nineteen runs on eighteen hits, eleven walks, and two errors) and the fact that he struck out twice, Gehrig was probably somewhat less than elated. The next afternoon, against the Yankees' Binghamton farm team, he had a double and a triple.

In years past, whenever doubt or insecurity crept into his head, he had conquered it with the knowledge that his physical strength and God-given athleticism would pull him through. Now, a few months shy of his thirty-fifth birthday, Gehrig had overcome many of the inhibitions that had plagued him as a younger man. But for the first time he had reason to doubt the reliability of his body.

The season would open in five days.

CHAPTER 18

THE LONGEST SUMMER

Gehrig had always loved playing baseball in April, when the cool breezes of spring made everything new and anything possible. He labored sometimes in March. But when the real competition started, when the 154-game schedule stretched out before him like a road map full of familiar destinations, he had always come through.

In 1938, things were different.

On opening day, against the Red Sox, he was held without a hit by Jim Bagby Jr., a rookie who had never before thrown a big-league pitch. The next afternoon he went 0-for-4 and 0-for-3 in a doubleheader. Then came an 0-for-5 game. In the Yankees' first home game of the season, against the Senators, he went 0-for-3 and could no longer hide his frustration. "Every time up there, it's something else," he muttered as he walked back to the dugout after one at-bat.

Sometimes a player feels good at the plate but still slumps. He hits whistling line drives straight at a defender's glove, or he's robbed by a succession of terrific defensive plays, or he hits the ball to the deepest part of the park, where an outfielder has room to run it down. This was not one of those slumps. Gehrig wasn't hitting the ball hard, and he wasn't comfortable at the plate. He tried changing his stance. He reminded himself not to lunge at the ball. He ran extra laps around the field before games to get his legs in shape. Nothing helped.

On April 23, the Yankees played their second home game of the year. It was a cool afternoon but perfect for baseball. The sun burned bright through cottony clouds. The crowd of 25,000 hummed, happy to be back again at the ballpark, drinking beer, munching hot dogs, puffing cheap cigars. In the first inning, with two outs and a runner at third, Gehrig came to bat against the veteran pitcher Wes Ferrell. Ordinarily, this was the sort of moment the Yankee captain relished — a chance to drive in a run and put his team in the lead. With one pitch he could jumpstart his season. He dug in and waited. Ferrell threw. Finally, Gehrig hit one on the button to a spot where no one could catch it. The crack of the bat gave way to the call of the crowd as the ball arced toward the deepest corner of right-center field. He rounded first, rumbled around second, and turned for third. It was a gutsy decision, especially for a man stuck so deeply in a slump. But Gehrig had always been aggressive on the bases, and he wasn't changing now. The relay from the outfield was perfect. Gehrig threw himself into a slide — but too late. On his first hit of the season, he made an out. The inning was over. The Yankees went on to lose.

Over the next eight games, Gehrig continued to play miserably, striking out six times and accumulating only four hits. He struggled even in batting practice. He had played 1,971 consecutive games in the big leagues and never suffered a drought like this one. It was almost as if another man — a weaker and less talented one — had put on his uniform and replaced him in the Yankee lineup.

The whole team got off to a slow start. Gehrig's failures no doubt contributed, but writers and fans pinned most of the blame on DiMaggio, who refused to play until Colonel Ruppert met his salary demands. After Gehrig had settled for $39,000, DiMaggio demanded $40,000. He and the boss weren't even in the same ballpark. The colonel offered $25,000 and vowed not to pay a penny more. The negotiations turned ugly. "DiMaggio is a very ungrateful young man, and is very unfair to his teammates, to say the least," Ruppert said. He repeatedly emphasized the athlete's youth and humble origins, as if to suggest DiMaggio had not yet earned the right to behave so haughtily. Joe McCarthy took the colonel's side and issued a less-than-subtle threat: "The Yankees can get along without DiMaggio."

Three days into the season, DiMaggio gave up, agreeing to $25,000. When he said he needed some time to travel from San Francisco before he could start playing, Ruppert docked the center fielder's pay. While the Yankees waited for DiMaggio, Gehrig continued in his funk, swinging weakly and at bad pitches. "The fly balls he hits haven't their former carry," wrote Harold Burr of *The Post.* When DiMaggio finally rejoined the Yankees on April 30, McCarthy made room in the lineup by demoting Gehrig from fourth to fifth in the batting order. Gehrig responded by going hitless in five tries. The next morning, when *The New York Times* printed its weekly list of major-league players ranked in order of their batting averages, his name was last, with a .133 average. He was the worst hitter in the American League.

When two more hitless games followed, McCarthy dropped Gehrig from the fifth spot to sixth. "Let Lou hit his way back to the clean-up spot," the manager said. Gehrig had no comment. He rarely spoke to the media during his difficult first month of the 1938 season. In trying times, he fell back on his old habits, preferring to suffer alone.

Everyone could see he was miserable. "Now, Lou," wrote Elizabeth "Babe" McCarthy, the Yankee manager's wife, in a typewritten letter, "don't become discouraged just because you are in a little slump — you know a bad beginning, a good ending so keep up your spirits, and I know all will be well. Joe is as strong for you as he ever was, and you know I am pulling and praying for you, so keep up a stiff upper lip, and Boy, when you start hitting that ball, it will be just too bad for the rest of the league. I'm praying for you Lou, and at Mass next Sunday, I will light a candle to the Sacred Heart of Jesus, invoking Him to help you, and when you hit that first homer, just say to yourself, Babe's prayers has done this for me."

Fans in Philadelphia and Washington took to mocking Gehrig when he came to bat, something they would never have dared before. Even one of the hometown papers, the *Daily News*, took a cheap shot, using quotation marks to add a note of sarcasm in referring to " 'Slugger' Lou

Gehrig." He was not the sort to let these things roll easily off his shoulders.

On the day of his second demotion, Gehrig scratched a single, breaking an 0-for-11 slump. The following afternoon he hit his first home run of the season. But even the home run arrived without the usual joy of a long-distance drive and a trot around the bases. It came on a sharply struck ball that scooted past center fielder Sammy West of the St. Louis Browns. While West chased after the ball, Gehrig took off, "galloping around the bags until he was breathless," as the *The Times* described it. Runner and ball arrived almost simultaneously at home. Gehrig made a headfirst lunge and slapped at the plate with an outstretched left hand. It wasn't pretty, but it counted.

In the days that followed, he at last started hitting. His batting average in May was .368. Still, his power numbers — seven doubles, one triple, four home runs, and twenty runs batted in — were far from Gehrig-like. He was connecting, but the ball wasn't going as far as it used to.

In all likelihood, he was learning to adapt to the changes in his body associated with the early onset of ALS. The nervous system works like a telephone network. Gehrig's brain was transmitting the same signals it always had: See the ball, hit the ball. The message went from the brain to the spinal cord and out to the arms and legs. But disease had begun to kill some of the lower motor neurons — the telephone transmitters — located on his spinal cord. The phone lines weren't dead, but the connection wasn't very good and some of the messages were getting lost. Some muscles were responding and some weren't.

Gehrig felt no pain, nothing to cause him concern, but there is evidence to suggest that he noticed the subtle change in his body. Like an aging opera singer who abandons the upper octaves and concentrates on improving her tone in the middle register, he adjusted his approach to the game. When the nerves fail to properly stimulate the body's muscles, the muscles atrophy. As the muscles in Gehrig's legs, shoulders, and arms began to atrophy, home runs became fly outs. Triples became doubles. Doubles became singles. He began to think about hitting for average instead of power.

By mid-May, after losses to Cleveland and Philadelphia, the Yankees were in third place, with a record of 14-9. The season had barely begun, but fans in New York had expected better. It was around this time that James Kahn of *The Sun* observed something he'd never seen. Spectators, he wrote, were booing the home team. Through past slumps, and even when the Yankees finished in third place under Bob Shawkey in 1930, crowds had remained polite. This new volatility, Kahn wrote, "is becoming as interesting as the Yankees themselves." The booing began when DiMaggio returned from his holdout, an expression of the fans' frustration with players who seemed increasingly spoiled and greedy. The notion of a high school dropout demanding $40,000 a year rankled many. But the razzing of DiMaggio was only the start. Gehrig could never be accused of greed, even though he was the highest-paid player in the league, simply because he had worked so hard through the years and seldom complained. Even so, the fans teased him about his Hollywood pretensions, shouting "Hi-ho, Silver!" when he came to bat, and heckled him when he failed to deliver with runners on base.

On May 22, with the Yankees in Cleveland to play the first-place Indians and their young flamethrower, Bob Feller, Gehrig, his average up to .267, was promoted from sixth to fifth in the batting order. He would remain in that slot for most of the season. Feller left the game with a sore shoulder after pitching three scoreless innings. In the sixth, with the Indians leading by eight runs, Gehrig came to bat against a relief pitcher named Johnny Humphries and banged a 435-foot double to right-center, knocking in the Yanks' first run. But as he ran the bases, he felt a sharp ache in his back and thigh. If he hadn't grabbed his thigh, he said later, he probably would have collapsed on the infield dirt. He limped into second and asked one of the umpires to call timeout. Doc Painter, the Yankee trainer, trotted across the infield and massaged Gehrig's back, easing the pain enough for Gehrig to stay in the game. Two batters later, he hobbled home on a base hit. But at the start of the next inning, Babe Dahlgren replaced him at first base. Gehrig went to the clubhouse, where Painter slapped some plaster on his back to form a cast.

"When he gets these attacks," wrote Kahn in *The Sun*, "they take his breath away and he has sharp pains through the small of his back. He can't straighten up, but he nettles when someone says he has lumbago or something else that is chronic."

"It's just a cold," Gehrig said. "The only difference is it doesn't come out on me. It settles in my back."

After the game, Gehrig was shuffling around the clubhouse, scratching at his plaster cast. He said he had no doubt he would be ready to play by the following afternoon. His streak was about to reach another milestone. He needed only eight more games to play his 2,000th in a row, and he had no intention of stopping now.

A heavy rain soaked League Park the following morning, forcing cancellation of that afternoon's game. Gehrig had been prepared to start, though his aching back probably would have limited him to a brief appearance. With a sense of relief and a fresh coat of plaster on his back, he went to the movies. Later that evening he talked to some of the reporters hanging around the team's hotel. Though he admitted he was still in pain, he said he was certain he would be well enough to play the next day. In fact, he played all nine innings, doubling, walking, and scoring twice as the Yankees lost, 9-5.

A few days later, McCarthy moved him back to the cleanup spot; he went hitless in four at-bats. All season long it seemed as though a strikeout followed every hit, a bad day every good one. He never enjoyed one of those long, wonderful stretches in which swing after swing resulted in the sweet crack of wood on horsehide and balls ricocheting around the park.

Gehrig had always employed a simple style of hitting — not like Mel Ott with his enormous kick, or Babe Ruth with his wild uppercut — and believed that his economical approach made him more or less immune to long slumps. Now, he began to tinker with his mechanics more dramatically than at any time in his career. He not only experimented with his batting stance, he also tried changing bats. Throughout most of his career, Gehrig used an ash bat that measured 36 inches in length and weighed between 36 and 37 ounces. From 1934 to 1937, almost all of his bats weighed 36¼ ounces. He began the 1938 season using more of the same. But as his slump stretched on through April and into May, he placed another order with the Hillerich & Bradsby Co., maker of the Louisville Slugger brand. The new bats he ordered, at 35¼ ounces, were the lightest the company had ever made for him. In most seasons, Gehrig placed three or four orders with the company, rarely adjusting the weight of his bats by more than a quarter ounce from one shipment to the next. He tended to order when his old bats broke, not because he wished to experiment, and he usually needed no more than a dozen bats to get through a full season. But in 1938 he placed ten separate orders for a total of thirty-four bats. He tried lighter bats, shorter bats, thinner bats. He tried longer bats that were not so heavy and heavier bats that were not so long. He tried everything.

"Lou, I've got an idea," Eleanor recalled telling her husband on the morning of May 31. "Don't go to the stadium today. Tell them anything you want, but skip it."

The day before, in a doubleheader against the Red Sox, Gehrig had played in his 1,998th and 1,999th consecutive games. This was to be a big day. He was standing at the door, dressed, ready to leave for work, ready to punch the clock for the 2,000th consecutive time.

"Skip it?" he said, according to Eleanor's memoirs. "You know I can't just skip it."

Eleanor made the case that a streak of 1,999 games would be much more memorable than one that stretched on to two-thousand-and-some-odd games. Why not end it now, she asked, when it's a matter of choice, instead of waiting for old age or an injury to force the matter? "Besides," she continued, "let's just do it for the sake of doing it. We can stay home and drink champagne."

Eleanor was so enthralled with her plan that she called Christy Walsh to enlist his support. Walsh said he liked the idea. Eleanor kept pushing.

She had changed her man in many ways. She'd introduced him to the arts. She'd taught him to pause and sign autographs instead of sneaking in and out of Yankee Stadium like a burglar. She'd turned him into a small-time movie star and improved his rapport with the press. She'd even helped him loosen the cord that bound him to his mother. But there were some things she couldn't do. Gehrig would not allow Eleanor or anyone else to end his streak. After all the broken bones, the bumps on the head, the bruises, backaches, and bad colds, he wasn't about to step aside voluntarily.

"I couldn't," he said.

Then he was out the door.

In one sense, Eleanor was probably right. Her husband would have received much more attention for ending his streak voluntarily than he did for continuing it that day. In fact, Gehrig's 2,000th game did not attract a lot of attention. He posed for pictures before the game. In one shot he lay down on the field next to a bunch of baseballs lined up in the shape of the number "2,000." In another he stood with his teammates and grinned sheepishly as they waved their caps in the air. But no official ceremony was held on the field. He received no gold watch, no trophy, no certificate of merit. There was no marching band, no visit from the mayor. Gehrig offered no remarks to the sparse crowd of 7,000. Joe McCarthy bestowed the nicest honor that day when, speaking privately to a reporter, he appraised Gehrig as "the greatest player of all time."

Yet again Gehrig was asked to defend his decision to play every day. The questions exasperated him. "I can't see why anyone should attack my record," he said. "I have never belittled anyone else's. I intend to play every day and shall continue to give my best to my employers and the fans. What about the guy who pays $1.10 to see the game? What if I sit on the bench and say I'm resting?"

When the game began, the paying customers cheered more loudly for DiMaggio than Gehrig, same as they did most days. Gehrig walked in the first inning, grounded out in the third, hit into a double play in the fifth, and popped out in the sixth. Finally, in the eighth, with shadows falling across home plate and the Yankees leading 8-5, he slapped a soft shot just over the pitcher's head and into center field, driving in a run. It was his only hit for the afternoon. His average for the season stood at .280, with four home runs and nineteen runs batted in.

After his 2,000th game, some newspapers, including *The Sporting News*, ran side-by-side photos showing Gehrig in 1925 and 1939. Most men thicken somewhat as they near middle age, but Gehrig appeared to have grown leaner. His shoulders, once famously compared to the great limestone promontory at Gibraltar, had clearly begun to crumble. His 1938 uniform appeared several sizes larger than the one he had worn in 1925. Some variation may be attributable to changes in style, but there's little doubt that Gehrig had lost some of his heft. Still, most writers who commented on the status of Gehrig's career at this milestone seemed to think he had a lot of good baseball left in him. Gehrig agreed. Asked if he might skip a game and get some rest soon, he said he didn't see any point: "I like to play baseball," he said, "and if I were to sit on the bench for a few games the worrying and fretting would take too much out of me."

Three days before his thirty-fifth birthday, during a game in Chicago, Gehrig blasted a mammoth home run, his ninth of the year. Later in the game, while playing first base, he noticed that Red Rolfe, the Yankee third baseman, was out of position. When a runner for the White Sox noticed the same thing and tried to sneak from second to third, Gehrig sprinted across the diamond, hoping to take the throw and tag the runner. He was a hair too late, but his hustle caught the attention of everyone in the stadium, including his younger teammates. He might have slowed somewhat with age, but his desire to win was as strong as ever. In the 1920s, the men in pinstripes had been swashbucklers — singing, drinking, and laughing as they won game after game and pennant after pennant. But this version of the team was all business, and Gehrig was the outfit's stern CEO. He was never wildly praised when he came through with the clutch hit or turned a difficult double play, but fans had learned to count on him. Now, for the first time, he seemed worried about whether he would be able to continue to come through. He was reluctant to accept the possibility that he was beginning to slow down.

"A ballplayer, like any other athlete, lasts just so long as his legs last," he told one reporter as his birthday approached.

My legs are as strong and in every way as good as they were twelve years ago. This year I have read and heard people say I'm getting near the end of my big-league career, but I know I'm not . . . because I know my legs are not going back on me. When they begin to fail, I will be the first to know about it, and I will be the first to know when the end of my playing days is near. . . . I had a batting slump early this season, but that was not because my batting eyes were growing dim. A good hitter will always remain a good hitter. . . . Good batters, like good salesmen, hit slumps. All will pull out of them if they keep hustling.

If Gehrig seemed defensive about his health, and about his legs in particular, he had good reason. The evidence was piling up around him. It was about this time that Joe McCarthy began to suspect that something was wrong with his first baseman. "We were playing a midseason series with Washington," he recalled in a 1945 interview. "For some time I had noticed Gehrig wasn't getting his body into his swing, wasn't taking his full cut. I called this to his attention and his answer startled me somewhat."

"You know, Joe," Gehrig told his manager, "I think it's best for me to make sure I get a piece of the ball. If I get enough little hits I can lead the league in hitting."

But McCarthy was still supporting his slugger. Even a diminished Gehrig was better than most of the league's first basemen. "I wouldn't take Lou out even if he asked me," he said that summer. "Sure, he's not hitting the ball the way he should. But let the others take up the slack. If Dickey, DiMaggio and Selkirk were hitting at their best, no one would be pointing the finger at Lou. He'll come out of it. He's hitting the ball but is swinging only with his arms. His stride is all off, but he'll come around."

The sixth annual All-Star Game was held on July 6, 1938, in Cincinnati. Once again, Gehrig was elected to the team, though he didn't deserve it considering his performance in the first half. Hank Greenberg, on pace to break Babe Ruth's single-season home-run record, was more worthy of a spot on the roster. Even Hal Trosky, Cleveland's first baseman, was having a better year than Gehrig. But baseball fans are a sentimental bunch, and Gehrig's lifetime achievements and good character were not lost on them. They picked Jimmie Foxx to open the game (making it the first All-Star Game Gehrig didn't start) and selected Gehrig as his backup. The second-stringer came on in the fifth inning. In three trips to the plate, he managed an infield single.

After the All-Star Game, he started hitting again, banging out twelve hits, including three home runs, in thirty-three tries. Then came another drought. On July 19, in the middle of the dry spell, he told reporters he had fractured his thumb. He didn't say how or when. "X-ray examination of the injury last Sunday night at St.

Vincent's Hospital revealed the new fracture and several old ones Gehrig knew nothing about," the *Daily News* reported. He wore a cast on the finger during warm-ups that day but removed it when the game began. He went hitless in four tries, striking out once, as Cleveland won, closing to within half a game of the first-place Yankees. The cast went back on after the game. But with the division lead on the line, Gehrig wasn't going to miss the next game. "I'd play in this series if I had no thumb at all," he said.

When the Yankees gathered in the clubhouse the next morning, Gehrig was still at home. With a steady rain falling outside his apartment window, he waited to see if the game would be called off. It was. And he was doubly fortunate when the rain continued straight through Thursday, canceling the doubleheader scheduled for that afternoon. The Yankees enjoyed a rare treat that week: four consecutive days of rest. For Gehrig, it could not have come at a better time. The only catch was that the team would have to play five straight doubleheaders in August to make up for the cancellations.

As summer began to stretch its legs, Gehrig began hitting the ball better than he had all season. On July 27, in St. Louis, he smashed his sixteenth home run of the year. The next day he hit another. He had at least one hit in each of the eight games that followed. Still, even during this period, some who had watched him play through the years thought he looked different. "It is my conviction that Gehrig is a very tired man," Dan Daniel wrote in *The Sporting News.*

On August 5, in Cleveland, Tris Speaker sat in the press box recording the details of the game on a scorecard and chatting with reporters. Speaker had played twenty-two years in the big leagues, mostly with the Indians and Red Sox, retiring in 1928 with a .345 lifetime batting average. Now he told some of the men seated nearby that he thought Gehrig looked slow.

Charlie Wagner, a pitcher for the Boston Red Sox, sat on the bench one warm summer day and watched Gehrig go from first to second on a double into the right-field corner. "There was something stumbling about him," Wagner recalled. "I turned to Joe Cronin and said, 'Geez, what's wrong with the guy?' You could see things happening. . . . He could still get up and bump the ball, but you could see it in his running."

Bob Feller, the future Hall of Fame pitcher for Cleveland, had a similar memory from 1938, saying Gehrig looked clumsy at times. "He got his legs tangled up, and he was stumbling around first base a little bit. . . . One time, I remember I had him three balls and no strikes and I threw him three straight curve balls and he took them all for strikes. It was very unusual."

There's always something sad about watching a ballplayer age. It's like seeing a preview of death, played out pitch by pitch, game by game, in front of thousands of spectators. He loses a bit of speed. His eyesight fades just enough that he can't see the spin on the ball and can't judge in the necessary split second whether it's a fastball or a curve headed his way. The snap action in his wrist slows just enough that he can't catch up to the fastest of fastballs. Little by little, it all gets worse, and a player's mind invariably turns toward retirement. But Gehrig wasn't suffering from the normal aging process of an athlete. His skills were fading much faster.

August is the most grueling month in any baseball season. It's the month when the weak and old begin to fade and when rookies with seemingly limitless energy begin to comprehend the discipline of body and mind required to play 154 games. Woolen uniforms grow heavy. Trips between cities stretch on and on. Hotel rooms seem to shrink. Patience wears thin, and fights break out among teammates. If just two or three men fail to hold up well under the pressures of August, a whole team might fall apart.

For the Yankees, August of 1938 may have been the toughest month anyone on the team had ever seen. They played thirty-six games in thirty-one days in five cities. They played ten doubleheaders. In one stretch, they played doubleheaders on five consecutive days. One might have expected Gehrig to wilt during such a taxing string of games, or perhaps to sit out a few innings here and there. But he didn't wilt and he didn't rest. In fact, he played his best ball of the year, and the Yankees began to separate themselves out from the rest of the field contending for the American League pennant.

On August 12, for the first time all season, Gehrig stroked four hits in one game, including a double and a home run. Four days later, he did it again. On August 20, he hit a grand slam, the twenty-third of his career, and drove in two more runs with a double. During the five-day stretch in which the Yanks played those ten games, he hit .293 with two home runs, a triple, and nine runs batted in. By the end of the month, his batting average was up to .284, with twenty-four home runs and eighty-eight RBIs.

"Lou Gehrig has pulled himself out of the deepest batting slump of his career by changing his stance back to the old Gehrig style," wrote Drew Middleton of the Associated Press. "I dunno what did it," Gehrig told Middleton, "except going back to my old stance. I couldn't figure out how the other one was wrong, but it looks like it was. I won't monkey with it again."

The Yankees were running away with the pennant, and Gehrig seemed to be back in form. But was he? He hit his twenty-sixth home run of the season on August 26, but after that, he slumped again. He hit nothing but singles for the next eight games and went twenty-one games without a home run. In many ways, his collapse was reminiscent of the one in 1927, when his mother was sick and Gehrig, seemingly exhausted, ceded the home-run crown to Ruth. But in 1927, his disappointing numbers for the season's last thirty games included a .345 batting average, seven home runs, seven doubles, four triples, and twenty-six runs batted in. This time the fadeout over the last thirty games was much worse: He hit .306, with three homers, six doubles, no triples, and sixteen runs batted in.

Gehrig had entered the season with 464 career home runs (though record-keepers at the time thought he had 465). It had seemed a safe bet back in April that he would hit his 500th before the end of the 1938 campaign. Now, however, he was falling short. On September 9, the day he played his 2,100th consecutive game, he slapped four singles, raising his average over .300 for the first time. He remained above the .300 line for more than a week. Then, on September 19, with the Yanks in St. Louis to play the Browns, Gehrig rested. He didn't complain of illness or injury, but he removed himself from the game at the end of the first inning. He didn't even make an appearance at the plate before letting Dahlgren take over for him. Technically, it kept his streak alive, but it was the first time since his streak began that he had appeared in a game without even stepping into the batter's box. Ten days later in Philadelphia, he did the same thing, making only a token appearance and sitting out almost an entire game.

As the regular season wound down and thoughts turned to the World Series, he ordered two more Louisville Slugger bats. One weighed 34 ounces, the other 33½. Whether he recognized the changes occurring within in his body or not, he clearly recognized the need for a different set of tools to get his work done.

For years, critics had dogged Gehrig for not resting, especially late in the year, when games no longer mattered. Now, having rested twice, he came under fresh criticism. Wrote one anonymous fan in a letter to *The Times*: "This fellow Gehrig, first baseman of the Yankees, is all wet as far as playing consecutive games is concerned. He plays only one inning and calls it a game. . . . I am sick of seeing his name in the box scores." For the next two weeks, a debate raged among letter writers over whether Gehrig had diminished his achievement by exploiting the loophole in the rules that allowed him to appear for one inning and still get credit for having played another game.

"To my mind, Gehrig is the greatest first baseman ever, and I take my hat off to him for that," another fan wrote. "But this consecutive game drivel is a bit annoying because the streak is synthetic. . . . So, all hail to Gehrig as the game's greatest first baseman! But as for the 2,000-odd consecutive game record, let's forget it. Unlike Gehrig, the ball player, the record is just 'phoney.' "

Yet another writer came to Gehrig's defense: "As a rule he is on the field giving his all for the full nine innings. . . . If Joe McCarthy were not satisfied with the performance of Gehrig, he would have benched him long ago." Another reader suggested a rule change: Players ought to be required to last four and a half innings to get credit for an official game.

In the last game of the season, Gehrig played all nine innings against the Washington Senators, singling once in four trips to the plate. He finished with a .295 average, twenty-nine home runs, and 114 runs batted in. His home run against Washington pitcher Dutch Leonard on September 27, the 493rd of his career, would prove to be his last.

As the Yankees prepared to face the Cubs in the World Series, Hy Turkin and Jack Smith of the *Daily News* noted that many of the Yankees seemed to be slumping, none more than Gehrig. "Gehrig is far off stride," they wrote. "He fidgets at the plate and looks muscle-bound. He's lost his rhythm."

The Series opened in Chicago, where Cubs fans labored to convince themselves that the team had a chance to beat the Yankees. The entire Chicago team hit only 65 home runs that year; the Yankees hit 174. The Cubs scored 713 runs; the Yankees scored 966. Stan Hack, Carl Reynolds, and Frank Demaree appeared to be no match for DiMaggio, Dickey, and

Gehrig, even if Gehrig was off stride. The Cubs had the best pitching staff in the National League, but they entered the Series with a lot of tired arms. The staff ace, Bill Lee, pitched on four straight days in the last week of the season as the Cubs fought for the pennant. After Lee, the team's best pitcher was Dizzy Dean. But this was not the same Dizzy Dean who had baffled hitters so thoroughly a few years earlier. In 1937, while enjoying a fine season, he was hit by a line drive and broke his toe. In trying to return from the injury too soon he altered the mechanics of his delivery and ruined his arm. He was all but washed up at the age of twenty-six.

For Gehrig, the World Series meant a trip back to the place where his baseball glory had begun: Wrigley Field. It had been eighteen years since his home run there had helped ice the win for Commerce High and put his name — "Babe" Gehrig — in headlines.

On October 5, a stiff wind blew in off the lake. An ecstatic cry exploded from the capacity crowd when Hack opened game one with a single. But he was quickly thrown out trying to steal second, and from that point on, the Chicagoans found little reason to cheer. In the second inning, Gehrig walked and scored the first run of the Series. In the fourth, he watched two bad pitches go by, swung at the third, and singled to right. But when he pushed his luck and sprinted toward second base, trying for a double, Phil Cavarretta threw him out. "He didn't look quite right on the field and on the base paths," Cavarretta recalled years later. "And whenever he took a lead, he wobbled." In the sixth inning of the same game, Gehrig struck out on a pitch around the knees. In the eighth inning, facing a three-two count, he checked his swing and started jogging to first base, believing he'd walked. Umpire Charlie Moran disagreed, calling him out on strikes. Livid, Gehrig ran toward Moran and started shouting. Coach Art Fletcher had to run down the line and shove both hands into Gehrig's chest to stop the first baseman from going after the umpire. That was about as exciting a moment as the game had to offer. The Yankees rolled to a businesslike win, 3-1.

Dean, "the celebrated hollow shell," as one writer called him, pitched game two and did a pretty fair job, holding a lead until the eighth inning, when his arm grew weary and Crosetti scorched a home run into the bleachers. DiMaggio hit another homer in the ninth to put the game out of reach. Once again, Gehrig played little role in the outcome. He walked, singled, flied out softly to left field, and struck out.

Fans, provoked by the temper tantrum he had thrown the day before, booed him every chance they got.

In game three, Gordon and Dickey homered to give the Yankees another win. By then, the outcome of the Series was beyond doubt. In the fourth game, a wild throw by Chicago's shortstop, Billy Jurges, gave the Yanks three unearned runs and their third straight championship. Gehrig, the most productive hitter to that point in World Series history, was almost invisible throughout the competition. He finished with four singles in fourteen tries, for a .286 batting average. He walked twice and struck out three times. He drove in no runs. Gehrig's four hits, Cavarretta said, "had no oomph."

After the final game, the Yankees engaged in their usual celebration — singing in the shower, spouting clichés to the press, slapping backs, drinking beer. Only two things about the scene stood out. First, Jacob Ruppert missed the party. He was back at his Fifth Avenue apartment, bedridden with phlebitis. The other strange sight was Gehrig. Later that night, as the team celebrated at the Commodore Hotel, he started knocking back shots of hard liquor. At one point, he sat astride a chair and pretended to ride a horse, as if he were back on the set of *Rawhide*.

"You'd better look after Lou," one Yankee whispered to Eleanor. "He's drinking triples, and he's really bombed."

CHAPTER *19*
LIKE A MATCH
BURNING OUT

As winter draped New York in shades of gray, Gehrig's condition continued to slide. He tripped on curbs. He fumbled small objects. On the rink at the Playland Ice Casino, he fell so often that the other skaters mistook him for a beginner. Eleanor began to suspect that her husband had a brain tumor.

Though he felt no pain, Gehrig agreed to see a doctor. The doctor's name is unknown, but he was almost certainly a general practitioner. Had Gehrig seen a neurologist, the correct diagnosis might have been made immediately. ALS, for all its mystery, reveals itself quickly to a physician who knows what to look for. Most victims of the disease are over forty years old, but there are plenty of exceptions. If a neurologist sees twitching muscles, hyperactive reflexes, and atrophy in the shoulders, arms, or legs, and if the muscle loss is greater in one leg or arm than another, he begins to think about how to break the news. Then he conducts more tests, hoping his suspicions are mistaken. But in 1939, there weren't many neurologists. The American Board of Psychiatry and Neurology had granted credentials to only ninety-eight specialists in the field. For most doctors, the central nervous system remained a mystery. So it is not surprising that the physician who examined Gehrig latched on to something he could understand and thought he could fix. The diagnosis was gallbladder trouble.

The gallbladder is a small organ, roughly the size of a baseball, that stores and concentrates bile secreted by the liver. When the gallbladder clogs, gallstones form. Gallstones can cause sharp pain, flatulence, and bloating. When the gallbladder becomes inflamed, a patient may feel sluggish and nauseated. It's not clear that Gehrig exhibited any of these symptoms, and gallbladder trouble did nothing to explain his frequent stumbling and muscle loss. Still, the doctor assured Gehrig that this was the source of his problems, and he prescribed a diet of raw fruits and vegetables. Gehrig, relieved, became convinced he would soon regain his strength. He told Eleanor that he wanted to leave for Florida as early as possible to do some deep-sea fishing and start working out.

But first he had to attend a funeral.

Jacob Ruppert, seventy-one years old, had been confined to bed most of the winter. On January 4, he suffered a heart attack. Friends and former players hurried to his Fifth Avenue apartment to say their goodbyes. Babe Ruth visited on January 12 and assured the colonel he'd pull through, though both men probably knew better. By the following morning, as streets fell silent under a heavy snow, Ruppert was gone.

With his slicked-back white mane, his heavily lidded eyes, and his expensive suits — which he changed several times a day to fit his mood — Ruppert had stood for decades as one of New York's dandiest symbols of prosperity. His brewery was the biggest in the country. His real estate empire was one of the proudest in all of Manhattan, its value boosted by an aggressive Depression-era buying spree to more than $30 million (the equivalent of about $400 million in 2004). The Yankees were a relatively small business for Ruppert — they were worth no more than $10 million in 1939 — but they were a critical part of his empire. Owning the Yankees gave Ruppert widespread popularity, something that all the real estate in the world couldn't buy.

Ruppert had never been chummy with

his players. Even in private he had addressed them formally. It was always Mr. Ruth, Mr. Gehrig, Mr. DiMaggio. He frustrated his employees with his intransigence when it came to negotiating salaries. The working-class men who played for the Yankees had heard stories about all the money Ruppert spent on Chinese porcelains and pure-bred Saint Bernards. Ruppert never gave in. He paid no more than he needed for talent, and he made it clear to his employees that all of them were expendable. Still, the players could have had it worse. Other owners sold off or traded their best athletes when they began to demand high salaries. But Ruppert wanted to win as much as his players did, and he wanted the best team money could buy, a fact that was never lost on the New York City steel workers, delivery boys, and Wall Street traders who paid to see the Yanks play. Ballplayers, too, once their salaries were settled, couldn't help admitting their respect for the boss. "He was one of the outstanding sportsmen of the era and a most loyal friend," Gehrig said when he got the news of Ruppert's death.

More than 4,000 mourners filed into St. Patrick's Cathedral on Fifth Avenue for the funeral service. Into the church marched New York mayor Fiorello H. La Guardia and his predecessor, Jimmy Walker. Former governor Al Smith and U.S. senator Robert F. Wagner were there, too. From the world of baseball came Gehrig, Ruth, McCarthy, Barrow, Paul Krichell, Tommy Henrich, Joe Cronin, Honus Wagner, Eddie Collins, and Kenesaw "Mountain" Landis. Thousands more were turned away when the church became full.

On January 17, executors of the colonel's estate named Barrow president of the Yankees. The longtime general manager had been handling most of the team's business for years. Ruppert had stepped in mostly for newspaper interviews and contract signings, but Barrow had been the one deciding which players to hire and which to let go. Barrow was even tougher than the colonel in many respects. Baseball had a viselike grip on his heart and his mind. He tried golf — once. Being away from the game he loved made him too jumpy. Most players were intimidated by Barrow's mammoth eyebrows and stern jaw. The rest learned to fear, or at least respect, his granite determination.

Now, with Ruppert gone, Barrow made it quickly clear to players that he was fully in charge. When Henrich wrote to the new boss that winter and asked for a salary increase, he received the following answer: "Replying to your letter of January 31, beg to advise that Colonel Ruppert fixed the

1939 salary figures . . . and there is no one now living with authority to change those figures." Barrow no doubt had the authority to change whatever figures he wanted to. But he knew Henrich couldn't argue with a corpse.

Gehrig's negotiations were even more abrupt. This time, he would not threaten a holdout. He would not flirt with Hollywood. He would not sponsor a tea party at the Commodore to brag about his value to the team. He was coming off the most disappointing season of his career. Just when he had mustered a bit of courage and an appreciation of his value, just when he had learned to savor a few sweet morsels of celebrity, his mediocre performance in 1938 dented his confidence again. And the symptoms that sent him to the doctor that winter — lethargy and weakness in the extremities — could not have helped his self-esteem. Barrow offered $35,000, which represented a $4,000 cut, and Gehrig took it without complaint. In fact, he'd been expecting an even steeper reduction in pay. He told one reporter he was "thoroughly satisfied."

Gehrig left early for St. Petersburg. Eleanor joined him. On their first night in town, they visited their friends Fred and Mary Lieb. It was Mary, several years earlier, who had urged Gehrig to be more aggressive in his pursuit of a wife. Fred had tried to pacify Christina Gehrig when her son got married.

The Liebs were two of the most interesting people orbiting the world of baseball. Fred's knowledge of the game was greater than that of all but a handful of men. It wasn't that he'd been around longer than the rest: At fifty-one, he was far from a grand old man in the press corps. It was his memory that set him apart. He seemed capable of recalling every inning of every game he'd ever seen, and he'd seen thousands, beginning with a Rube Waddell shutout of the Tigers in 1904 at Huntington Park in Philadelphia. But he lived outside the press box, too. He practiced yoga. He believed in reincarnation. He studied telepathy and clairvoyance. He was convinced that his wife had been blessed with special psychic powers, and he wasn't afraid to say so in the company of some of the smartest men he knew. The Liebs had even made a believer of Jacob Ruppert. A year before Ruppert's death, Mary claimed to have received a telepathic message from one of the colonel's old friends, Fred Wattenberg, who had recently died. Lieb invited Ruppert to come by the house and speak to Wattenberg himself. Ruppert said he would come, but when the date arrived, he was too sick to keep the appointment. Fred and Mary, deciding to contact Wattenberg on their own, placed a Ouija board on their laps and gently rested their fingertips on the board. They asked Wattenberg what message he wanted relayed to the colonel and then watched as the pointer spelled a reply: "I WANTED TO TELL HIM THAT WITHIN A YEAR HE WOULD JOIN ME OVER HERE."

Babe Ruth, Miller Huggins, Connie Mack, John McGraw: They all dropped by to visit the Liebs at one time or another. Mary was never impressed with the celebrity athletes. "Men with sticks," she called them. But she liked men with complex personalities. In Gehrig, she recognized a sensitive spirit and an oft-times tortured soul.

When the Gehrigs arrived on an evening in late February, it was either Lou or Eleanor — Fred couldn't remember which — who suggested that Mary bring out the Ouija board. The Liebs said they had been in contact that week with a spiritual "entity" identifying itself through the board as "Mark Antony." As Fred and Mary and Eleanor and Lou balanced the Ouija board between them, Mark Antony began by spelling out a message for Eleanor: "YOU WILL SOON BE CALLED UPON TO FACE

THE MOST DIFFICULT PROBLEM OF YOUR LIFE."

"We were all somewhat startled," Lieb recalled. Eleanor said she and Lou had been thinking about adopting a child, but they were worried that Lou's mother would not approve. Lou was afraid that Christina wouldn't want a grandson who wasn't a genuine Gehrig.

"Is it about the adoption of a baby?" Eleanor asked.

Their hands on the board, the Liebs and Gehrigs awaited a reply. Mark Antony said "NO." But that was all he said.

Throughout the first two weeks of spring training, reporters refrained from writing what could have been the biggest story of the pre-season: Lou Gehrig looked like a bum. "He didn't have a shred of his former power or his timing," wrote Joe DiMaggio in his autobiography. DiMaggio, stunned, said he saw Gehrig swing and miss at nineteen consecutive batting-practice pitches, all of them easily crushable. It was a performance that defied comprehension. No one could be that far out of shape. No one could succumb to the ravages of age so suddenly and dramatically.

Something was wrong. That much was as clear as the big number 4 on his back. But no one wanted to be the first to say it, or at least to print it. "The old 'iron man,' " reported *The Times*, "is suffering from a little leg stiffness. . . . Nothing serious." For the first few days, everyone went through the usual drills, taking grounders, swinging bats, limbering up their arms, running around the edge of the outfield grass.

"The hardest part about spring training," McCarthy said during the first week of camp, "is to get the players' minds back on baseball. Maybe they've been running a filling station during the winter, maybe they have found themselves a girl, or there's a new baby. My job is to get 'em baseball-minded again." The stocky manager slipped a stick of gum out of his back pocket, tucked it in his mouth, and began to chew. While McCarthy spoke, the reporter conducting the interview watched Gehrig stand in the batting cage and take his cuts. His stride was too short. His wrists lacked the usual snap. All the problems that had bedeviled his swing in the late summer of 1938 were worse now. When he finished, he was short of breath.

By the second week of camp, the writers covering the Yankees began to drop hints. "Lou has been complaining of pain in his calves," wrote Dan Parker of the New York *Daily Mirror*, a clue suggesting that Gehrig might have been experiencing the cramping commonly caused by ALS.

"Father Time Scouting Gehrig" read the headline on James Kahn's March 2 story in *The Sun*. Kahn wrote that some people in the Yankee organization believed "the end of the trail was nearing for the Iron Man." The article went on to discuss possible replacements. Babe Dahlgren was still on the roster, but the Yankees were hoping to find someone with a bit more muscle. Ken Sears, the son of a National League umpire, was a good candidate, but he needed more seasoning. There was a lot of talk about converting Henrich from the outfield. There were high hopes, too, for a young Alabaman named Ed Levy. Before he joined the Yankees, Levy had been known as Ed Whitner, but Barrow suggested that the Irish-Catholic slugger would have a better chance to make the team if he used his Jewish stepfather's last name. The twenty-two-year-old went along with the idea. But as the spring progressed, it became clear that Levy was neither sufficiently Jewish nor sufficiently talented.

The first open expression of doubt about Gehrig came at the tail end of a story by Rud Rennie that appeared on March 8 in the *Herald-Tribune*. "Under the quiet surface of life in the Yankee camp," Rennie wrote, "there is a growing concern as to how Lou Gehrig, the iron man, will get along this year. Lou will be thirty-six in

June. He has not missed a game since 1925. Everything comes harder to him this year. He is working like a horse to get himself in condition. And all the while, the Yankee board of strategy is looking at the big, slugging rookies, regardless of whether they are outfielders or catchers, wondering whether any of them can play first base."

More startling to readers of the *Herald-Tribune* must have been the photo that appeared in the paper six days later. Gehrig, DiMaggio, Henrich, Dickey, and Gordon — the heart of the Yankee lineup — were posed in a formation no doubt arranged by the photographer: The men stood in a semicircle, pointed the barrels of their bats to a central spot on the ground, and leaned on the handles as if the bats were walking sticks. Gehrig stood out in the picture, partly because he was the only one wearing a sweatshirt instead of a pinstriped jersey. But there was something else. Even with his body shrouded beneath a gray sweatshirt, it was clear from the photo that his shoulder muscles had withered. His calves looked shrunken, too. None of the newspaper stories that spring made mention of Gehrig's weight, but he appeared at least ten pounds lighter than he had been a year earlier. Streaks of gray ribboned his hair just above the ears. Also, Gehrig was the only one in the photo who didn't lean on his bat. Instead, he held it a few inches off the ground, as if he were hesitant to bend over too far.

Did Gehrig know just how bad he looked in the first weeks of training camp? "He knew it," recalled Johnny Sturm, a young first baseman who joined the Yankees that month in St. Petersburg. Sturm, speaking German, asked Gehrig how he felt. "*Schlect,*" or "terrible," came the reply. "He said, 'I can't do it no more,'" Sturm recalled. "He was working out, working out, working out, and instead of getting better, he was getting worse." Sturm was so far down on the list of candidates for the first-base job that his name was never mentioned in the newspapers. But Gehrig offered him encouragement. "One of these days you'll be taking my place," Gehrig said, attempting a smile.

Sturm assured Gehrig that no one was taking his place yet. But Gehrig was inconsolable. He blamed himself for not working harder on his physical condition over the winter. He believed that he should have spent less time fishing and more time running. Instead of getting in the car to go two blocks for a newspaper, he should have walked. "Big strong guy like that, he hated to admit something was wrong," said Sturm. "People just went along with him.

They couldn't walk up to him and say, 'What the hell's wrong with you?' But it was plain to everyone who saw him."

"He was tired," Sturm said. "It was like a match burning out."

Before he made the big leagues as an infielder with the Reds, Eddie Joost used to pay to see Gehrig play in Yankee Stadium. "I never saw a guy hit line drives like he hit," Joost recalled. "He hit one off the scoreboard and smashed it to pieces. The thing started falling apart. The numbers were falling for twenty minutes." But in the spring of 1939, when Joost played in an exhibition game against the Yankees, he was shocked to see the change in Gehrig. "He wasn't good at all," Joost said. "You could see he wasn't well."

Bill Hitchcock, twenty-two years old that spring and trying to make the Yankees as an infielder, said he had been looking forward to seeing the team's star first baseman in camp. Gehrig had always been one of his idols. What he saw, however, left him shaken. "He'd stoop over to field the ball, and before he'd get his glove down, it would hit him in the shin," Hitchcock said. Then Gehrig would hobble around, chasing after the ball — too late to make the play. And that was in batting practice. Once the game began and the balls came at him more quickly, Gehrig didn't even get close enough to take a shot in the shins.

Bud Metheny, trying out for the Yankees as an outfielder that spring, was another player who never forgot his brief encounter with Gehrig in the spring of 1939.

"Lou, how do you feel?" Metheny recalled asking one day on the practice field.

"Like hell," Gehrig said.

On March 17, against the Boston Bees, Gehrig let two ground balls trickle through his legs, plays "that even your eight-year-old kid would have handled with his eyes closed," wrote Charles Segar of the *Mirror*. When he came to bat during the game, he turned to Boston's catcher, Al Lopez, and asked for advice. Lopez recalled the conversation sixty-five years later.

"Al, you've caught me before," Gehrig said. "What am I doing wrong?"

"I don't think you have any snap to your swing. You're kind of pushing it," Lopez answered.

"That's how I feel," Gehrig said.

By that time, reporters in the press corps could no longer ignore the story. Joe Williams, writing in the *World-Telegram*, said, "He isn't hitting the ball well . . . isn't getting the balls he used to get. . . . His bones creak and his lungs wheeze as he labors his way around the bases. . . . On eye-witness testimony alone, the verdict must be that

488

of a battle-scarred veteran falling apart." *The Sun* left cause for hope: "He runs and throws and bats with more effort. He looks slower. . . . He is touchy and sensitive about any suggestions that he isn't the Gehrig of old." Harold Burr of the *Post* reserved judgment: "There's still rust in the old Locomotive. . . . He's still falling away from the pitch and not getting his old drive." The *Herald Tribune* was terse: "Gehrig never has been a good hitter in spring training. But this year he is not only not a good hitter, he is not a good ball player. He looks pretty bad. . . . It looks as if the Iron Man is beginning to crumble." Jack Miley of the *Post* cracked wise: "Gehrig's ambition to play in 2,500 consecutive games is slimmer than a bathing beauty's ankles." Eleanor by now had gone home to New York. She clipped these articles from the newspaper and pasted them in her giant black scrapbook — the one with "Lou Gehrig" embossed on the cover in gold letters — the same as she had clipped stories of his triumphs.

At last, after more than three weeks of stumbling and striking out, Gehrig, collector of three hits (all of them singles) in thirty-five at-bats, spoke for himself.

I've been worried since 1925. I always

worry. I don't enjoy going without my base hits. But you know I never hit in spring training. Whether I'll get to hitting when the season starts and have a good year is something that cannot be foretold. I'm not a guy to pop off and claim that I'll do this or that. I'm doing the best I can. If it isn't good enough, McCarthy will get me out of there. If it is, then I'll stick. I feel fine. So far as I know, I haven't changed my style at bat. I just don't hit in the spring, that's all. And as you get older, it takes longer to get in the swing of things. I'd like to help you and say something, but what can I say? The batting averages will tell the story when the time comes.

After reporting Gehrig's comments, the *Herald Tribune* reviewed his recent performance. "He isn't taking that big, full cut at the ball. . . . He does not throw as he did. He doesn't dig balls out of the dirt. He falls on foul flies."

On the day the story appeared, Gehrig booted a ground ball in a game against the Newark Bears. He singled in the second inning but was picked off first base. The next day, when the Yanks played against their minor-league squad from Kansas City in Haines City, Florida, he was benched. "McCarthy figured a day off would do

Gehrig more good than another game, so he sent Henrich to first," said the *Daily News*.

Gehrig used the opportunity to go fishing. Bill Dickey, nursing a charley horse, took the afternoon off, too, and joined his pal somewhere off the coast of St. Petersburg. The next day, Gehrig returned to the lineup. After drawing a walk, he was caught off the base when Joe Gordon lined out. The consensus in the press box was that Gehrig should have had plenty of time to get back. In the eighth inning, he cracked a sharp grounder past the pitcher. If he'd run hard to first, he probably would have beaten the throw. Instead, he trotted and was thrown out. A day later, Jimmy Powers of the *Daily News* declared Gehrig "all washed up" and added that there was some doubt as to whether he would even last through spring training. "Gehrig was bad enough last year," wrote Powers. "Players always talked about him in the clubhouse. He caused the nearest thing to dissension on the club. A group almost went to Manager Joe McCarthy to ask him to lift Lou out of the lineup. McCarthy is in a tough spot. He has a certain amount of loyalty to Lou and will play him as long as possible. But if he plays him too long he may wreck the team. Meanwhile Lou has everyone's sympathy because he is just about the most popular man in the American League."

Wes Ferrell, who joined the Yankees late in the 1938 season, arrived in spring training feeling like an old man. At the age of thirty-one, he had already pitched 366 games. His arm was just about shot, his fastball mostly a memory. But, like Gehrig, he was trying to prove that he had a couple of good years left. One day in the clubhouse, he commiserated with Gehrig about the challenges of getting a middle-aged body in shape. "All of a sudden," Ferrell said, "he fell backward, down to the floor. He fell hard, too, and lay there frowning, like he couldn't understand what was going on."

Ferrell said he accompanied Gehrig the next day to watch Sam Snead, Gene Sarazen, Ben Hogan and other professional golfers play in the St. Petersburg Open at the Pasadena Golf Club. Ferrell wore his golf cleats, but Gehrig wore a pair of sneakers and slid his feet along the well-groomed grass.

A few days later, Ferrell did Gehrig a favor. In batting practice, he tossed him one cream puff after another until Gehrig managed to knock three balls over the right-field wall. Later that afternoon, in a game against the Brooklyn Dodgers, Gehrig rapped two hits. One of them was a solid shot that should have been a double, but Gehrig was thrown out at second.

Under cloudless skies on the evening of March 30, the Yankees' train pulled out of the station in St. Petersburg, headed north and west. The team was setting out on a tour of eleven cities in fifteen days. The competition would be weak. McCarthy would use this time to fine-tune his lineup and take one last look at the players he was thinking about cutting before the season began. Gehrig had traveled this circuit many times, but the games had never mattered so much. The Yankees would never cut him, but they were thinking about benching him if he didn't come around. "I will not play Gehrig unless he improves considerably in the next two weeks," McCarthy said. "We know he's bad, but we hope he'll pick up as we move north. I'll play him every day for the rest of our exhibition schedule and see what happens." If Gehrig were a rookie, the manager said, the Yankees would have already let him go.

"Give me a little time," Gehrig told the writers. "I know I'll be alright by the start of the season. Right now, I can't get my bat around on the ball. Sometimes I can't even get my eyes focused on it as it comes up to the plate. But I know I'll be okay soon." He said there was nothing wrong with him that a little more practice couldn't cure, and now he had two weeks to prove it.

The first stop was Tallahassee, Florida. On March 31, facing a pitcher named Oliver "Dill" Pickle of the Tallahassee Capitals, the Yankees cranked twenty-two runs on twenty-three hits. Even Ferrell, the Yankee pitcher, stroked three hits. At one point, some joker propped a couple of ladders against the center field fence to give the Capital outfielders a better chance to haul down the Yankees' long drives. Gehrig was the only Yankee starter without a hit. In the fifth inning, when the Yankees sent twelve men to the plate, Gehrig came to bat twice and made two outs.

Against the New Orleans Pelicans the next day, on a hot and humid afternoon, Gehrig redeemed himself. He singled twice, doubled, and drove in six runs. The double, though, came with an asterisk. His shot to left field would have been a single had the left fielder not fallen down. In Houston the next afternoon in a game against the Buffaloes, Gehrig singled, drove in a run, and made a nifty grab on a line drive slapped sharply to his left. He played all nine innings in 90-degree heat, sweating through his gray wool uniform, and allowed himself a smile when the game was done. "I'd like to see anyone tell me he's through," shouted a fan sitting behind the press box. In San Antonio, where the Yankees played the Missions, Gehrig went hitless in three tries and was removed from the game after getting hit with a pitch. In Fort Worth, against the Cats, he made a one-handed running catch on a foul ball, singled, and scored a run. "Gehrig's getting stronger, and he'll be better," McCarthy said as the train rolled out of Fort Worth, heading for Oklahoma City. "I'm not worried about him."

The Oklahoma City game was canceled when icy weather blew into town, so the Yankees moved on to Tulsa, Oklahoma, where Gehrig and a few teammates visited a twelve-year-old boy at St. John's Hospital. In the game that afternoon, Gehrig lost a pop fly in the sun and wind. He had no hits in four tries. In Little Rock, Arkansas, where the Yankees played two games, he singled in the first game and hit a ground-rule double, his sharpest blow of the spring, in the next. The following day, playing in Atlanta, he walked three times and singled. He had a three-game hitting streak, but it did nothing to improve his outlook. Doing all the same simple things he'd been doing for years, throwing and catching and swinging a bat, he didn't feel right at all, and he still hadn't hit his first home run.

Gehrig's somber mood cast a shadow over much of the Yankee clubhouse. "If he strikes out, pops up or foozles a bunt he walks silently back to the dugout and broods," Jimmy Powers wrote in his column. "His fellow players sympathetically keep quiet. They avoid his eyes. He takes a drink of water in a dead calm. No one says a word for fear of causing a blowup. Tension mounts. Lou would like to talk about his slump. His teammates awkwardly give him a community poker-face. They think they are doing the right thing. 'Oh, leave him alone. He'll snap out of it!' is the way Dickey expresses the team's sentiment."

After stops in Greenville, South Carolina (0-for-2), and Charlotte, North Carolina (1-for-4), Gehrig and the Yankees had just one more game to play before heading home. Norfolk, where Gehrig had been plunked on the head by a pitch in 1934, was the final destination on the circuit. The Yankees and the Brooklyn Dodgers had agreed to travel north on the same train, playing four exhibition games along the way. They had already played three times by the time they pulled into Norfolk. For the road-weary players, this was a game to be dispensed with quickly. But for Gehrig, every game was a chance to turn things around. Despite a month in the sun, he looked washed out and worn, said Ernie Koy, who played that year for the Dodgers and counted Gehrig as a friend. "He wouldn't talk," Koy said in an interview. "[Lefty] Gomez would make him talk a little bit, but he wouldn't say very much." Then, during warm-ups before the Norfolk game, something happened that must have jolted Gehrig as much as it jolted everyone else who saw it.

All spring, Yankee management had been talking about finding a replacement for Gehrig. But none of the prospective fill-ins ever impressed McCarthy enough to claim the position of front-runner. Henrich hadn't had enough time to learn the position. Levy wasn't hitting the ball. Babe Dahlgren had been working out exclusively at third, where he was expected to fill in from time to time for Red Rolfe. But before the game at Norfolk, when Gehrig was taking ground balls at his usual spot on the infield, McCarthy told Gehrig to knock off and let Dahlgren field a few. It was the first time all spring Dahlgren had put on a first-baseman's mitt. Suddenly, it was clear that McCarthy had settled on a replacement. It was only practice, but just watching Dahlgren work out at first base — he had such beautiful footwork, such soft hands — reminded everyone of precisely how bad Gehrig looked.

It might have been the threat of losing his job to Dahlgren, or the lousy Brooklyn pitchers, or the short fences at Bain Field. Whatever the reason, Gehrig had his best day at the ballpark since August of 1938. Before a crowd of 7,000 in a game that didn't matter, he enjoyed one last moment of athletic greatness.

On the mound for Brooklyn was an old acquaintance — Fat Freddie Fitzsimmons, who had given up a big homer to Gehrig in 1936 during the World Series against the Giants. Fitzsimmons (more chunky, really, than fat) was thirty-seven years old and looked as if he would be pitching in the big leagues forever. He threw an infuriating combination of curves and knuckleballs. As long as his flutter balls fluttered and his curves curved, he was tough to hit. Gehrig couldn't have asked for a more ideal pitcher that afternoon. His reflexes by now were too slow to catch up to a good fastball, but he had no trouble timing his swing to hit Fitzsimmons. In the third inning, Fitzsimmons threw one high and outside. Gehrig didn't get all of it — he hit it toward the end of his bat rather than on the sweet spot — but he got just enough to send it over the short wall in right field. It was his first home run of the year. Is it possible that Fitzsimmons might have let Gehrig hit the ball hard? Koy, who sat in the dugout that day, was infuriated by the suggestion. "He didn't let him, no," said Koy. "He was bearing down the whole time. Fitz was a tough guy."

In the ninth inning, with the Yanks trailing Brooklyn by eight runs, Gehrig came to bat one more time. It had already been his best day of the spring. In addition to his home run, he had also smacked two line-drive singles. Now, with a man on first and a new pitcher, Red Evans, in the game, Gehrig floated another high fly over the fence in right field.

Gehrig's two homers, wrote Kahn in *The Sun*, were not like his "whistling drives" of old. Even so, Kahn wrote, "This sudden outbreak came at a time when speculation on just how long Lulu could stick in the lineup was at its height. Gehrig never has been a diamond dramatist, but if he was he couldn't have timed his explosion any better."

The four hits were not enough to convince anyone that his troubles were behind him. "It would have been easy to say 'Oh, boy, he's coming back,' " Henrich recalled. "But we didn't say that."

CHAPTER 20
LAST CHANCE

Mayor La Guardia threw out the first baseball of the 1939 season on Wednesday, April 20, but it hardly seemed like spring: The skies over New York were cinder-block gray, the air chilly and damp. Yankee Stadium was half empty.

About three o'clock, Gehrig jogged to first base and began tossing a baseball around the infield, getting ready for the game to begin.

Over his right shoulder flew the Yankees' latest championship banner. In front of him, by the Yankee dugout, sat his wife, Eleanor, her smart hat worn at a slant, a white corsage fixed to her lapel, a mink stole around her shoulders. She wore her hair a few inches longer now than she had when she and Lou met, but her appearance had not changed much. She was still slender and youthful, with that impish smile, and she still knew how to strike a fetching pose when the cameras pointed her way. To Eleanor's right sat Christina

Gehrig, with no bow in her hat and no flower on her lapel, wearing a practical wool coat. To Eleanor's left sat Heinrich — or Henry, as he preferred to be called — one of the few men in the stadium with a bare head. He wore a suit and tie and an overcoat and held a program in his meaty left hand. The family did not often sit together at the park, but opening day was a special occasion.

Gehrig, not yet thirty-six years old, was beginning his fourteenth full season. Over the course of those seasons, his streak of consecutive games had grown quickly, the numbers flying by like fluttering calendar pages in a cinematic montage. Every time a sports fan opened a newspaper, it seemed, Gehrig was being honored for having reached another milestone . . . 1,000 games . . . 1,500 . . . 2,000. And he had made it look easy. Now, though, after 2,122 games, each addition to the record loomed large, like the steep, final steps of an arduous climb. Newspaper reporters were saying the string might snap at any time. Suddenly, the dullest record in the book was packed with high-wire drama. And the fans knew it. Gehrig, for one of the few times in his career, was the center of attention.

Game 2,123, April 20; Yankee Stadium: In the first inning, Gehrig stepped to the plate with a chance to start things right, to prove that the rumors of his demise were premature, and to reward the fans who cheered him so lavishly. "Never in his palmiest years did Gehrig receive a more generous first day hand from the crowd," *The Times* reported. Two men were out; two were on base. The stadium noise reached a crescendo. The great Lefty Grove was on the mound for the Boston Red Sox. Gehrig had always hit him well, with nine home runs over the course of his career. Like Gehrig, Grove had been playing the game a long time, and like Gehrig, he was beginning to hear questions about how much longer he could last. Gehrig curled his fingers tight around the handle of his bat. As the pitch came, he timed his swing perfectly and hit the ball fairly hard — but right at Ted Williams, the rookie right fielder. "He didn't really rip it, just a mediocre line drive," recalled Williams, who made an easy catch to end the inning.

The rest of the afternoon only got worse. In the third inning, after DiMaggio singled, Gehrig hit into a double play. In the fifth, with one out and a man on third, Grove walked DiMaggio intentionally, preferring to take his chances with Gehrig. Yet again Gehrig had a chance to drive in runs and break open a close game. Yet again he hit the ball hard. But this time it went straight to the second baseman, Bobby Doerr, who caught it and threw quickly to first, catching DiMaggio off the bag for a double play. Gehrig had made solid contact on all three trips to the plate, but the ball had none of its usual zip coming off his bat. A little extra muscle and he might have been 3-for-3. More than six decades later, Doerr still remembered how anemically Gehrig swung the bat that afternoon. "Geez, I wonder what's wrong with him?" he thought at the time.

In the ninth inning, with the Red Sox batting, Gehrig caught a throw in the palm of his mitt and reached out to tag a runner. The first baseman had been using the same brown leather Spalding mitt for ages. It had a wool-lined strap on the back that he buckled across his wrist. He had reinforced the webbing between the thumb and index finger with white tape. He knew this piece of pliable leather as if it were an extension of his own skin. But now, inexplicably, it failed him. As he moved his arm to apply the tag, the ball slipped from his grasp and fell softly to the dirt. "A childish error," one writer called it. Fortunately, the runner didn't score, and the Yankees held on to win, 2-0. In the clubhouse after the game, Gehrig wore a scowl. Jimmy Powers of the *Daily News* described him as "pretty cheerful for a corpse." The players dressed quickly and boarded a train for Washington.

Game 2,124, April 21, Griffith Stadium: While the Yankees took batting practice, an eighteen-year-old pitcher named Walt Masterson stood behind home plate and stared, like a kid with his face pressed to a toy store window. Masterson had not yet thrown his first pitch in the big leagues, and he couldn't wait to see how well his sweet, snapping curve ball would work against the game's best hitters. He'd been a fan of Gehrig's most of his life. Now the Yankee legend was a few feet away, stepping into the box to take batting practice. It was a scene Masterson would never forget. "The stroke and everything looked good," he said, "but the ball wasn't going out of the infield. It was like he was hitting with *The Washington Post.* It was most unusual to see. . . . He was making contact, but the ball was just rolling. No line drives."

In the bottom of the first inning, with a man on first, Buddy Lewis of the Senators hit an easy grounder to Gehrig. Gehrig had made the same kind of play hundreds of times — maybe thousands — but this time he fumbled it. Both runners were safe. The official scorer, perhaps wishing to be kind, decided not to call it an error. The rest of the afternoon wasn't so bad. Gehrig walked twice, scored a run, beat out a hit on a slow roller to second base, and popped out to third. The Yankees won.

After the game, he tried sneaking out one of the back doors at Griffith Stadium. When twenty screaming youngsters mobbed him, he turned and headed back toward the stadium. When the kids cut him off, he gave up and signed autographs until they all went home satisfied.

Game 2,125, April 22, Griffith Stadium: In the third inning of the team's third game of the season, Gehrig let a line drive go off his glove. Two batters later, Sam West of the Senators rifled another shot toward first base. Gehrig almost fell over trying to get out of the way. Neither play was ruled an error, but three runs scored in the inning. At the plate, he had nothing but feeble swings, resulting in two groundouts and two soft fly balls to the outfield. The Yanks lost, 3-1.

Game 2,126, April 23, Griffith Stadium: The box score would reveal neither triumph nor failure. Gehrig walked once and hit four soft ground balls that went for routine outs. But beyond the box score, one play stood out. After Gehrig's walk in the first inning, Dickey smashed a long drive off the right-field wall. Everyone in the park assumed Gehrig would score from first on the play — until they looked out on the base path and saw him running. He was churning his legs as if someone had replaced the infield dirt with flypaper. Gasping for air, he stopped at third. "He couldn't hardly move," recalled Cecil Travis, who played shortstop that day for the Senators and watched Gehrig go by. One writer said Gehrig looked like he was running uphill.

Game 2,127, April 24, Yankee Stadium: Back home for their fifth ballgame in as many days, the Yankees this time were taking on the Athletics. In some parks, batters' names were announced over the loudspeakers each time they came to the plate. Yankee Stadium, where custom tended to change slowly, had not yet adopted the innovation. Only new players were announced mid-game. Gehrig, of course, needed no introduction, and the fans needed no prompting when they saw the man with the number 4 on his back emerge from the dugout. Every time he grabbed a bat and stepped to the plate, he was cheered as if he had just hit a game-winning home run. The jeering he had heard last year was gone. Fans could see he was suffering and wished him well, and they knew the Yankees would be a better team if he would finally come around. On this, another disappointing day, he needed the support, as he struck out, grounded out, walked, and fouled out.

Game 2,128, April 25, Yankee Stadium: In the bottom of the second inning, Gehrig grounded weakly back to the pitcher. In the top of the fourth, he let an easy grounder carom off his glove. The official scorer ruled it a base hit. In the bottom half of the inning, Gehrig singled for his first hit in thirteen tries. In the fifth, with runners at first and third, he dribbled a grounder to first base. The runner on third scored on the play, giving Gehrig his first run batted in of the year and the last — number 1,995 — of his career.

As the game entered the late innings, Gehrig had reason to be encouraged. The Yankees were winning, 6-4. He had a single and an RBI and one more chance coming. Another hit would make for a pretty respectable afternoon of work. Leading off the bottom of the eighth, he hit a lazy fly to left field that landed softly in the grass. Bob Johnson, the left fielder, had been expecting Gehrig to pull the ball. Now he had to make a long run to recover. Gehrig knew right away he had a chance for a double.

Dario Lodigiani, playing second base that day for the Athletics, recognized the same thing. Probably a double, he told himself, and so he sprinted to second base, straddled the bag, and waited for Johnson to throw him the ball. Lodigiani, twenty-two years old, had seen Gehrig play in 1938. "He was pretty fast for a big man," Lodigiani recalled in an interview. "And you could hear him when he put his feet down. Boom! Boom! Boom! So while I waited for the throw, I thought 'Geez, he's going to slide and knock me into left field or something.' " The throw from Johnson was on the mark. Lodigiani grabbed it with both hands and braced himself for the impact. "I wheeled around and" — Lodigiani paused and took a breath — "Geez, he was only halfway to second." Gehrig had two choices when he saw Lodigiani holding the ball: retreat to first or keep going to second. In either case, he was almost certainly out. But he didn't run for first or second. He just lowered his head and jogged slowly back to the Yankee dugout. "I never even tagged him," Lodigiani said. "He knew. He called himself out." The crowd hushed. It was almost as if 7,268 spectators were trying simultaneously to look the other way.

When he got back to the dugout, Lodigiani asked his manager, Connie Mack, if he had done the right thing. Should he have chased after Gehrig and applied the tag even as Gehrig headed for the bench? Mack, who had been playing or managing in the big leagues since 1894, said he didn't know. He'd never seen anything like what had just happened.

Gehrig was discouraged by his play. But if he was embarrassed, he didn't show it. "I wish you would tell everybody how much I appreciate their kindness," he told one writer after the game. It was the first time in weeks he had made any significant remarks to the press. He continued on the theme in a conversation with another reporter:

First, I want to tell the fans how grateful I am for the way they've been treating me. That's something I've never had a squawk about. They've always been great to me. But now I'm appreciating it more than ever. I hear their applause, and I know that they're still pulling for me, and that means everything when you're out there having a tough time getting started. Then, everyone on the club has been swell. Joe McCarthy is a great boss. He has never said a thing to me all spring that hasn't been encouraging and comforting. The other fellows have tried to help me in every way. No one has done a thing all spring to indicate to me that they've lost any confidence in my ability to get going and help the club win another pennant. All of that has been great, and

I appreciate it, and that's what I want to say. When you're down on yourself it means everything to have the fans and the fellows on your own team slap you on the back and say you're going to be okay. And I will be, just as soon as I can shake myself out of this frame of mind this bad spring has put me in. I can feel the difference in myself. Things are getting easier. I'll be all right.

That same day, Gehrig placed an order with the Hillerich & Bradsby Co. for three new bats. These bats, at 33 ounces each, were lighter even than the ones he'd tried down the stretch of the 1938 season. They were the lightest bats he'd ever owned as a big leaguer. Yet while the bat order reveals a good deal about his physical condition, it reveals a good deal more about the player's psychological state. Gehrig wasn't kidding when he told reporters he thought he would be OK. He expected to continue playing ball.

Game 2,129, April 29, Yankee Stadium: More rain meant more rest for Gehrig and the Yankees. After bad weather canceled a home game against the Athletics and two road games with Boston, the Yanks faced the Senators again. McCarthy was not wavering in his support of Gehrig. When he filled out his lineup card, Gehrig was still in there — playing first base and batting fifth. Gehrig had stood at first base almost as long as there had been a first base at Yankee Stadium. He was a living monument, an icon, and McCarthy had apparently made up his mind that he would not be the one to change that.

Gehrig didn't play especially well in his first game after the break, but neither did he disgrace himself. He made thirteen putouts at first base without committing an error or miscue. In the second inning, he walked and stopped at second on a single to right field by Joe Gallagher. DiMaggio scored from second on the play, which suggests that another runner in Gehrig's position might have been able to take third. But Lou was learning his limitations.

In the third inning, DiMaggio hurt his ankle chasing a fly ball and had to be carried off the field. The Yankees, trailing 3-1, needed Gehrig more than ever to deliver some offense. In the fourth, he responded with a single — hit number 2,721 of his career. But once more he ran the bases with caution, stopping at second on a base hit by Dickey, and failed to score. In the fifth inning, with two on and two out, Gehrig flied out to center field. In the seventh, he came to the plate with a man on base and rolled gently to second base, once more dashing any chance for a rally.

The Yankees lost, 3-1.

Game 2,130, April 30, Yankee Stadium: While 23,000 people marched through the turnstiles to watch baseball on this cloudy Sunday afternoon in the Bronx, a far bigger attraction took place to the southeast, in Queens, where 600,000 attended the opening of the World's Fair. The Fair, decked out with pylons, sundials, statues, lightning bolts, Saturn rings, flower beds, and fountains, seemed to come from somewhere near the far edge of the human imagination. The titans of American industry — Hoover, Chrysler, and AT&T — all built dazzling art deco temples, suggesting to consumers that they were on the verge of creating a new world, not just new products. The thrill of it was enough to help visitors forget about the stubborn tenacity of the Depression and Hitler's brazen advance in Europe. Instead, they entertained thoughts of a future filled with speedy cars and super highways and a million other things to make life faster, longer, and better.

The fairground, built atop an ash dump, was an optimist's playground full of new ideas and bold promises. The biggest promise of all came in a relatively small box: television. Most Americans had heard of the invention, but few had seen it prior to the Fair. So when President Roosevelt's speech at the opening ceremony was broadcast over a fifty-mile radius in and around New York, that made big news, even though no more than two hundred television sets in the region picked up the signal. A few weeks later, on May 17, Princeton and Columbia would play the first televised baseball game. That almost no one watched hardly mattered. Everyone could see the potential. *The Times* predicted that April 30, 1939, would be remembered as the birthdate of an important new industry and an enormous popular craze.

In the Bronx, history of an entirely different sort was being made, though no one knew it at the time. The game between the Yankees and Senators chugged along without a hint of drama. There were no big home runs, no great defensive plays. For six and a half innings, there was no scoring at all. The weather was warm. Sunny skies turned gray as one inning rolled into the next. The game paused briefly in the seventh after a thick cloud dumped rain on the field. When the action resumed, the Yankees scratched out a run on a couple of infield hits. Washington answered in the next inning with three runs to take the lead.

Gehrig had no hits and committed no errors. He did nothing much to help his team, nothing much to hurt it. Even so, he was deeply disturbed by his performance. It wasn't simply that he couldn't scratch a hit. He'd had plenty of 0-for-4s in this frustrating season. The thing that gnawed was his failure to drive in runs. Every time he came up, he had at least one man on base. RBIs had always been his specialty, his meat and potatoes. Cobb slashed singles. Ruth hit homers. Gehrig drove in runs. Only now he didn't.

His final at-bat came in the eighth inning against Pete Appleton, a right-handed journeyman relief pitcher. With two men on base, Gehrig had one more chance to get the Yankees back in the game. He had one more chance to resuscitate his spirit. He swung and hit the ball hard — harder perhaps than he'd hit it all season — and the ball flew on a long arc to straightaway center field. Had he started his swing a fraction of a second sooner and pulled the ball to right field, he might have had a home run. Instead, George Case ran it down for the out.

"A hit would have won the ballgame for the Yankees," Gehrig said later, "but I missed. . . ."

In the top of the ninth inning, another play unfolded that would haunt him in the days and weeks to come. With no runners on base, Buddy Myer hit a grounder to first. It was a routine play, not requiring much movement or agility. Ordinarily, Gehrig would have grabbed the ball, dashed a couple of steps to his left, and stepped on the base for the out. But by the time he got his glove on the ball and set his feet, he could see that he wasn't going to beat Myer to the base. The simple act of shifting his momentum from right to left had taken too much time. Motions that he had once made reflexively now required slow, separate actions, as if his brain were pausing to glance at an instruction manual. Johnny Murphy, pitching in relief for the Yanks, saw that the first baseman was in trouble and sprinted from the mound to help out. Gehrig flipped the ball to Murphy, who stepped on first for the out.

When Gehrig got back to the dugout, some of his teammates slapped him on the back and offered congratulations for making the play. He watched as the Yankees tried and failed to score in the bottom of the ninth, losing the game, 3-2. But all he could think about were those slaps on the back. Had his level of play slipped so much that he deserved congratulations for making easy outs? "Heavens," he asked himself, "has it reached that stage?"

With DiMaggio out with a lame ankle and Gehrig playing so poorly, Joe McCarthy announced plans to scramble his lineup. The Yankees were about to embark on a two-week trip out west, visiting Detroit, Cleveland, Chicago, St. Louis, and Philadelphia. But the manager still had no intention of giving Gehrig a rest. At worst, he said, he might drop him to a lower spot in the batting order. Some of the writers were skeptical, predicting that Gehrig would be benched before the team returned to New York.

The day before the start of the road trip, the Yankees enjoyed a break in the schedule. Gehrig stayed home. Eleanor described her husband's condition that day as "troubled, shaken, even shocked."

"They don't think I can do it anymore," he told her. "Maybe I can, maybe I can't. But they're talking about it now, they're even writing about it. And when they're not talking, I can almost feel what they're thinking. Then, I wish to God that they would talk — you know, say anything. . . ."

"Sweetheart," Eleanor replied, "you've done it for thirteen years without a day off. The only thing that matters is whether you get the same feeling of satisfaction out of it."

"How can I get the same feeling of satisfaction out of it? I'm not giving them the same thing, so I'm not getting the same thing. You think they're hurting me. But I'm hurting *them*, that's the difference."

CHAPTER 21

PITCHERS ONCE
FEARED HIS BAT

The Yankees arrived in Detroit on the morning of May 2 and checked into the Book-Cadillac Hotel.

Bob Murphy, a writer for the *Detroit Times*, pen and pad in hand, approached Gehrig in the lobby.

"Off to a slow start," the reporter said. It wasn't much of a question, but it was enough to get a response.

"Yes," Gehrig said, forcing a smile, "off to a very bad start, if you want to be truthful. . . . I've been getting off to bad starts for several years now. Only this one is the worst."

Murphy asked if Gehrig thought he would start hitting soon.

"I only hope," he said. "You never lose hope in baseball."

Later that morning, he sat in the hotel restaurant and ate breakfast with Dickey. After breakfast, Gehrig was sitting in the

lobby reading a newspaper when Joe Mc-
Carthy arrived. Gehrig spotted the manager at the cigar counter, dropped his
newspaper, and got up.

"Joe, I want to talk to you about an important matter," Gehrig said, according to
Charles Segar of the New York *Daily
Mirror*, who noted in his newspaper story
that day that he was sitting next to Gehrig
in the lobby when McCarthy came in.

The men, escorted by a bellhop, went to
McCarthy's room. When the bellhop was
gone, Gehrig blurted his news. He said he
was ready to take a seat on the bench.

McCarthy asked if he was sure.

Gehrig said he was. He said he was
doing it for the good of the team.

McCarthy walked back to the hotel
lobby and asked the reporters to gather
around. He had an announcement.

"It's a black day for me," he said, his
voice choking. "And the Yankees."

Gehrig spent much of the early afternoon
chatting with sportswriters, both at the
hotel and at the ballpark. He seemed glum,
the writers said, but he was being a good
sport. If Gehrig had been forced from the
lineup by McCarthy, as some writers have
suggested, it seems unlikely that the manager would have made the move after such
a brief consultation with Gehrig. It also

seems unlikely that Gehrig would have been so eager to talk.

"I haven't been a bit of good to the team since the season started," he told one reporter. "It would not be fair to the boys, to Joe or to the baseball public for me to try going on. In fact, it would not be fair to myself, and I'm the last consideration. It's tough to see your mates on base, have a chance to win a ballgame, and not be able to do anything about it. McCarthy has been swell about it all the time. He'd let me go on until the cows came home, he is that considerate of my feelings, but I knew in Sunday's game that I should get out of there."

Gehrig said he would probably sit out "a couple of games." After that, he'd see how he felt. If the warm weather revived his strength, he felt certain that his confidence would also return. "I've got to remain in baseball," he said. "For one thing, I'm crazy about the game. For another thing, I am not quite thirty-six. In other walks of life, a man begins to do his best work at that age. . . . If by chance the legs do not respond and the swing does not come back — well, I am taking my hurdles as I come to them."

Gehrig went out of his way that afternoon to apologize to Bob Murphy. He felt badly about implying in his earlier conversation with the writer that he intended to keep playing. But he hoped Murphy would understand that he couldn't very well share the news with the press before telling his manager.

By one o'clock, the Yankees and Tigers were at the stadium getting dressed for their game. The Yankee locker room seemed quiet — much quieter than usual, according to Babe Dahlgren, who wrote an article filled with his recollections fifteen years later. Word of Gehrig's decision had begun to spread, but Dahlgren hadn't heard yet. As he finished dressing and sat on his stool, checking the lacing on his glove, Dahlgren felt a tap on the shoulder. It was coach Art Fletcher, who leaned in close and whispered, "Babe, you're playing first base today." Since 1925, no Yankee but Lou Gehrig had heard those words.

"Are you kidding?" Dahlgren asked.

But Fletcher was already walking away.

"Good luck, Babe," he said over his shoulder.

Slowly, Dahlgren's teammates began to approach to offer their encouragement. When Dahlgren walked down the ramp to the dugout and out on the field, he saw Gehrig surrounded by reporters and photographers. The photographers asked Gehrig to pose with his replacement, then with some of the Tigers, then alone on the bench, looking wistfully out at the field. For the latter photo, someone at *The Times* came up with a headline that sounded like an epitaph: "Pitchers Once Feared His Bat."

Fred Rice, working as an usher that day at the stadium, recalls watching Gehrig put on a mitt before the game and play catch with Dickey. But when one of Gehrig's throws bounced short and rolled to Dickey, the game of catch ended abruptly. "Lou just looked at him," Rice recalled. "He dropped his glove, stumbled around to pick it up, and then walked toward the dugout." Gehrig didn't take any practice at first base.

Moments before the start of the game, Dahlgren shared a private moment with Gehrig, away from the cameras and from the rest of the team. He offered Gehrig one last chance to change his mind.

"Come on, Lou, you better get out there," Dahlgren said, his voice cracking. "You've put me in a terrible spot."

Gehrig slapped him on the back. "Go on, get out there and knock in some runs."

McCarthy asked Gehrig to carry the lineup card to home plate, a job he occasionally performed in his role as captain but which more often fell to one of the coaches. No doubt McCarthy wanted to give the audience of 11,000 a chance to show its appreciation for the greatest first baseman to ever play the game. As Gehrig handed off the lineup card and shuffled back toward the dugout, Tiger announcer Ty Tyson used the public address system to inform members of the crowd that they were witness to an important moment: "How about a hand for Lou Gehrig, who played 2,130 games in a row before he benched himself today?" It took a few seconds for the news to register, but as it did, the fans began to cheer and clap. Gehrig tipped his hat and disappeared into the dugout. He bent over the water fountain and took a long drink, trying to hide his face. But his teammates could all see that he was weeping.

Once the applause quieted and Gehrig found a seat on the bench, the stadium fell silent. "The crowd was pretty quiet there for a while," recalled Floyd Giebell, a twenty-nine-year-old rookie pitcher for the Tigers at the time. "It must've been about three or four minutes, everyone was very somber." The Yankees could have been distracted by Gehrig's departure from the lineup. Instead, they played with energy and focus, breaking out of their offensive slump in a big way. Though they were without Gehrig and DiMaggio, the team scored twenty-two runs, cruising to an easy win. Dahlgren showed no evidence of butterflies. He homered, doubled, and drove in two runs.

At some point during the game, reporters wandered into the grandstand to interview Wally Pipp, a resident of Grand Rapids, who happened to be in Detroit on business that day and had decided to take in the game. "Lou looks ill to me," said Pipp, now forty-six years old. "Back when he joined the Yankees he seemed bigger and broader."

In the seventh inning, with the victory all locked up, the new first baseman approached the old one and asked if he wanted to play an inning or two, just to keep his streak alive.

"They don't need me out there," Gehrig told Dahlgren. "You're doing fine."

The next day, Gehrig picked up a piece of Book-Cadillac hotel stationery and wrote a note to Eleanor. The undated letter, written in a graceful hand, was found by archivists at the Baseball Hall of Fame among papers donated by Gehrig's wife. The end of the letter has apparently been lost, or else Eleanor chose not to preserve it. Historians have debated whether Gehrig wrote the letter after ending his streak, or later, after his illness was diagnosed. But given that the letter came from the Book-Cadillac and that Gehrig made reference to an event "yesterday," it seems almost certain that he was referring to the end of his streak, which would mark the date of the letter as May 3, 1939. He wrote:

My sweetheart — and please God grant that we may ever be such — for what the hell else matters — That thing yesterday I believe and hope was the turning point in my life for the future as far as taking life too seriously is concerned — It was inevitable, although I dreaded the day, and my thoughts were with you constantly — How would this affect you and I — that was the big question and the most important thing underlying everything. I broke just before the game because of thoughts of you — not because I didn't know you are the bravest kind of partner, but because my inferiority grabbed me and made me wonder and ponder if I could possibly prove myself worthy of you — As for me, the road may come to a dead end here, but why should it? — Seems like our backs are to the wall now, but there usually comes a way out — where, and what, I know not, but who can tell that it might not lead right out to greater things — Time will tell —

As for our suggestion of a farewell

tour and farewell day Joe had a different but sensible idea — He said there wasn't anybody more deserving of the remaining salary — and he wasn't afraid of Ed [Barrow], but with this new setup that question might arise, and if we planned a farewell day to record, newspapermen would interpret it as the absolute finish and that might cause quite a squabble among all the new directors, whereas if we said just a temporary rest and lay off — to come back in warmer weather, there could hardly be any doubt — I couldn't tell you this over the phone because Bill [Dickey] was . . ."

And there the letter broke off.

CHAPTER 22

THE BITTER WITH
THE SWEET

He was right. The team didn't need him.
With their captain on the bench, the Yankees went on a terrific run, winning so easily
and with such regularity that the pennant
seemed already assured. The only mystery
was when — or if — Lou Gehrig would get
back into the lineup.

Gehrig carried on with all the rituals and
routines of his former life. He sat in front
of his locker, smoked his pipe, and pulled
on his pinstriped pants. He checked the
laces on his glove and curled the brim of
his cap. He stuck a piece of gum in his
mouth, jogged onto the field during warm-
ups, and tossed the ball back and forth
with his teammates and coaches. He did
everything he'd always done. Except play.

He was an athlete without a sport, a
competitor with no opponent. His teammates tried to kid him about riding the
bench. "Just think, Lou," said Lefty

Gomez, "it took fifteen years to get you out of there. I'm out sometimes in fifteen minutes." But Gehrig wasn't laughing, and as it became clear that the time off wasn't doing him any good, physically or emotionally, the joking ended. With each day, he grew weaker and clumsier. As the Yanks continued their road trip, players around the league witnessed his diminishing condition. One day in Cleveland, Bob Feller walked into the Yankee clubhouse and spotted Gehrig "stripped to the waist and shockingly thin . . . sitting there with his head between his shoulders." When the Washington Senators went to Detroit and checked into the Book-Cadillac, they heard from some of the bellhops that Gehrig had fallen down the lobby staircase on his most recent visit. Soon the rumor spread all around the league.

When the Yankees returned to New York on May 16, a Tuesday, only 6,500 fans turned out to see them play. The newspapers didn't mention whether Gehrig was at the park, or if he took the lineup card to home plate, as had become his custom since the benching. Whether he made an appearance or not, though, it was a momentous occasion: the first time since the summer of 1925 that someone other than Gehrig started a game at first base for the Yankees in Yankee Stadium. In replacing Gehrig, Babe Dahlgren had taken a humble approach. He sought no media attention. When reporters quizzed him, he said the same thing almost every time: I'm no Lou Gehrig and I never will be. In his New York debut, though, against the Browns, Dahlgren offered a pretty fair imitation of the original item. In the top of the eighth inning he made a spectacular catch on a bases-loaded line drive, saving at least two runs. In the bottom half of the same inning, he cracked a three-run, inside-the-park home run.

For the two weeks that the team remained in New York, Gehrig's name was scarcely mentioned in the press. His sudden plunge from greatness was like nothing the writers had seen before. Legends were supposed to fade, not nosedive. It would seem that no one knew what to say or write. One day during the Yankee home stand, McCarthy visited the Court of Sport at the World's Fair, where he spoke to a crowd of about a thousand children. One boy raised a hand and asked the manager when fans might see their favorite first baseman back in the lineup. "That's entirely up to Gehrig," McCarthy said. "When he feels he's ready, I'll give him another chance."

On May 29, the Yankees hit the road

again, traveling to Boston, where Red Sox pitcher Elden Auker spotted Gehrig smoking a cigarette in the Fenway Park dugout before the game. Auker, like a lot of Gehrig's friends, had always enjoyed testing the big first baseman's strength. Auker liked to sneak up and try to wrestle him to the ground, or tie him up in a headlock. Though Auker was the taller man, Gehrig was much more solidly built. Their wrestling matches usually ended in a matter of seconds, with Auker brushed aside like dandruff. This time, though, when Auker threw his arm around Gehrig's head and neck, Gehrig's knees buckled and he began to fall.

"Oh, God, Elden," he said, "don't do that."

"What's the matter, Lou?" Auker asked.

"I don't know. There's something wrong with me," he answered as his friend helped him to his feet. "It started over the winter. I lost weight and I felt like I was getting weak. This spring it just seems like I'm weaker and weaker and weaker. . . . I don't know what it is."

The same baseball experts who had declared weeks earlier that Gehrig was the victim of age, or poor conditioning, or the strain associated with his streak, were beginning to revise their views as the season continued and he showed no indication of regaining his form. "There must be something organically wrong with Gehrig," said Barrow. "I've been in baseball 50 years and I never saw a great hitter go to pieces all at once before."

Gehrig, at first, seemed reluctant, at least publicly, to accept the possibility that he might be ill. "I just can't understand," he said. "I am not sick. The stomach complaint which was revealed last year in three separate examinations . . . has been cleared up by my observance of a strict diet. My eye is sharp, yet I am not swinging the bat as of old." He would suggest in later interviews that he had seen a doctor again in May, when the Yankees were playing at home. But he never named the doctor or said if he'd seen a specialist. At this point, given the symptoms, even a general internist might have begun to suspect that Gehrig's problems were rooted in the neurological system. But it still wasn't likely that a doctor would have considered amyotrophic lateral sclerosis. Even if the doctor had heard of ALS — no sure thing — he might have assumed that Gehrig was too young to get it. Whatever the doctors told Gehrig, it wasn't enough to chase the troubling thoughts from his mind. Though he felt no pain, he knew something was wrong. He knew it every time he picked up a bat and took a few swings or tried to jog across the field during practice.

By the end of May, he had stopped taking batting practice and had quit working out at first base. He sounded as if he'd given up hope of returning to the lineup. "These hot days make it awful hard on a fellow sitting on the bench," he said. "I'd like to get these dogs out there and give them a good workout. But the boys seem to be doing okay without any help — if I could give it to them."

In an interview with Frank Graham of *The Sun*, he sounded like a man who was worried about more than the end of his playing career. "My friends slap me on the back and say, 'Don't worry, Lou.' Don't worry? How can I help it?"

On June 1, with the Yankees in Cleveland, bullpen coach Johnny Schulte spoke to a Knights of Columbus group and let slip a secret. "Lou is a sick man," Schulte said. "Some time in the next few days he's going to Rochester to find out what it is that's been sapping his strength. We hope it's nothing serious, though it doesn't look good now." Schulte was referring to the Mayo Clinic in Rochester, Minnesota.

Gehrig must have told his manager, and perhaps a couple of his friends, that he intended to make the trip, but he had not planned on making his decision public. At first, he told reporters that Schulte was mistaken. "Just another rumor," he said. Two days later, though, he confirmed he would indeed be going to the clinic, and he apologized for having lied. "I hadn't made up my mind about what I was going to do," he said. "I thought I could kill the whole story by denying it. Even my wife did not know I had anything like that in mind. She was all upset and on the telephone in no time wanting to know what was the matter. Now I look like a dope, and I feel bad about the way the whole thing has been balled up. I'm not sick. I feel fine. Never better in my life. But there must be something wrong. A ballplayer of my age and physique doesn't lose his ability as suddenly as I did. There must be a reason for it."

But before leaving for Minnesota, he spent one more week traveling with the Yankees — and on June 12, in Kansas City, he tried one last time to play baseball.

"Oh, it was a sad day," recalled Phil Rizzuto, then a twenty-one-year-old shortstop for the Kansas City Blues, the Yankees' AA farm team. But it began for Kansas City baseball fans as the most exciting day of the year. The city was delirious over the arrival of the Yankees. All

532

over town, people were talking about how the Blues were going to give the big shots from New York a whipping. The Blues were no ordinary bunch of minor-leaguers. With Rizzuto at short, Johnny Sturm at first base, Vince DiMaggio (Joe's brother) in center field, Jerry Priddy at second, and Clyde McCullough catching, they were one of the finest minor-league teams of all time and probably could have beaten a few big-league clubs. They went on to win 107 games that year, losing only 47. Fans anticipated a terrific battle.

It began as a brilliant day, the heat and humidity rising as if to match the city's enthusiasm. By noon, with more than two hours to go before the start of the game, every seat in Jacob Ruppert Stadium had been sold. By game time, more than 24,000 fans swarmed the park. All available surface areas — stairways, aisles, fences, even concession stand roofs — were jammed. Jackets came off and ties came loose.

Maybe Gehrig was inspired by a desire to please the big crowd. Or maybe anxiety over his upcoming physical examination motivated him to conduct an exam of his own by taking a few swings and fielding a few throws in a real game. Baseball had always been his security blanket. As a small boy, when he was taunted as a "Heinie," he had won respect on the schoolyard by showing he could hit and throw the ball harder than children twice his age. In high school and college, when he was too shy to make friends any other way, he earned the admiration of his teammates by playing with vein-popping intensity. Now he turned to the game again. Twenty years after his first foray into organized baseball, at Commerce High School, he played his final game.

Gehrig was warming up on the infield when Sturm, the Blues' first baseman, came over to say hello. "He looked kind of thin, kind of beat up a little bit," Sturm recalled. The twenty-three-year-old minor-leaguer remembered how friendly the Yankee star had been in spring training. Sturm asked how Gehrig was feeling. "All right" was the response. Sturm got the feeling he didn't want to talk.

McCarthy had left the team a few days earlier to attend a celebration at the Baseball Hall of Fame in Cooperstown, New York, in honor of the game's centennial. Thousands of people gathered in the picture-book village to see and meet some of baseball's greatest legends, including Ty Cobb, George Sisler, Grover Cleveland Alexander, Nap Lajoie, Walter Johnson, Eddie Collins, Connie Mack, Cy Young, and Babe Ruth. Meanwhile, in Kansas

City, Art Fletcher, filling in as manager for the Yankees, agreed to let Gehrig play first base. Fletcher penciled him into the lineup as the eighth hitter. In the bottom of the first inning, as the Blues came to bat, Gehrig slid on his tattered brown Spalding baseball mitt and walked across the infield. Rizzuto grabbed a bat and stepped toward the on-deck circle, his eyes glued to Gehrig. Growing up in New York and cheering the Yanks, Rizzuto, a little man, had always been awed by the sight of the first baseman's mammoth frame — "so wide and solid" — and the thunder in his swing. Now he noticed that his childhood idol was having trouble walking.

In the top of the second inning, the crowd gave Gehrig a standing ovation just for stepping to the plate. He swung and made contact. The ball rolled softly to second base, where Jerry Priddy gloved it and threw to Sturm for the easy out. In the bottom half of the inning, Gehrig returned to his position at first base. He made two errors — dropping one throw and letting another sail by — but was charged with neither by the official scorer. Clyde McCullough, the Kansas City catcher, remembered one more play that didn't show up in any of the press accounts of the game. In the third inning, McCullough wrote in 1982, a left-handed hitter drilled a line drive in Gehrig's direction. Gehrig raised his mitt to make the catch, but the force of the ball "knocked him down and he fell on his back," McCullough wrote. When the inning was over, Gehrig quit the game and went back to his room at the Hotel President. That evening, in the hotel dining room, he said goodbye to his teammates.

The next afternoon, he flew on choppy air to Rochester, Minnesota. Eleanor remained in New York. Dressed in a blue sport coat and gray trousers, and carrying a copy of the *Saturday Evening Post*, Gehrig stepped down the stairs of a Northwest Airlines DC-3 and onto the tarmac. The gusts from the plane's propellers mussed his hair. Readers of the *Rochester Post-Bulletin* had been expecting him to arrive by train the night before, so no big crowds were on hand at the airport. A reporter and a photographer approached. Gehrig nodded, signaling to the photographer that it was OK to take pictures. A smile flashed across his face. The reporter, Joe Kernan of the *Post-Bulletin*, introduced himself and asked Gehrig if he wanted a ride into town. Seeing no cabs nearby, Gehrig accepted.

Kernan drove slowly and indirectly to the Kahler Hotel. Gehrig rubbed his chin and said he was eager to get to his hotel and have a shave, but Kernan ignored the hint, taking his passenger on a short tour of downtown Rochester. He had a big story in his car, and he was angling to hold on to it for as long as possible. Gehrig looked tired and anxious, according to Kernan's story, but he smiled politely.

"Where do you feel the worst, Lou?" Kernan asked. Gehrig said he was in no pain and doubted the doctors at Mayo would find anything wrong. "I'm not hiding a thing," he said.

Kernan turned to baseball, probably thinking he'd have better luck getting a good quote. He asked whether the Yankees of the 1920s had been better than the Yankees of the 1930s. Now Gehrig got snippy. "That's not a question for a contemporary ballplayer," he said. "Wait until I'm all washed up."

When they arrived at the Kahler, Kernan hopped out of the car and reached for his passenger's suitcase. Gehrig waved him off, chuckling and reminding the reporter, "I'm bigger than you." The desk clerk welcomed Gehrig and asked if he wanted to look at a selection of rooms. "I'll take anything you've got," he said. "I'm not fussy." Gehrig went upstairs, perhaps to shave, and then walked a block to the Mayo Clinic. Though it was already late in the afternoon, he didn't want to waste the day.

To many first-time visitors, the Mayo looked like the Land of Oz, a magical kingdom of modern medical geniuses and whizbang machines plopped down stunningly among the rolling hills of southern Minnesota. The clinic's headquarters, seventeen stories tall and topped with a four-story bell tower, shot up over Rochester like an elm tree in a field of alfalfa. In 1939, roughly a hundred thousand patients came through its massive bronze doors. The Mayo was a mecca for hypochondriacs as well as for the seriously ill. In the late 1930s, only one doctor in a hundred worked in a group practice, and the average group practice contained only eleven doctors. The Mayo, with five hundred doctors and specialists in every imaginable discipline, was unique. The rich and famous arrived from around the globe. The poor scraped and borrowed to get there. Pullman cars on trains from Chicago to Rochester were equipped with extra-wide doors to accommodate stretchers. Passengers flying on Northwest Airlines traveled in pajamas, slippers, and bathrobes. *Life* magazine in 1939 called it a hospital for the industrial age, with surgery served up as if on a production line.

If Gehrig had arrived at the Mayo a few months earlier, one of the founding Mayo brothers — William or Charlie — might have supervised his care. At the very least, one of the Mayo brothers probably would have greeted him and introduced him to the physicians who would be leading his examinations. But Dr. Charlie had died a few weeks before Gehrig's arrival, and Dr. Will was gravely ill; he died a few weeks later. So Gehrig in all likelihood entered the clinic alone. As he stood at the first-floor registration, he would have glanced at a long, marbled hallway, where patients sat in wicker chairs, awaiting their appointments. At the desk, he would have been given a brown envelope with his name and patient number on it. From there, he would have walked down the hallway to a bank of elevators. As Gehrig rode the elevator, his medical records would probably have traveled by hidden conveyor belt from the first floor to the eighth.

Dr. Harold C. Habein was the first Mayo doctor to examine Gehrig. Normally, patients were assigned to an examination room and met by whichever doctor happened to come up in the rotation. But Gehrig got special treatment. Habein was one of the hospital's top doctors, and he was often assigned to conduct the initial exam when wealthy or famous patients came to the clinic. Benny Goodman, Eddie Duchin, and Sid Luckman were among the men who started out as Habein's patients and eventually became his friends. Habein decided to see Gehrig in his office, where he thought they would be more comfortable than in one of the floor's small exam rooms. When he asked Gehrig if he'd been having any problems, Gehrig said he'd been feeling "a bit clumsy" with his left hand. Otherwise he felt fine. The doctor asked him to undress.

"When he took off his clothes for the examination, the diagnosis was not difficult," Habein later wrote in his unpublished memoirs. "There was some wasting of the muscles of his left hand as well as the right. But the most serious observation was the telltale twitchings or fibrillary tremors of numerous muscle groups. I was shocked because I knew what these signs meant — amyotrophic lateral sclerosis. My mother had died of the disease a few years before." Habein didn't tell Gehrig that he suspected ALS. He wasn't a neurologist. Even if he had been, he wouldn't have wanted to rush such a serious diagnosis. He phoned Dr. Henry W. Woltman, the head of the Mayo's department of neurology. If Dr. Israel Wechsler of Mt. Sinai Hospital in New York was the Babe Ruth of American neurology in 1939, then Woltman was its Lou Gehrig — a heavy hitter who spoke softly and shunned attention.

Woltman bore a strong resemblance to

the farmer with the pitchfork in Grant Wood's famous painting *American Gothic.* He was forty-nine years old, tall, and slender, with thinning hair, an egg-shaped head, and rimless glasses. He was a mild man by nature. His peers would sometimes forget he was in the room during staff meetings, until he raised his hand and asked a brilliant question. He appeared to be so meek and unprepossessing that his patients sometimes insisted on seeing another doctor, one who seemed a little more confident. Farmers and gas station attendants who drove cross-country and chief executives flying in from the coasts expected to be treated by God-like men, not by this milquetoast. Woltman didn't mind. He'd turn away, walk to the phone, and dial one of his colleagues. "Would you step in here, please?" he would ask. The junior doctor, embarrassed, would explain to the patient that Woltman was the chief of neurology and one of the best neurologists in the world. The patient would acquiesce and Woltman would return to the room, quiet as ever.

When Jean-Martin Charcot identified ALS in 1874, there were no medical books or manuals that listed the correlations between symptoms and diseases. Forty years later, when Woltman finished medical school, there were still no formal courses offered for the practice of neurology and no standard diagnostic practices. When he arrived at the Mayo Clinic, becoming one of only two neurologists on staff, he began to develop a checklist of the reflexes and sensory responses that a doctor should expect to find in a healthy person. His checklist is still in use at the Mayo today. Before running down the roster of symptoms, Woltman would usually ask the patients why he had come to the clinic and why he was seeing a neurologist. He was a terrific interviewer, guiding patients so gently that they barely recognized the examination had begun. While his patients spoke, Woltman would quietly take notes. His handwriting was small and nearly illegible. Gehrig was the sort of patient Woltman loved to work with. Assessing the physical condition of an accountant or a university professor could be tricky, because men in those professions tended to sit at desks all day, muscles wasting away undetected. But a professional athlete pays attention to his body, and so do the thousands of sports fans and writers who watch him play every day. When did he start to lose power as a hitter? Woltman might have asked. Did he feel any different running the bases? Had he been making more errors? If there had been any doubt, Woltman could have found his answers in the box scores.

As he progressed to more specific questions, the doctor usually moved from head to toe: Any problems speaking? Chewing? Swallowing? Keeping your head up? How's the strength in your arms? Having any trouble walking? Climbing stairs? Any problem breathing while you sleep? Are you out of breath when you run? Noticed any loss of muscle? Any twitching or cramping?

When the interview was done, Woltman would begin the physical exam. Once more working from head to toe, he would look for signs of muscle atrophy in the face, tongue, jaw, and throat, moving down to the shoulders, arms, chest, and stomach, and on to the legs and feet. With a heavily muscled man such as Gehrig, muscle loss or twitching in the biceps or triceps might have been obvious in an instant. But Woltman liked to take his time. He pulled at his patient's fingers, because muscle loss in the hands tends to be easy to detect. He would have tapped the flesh around his patient's mouth to see if it prompted a sucking reflex. Then out would come the doctor's Tromner hammer — a sleek, steel instrument with rubber tips that he had discovered on a trip to Europe — to test the patient's reflexes. People with ALS usually have an overreaction to a tap of the hammer, an indication of upper motor neuron loss.

Woltman was a cautious man, so cautious that he would sometimes take out his Tromner hammer and test his children's reflexes if they complained they weren't feeling well. Even when logic told him his children had nothing more serious than a sore throat or cold, out came the hammer. It became a joke among the kids when they got older. But they understood that this was something their father needed to do to calm his own nerves. His first instinct, whether with a patient or with his own three children, was to eliminate the worst-case scenario. ALS was the worst case.

By the time he had tapped Gehrig's knees, ankles, and elbows with his Tromner, Woltman probably knew that Habein's hunch was right: Gehrig had ALS. Looking at a case of ALS is "like looking at an orange," said Dr. Donald Mulder, who joined the Mayo Clinic as a neurologist in 1950 and trained under Woltman. "There are certain characteristics you look for" — uneven muscle loss, hyperactive reflexes, twitching — "and you are not often mistaken."

For Woltman, the cause of Gehrig's physical decline was no longer a mystery. He would spend the rest of the week running more exams, hoping that he might somehow turn up evidence that his diagnosis was incorrect. Anything else, even a tumor on the spine, would have qualified as good news.

After his second day of tests, Gehrig emerged from the clinic in a black sport coat and tie. Joe Kernan of the *Post-Bulletin* and at least one other reporter sat waiting. "I don't know any more than when I started, so far as my health is concerned," Gehrig said. "They didn't tell me a thing. All I know is that I got a pocket full of envelopes." The envelopes contained instructions for Gehrig's next set of appointments. "Great fellows, these doctors," he continued. "Friendliest bunch you'll find any place."

The reporters asked Gehrig if he wanted to join them for a round of golf. Gehrig said no. He didn't want word to get back to New York that he was enjoying himself. Then one of the reporters asked Gehrig if he wanted to go say hello to Julie Wera, who had been one of his teammates on the 1927 Yankees, a third baseman who appeared in thirty-eight games before blowing out his knee. He had tried a comeback in 1929 but had given up and moved back home to Minnesota. Gehrig became excited. "Julie? In town here? Where is he?" The reporters said he was working as a butcher at the Piggly Wiggly a few blocks away. They offered to take him there.

"Gosh sakes!" said Wera, as he saw Gehrig walking through the grocery store and heading for the meat department. The men shook hands and joked for a few minutes, until a customer complained that Gehrig ought to wear an apron if he planned to stay behind the counter all afternoon. He smiled and put one on. The photographer flashed a picture.

That evening, Gehrig had dinner at the home of Dr. Paul O'Leary. O'Leary was a well-rounded physician. As a specialist in dermatology, he devoted much of his time to treating patients with syphilis. Syphilis, when untreated, can cause damage to the central nervous system. So O'Leary might have been familiar with ALS and other nervous system diseases. It was perhaps more important, though, as far as Gehrig was concerned, that O'Leary knew how to translate complicated medical terminology into simple English. He was a handsome man with thinning white hair and big eyes that worked like a sedative — one look provided relief. "You couldn't help but fall in love with Paul O'Leary," said his nephew, Jay Youmans. "He made people feel at ease." Mayo administrators often called on O'Leary to usher the clinic's most famous patients, making sure they saw only the best doctors and were never kept waiting. Everyone from Gloria Swanson to John F. Kennedy fell under the O'Leary spell.

After dinner, Gehrig and O'Leary watched a softball game at Soldiers Field in Rochester. Gehrig, having never seen a softball game before, was not impressed. "There's too much loafing in this game of softball," he said. "There's no pep, no ambition, no get-up, no zing there. Why, one fellow out in the field stood there yawning and looked like he was ready to be hitched to a cart."

Gehrig spent a full week in Rochester, arriving on a Wednesday afternoon and departing on the following Tuesday. Eleanor remained in New York. His medical records have been permanently sealed despite frequent requests by doctors and journalists to have them opened. Given the duration of his stay in Rochester, it's most likely that his doctors broke the news of his diagnosis gradually, first saying that the examination showed symptoms consistent with ALS but adding that more tests were in order. Woltman most likely delivered the diagnosis and began teaching Gehrig about ALS even as he searched for other possible explanations for his illness.

If Gehrig did in fact learn over the course of the week that he faced such grim prospects, his demeanor remained remarkably sunny. He smiled everywhere he went. When a couple of ten-year-old kids knocked on his hotel room door and asked if they could have an interview for their neighborhood newspaper, he invited them in and spent an hour answering questions. He dropped by the Civic Center one day, where he grabbed a bat and demonstrated his swing for kids who played in the Legion Junior Baseball League. He sat in the stands, mosquitoes buzzing around his head, and watched Little Leaguers in baggy uniforms play baseball. He dined at the homes of his doctors most evenings. Whenever word got around that he was up on Pill Hill, the neighborhood where most of the town's physicians lived, kids would wait outside with balls and gloves, hoping to lure him into a game of catch. By the end of the week, it seemed as if every kid on Pill Hill had an autographed baseball. Nancy Bragden (née Horton) remembers that her brother Tommy told Gehrig a dirty joke, one involving "doo-doo" and breakfast cereal. Gehrig got a huge laugh out of it, she said, and Tommy got a lecture from his mother.

Gehrig wrapped himself in the blanket of Rochester's innocent charm. Away from the big-city reporters and expectant teammates, away from his anxious wife and parents, he unwound completely. But it wasn't just the soft hum of small-town life that Gehrig found so pleasing. After weeks and months of uncertainty, after a period in which self-doubt had corroded his spirit like acid chewing through steel, he was at last getting answers. They were not the answers he wanted. But they were answers. Now he knew why he couldn't hit a ball.

On Saturday, Gehrig and O'Leary went for an overnight cruise on Lake Pepin. By now, the men had probably discussed the details and dynamics of ALS. Gehrig had probably begun reading literature on the disease. He was beginning to get a sense of what would happen to him. There was nothing the doctors could do to cure the disease, or even slow it. But there were plenty of things they might do to give the patient an ember of hope as his motor neurons and muscles began to die off. The 1930s were a time of fantastic scientific progress. Insulin had been discovered in 1921, radically improving life expectancy for diabetics. Scientists were rushing to prepare the first shots of penicillin for humans. And right there in Rochester, Dr. Edward Kendall had just isolated cortisone, an anti-inflammatory that offered fast relief for sufferers of arthritis, a discovery for which he would, in 1950, earn a share of the Nobel Prize. While it was true that

ALS remained incurable, the attitude prevailing among scientists was that it might not remain so for long. Vitamins, first identified in 1912, were still new, and doctors were racing to see what could be done with them. There was strong evidence to suggest that vitamins B and E might help fight certain neurological disorders. In New York, Dr. Israel Wechsler was experimenting with vitamin E to treat ALS patients. And in Rochester, an optimistic doctor named Bayard T. Horton — whose son Tommy told Gehrig that dirty joke — believed that histamine shots might be the cure for everything from headaches to baldness. He wanted to try his wonder drug on ALS patients.

Gehrig agreed to do whatever the doctors told him. But he said he was not prepared to stay home reading the paper and awaiting his next doctor's appointment. He knew he would never play baseball again, but he nevertheless wanted to spend the remainder of the season with the Yankees. He wanted to feel useful. Even if he did nothing more than carry the lineup card to home plate and hit a few fly balls to help the outfielders warm up, he wanted to be part of the team. He also wanted to stick around long enough to collect a full year's pay. He told one writer, in fact, that he couldn't afford to quit the game because poor investments, heavy taxes, and family problems had cut into his bank account. "I haven't got the kind of money you fellows think I have," he said. So the doctors at the Mayo prescribed daily doses of vitamin B, vitamin C, and niacin (a vitamin in the B family). In theory, these antioxidant vitamins were promising. Since scientists believed (and still believe) that excessive oxidation might be responsible for destroying cells within the body, it made sense that antioxidants might reverse the damage. In reality, though, they had no effect on ALS. Nothing did.

On Monday, the day after he returned from his boat trip, Gehrig received a telegram from his teammates, wishing him a happy thirty-sixth birthday. Employees of the Kahler Hotel baked him a white cake with a baseball frosted on the top. A picture of Gehrig getting ready to blow out the candles appeared in the local paper. The headline was in the form of a question: "HAPPY BIRTHDAY?" That morning, he phoned his wife and said he would be calling back later to give her the official word on his diagnosis. Eleanor asked Fred and Mary Lieb to come over so she wouldn't be alone when the call came from Minnesota. When the phone rang in the afternoon, Eleanor and the Liebs were sitting in the living room. Eleanor excused herself and picked up the extension in the bedroom.

When she emerged, she appeared shaken.

"I guess I need a drink," she said. "A real stiff drink."

The Liebs waited.

"You know what the Dutchman just told me?" she asked. " 'Don't worry, Ellie, I have a fifty-fifty chance to live.' Just as though he were asking about the weather in Westchester County. Something is really wrong with him, and I think his spinal cord is affected."

Gehrig also sent his wife a letter, a copy of which is held in the archives at the Baseball Hall of Fame. It reads, in part:

The bad news is "lateral sclerosis," in our language infantile paralysis. There isn't any cure, the best they can hope is to check it at the point it is now and there is a 50-50 chance for that. My instructions and my physicians will be furnished by Dr. O'Leary. There are very few of these cases . . . it is probably caused by some germ. However, my first question was transmission. No danger whatever. Never heard of transmitting it to mates. If there were (and I made them doubly assure me) you certainly would never have been allowed within 100 feet of me. There is a 50-50 chance of keeping me as I am. I may need a cane in 10 or 15 yrs. Playing is out of the question and Paul [O'Leary] suggests a coaching job or a job in the office or writing. I made him honestly assure me it will not affect me mentally. They seem to think I'll get along all right if I can reconcile myself to this condition which I have done but only after they assured me there is no danger of transmission and that I will not become mentally unbalanced and thereby become a burden on your hands for life. I adore you sweetheart.

Underneath was a postscript from O'Leary: "Sorry Lou's report is not more encouraging. He has shown a remarkable spirit and if he tends to the treatment program will be all right."

Gehrig's letter and O'Leary's postscript strongly suggest that the doctors at the Mayo were breaking the news gently — perhaps too gently. If they were permitting Gehrig to believe that ALS could be checked, they weren't really breaking the news at all.

O'Leary no doubt knew the truth. He knew that ALS would hinder Gehrig's walking until he needed a cane, and then it would leave him unable to walk at all. It would weaken his hands until he couldn't button his shirt, until they became useless claws. It would immobilize his jaw until he couldn't chew solid foods or swallow. It would paralyze his tongue until he couldn't speak. Finally, it would cut off his breath and he would die. Is it possible, though, that O'Leary and the rest of the doctors at the Mayo spared their patient the grim details? It's possible, but highly unlikely. Woltman, the chief of neurology, was a soft-spoken man, but he was a stickler for doing his job properly. Those who worked with Woltman say they can't imagine a circumstance in which he would permit a patient to leave his office without a thorough understanding of his condition and prognosis.

It's possible, of course, that Gehrig received a complete and honest report but chose to overlook some of its unpleasant details. He would not be the first or last terminally ill patient to do so. It's also possible he understood perfectly well but decided to spare his wife.

On his last day in Rochester, Gehrig met once more with Harold Habein. The doctor handed over a typewritten letter explaining the outcome of Gehrig's examination. Gehrig planned to give the letter to either McCarthy or Barrow. It read:

To whom it may concern:
This is to certify that Mr. Lou Gehrig has been under examination at the Mayo Clinic from June 13 to June 19, 1939, inclusive.
After a careful and complete examination, it was found that he is suffering from amyotrophic lateral sclerosis. This type of illness involves the motor pathways and cells of the central nervous system and in lay terms is known as a form of chronic poliomyelitis (infantile paralysis).
The nature of this trouble makes it such that Mr. Gehrig will be unable to continue his active participation as a baseball player, inasmuch as it is advisable that he conserve his muscular energy. He could, however, continue in some executive capacity.

When he was finished at the clinic that day, Gehrig visited a Boy Scout camp, where he signed an autograph for fourteen-year-old Mike Paulios. Sixty-three years later, Paulios would recall that Gehrig looked like a superhero, big and strong and handsome — not at all sick. From the Boy Scout meeting, Gehrig went back to the

Kahler, where he had dinner with some of his doctors. The next day, he flew on United Airlines from Minnesota to Newark, landing at eight-thirty in the evening. He smiled as he stepped off the plane and embraced his wife. Reporters asked for a report on his condition. Gehrig said he had an envelope in his pocket that would explain everything, but he wouldn't reveal its contents until after he had spoken to McCarthy and Barrow.

On Wednesday morning, several hours before game time, Gehrig made the trip from Larchmont to Yankee Stadium, where he met with his bosses and handed over the letter from Habein. Gehrig left the meeting and walked into the clubhouse, where his teammates let loose a cheer when they spotted him. He pulled on his uniform, laced up his shoes, and made his way toward the field.

A little bit later, Barrow made the announcement to the media. "Gentlemen," he said, "we have bad news. Gehrig has infantile paralysis. The technical word for his illness is chronic poliomyelitis. Gehrig has been given a chart of exercises and a list of doctors by the Mayo Clinic. . . . The report recommends that Lou abandon any hope of continuing as an active player."

Barrow released to the media a copy of Habein's letter. But there was nothing in the letter or in Barrow's comments to suggest that Gehrig's disease was deadly. In preparing their stories, reporters assumed that he would probably be crippled, but they never suggested, and never guessed, that he had only a short time left to live. The misunderstanding stemmed from one word contained in Habein's letter. The word was "poliomyelitis." Everybody had heard of polio; polio was FDR's disease. When a new charity called The March of Dimes asked Americans to help fight polio by sending dimes to the White House in 1938, more than 230,000 dimes arrived in the first three days. It's not clear whether Habein employed the reference to polio to help the public better understand Gehrig's illness or because he was hesitant to break the bad news in complete detail, but he and his colleagues at the Mayo surely knew that ALS and polio were far from the same. By simplifying the diagnosis, the doctors may have left the impression that Gehrig would likely survive.

Gehrig didn't do much to clarify matters. As he sat in the clubhouse next to Dickey and laced his shoes, he told one reporter that he believed the disease had been checked and that his condition would get no worse. Then he moved from the clubhouse to the dugout, where he sat on the steps and offered his teammates more detail on the results of his examination.

"They were particularly interested in my head," he said. "I told them I'd been hit on the head several times. They must have taken sixteen X-ray pictures of my head. But they found nothing." Everybody laughed at the old joke. Gehrig continued, explaining to the men that his diseased nervous system was working like a poorly wired telephone network. "It's like calling up New York and getting it by way of Chicago, St. Louis, New Orleans, Memphis and Duluth," he said. "It's not quick and direct. And that's the way I am. It's a wonder I haven't been hit by a pitched ball this year."

Someone in the dugout asked how he felt.

"I feel fine," he said. "I have no aches or pains. I eat well and I sleep well."

"Is what you've got curable?" he was asked.

"I don't know," he answered. "They gave me a list of doctors, one in every city we go to. My wife is making an appointment for me to see the one I have to go to here. Only time will tell."

CHAPTER 23

LUCKIEST MAN

When Gehrig announced that he was through playing ball, he also announced that he intended to more or less disappear from view. When he did step on a ballfield, he made sure there were teammates by his side so fans wouldn't notice his awkward gait. He would continue to travel with the Yankees and to sit in the dugout while the team played, but he would no longer carry the lineup card to home plate before each game. He made an exception in Philadelphia on June 29, when the legendary manager Connie Mack asked him to step onto the field before that afternoon's game. The crowd stood and cheered for eight minutes as Gehrig wiped the tears from his eyes. In Washington, D.C., a group of boys broke into spontaneous applause when they spotted him walking through Union Station. Gehrig shook his head, as if amazed. But as much as he appreciated the displays of affection, he no longer wanted to hear the applause of the crowd each time he walked onto the field or passed through a train station. "I'm not going to make that play for sympathy," he said.

Most baseball fans were still operating on the assumption that Gehrig's unpronounceable disease would render him an invalid, to use the language employed by several newspaper writers. A reporter for the Associated Press interviewed experts at the American Medical Association and wrote a story that described ALS in near perfect detail. The article said ALS should not be confused with infantile paralysis, which "is directly traceable to an infectious agent, or virus." No one knows the cause of ALS, the Associated Press reported, but it is almost certainly not contagious. The story went on to note that victims wasted away until they resembled living skeletons and that no treatment existed. The writer stopped just short of delivering the knockout punch.

Some sportswriters went so far as to suggest that the doctors at the Mayo Clinic had concocted the ALS diagnosis to explain away Gehrig's faltering skills. "Personally, I don't care what Gehrig's got," wrote Jack Cuddy of the United Press syndicate. "But I'd like to exchange my body for his during the next 40 or 50 years, let us say. And I'm pretty sure I'd do all right — regardless of the experts' argument over the Latin or Greek declensions of what Larruping Lou may or may not have." Monty Stratton, a pitcher for the White Sox who had blown off his leg in an off-season hunting accident, was far more deserving of sympathy than Gehrig, Cuddy argued.

Some people in and around the game, meanwhile, continued to speculate that Gehrig had made himself vulnerable to disease by pushing too hard in pursuit of his consecutive-game streak. "If he had been content to break my record, then piled up a hundred more games or so, and taken things easier after that, he would have lasted longer," said Everett Scott, the retired shortstop who once held the record for consecutive games played.

Only the people closest to Gehrig knew the truth. As soon as Fred Lieb heard Eleanor say that her husband's chances were fifty-fifty, Lieb went home and phoned his doctor to ask him about ALS. Eleanor, too, called one of the doctors at the Mayo Clinic and received an honest appraisal of her husband's chances of survival. Barrow knew the truth as well. But word never spread much beyond that small circle, in part because Gehrig kept insisting that ALS could be beaten. Most reporters and most of Gehrig's teammates never bothered to verify his claim. "Nobody knew what the heck that disease was," Tommy Henrich said.

At first, the Yankees planned to honor Gehrig in a manner befitting his modest personality. His teammates took up a collection to buy him a fishing rod, and they asked the writer John Kieran of *The Times* to compose a poem they would have engraved on the base of a trophy. The players planned to make the presentation in the privacy of the clubhouse. But some of the writers who covered the team began campaigning for a public ceremony, a Lou Gehrig Appreciation Day, and Barrow relented. Usually, teams scheduled appreciation days on dates when they wanted to boost attendance — on a Thursday afternoon, for example, with the miserable St. Louis Browns in town. But Barrow scheduled Gehrig's day for July 4, 1939, between games of a doubleheader with the Washington Senators, when a big crowd was already assured. He ordered workers to hang bunting from the stadium's façade, as if it were the World Series. And to commemorate the span of Gehrig's career, the team president invited members of the great 1927 Yankees to return to the ballpark for a reunion. Barrow even agreed to pay travel expenses for those coming from out of town. Babe Ruth, Bob Meusel, Earle Combs, Joe Dugan, Tony Lazzeri,

Mark Koenig, Herb Pennock, George Pipgras, Waite Hoyt, Wally Schang, Benny Bengough, Everett Scott, and Bob Shawkey all agreed to be there. So did Wally Pipp. Gifts would be presented. Mayor La Guardia would make a speech. The Yankees expected their biggest crowd of the year.

Gehrig was dreading it.

On that hot, muggy Fourth of July, they threw open the gates to Yankee Stadium at ten in the morning, hoping to avoid a crush. Beneath a hazy scrim of clouds, fans began pushing through the turnstiles at Yankee Stadium and finding their seats. By eleven, the sun had burned away most of the haze. A pale yellow light fell over the high stadium arches and onto the field. The players began warming up. The crowd hummed with anticipation.

Before the first game, a small ceremony was held at home plate in honor of Johnny "Legs" Welaj, a rookie outfielder for the Senators playing for the first time in front of his family and friends. Busloads of people from Manville, New Jersey, had made the forty-five-mile trek to see their hometown hero. To them, it was Johnny Welaj Appreciation Day. Many in the Welaj family learned only after they arrived that Lou Gehrig would also be honored.

While the Welaj family brought dozens

of friends and relatives to the game, the Gehrig party consisted of only four people: Eleanor, her brother Frank, and Christina and Henry Gehrig. They shared a set of box seats behind the Yankee dugout. A reporter for the *Daily News*, Rosaleen Doherty, sat with the family and took notes for at least part of the afternoon.

"Has this made much difference to your life?" Doherty asked Eleanor.

Eleanor hesitated. "Of course, it's changed our life," she finally said, "but maybe not in the way you think I mean. The game is over for us, but there is a lot left. . . . We are going to get along, and Lou — who is a good soldier — is going to do what the doctors told him and get well. I had a bad moment when I first heard that he was through — I won't deny that — but it is over now."

While Gehrig dressed in the clubhouse, some of his old teammates dropped in to say hello. Babe Ruth hadn't yet arrived, and everyone wondered whether he would show up, but Bengough, Dugan, Hoyt, Koenig, Lazzeri, Meusel, Pennock, Pipp, Schang, Scott, and Shawkey were all there. When they barged in on the younger men now using their lockers, it was as if the lights in the room had just gotten brighter. The electricity was palpable.

"Take those uniforms off and give them

to us," shouted Waite Hoyt. "We'll handle the Senators for you."

Looking up from their stools, the younger Yankees might have wondered briefly if Hoyt was serious. Most of the old men still looked as if they could play. They settled into the clubhouse and began to reminisce about all the late nights, all the games played on queasy stomachs, all the busted curfews and splitting headaches. They remembered the games won in dramatic style — five o'clock lightning, they'd called it — and one in particular in which an extra-inning home run by the Babe prompted a giddy rush for the train station. They remembered the barbecued ribs and beer. They remembered nervous little Miller Huggins pacing in the dugout during the fourth game of the 1927 World Series, the only man on the planet, it seemed, who doubted the Yankees would win. The mood was ebullient, like a high school reunion at which every old classmate is confident, rich, and handsome. Gehrig, overwhelmed with emotion, left the men for about thirty minutes, retiring to the privacy of Joe McCarthy's office. When he returned, he apologized to his old teammates for not having thought to order a keg of beer.

Then everyone cleared out of the clubhouse. The young Yankees took the field, the old Yankees took their seats in the stands, and Gehrig assumed his position on the bench next to McCarthy. There wasn't much action in the game. Even the men on the field seemed bored, or distracted. As he watched the innings roll, Gehrig begged McCarthy for a reprieve from the fast-approaching ceremony. "I'd give a month's pay to get out of this," he said. McCarthy didn't answer.

When the game finally ended, with the Yanks losing, 3-2, preparations got under way. A brass band marched across the field, drums rattling and horns blaring. The modern Yankees lined up on the third-base side of the dirt path between home plate and the pitcher's mound. The Senators stood facing them on the first-base side. The 1927 Yankees and the rest of the visiting dignitaries, including Mayor La Guardia and U.S. Postmaster General James Farley, stood near home plate. La Guardia wore a cream-colored double-breasted suit. Babe Ruth, having arrived in plenty of time for the ceremony, also wore a cream-colored suit, though his was twice as big and a lot flashier than the mayor's. Several microphones were perched on tripods atop home plate, marking the spot reserved for the guest of honor.

Gehrig stepped gingerly from the dugout. Barrow, wearing a straw hat and big sunglasses, gripped Gehrig's left arm with both hands, as though pushing him and holding him up at the same time. The two men walked toward home plate. When they drew near, Barrow released his grip, letting Gehrig complete the journey alone.

He had about ten yards to go. He lowered his head, avoiding all eye contact. He walked slowly and awkwardly. His pants were pulled up high around his waist. His shirt, far too big now for his chest, fluttered slightly in the breeze. The fans stood and cheered. Gehrig never acknowledged them.

He stopped when he reached home plate and took a position opposite the grove of microphones that marked center stage. If he had looked up, he might have seen his wife and parents. He might have seen the uncomfortable looks in the eyes of some of his teammates. He might have seen the fans standing against the screen behind home plate, their fingers wrapped tightly in the netting that protects spectators from foul balls. But he didn't look up. He hung his head and began to cry as Sid Mercer, the master of ceremonies, introduced the first speaker.

La Guardia stepped to the microphone, put his hands on his hips, and called Gehrig "the perfect prototype of the best to be found in sportsmanship and citizenship." Postmaster General James Farley said the guest of honor would "live long in baseball." Then came McCarthy, Gehrig's manager and friend, who sobbed as he spoke into the microphone: "Lou, what else can I say except that it was a sad day in the life of everybody who knew you when you came to my hotel room that day in Detroit and told me you were quitting as a ballplayer because you felt yourself a hindrance to the team. My God, man, you were never that."

Ruth took a turn. Though their relationship had been troubled, and though the Babe could be foolish and crude, he never held a grudge. Now, he seemed genuinely happy to be reunited with his old pal. "In 1927," he said, "Lou was with us, and I say that was the greatest ball club the Yankees ever had." He rattled on for a minute or so, encouraging Gehrig to catch a lot of fish in his free time.

The gifts piled up at his feet. He accepted a fishing rod and tackle from his teammates; a framed parchment with the words "Don't Quit" across the top from the Senators; another parchment from the Old Timers' Association of Denver; a ring from the jewelers Dieges & Clust; a fruit bowl and two silver candlesticks from members of the New York Giants; a silver pitcher from the Harry M. Stevens firm, which employed the young men in white jackets who sold concessions at the stadium; two platters from the Stevens employees; a smoking stand from the newspaper writers who covered the team; a silver cup from the Yankees' office staff; and a silver serving set from the team's management.

When McCarthy presented a trophy with an eagle perched atop a baseball, Gehrig bent over immediately to set it down in the grass, as if the weight were too much for him.

Throughout the ceremony, Gehrig looked as if he couldn't wait to get it over with. He twisted his baseball cap in his hands. He pawed at the dirt with his cleats. He removed a big white handkerchief from his back pocket and wiped his tears. He shifted his weight from left to right and stared at the ground. McCarthy, afraid that Gehrig might collapse, asked Babe Dahlgren to be prepared to step in and make the catch.

When all the speeches and presentations and introductions were through, Mercer stood quietly in front of the microphone for a moment and waited to see if Gehrig would address the audience.

Another big blast of noise came from the crowd. "We want Lou!" the people chanted. "We want Lou!"

Gehrig had given some thought to what he might say. Eleanor, in her memoirs, would say that Gehrig had written an outline of his remarks but hadn't rehearsed. Now, overwhelmed by emotion, he didn't think he could go through with it. He shook his head, no. The master of ceremonies leaned into the microphone and told the crowd that he was sorry, but Gehrig was too moved to speak. In the grandstand, his mother and father both sobbed. Eleanor's eyes were dry, but her body trembled.

"We want Lou!" the crowd bellowed.

Gehrig turned toward the dugout. Workers stepped toward home plate, getting ready to haul away the cables that snaked through the grass and led to the microphones at home plate.

Suddenly, Joe McCarthy moved to Gehrig's side, put a hand on his back, and spoke softly in his ear, encouraging him to speak. Gehrig nodded and moved slowly toward the microphones. He had never been able to disobey orders.

He lowered his head and ran his right hand through his hair. There was one more wave of noise from the crowd and then dead silence. Every man and woman, every peanut vendor and usher, every ballplayer and batboy, every photographer and writer seemed to stare and wait. Even the men in the press box stopped typing. Gehrig swallowed hard. He wiped his eyes again. The wind blew softly from right field to left, snapping the flags above the grandstand.

"Over 60,000 people and there was not a murmur, not a sound," recalled Jim Walls of Fort Thomas, Kentucky, who watched from a seat in the grandstand on the third-base side. "I felt thrills up and down my spine."

Minutes seemed to pass. At last, Gehrig bent over slightly in the direction of the microphones, took a deep breath, and began to speak.

"For the past two weeks, you've been reading about a bad break," he said, his voice cracking so that the last word of the sentence came out "brag." He stopped, dropped his head again, and swallowed. "Today I consider myself the luckiest man on the face of the earth."

He paused as his voice echoed through the ballpark, but he didn't look up. The sorrowful expression on his face never changed.

"I have been in ballparks for seventeen years and have never received anything but kindness and encouragement from you fans," he said.

"When you look around, wouldn't you consider it a privilege to associate yourself with such fine-looking men as are standing in uniform in the ballpark today? Sure, I'm lucky. Who wouldn't consider it an honor to have known Jacob Ruppert? Also, the builder of baseball's greatest empire, Ed Barrow? To have spent six years with such a grand little fellow as Miller Huggins? To have spent the next nine years with that smart student of psychology, the best manager in baseball today, Joe McCarthy? Who wouldn't feel honored to room with such a grand guy as Bill Dickey? When the New York Giants, a team you would give your right arm to beat, and vice versa, sends you a gift — that's something. When the groundskeepers and office staff and writers and old timers and players and concessionaires all remember you with trophies — that's something. When you have a wonderful mother-in-law who takes sides with you in squabbles against her own daughter — that's something. When you have a father and mother who work all their lives so that you can have an education and build your body — it's a blessing. When you have a wife who has been a tower of strength and shown more courage than you dreamed existed — that's the finest I know."

He swallowed hard.

"So I close in saying that I might have had a bad break, but I have an awful lot to live for. Thank you."

Even as the final words tumbled out of his mouth and reverberated through the grandstand, he began to back away from the microphone.

The band began to play a German folk song, "Du Du Liegst Mir im Herzen" (You Are Always in My Heart). Babe Ruth moved in, reached for a handshake, and then grabbed Gehrig in a hug. The photographers went crazy. Gehrig managed a small, crooked smile. Cheers rolled over the ballpark and continued until Gehrig disappeared into the dugout.

In the press box, where the typewriters began to clack again as soon as Gehrig finished, the power and importance of his speech registered instantly. Dan Daniel of the *World-Telegram* described it as "the most dramatic demonstration in the annals of the sport."

"Gehrig was never greater," Rud Rennie wrote that afternoon for the *Herald-Tribune.*

"He pulled a classic," typed Jack Miley of the *Post.*

"I saw strong men weep this afternoon," wrote Shirley Povich of *The Washington Post.*

Richards Vidmer summed it up best in the *Herald Tribune*:

Throughout Lou Gehrig's career there was always the feeling he lacked that mythical something called color. Perhaps he did. And yet now that his playing days are over he has more color than almost any athlete in the game. Somehow I felt that at the Stadium yesterday they were honoring not a great baseball player but a truly great sportsman who could take his triumphs with sincere modesty and could face tragedy with a smile. His records will attest to future generations that Lou Gehrig was one of the greatest baseball players who ever lived, but only those who have been fortunate enough to have known him during his most glorious years will realize that he has stood for something finer than merely a great baseball player — that he stood for everything that makes sports important in the American scene.

After resting for a few minutes in the clubhouse, Gehrig returned to the dugout and watched the Yankees beat the Senators in the second game of the doubleheader. He joked with his coaches and teammates and confessed that he had never been more frightened in his life than in the moments before he spoke. But now that it was over, he seemed relieved, even happy.

When it came time to go home, he went back to his locker and changed from his uniform into a jacket and tie. He was exhausted but smiling.

"Feel my undershirt," he told one writer as he dressed to go home. "It's wringing wet. . . . I'm going home and go to bed."

CHAPTER 24
THE BUREAUCRAT

It took the first sign of weakness to make baseball's strongest man seem human. In the weeks following his tearful speech, Gehrig received more fan mail than he had throughout his entire career. So many letters arrived at Yankee Stadium that he had to haul them home in boxes. They came from ordinary Americans who had faced extraordinary battles with illnesses and wanted to tell Gehrig not to lose faith. They came from baseball fans who suddenly recognized that Gehrig's heroism transcended the game. And they came from doctors and scientists who promised cures. In all, there were some thirty thousand letters.

Gehrig and his wife were particularly interested in the letters that contained promises of a cure for ALS. They threw out the far-fetched ones and sent the rest to the Mayo Clinic for evaluation. "I hate like hell to bother you with these wild goose chases," Gehrig wrote in one letter to Paul O'Leary, "but I do want to keep you informed when I feel that reliable people are recommending a reliable practitioner."

As he grew accustomed to the fact that he would never again play for the Yankees, Gehrig began to treat the Mayo Clinic as if it were his new team. He wrote letters to his doctors in Rochester, thanking them for their time and attention, and vowing to follow their advice throughout his treatment. Over and over, he expressed his gratitude. In one letter, Gehrig hinted that he might have been given a discount on his hospital bill. Most of all, though, he appreciated the personal attention he'd received in Rochester — from doctors, from hotel workers, from neighborhood kids, even from the local press. Gehrig had never been so coddled and so warmly embraced in all his life as he had been during his week of exams at the clinic. Tender loving care was not exactly a specialty in the rough and sweaty world of baseball, and neither had it been abundant in Gehrig's childhood home. In any case, he soon began showering the men, women, and children of Rochester with gifts from New York. He sent dozens of autographed baseballs and photographs. He collected old gloves and balls from the Yankee clubhouse and shipped them out west to help supply some of the town's youth baseball teams. He gathered autographs at the All-

Star Game in New York and sent them to some of his doctors. If the doctors at the Mayo had cured him and returned him to the Yankee starting lineup, Gehrig could hardly have been more generous.

He reserved his most extraordinary act of munificence for O'Leary, the physician who had been his unofficial host during his visit to Rochester. O'Leary was conservative in both appearance and manner, but he emitted warmth like a radiator, silently and with no visible effort. "He was very impressive, and he had a delightful personality," said Donna Ivins, his former secretary. "He was mostly quiet, except for one time when he took me down the hall by the ear because I misbehaved. It was all in fun. Oh, he was very charming." One day in July, O'Leary opened a package from New York and found the 14-karat white-gold pocket watch that the Yankees had presented Gehrig for his role in the 1932 World Series. On the back of the watch, Gehrig had engraved the words: "To Paul, May I always be worthy of your friendship."

Gehrig believed unconditionally in his doctors and in the course of treatment they had designed. He required no second opinion. The Mayo Clinic, he informed acquaintances, was "the greatest institution on the face of the earth." He told his friends that if they weren't feeling well, or if they were unhappy with the care they were receiving from their doctors, they needed to go to the Mayo. Three weeks after his visit to Rochester, he had already referred at least half a dozen friends. Among them were Art Fletcher, the Yankee coach, who needed a routine checkup, and Babe Dahlgren's wife, who was suffering dizzy spells. When the relief pitcher Johnny Murphy mentioned that his sister was unhappy with the results of a recent operation on her sinuses, Gehrig offered to contact the clinic and arrange a visit. He assured Murphy that the Mayo's surgeons would fix whatever damage the East Coast doctors had done and that a reasonable fee would be arranged.

Gehrig had always functioned best as part of a team. In high school and college he forged his identity not in the classroom or in social settings but on ball fields, where a man could stand out without standing alone. As a professional athlete, he enjoyed the game more than the platform for celebrity it afforded him. He seemed happiest when he could master a specific task and see direct results — runs batted in, games won, championship flags hoisted. He took comfort working for strict bosses and following precise rules. It's ironic perhaps, considering that so much of

Gehrig's public image was built on his health and durability, but, in a sense, he made for an ideal patient. In the Mayo Clinic he found an organization as proud and well-run as the Yankees. Just as the Yankees required players to wear coats and ties when they traveled, the Mayo Clinic required doctors to dress formally when making rounds. Brothers Will and Charlie Mayo would chastise doctors if their shoelaces weren't tied, or if they loosened their ties on warm days, and those standards were upheld long after the famous founders were gone. At the Mayo, Gehrig found doctors as learned about medicine as Miller Huggins was about baseball and as demanding as Joe McCarthy. He found an approach to medicine that stressed collaboration, where doctors were encouraged to share their patients so that specialists in several fields might help treat various symptoms. And he was assigned a treatment program that demanded the same discipline he had applied to his performance on the ball field. The Yankees may not have needed him anymore, but at the Mayo Clinic, where exciting breakthroughs in medicine were happening all the time, and where hope for his own recovery seemed to rest, Gehrig had important work to do.

Twelve days after his farewell speech, the

Yanks were in Cleveland to play the Indians. Gehrig picked up a piece of hotel stationery and jotted a letter to O'Leary. "Just a line to say hello," he wrote, "and also report the splendid progress I am making." He noted that he had gained "7 to 9 pounds." He added: "Seem a little more secure in my legs, and in general feel great." While he felt strong enough to go for a walk, Gehrig wrote, he had resisted the temptation. The doctors wanted him to rest. Gehrig followed their order.

In the months to come, Gehrig and O'Leary would exchange more than a hundred letters and telegrams, amounting to nearly two hundred pages in all. Gehrig would come to depend on O'Leary to restock his supplies of medicine and to boost his sagging confidence when his health took a precipitous drop. He would complain about his struggle to quit smoking and joke about laboratory experiments on monkeys. Throughout the correspondence, he made almost no mention of baseball or his Yankee teammates. Most of the letters concerned his condition, and it is here that they are most illuminating. Gehrig today is as famous for his disease as he is for his athleticism, yet until now precious little has been known about the course of his personal illness. In his letters, however, Gehrig provided precise details of his medical regimen and his deteriorating physical form, day by day and week by week. The letters also detailed the experimental treatments that Gehrig believed, almost to the end, might save his life.

Gehrig never gave up. Several times, however, when his condition began to slide sharply, when tremors shook his body and the simple act of getting up from his chair felt like a Herculean labor, he would begin to express doubts. On these occasions he would beg O'Leary to put aside the niceties and tell him the truth. He promised that he wouldn't fall apart. He promised not to give up. But he insisted on knowing: Was there really a chance he might survive?

O'Leary, faced with a difficult choice, behaved more as a good friend than as a good doctor. He offered Gehrig hope.

After his speech, Gehrig received one more formal honor. At the seventh annual All-Star Game, played that year on July 11 at Yankee Stadium, he was named honorary captain of the American League team. In the locker room, his teammates averted their eyes as Gehrig struggled to dress himself.

Two days later, the Yankees left for an eleven-day western swing. Gehrig went along. Joe DiMaggio recalled watching his teammate's physical abilities slip over the course of that long road trip. It was as if Gehrig had aged forty years in the blink of an eye. The deterioration was most evident during card games. "At the beginning of this trip," DiMaggio wrote, "Gehrig shuffled the cards with difficulty, but before the trip was over someone else had to take over his deal for him."

A month later, the Yankees traveled west again. On August 20, after splitting a doubleheader with the Athletics and running their record to seventy-eight wins and thirty-four losses, the team boarded a train for Chicago. Gehrig went along again, but this time he didn't intend to complete the trip. He changed trains at Union Station in Chicago and continued on to Rochester for his second round of appointments at the Mayo. "The doctors at the clinic will check my condition and see what progress I'm making," he told reporters.

When he arrived in Rochester at nine-forty that evening, O Leary and his two children were there to meet him at the station and to drive him to the Kahler Hotel. The next morning, Gehrig visited the clinic for his checkup. He saw all the same doctors he had met in June: Woltman, Habein, and O'Leary. When he wasn't with the doctors, he continued to make the social rounds in Rochester. He chatted with reporters from the *Post-Bulletin*, dined with the O'Learys, and went for a swim at the home of O'Leary's mother-in-law, Ruth Youmans. In a series of photographs taken near the pool, Gehrig wore nothing but swim trunks. His body was entirely different from the one on display three years earlier in the glamour shots taken as part of his Tarzan audition. His shoulders and biceps now looked thin, as if he had done little if any hard work or exercise in recent years. His flesh on his chest drooped. His legs looked normal, but not for Gehrig, whose lower body had always been so big. If he really had gained weight, as he said in his letter to O'Leary, it was only because flab had replaced muscle.

As Gehrig prepared to leave town, Habein issued an updated report on his patient's condition and released it to the media: "The general condition of Lou Gehrig is definitely improved. He has gained weight and feels well in every respect. As for his trouble in regard to the nervous system, there is no evidence of progression. We will continue along the same line of treatments, with few modifications." Once again, Habein described the illness in vaguely optimistic terms and made no attempt to clear up the confusion created by his earlier statement about poliomyelitis and infantile paralysis.

Gehrig, interviewed that evening at O'Leary's house, where he was a dinner guest, continued to express optimism. "I've been feeling right along that I was getting better," he said. "But it is good to get the news direct from headquarters."

Over the next several months, he continued to attend every Yankee game, home and away, playing the part of cheerleader. He stood on the field as his teammates warmed up and sat on the bench when they played. He shouted at umpires and barked at opposing pitchers. But if baseball offered a distraction, it didn't keep him from thinking about his future. Though the worst of the Depression was over, jobs were still far from abundant in 1939, and the economy would not fully rebound until the United States entered World War II. The Yankees could have offered Gehrig a job as a coach, or a scout, or an executive of some kind. But they never did. If the team's hesitancy perturbed him — and Eleanor would suggest in later years that it did — Gehrig didn't let on at the time. Still, he had other options. At least one restaurant owner had offered him $30,000 to lend his name to a new eatery. A nightclub promised to pay him $750 a week to greet customers. No doubt there were other opportunities to trade his name and image for cash. But the offer that intrigued Gehrig most came not from private industry but from Fiorello La Guardia, who asked Gehrig to become a commissioner on the city's parole board.

It sounded, in many ways, like an awful job. Gehrig would get a drab office and only $5,700 a year. He and Eleanor would be required to move from Larchmont back to New York City, where all municipal employees were required to make their home. And the work itself was nothing to get excited about, especially for a man who had worked at play all his life. He would be required to visit prisons, counsel inmates, and evaluate cases to decide whether criminals should be released. But Gehrig didn't need much time to think about it. Faced with a choice between a frivolous job that paid well and a meaningful one that didn't, Gehrig chose the meaningful. In a letter dated August 14, 1939, two months before news of the job offer was released to the newspapers, Gehrig wrote to the mayor:

I have forwarded your request for reservations for the World Series to Mr. Barrow (provided we win the darn thing), and I also took it upon myself to suggest to Mr. Barrow that you might like to travel with us on the baseball special which is composed only of newspaper men, baseball officials and baseball players. I hope this latter meets with your approval.

I have been giving the matter that we discussed considerable thought, and the more I think about it, the more the proposition appeals to me.

If I were to accept, I would want to feel that ultimately you would be proud of your selection, and therefore, I would appreciate it if you would have your secretary forward the literature explaining the work. In this way, I could have a better idea of the duties involved and I would have a clearer idea as to whether I could fill the bill to your complete satisfaction.

Whatever my decision might be I want you to know that you gained an admirer on the day of our meeting. It is heart warming to receive the sympathy and plaudits of the crowd, but it is something more to receive a simple, honest and unbiased offer such as you extended me. For that reason the present Mayor of New York City will always have my sincere friendship.

La Guardia sent Gehrig a pile of books, along with a note encouraging him not to fear the complexity of the job: "It all boils down to a matter of just plain, ordinary, every-day common sense — is the individual worthy of being helped — will giving him a chance serve the community and him better than keeping him in jail — is he a victim of circumstances or just a plain, ordinary, hard crook — what is the condition of the family — will he do them more good in jail than out of jail. As you see, these are just questions of every-day life that common sense and impartiality can judge. This is something that one cannot get out of books."

Though Gehrig and La Guardia had essentially come to terms, they decided not to announce the appointment until after the baseball season.

The Yankees ran away with the 1939 pennant, finishing seventeen games ahead of young Ted Williams and the Red Sox. DiMaggio flirted with a .400 average much of the season and wound up at .381. Rolfe, Selkirk, Dickey, and Charlie Keller all batted better than .300. Joe Gordon hit twenty-eight homers and drove in 111 runs. Dahlgren hit only .235, but he fielded his position beautifully and drove in a respectable eighty-nine runs. The team's greatest strength was in its pitching. "We don't go out and overpower the opposition as we used to," Gehrig said, sitting in the dugout before one late-season game and chatting with a writer. "We just wait for the other team to give us an opening. Sometimes it comes in the third inning, sometimes in the fifth, sometimes in the seventh. But when it does, we haven't given them anything too big to overcome."

Gehrig still wished he could play. "But I guess there's nothing new about that," he said. "I suppose a lot of fellows before me have wished they could go on after they're all through." The writer pointed out that Gehrig wasn't like those other fellows, though. He might have played another four or five years if not for his illness. He was entitled to feel some regret. Gehrig refused to reveal any anger or remorse. "Maybe you're right," he said. "Maybe I did have my playing days cut short a few years. But look, I had seventeen years in the big leagues [including partial seasons] and I'm grateful for those. Not many fellows get such a good break as that. I certainly haven't any kick coming."

On the morning of the first day of the World Series, Eddie Joost, Paul Derringer, and Bucky Walters of the Reds took a taxi from the team's hotel to Yankee Stadium. As they were getting out of the cab, a Packard pulled to a stop in front of them. From a distance of fifty feet, they couldn't make out the driver, but they watched as he got out of the car and fell to the curb, pawing at the door of his car and trying to pull himself back up.

"So we went over to help," Joost recalled. "When we got to him, we saw it was Gehrig. We said, 'Hey, what the hell's going on? Are you OK?' He said, 'Yeah, yeah, I'll make it.' He wasn't embarrassed by it." The men walked together into the park, chatting about the game. Joost looked down and noticed that Gehrig was shuffling his feet like an old man in slippers as they headed toward the clubhouse.

As the World Series began, Gehrig received the celebrity treatment, even though he wasn't playing. Reporters and photographers crowded around, recognizing no doubt that they might never again see him in pinstripes. In New York, Babe Ruth dropped by to have his picture taken with his old home-run hitting partner. In Cincinnati, Gehrig signed an autograph for Frank Sinatra, a twenty-three-year-old singer who had just joined the Harry James band and recorded his first hit songs. Sinatra grinned from ear to ear as he stood before Gehrig in the Yankee dugout, the autograph gripped tightly in his left hand.

Gehrig didn't step onto the field during the Series, not even to present a lineup card. One writer speculated that Joe McCarthy didn't want fans to see how poorly the former first baseman walked.

The Yanks swept the Reds in four games, confirming their place as one of the game's greatest teams of all time. For the Yankees, championships had once again come to seem routine, as they had in the early days of Gehrig's career. From 1927 to 1939, the Yankees won seven out of thirteen championships. In World Series play over that stretch, they won twenty-eight games and lost only three. Gehrig probably didn't feel as if he'd added much in the most recent campaign, but he had been a critical player — perhaps *the* critical player — in an era of remarkable Yankee domination. Though he didn't play in the 1939 Series, he was listed as an active member of the team and received a full share — $5,542 — of the team's World Series income. He joined his former teammates in the clubhouse for one last victory celebration, one last chorus of "The Beer Barrel Polka."

CHAPTER 25

OUR BOY IS PRETTY DISCOURAGED

On a clear morning in October, a whiff of summer still clinging to the air, Gehrig and his wife set out to go fishing. But before they could get out the door, a newspaper reporter appeared at their apartment in Larchmont. Mayor La Guardia had just announced that Gehrig would soon be sworn in as the city's newest parole board commissioner. "He expects to devote his life to public service," the mayor had said.

"This is the greatest thrill of my life!" Gehrig told the reporter. "I feel mighty proud — you can understand that. It more than makes up for having to quit the good old game."

After he got back from fishing, changed his clothes and put on a pair of slippers, another reporter arrived at the apartment. Gehrig posed for photographs before a stack of law books, most of which he'd borrowed from the mayor, and went on at length about his new career.

"I think I'm going to get a bigger kick out of being a parole commissioner than I've ever had before in my life," he said. "Don't think me egotistical if I say I think maybe I've got something to offer. Some kid who comes before me after he's been in a jam with the law will start to tell me what a tough break he's had. And I can say, 'What about me, fellow? I know what tough breaks are.' "

The reporter asked Gehrig how he was feeling.

"The docs say now I may get a break myself," he said. "They say there's better than a fifty-fifty chance that this thing can be checked. Today when my wife and I went out in the boat in Larchmont Harbor it seemed to me that I got around better than I did a few days ago." But he didn't want to talk anymore about his health. He didn't want to talk at all about what had really been happening to his body, about the cysts bursting bright red from his skin, the fibrillations shaking his bones, the growing weakness in his hands and legs, the difficulty sleeping, the increasing wobbliness of his gait. The topic for the day was crime and punishment, and he was sticking to it.

"I've always been interested in kids and young fellows," he said. "Been talking to them and their dads for years at father-son banquets and such. Maybe now I'll be able to say the right word at the right time to fellows who need it most. Maybe they'll take it from me because they know me and pay attention to me more than they would some man who was only a stranger on a board they were scared to death of. I want to visit all the prisons, learn as much as fast as I can to get down to work as quick as I can."

The following week, La Guardia administered the oath of office. Gehrig was expected to serve a ten-year term. Meanwhile, he and Eleanor began making plans to move from Larchmont to New York City. The couple found a charming little house in Riverdale, a well-to-do, thickly wooded section of the Bronx where, as Eleanor remembered it, "pheasants roamed the lawns and wild roses bloomed along the driveways and walks." They moved in a few days before Christmas. Nell Twitchell, Eleanor's mother, had already been living with her daughter and son-in-law for several months. She planned to join them in the new house.

As his condition deteriorated, Gehrig relied more than ever on his wife. At the same time, relations between Eleanor and Christina grew more toxic. Christina accused Eleanor of contributing to Gehrig's illness with her inept cooking. "Pea soup is no good," she said, according to one of Nell Twitchell's letters. "Dry beans are better for vitamins." The argument grew more intense, as if years of barely submerged tension were finally rising to the surface. Gehrig wasn't in the room at the time of the quarrel, according to the letter, but when Eleanor told him what had happened, he vowed never to see his mother again.

The new home was lovely, built in 1929 by the architect Dwight James Baum, a distant relative of L. Frank Baum, author of *The Wizard of Oz*. Dwight Baum built more than 140 homes in Riverdale. The Colonial-style wood-frame home that the Gehrigs rented, at 5204 Delafield Avenue, had been erected atop an enormous boulder, and rather than trying to remove the rock, Baum had decided to build around it. The house sprouted beautifully from the forest, like a white stucco mushroom, but Baum's earthy design made life difficult at times for the home's inhabitants. In building atop a rock rather than a concrete foundation, Baum had been forced to improvise, making the west side of the house several feet lower than the east side. Getting from the dining room to the living room required a three-step climb. On the second floor, going from the master bedroom to the smaller bedrooms required three more steps. There were twenty-five stairs from the mailbox to the front door, thirteen stairs from the first floor to the basement, and twelve stairs from the first floor to the master bedroom. For Gehrig, losing mobility daily, the place must have come to seem like a cruel joke.

When he had lived in New Rochelle with his parents, Gehrig, a single man with spare time on his hands, had enjoyed having dogs around the house. He'd been in apartments and without pets since his marriage to Eleanor, who was no animal lover. But when he moved to Riverdale, Gehrig brought with him a new dog — a white terrier with black patches — and had a fence built around the backyard to keep the animal from running away. The dog's name was Yankee. It may have been a gift from someone connected with the team, according to Louise Goode, who lived with her parents in the house next door. Gehrig adored the animal. Eleanor hated it. The dog barked too much and sometimes clawed its way under the fence and into the neighbors' yards. But Goode, a teenager at the time, didn't mind. Sixty-four years later, the dog remained part of a special memory for her. She still recalled Gehrig shouting in his high-pitched voice so the whole neighborhood could hear: "Yankee! Yankee!"

By winter, Gehrig was no longer writing letters by hand, his penmanship having become as sloppy as his fielding had been six months earlier. On December 2, he dictated a letter to Paul O'Leary. It's not clear whether Eleanor, a nurse, or someone else typed it for him.

"Dear Paul," he began. "Thank you for your kind letter, and I am making every effort to follow your instructions to the letter T. Yesterday I doused the cigarette that I was smoking on the arrival of your letter, had four puffs at long intervals, smoked one after dinner and one about midnight. This morning I tried one after breakfast and it tasted lousy, made me half dizzy so I put it out." Before the doctor told him to cut back, Gehrig had been smoking heavily.

He went on to ask if O'Leary might arrange for a test to check for tumors on his spine. "I have been troubled with my back for the past ten years as you know," Gehrig wrote.

But never before has it hit me when I haven't been indulging in strenuous exercise. About three weeks ago I had an attack which began on the left side, I would say on the outer edge of the lung, and the same as usual, in three or four days it worked itself up to that identical section of the spine where it has always ended. Now I have noticed my cysts to work the same way. I would have three or four days of infection where they would swell tremendously and be sore as hell, and then taper off back to normalcy. Please assume that this is a dumb ball player talking, but the logic in my mind seems to think that there is one chance of there being one of these cysts at that point on my spine that starts to rare up every so often.

A bit deeper into the letter, Gehrig mentioned an encouraging meeting with Al Reiser, a New York orchestra leader who had been "similarly infected" with ALS. Reiser had at one time lost most of the motion in his legs and arms. Breathing and swallowing had become difficult. "And yet today," Gehrig wrote, "two years after he was stricken he professes almost normalcy. . . . This does look encouraging, doesn't it? As far as I can see, he was taking pills and three injections weekly, which seems to be about the same treatment that I am getting now."

Gehrig made reference in his letter to his last meeting with O'Leary, which took place in New York on November 1:

At that time, I was a little discouraged, but your explanation and your visit picked me up quite a bit. Paul, I feel you can appreciate how I despise the dark, but also despise equally as much false illusions. Now Al Reiser is definitely an encouraging sign. Two doctor friends of Mom's have told her it would be a matter of three or four years, and I would start to pick up. Another friend's doctor who is supposed to be one of those reputed doctors (or racketeers), seems to think along the same lines, that in several years I might get up one day and be practically normal. You are well aware of my thoughts of these New York bastards. That is why I am mentioning these facts to find out from a truthful organization what your experiences have been and what my hope for encouragement is. Incidentally, before I forget, Al Reiser told me that the big thing I need now with my excellent attention is courage. I do not want to be a hero, and I would hate like hell to be a cry baby, but I would also like to know the facts if any.

He went on in the letter to say that a test

of his hand strength, performed by a doctor in New York, indicated further loss of muscle, while his walking had gotten neither better nor worse.

"I definitely feel I am doing as well as can be expected. What I am looking for Paul is a confirmation, but it must be on the level, of Reiser's statement 'keep that chin up and keep your courage, and in two or three years you will be all right.' Have you ever had any such experience as Reiser's with any of your patients?"

The letter concluded on the fourth page with a few scattered thoughts. Gehrig reported his fibrillations had "toned down considerably," although the twitching in his right elbow "has been really raising hell." He said he was looking forward to the O'Leary family's upcoming visit to New York, and that he hoped to get tickets for the doctor's children to see *Hellzapoppin* and for the adults to see either *Life with Father* or *Streets of Paris*.

He signed the letter "Cordially, Lou Gehrig," in slightly larger than usual script. Beneath his signature he wrote by hand: "A specimen of my handwriting for Dr. Woltman." His penmanship, while sloppy, was still perfectly legible.

O'Leary responded to Gehrig in a letter dated December 8, 1939:

I was happy that Al Reiser and you got together because I know by innuendoes you have the impression that people do not arrest the progress of amyotrophic lateral sclerosis. Al Reiser is just one of a group that have been improved and I trust that in seeing him you have been reassured that there is a damn good probability that you will do likewise.

You remember [in] our last talk . . . I tried to emphasize the point that you would probably progress to a certain degree, following which you would either remain stationary with some residual signs like numbness in your fingertips and a little difficulty in walking or that there would be even an improvement in many of these temporary inconveniences. If you reach this point by next summer I will think that you have done swell.

O'Leary went on for four pages, urging his patient to "continue pounding along with treatment." He told Gehrig to get used to the fact that "little things cropping up from time to time" might make him feel that the illness is progressing. But the doctor urged his patient not to worry. In the end, he wrote, "courage and persistence in treatment invariably result in an arrest of the process such as you have."

The doctor's encouraging words were misleading, at best. O'Leary knew that Reiser didn't have ALS (it was probably a milder form of sclerosis). And he almost certainly knew that "courage and persistence" would not stop ALS from attacking a man's body any more than it would stop a bullet from penetrating his flesh. But while physicians are bound not to lie to their patients, they often walk a fine line. To this day, doctors don't understand why some victims of ALS last longer than others. Some doctors say their more optimistic patients tend to take better care of their bodies and succumb more slowly to the corrosive effects of the disease. So if the patient wishes to swallow a small dose of false hope along with his vitamins and mineral oils, his doctor isn't going to stop him.

On December 10, Gehrig, encouraged again, wrote back to O'Leary: "Up until now, I was under the impression that every inch of ground lost could never be regained, but since talking to Reiser and having it confirmed by you . . . I believe . . . that I will be well on the way to recovery very shortly."

He went on to offer evidence of his improving condition: "A week ago Saturday, were just low dopey days for me, followed by three swell days, Wednesday, Thursday and Friday, days where my energy just seemed inexhaustible and loaded with pep." He said that he understood some of his pep might be a result of his encouraging meeting with Reiser and the good news contained in O'Leary's letter. Also, he noted that he might be getting used to his physical limitations and learning better to cope with them. "Considering all these things," he writes, "I still say I had three marvelous days."

On December 7, the Baseball Writers Association of America voted to waive its normal election process and immediately nominate Gehrig to the Baseball Hall of Fame. It was the first time that a player had been named to the Hall of Fame the same year he departed the game. Shortly thereafter, Barrow announced that the Yankees had retired Gehrig's number. Never before had a player's number been retired. Never again would a Yankee player wear Number 4 on his back. Barrow also told the press that Gehrig's locker would never be used by another player. "We always want Lou to feel he is still one of us," Barrow said, "and that he will always be welcome to use his locker whenever he wants to."

Gehrig's first round of medical experiments began on a Friday night, January 5, 1940. Making his third trip to Rochester, he was placed under the care of Dr. Bayard T. Horton, one of the clinic's most famous scientists and one of the most optimistic men in modern medicine.

A slender man with delicate features and a piercing gaze, Horton was on the brink of greatness, or so he believed. And the greatness awaiting him was not the mundane kind attendant upon becoming a top doctor in one's chosen field or a department head at an important hospital. Horton believed that his name would soon rank with the giants of scientific research — men like Sir Alexander Fleming, whose observations on bacteria had led to the development of penicillin; Frederick Banting and Charles Best, the discoverers of insulin; and Will and Charlie Mayo, his nearest and dearest heroes, the pioneers of modern surgery and group practice. "The history of medicine, like the history of the world, is the history of but a few people," Horton once wrote. "It is only the few who leave their footprints on the sands of time; if a man expects to do so, he must wear his working shoes."

Few worked harder than Horton. Few exhibited more passion. And in 1940, Horton believed he had found his ticket to immortality: Histamine, he told his friends and colleagues, was going to change the world of medicine as dramatically as insulin had. It would "make the lame to walk, the deaf to hear, and the blind to see." He believed it might also allow Lou Gehrig to live long and walk without a hitch.

Histamine occurs naturally in human tissue and in the bloodstream, causing dilation of the capillaries and contraction of muscles, among other things. When human tissues are hurt or infected, cells in the tissue naturally release histamine, which causes the blood vessels to dilate. That allows fluid and cells from the immune system to leak from the bloodstream, flooding the site of the injury so healing can begin. The presence of histamine in human tissue had been discovered in 1927. Almost immediately, scientists began testing its therapeutic effects.

Dr. Horton grew up in Gate City, Virginia, a small town in the heart of Appalachia. Though he wasn't trained in the Ivy League, as many of his colleagues had been, he was as bright and confident as any of them. With his warm accent and gift for storytelling, he charmed people first, and then impressed them with his intelligence. Horton was the first scientist to identify the characteristics of cluster headaches, which later became known as Horton's cephalgia. But histamine, he believed, would eventually make his other discoveries seem minor. He would follow histamine — "like a cat following a patch of sunlight," as one scientist wrote years later in an assessment of Horton's career — for the rest of his life.

Will and Charlie Mayo were strong supporters, and they permitted Horton to establish his own clinic on the fourth floor of St. Mary's Hospital in Rochester, a place where he turned down the lights and soothed his patients with gentle music as they waited for histamine to chase their headaches and various other maladies away. Before long, patients with multiple sclerosis, Ménière's syndrome, Alzheimer's, macular degeneration, baldness, and other ailments were settling into the cozy confines of Horton's lab and taking injections of histamine. Horton told Gehrig that he thought histamine might even help pitchers with worn-out arms recover their strength. Some of Horton's colleagues were skeptical, wondering if the doctor's powers of suggestion were more powerful than his prescriptions.

By the time Gehrig came along, Horton had tried histamine on four patients with sclerosis. It's not clear how many of them, if any, were ALS patients. The doctor planned to saturate Gehrig's body with histamine and send him home with instructions to take two injections a day.

While Gehrig was undergoing the treatment, O'Leary wrote to the patient's wife, saying that two of Horton's sclerosis patients were doing fairly well and two showed no improvement. "I wish I knew, Eleanor, what the histamine would do," O'Leary wrote. "There is no way we can forecast it; however, I do think that he must keep plugging and that we must keep our chins up in an effort to encourage him further."

As much as he remained committed and loyal to his doctors at the Mayo Clinic, Gehrig also remained open-minded about new treatments. When he read an article in the newspaper about the benefits of testosterone injections, or when he received a package of mineral pills from the Colloidal Institute in Lakeland, Florida, or when a doctor from Portland, Oregon, told him apple seed oil might cure ALS, Gehrig wrote to his friends at the Mayo and asked whether there might be any value in these approaches. He tried a few of the oils and vitamins sent his way.

Still, Gehrig remained wary of doctors — especially East Coast doctors. He admitted in one letter to O'Leary that he'd been angered by the failure of his doctors in New

York to diagnose his condition. But there was one man in New York Gehrig couldn't dismiss, a physician who probably knew more about ALS than anyone in the United States. Gehrig first visited Dr. Israel Wechsler on January 27, 1940, at the doctor's private office at 83rd Street and Park Avenue.

The office reeked of genius. The bookshelves were lined with medical journals. Walls were covered with framed photographs: Albert Einstein, the Hebrew poet Chaim Bialik, Louis Pasteur. On his desk, Wechsler kept a tin box in which he collected contributions to help Jewish immigrants who were fleeing Hitler's armies in Europe and settling in Palestine. But the box was usually empty. Whenever one of his patients leaned forward to stuff in some coins or a bill, Wechsler would snap out of his chair and put his hand over the lid. "That's not for you," he would say. Later, perhaps over lunch, he would talk to the patient about making a much larger donation, or becoming a volunteer.

Wechsler was a difficult man to say no to. He was a man of powerful opinions, brilliant insight, and enormous charisma. He studied Torah with some of the city's rabbis, though he cared little for organized religion. He adored classical music, but thought it best not to listen too much or

608

else risk becoming intoxicated by its beauty. He was the chief of neurology at Mount Sinai Hospital, but he also practiced psychiatry, and he believed that most patients could be cured quickly, whether their troubles were psychological or neurological. Once, a wealthy woman visited his office and complained that she had developed a terrible fear of injuring her children. She was afraid to give the children baths for fear she might scald them, afraid to serve dinner for fear she might cut them with a knife. Wechsler, who had corresponded with Sigmund Freud and considered him an important influence, listened and pronounced that the woman was responding to subconscious anger because her children had curtailed her active social life. He assured the patient that her feelings would not materialize into actions and declared her cured. The doctor's confident judgment was all the patient needed. She never worried again about injuring her children, according to Dr. Louis Linn, who shared an office with his famous father-in-law. Joseph Fuchs, a promising young violinist, once came to Wechsler complaining of paralysis in one of the fingers on his left hand. Other doctors had told Fuchs the problem was in his head, that he had developed a severe case of performance anxiety. Wechsler disagreed. He recommended surgery on the violinist's ulnar nerve. The surgery was a success. Fuchs went on to a brilliant career.

Early in 1940, Wechsler was dashing madly to publish the results of his latest experiment, in which ALS patients were treated with heavy doses of vitamin E. Vitamins were new. Pharmaceutical labs were still developing new varieties, and doctors were only beginning to explore their potential. Wechsler had heard of another neurologist conducting similar studies at Montefiore Hospital, and he didn't want to let this other doctor publish first. When Gehrig came into Wechsler's office, the doctor was delighted to have another subject for his study. After listening to Gehrig's story, he told his newest patient that his vitamin E levels had been badly depleted by the diet he'd undertaken to improve his gallbladder. In conducting his physical examination, he found that Gehrig's disease had already done severe damage.

"When first seen," Wechsler wrote of his meeting with Gehrig, "he had marked spasticity in both lower extremities . . . generalized fibrillations, weakness of the shoulder and arm muscles and almost complete paralysis of the hand muscles, atrophy of the supra- and infraspinati [shoulder muscles], deltoids, pectorals and all the small muscles of the hands."

Gehrig returned a week later to begin treatment. Wechsler urged his new patient to give up his histamine injections and to increase his vitamin E intake from three pills a day to five. Wechsler was right — histamine was more likely to cause headaches than do any good — but Gehrig had a difficult time believing that anyone at the Mayo Clinic would have given him bad advice. "Unless I am a rotten judge and sadly mistaken," he wrote, "I do not believe that Dr. Horton or the clinic would be giving such great attention to histamine if it were of such little importance as Wechsler seems to think." Gehrig was so thoroughly sold on histamine, in fact, that he wrote to Gabby Hartnett, manager of the Cubs, telling him that he should send Dizzy Dean to Rochester to get some shots for his limp right arm. "Why I should take an interest in this publicity crazed ape, I shall never know," Gehrig wrote to O'Leary, in reference to Dean, "but I personally believe it is more to help a swell personality like Gabby Hartnett than it is to do anything for Diz. There is only an outside chance that he will arrive there but if he does you will come in contact with a boy who thinks he knows all the answers and who, I would judge, has an I.Q. much below par."

Gehrig remained so enamored of the

doctors at the Mayo that he was slow to embrace Wechsler, despite the New York doctor's considerable energy and charm. Gehrig wrote:

Wechsler said he has experimented a great deal on monkeys, and he has found that when he deprives a monkey of bananas and walnuts (which are supposed to be rich in vitamin E) he definitely notes an atrophy in the muscles. And again, when he administers large quantities of vitamin E to these monkeys they respond almost immediately. Maybe I'm nuts, but I'm inclined to believe that for thousands of years the monkey's digestive tracts have been trained along a very limited diet and when you deprive the animal of this limited diet certainly the bottom must fall out of somewhere. My comparison would be if I told you to stop eating soups, vegetables, bread and butter, meats and desserts, that something drastic would happen to you in time. At any rate this amused me a great deal.

Gehrig followed with an update on his condition: His color was good. He found it easier to walk with heeled shoes than slippers. He was napping every day around noon and getting plenty of sleep, but still felt tired at times. For the most part, he wrote, there had been no great change.

Two weeks after his first appointment with Wechsler, Gehrig began to express more trust in his new doctor. "He mellowed considerably and didn't make any bold statements with the exception that he is more convinced than ever that vitamin E is the solution," Gehrig wrote. "He also seems convinced that the reason the pills had no effect on me in the two weeks' trial was that my system is unable to absorb this vitamin via the digestive tract." Wechsler prescribed between thirty and fifty milligrams a day of Ephynal, a vitamin E tablet made by the Hoffmann-LaRoche company, and told Gehrig to eat a lot of lettuce, kale, whole wheat bread, coarse cereal, butter, bananas, fresh corn, fresh peas, beans, egg yolks, and fatty beef. He also ordered him to take two teaspoons of wheat germ oil every day to help absorb the vitamins. Boxes of the oil were selling for $2.50 each, which seemed a bit high, so Gehrig asked O'Leary to send him free samples from the Mayo Clinic. O'Leary complied.

After three weeks, Wechsler told Gehrig he detected "a hairline improvement." Gehrig said he felt as if his legs had gotten no worse since November, but his hands and arms had continued to lose strength.

The headline — "REMEDY IS FOUND FOR 'GEHRIG DISEASE' " — appeared on page 24 of *The Times* on March 13, buried between a story about plans to build the new Battery Brooklyn Tunnel and another about a thief who made off with $15,000 in jewels from an Upper East Side apartment. The article reported that Dr. Israel Wechsler had documented the "first successful treatment of the hitherto incurable disease of the central nervous system known as amyotrophic lateral sclerosis, popularly known as 'Lou Gehrig's Disease.' " Wechsler reported his findings at a meeting of the New York Academy of Medicine. A few days later, he published the results of his research in the *Journal of the American Medical Association.*

Wechsler documented only two cases and noted that his conclusions were preliminary. Even so, he wrote, the results were "so spectacular" that he couldn't wait to publish. In both cases, ALS patients taking vitamins were regaining strength and mobility. The doctor said he would need at least a year to determine whether the new treatment might bring permanent relief. In his published paper and in his comments before the academy, Wechsler made no mention of his most famous patient, the man for whom the disease was now unofficially named. In fact, he never told anyone he was treating Gehrig. By keeping quiet about his most renowned patient, he went a long way toward earning Gehrig's confidence.

When journalists called Gehrig to ask for a quote on the encouraging new medical report, he declined to comment.

From the tone of Gehrig's letters, one might get the impression that his thoughts and efforts were devoted entirely to his medical treatment. In fact, he was reporting to work every day at the Parole Commission, at 139 Centre Street in downtown Manhattan. Gehrig insisted on driving, despite Eleanor's protests. He arrived most mornings at nine o'clock, parked the car, and took an elevator to his fourth-floor office, where "Mr. Gehrig" was painted with gilt letters on the door. His tidy desktop contained an in-box, an out-box, and a tray full of paper clips that were probably too small for his fingers to grasp. He spent most of his time there thumbing through paperwork. Once or twice a week, usually on Tuesdays and Fridays, he would visit inmates at "the Tombs," the city penitentiary on Riker's Island, or the House of Detention for Women on Greenwich Avenue in Manhattan. When he wasn't interviewing prisoners, he was reviewing their case files and preparing recommendations to the board on who should receive parole. The commission handled about six thousand cases in 1940, but there is no record in the municipal archives to suggest how much work Gehrig shouldered.

Thomas Rocco Barbella, who later changed his name to Rocky Graziano and became a champion middleweight boxer, claimed to have seen Gehrig at work in his new job. Barbella said he was incarcerated in the Tombs when the city's most famous parole commissioner visited him. "You've been in your share of trouble, haven't you?" Gehrig asked, according to an interview that Graziano gave Gehrig biographer Ray Robinson. "You've caused your mother a lot of grief, haven't you?" When Gehrig announced that he thought Barbella ought to go back to reform school, the young man cursed. "I felt like killing him," he recalled in the interview.

Careful observers visiting Gehrig's office might have noticed signs of his creeping illness. His shirt collar sometimes poked from beneath his sweater and his tie was at times askew, suggesting that he lacked the fine motor skills to make the necessary adjustments. He held the telephone awkwardly and turned pages in books with great difficulty. When papers passed his desk requiring a signature, he used a rubber stamp.

His personality had always been well

suited to certain desk jobs. Once, as a collegian, he thought seriously of becoming an engineer. Now, he enjoyed the unambiguous nature of his work. There were numbers to tally, yes-or-no votes to cast, dull but important forms to fill out. Gehrig treated it seriously. He needed the job, enjoyed having someplace to go every morning, and wanted to feel useful. "It came just at a time when I needed to take my mind off myself and become interested in some new field," he said. "The work is unbelievably interesting."

Gehrig was beginning to believe more strongly in the power of vitamin E — and in Wechsler. "As a matter of fact, Paul," he wrote on March 23, 1940, "I have kept this from everybody, but the last two or three weeks have made me definitely feel that a change is taking place. The change is so minute I can barely put my finger on it, but there are just little things that I seem to think that I am doing just a little bit better than I used to, and I pray to God that this is not my imagination, but the truth. You know I am pretty cynical, and when I say this, I say it truthfully about my improvement."

Eight days later, though, on March 31, his optimism began to fade. He wrote to O'Leary again:

From what I am going to write, please don't judge me a cry baby, or believe me to be losing my guts, but as always I would like to know the actual truths and not continue to receive encouraging reports which have little or no chance of materializing, or to continue to live in false hopes. There is definitely something going on within my body which I do not understand and which I would appreciate immensely if you would discuss with Dr. Woltman and PLEASE reveal to me the honest opinions. A week ago yesterday Wechsler assured me one hundred percent that the progress of my ailment had definitely been arrested. Then on Wednesday afternoon my left side began to fibrillate rather violently. Then Wednesday, Thursday and Friday were very listless and depressing days. My left thumb and middle finger both hang, and it is only with great effort that my left wrist does not continually sag. During these three nights my left leg (in bed) did considerable jumping. Then Saturday fibrillations quieted down, and today I feel pretty good again. Now my point is this: you have in all probability noticed from my letters that I am having my ups and downs (as you predicted last August) much more frequently in the last two months than I have had prior to that time.

He went on to give a brief account of the past two months of ups and downs, and then asked: "What is your conclusion? And honestly, please."

You said you have seven or eight patients at St. Mary's which have been under the vitamin E therapy, and what do you find. Wechsler says that he has twenty patients now, and he is more convinced than ever that they are on the right track. Of course I stopped taking vitamin E orally about six or seven weeks ago, when we started the injections, and three weeks ago as I informed you he decided to give it both orally as well as the injections. The others are showing such remarkable results, and I fully realize that we have only been using the stuff an exceptionally short time, I am naturally wondering whether I am doomed to an only arrested stage instead of a recovering stage. And as you know, I am not a cry baby, but this question to me right now is one of the most important that I have confronting me, and I feel you can appreciate my thoughts and position. I am not dumb, or unreasonable enough to ask the impossible, for I fully appreciate and believe that no person alive today can answer the questions I have confronted you with. . . .

Please don't think, Paul, that I am overly depressed, crying, or quitting, for I am not. Last New Year's you assured me of a 45% chance of making some sort of a recovery, and you also assured me that I need not look for a turn until around July. I have thoroughly reconciled myself to these facts and to the honesty of your statements, but you can readily appreciate why I am in a quandary when a fellow like Wechsler announces unbelievable results in a period of five or six weeks, and the above facts are happening to me.

I hate like hell to bother you with these additional burdens of mine, for the Lord knows you have enough misery out there each day and week, but I know you will also appreciate the confidence I have in you and your organization, and for that reason an honest opinion coming from you people is of vital importance to me.

The next letter to O'Leary came not from Gehrig but from his wife. "Our boy is getting pretty discouraged," she wrote on April

9. "There is no question that he is continually losing ground, especially in the use of his hands.

"I am worried about his spirit and courage as this thing progresses, and I believe we should keep him on the optimistic side by hinting about other cases on record which have become practically bedridden, and then gradually improved because of some mysterious working of nature. He will believe this because of Al Reiser's case. . . . I don't believe he had the identical disease, but I am glad he impressed Lou that he had."

Eleanor wrote that Gehrig was getting all the fresh vegetables she could pour into him and visiting Dr. Wechsler every week. She concluded with these words: "It must be very difficult for you to answer his last letter to you, and I feel we must all lie like mad. I want him to keep a thread of hope; there is no point in adding mental torture to the horrible experience he is now going through."

If he wished to reply to the letter, Eleanor instructed O'Leary, he should write to Ed Barrow's home in Larchmont so that Gehrig wouldn't open the mail. Barrow would pass along the letter without arousing suspicion. O'Leary did as he was told.

"I have always disliked to tell falsehoods," he wrote to Eleanor in a letter dated April 16, "but I feel that with Lou we must keep his morale up, not only for the benefit and help it may be to him, but also in order to save him the shock that accompanies such discussions." Here, for the first time, he confessed to Eleanor what she already seemed to understand: ALS cases at the Mayo "have not done well." He continued: "I hope Lou keeps up his enthusiasm for Wechsler and that our disappointments thus far will soon turn to encouragement."

Gehrig was clearly beginning to doubt the encouraging words of his friend and doctor. But every time he appeared ready to accept his grim fate, some encouraging bit of news or innovative scientific development came along to prop him up.

In May, the boost came from Wechsler, who wrote to Dr. Woltman in Rochester that he believed Gehrig's disease had been checked. At the same time, Wechsler was preparing to publish a follow-up to his first paper on vitamin E. This report — eventually published in the *American Journal of Medical Science* — would be even more encouraging than the last. The doctor said that eleven of his twenty ALS patients were showing improvement. Two had recovered completely, four had shown marked improvement, and five had experienced moderate gains. Gehrig, referred to in the study as "L.G., male, age 36," fell into the "moderate gains" group. "The fibrillations have practically disappeared, walking is somewhat improved and some power has returned in both thumbs," Wechsler wrote in regard to this poorly disguised patient. "The case may be regarded as definitely arrested and somewhat improved."

Gehrig was somewhat amused by the doctor's excitement about the improved range of motion in the tip of his left thumb. Less than one year earlier, he had still entertained hopes of returning to the Yankee lineup and resuming his career. Now, his doctor was calling for celebration because Gehrig had managed to wiggle his thumb. And yet he wanted to believe in the doctor's pronouncement. "This may sound ridiculous," he wrote to O'Leary, "but I know you can appreciate how important it is to me."

Dressed in a suit and tie, Gehrig attended a handful of games at Yankee Stadium, sitting stiffly on the bench next to Joe McCarthy. He and everyone else believed the Yanks were a lock to win the pennant. But the cool efficiency with which the team had won in 1939 somehow turned to cold stiffness in 1940. This time, the lineup never clicked. DiMaggio was pounding the ball as hard as ever, but most of the other players looked lost. Frankie Crosetti, hitting only .150, was benched in May. His 420-game streak of consecutive games — the longest among active players — was over. Gordon, Rolfe, Dickey, and Selkirk were having miserable seasons, too. The splendid pitching staff that had carried the team in 1939 was merely average. Fans and writers were astounded at how quickly and completely the Yankees had come apart.

By mid-August, the team was in fifth place, more than ten games behind the Cleveland Indians, when Jimmy Powers of the *Daily News* published an article containing a novel theory explaining the team's underachievement. The story began:

> The Yankees, who for the past four years have been one of the greatest baseball machines in history, and almost universally selected to win the pennant again, have collapsed.
>
> Why?
>
> Has the mysterious "polio" germ, which felled Lou Gehrig, also struck his former teammates, turning a once-great team into a floundering non-contender? According to overwhelming opinion of the medical profession, poliomyelitis, similar to infantile paralysis, is commu-

nicable. The Yanks were exposed to it at its most acute stage. They played ball with the afflicted Gehrig, dressed and undressed in the locker room with him, traveled, played cards and ate with him. Isn't it possible some of them also became infected?

It's hard to believe mere coincidence can explain away the wholesale failure of the individuals. In Gehrig's case, one of the most prominent symptoms was loss of muscular power. The same symptom can be found in many of the Yanks today. So far no one has been able to advance a satisfactory reason for it.

The newspaper published a drawing of a Yankee player crumbling to the ground, his bat and glove fallen at his side, menacing clouds gathering overhead. The story included a chart listing the conditions of the so-called "Slumping Champs." Red Ruffing, according to the article, had "unexpectedly lost his overpowering fast ball"; Lefty Gomez was throwing "with hardly any power at all"; Monte Pearson suffered from "trouble in shoulder muscles"; while Johnny Murphy had "lost the sharp break in the famous curve ball." The list went on to name six more players suffering from myriad maladies and meltdowns. Powers asked: "Can coincidence explain these simultaneous ailments? Couldn't the 'polio' germ be the cause?" The writer concluded: "If Gehrig passed through a stage in which the cause of his ineffectiveness was undetermined, isn't it possible such is also the case with many of the Yanks today?"

Gehrig was livid. In a letter to O'Leary he referred to Powers as a "yellow bastard" and a "yellow so and so who hasn't got a gut in his body." Two days after the story appeared, he filed a million-dollar libel suit against Powers and the owners of the *Daily News*. Later, Gehrig would add as a defendant the Tribune Co., which owned the *Chicago Tribune*. Gehrig's complaint, filed at the New York State Supreme Court in Bronx County, claimed that the former athlete was "greatly injured in his credit and reputation and in the social intercourse with his friends and suffered great pain and mental anguish."

Lawyers for the *Daily News* blamed the misunderstanding on Gehrig's doctors at the Mayo Clinic and on Yankees officials, who originally described the disease as a form of poliomyelitis, or infantile paralysis, which, unlike ALS, is a communicable disease. If Gehrig did have poliomyelitis, as the Mayo Clinic indicated in Dr. Habein's poorly worded 1939 statement, the men who shared a locker room and dining car with him could conceivably have become infected. Lawyers for the newspaper pointed to the case of a Loyola University football player who apparently transmitted poliomyelitis to two of his teammates. After Gehrig filed his suit, a lawyer for the *News* traveled to Rochester and interviewed some of the doctors who had diagnosed Gehrig. Only then, the lawyers for the newspaper claimed, did reporters and editors learn that Gehrig had ALS and that ALS was not a form of polio. The paper published two quick stories, attempting to set the record straight, but for Gehrig, the gesture was not enough. He pushed ahead with the lawsuit.

Powers had bungled the story, but Gehrig's lawyers knew that they would have to prove that the journalist acted out of malice in order to win a libel suit. There was no evidence that Powers had anything but respect for the former ballplayer. The lawyers also knew their client was in no condition for a long legal battle, that whatever time he had left ought not be spent in law offices and courtrooms.

The case never went to trial. The newspaper publishers paid Gehrig $17,500 to settle the suit. On December 19, Gehrig signed the one-page agreement in a hand so shaky it would appear to have been written by the passenger of a car rumbling down an unpaved road.

That winter, O'Leary urged Gehrig to quit his job. Still possessed of dogged work habits, Gehrig refused. He was proud of the fact that he was still able to walk, albeit clumsily. Besides, he said, sitting at the office required no more energy than sitting at home. His greatest exertion involved getting from the driveway to the first floor of his house, and then from the first floor to the master bedroom on the second floor. Gehrig told O'Leary he wasn't ready yet to become homebound.

When Gehrig wasn't downtown at the Parole Commission office, Eleanor often invited guests to drop by the house. Pitzy Katz, the actor and comedian, was a frequent visitor whose ethnic jokes never failed to make Gehrig laugh. Bill Robinson, the famous tap dancer, came around to say hello. Songwriter Fred Fisher entertained on the Gehrigs' piano. Actress Tallulah Bankhead also stopped by on occasion. Bankhead — who reportedly smoked more than a hundred cigarettes a day, drank heavily, and traveled with a suitcase full of sleeping pills — hit a room with the subtlety of a tornado. The actress was probably a friend of Eleanor's, but she and Gehrig had at least one thing in common: both were heavily medicated. Gehrig, after listening to Bankhead describe her assorted aches, pains, and maladies, tried to persuade her to visit the Mayo Clinic. Bill Dickey and his wife Vi dropped in, as did some of the other members of the team.

Sportswriters came around for interviews, too. One of them, Bob Considine, asked Gehrig how he was feeling.

"Oh . . . can't complain, still punching," Gehrig said with a chuckle. "They're still hoping to hit on something that will check this thing I've got. No, I haven't been back to the Mayo Clinic. Probably won't go back there, unless they tell me they've developed something new, and send for me. They turned me over to a fine doctor here in New York. He's making some fine progress."

Considine said that was wonderful news.

"Yes, it certainly is," Gehrig replied. "He's prepared a paper for the Medical Association about treating cases like mine."

Gehrig was referring to yet another of Wechsler's updates on vitamin E research. Considine asked if Gehrig's case would be included in the next published report.

"Well, no," Gehrig said. "It's about seven other persons with similar trouble. They're coming along fine with those new injections. I'm not included. But I'm glad to say those others are coming along swell."

Considine, searching for some sign of hope, asked if the other patients had been receiving treatment longer than Gehrig.

"Not as long," Gehrig said.

Eleanor invited as many distractions as possible. There was only one distraction she couldn't endure, and that was her mother-in-law. Christina Gehrig wasn't welcome in her son's home. If Gehrig was upset, or if he missed his mother, or if he sneaked up to Westchester for visits while he was still able to drive, he never mentioned so in his letters. During the last week of the year, Eleanor finally relented and allowed Christina to visit. But even then, she couldn't bring herself to extend the invitation personally. Instead, she sent Dr. O'Leary, visiting that week from Minnesota, to meet with Gehrig's parents and to tell them that they should go see their son while there was still time.

For Gehrig, eating was becoming increasingly difficult. Though most of the food he ingested was soft, he still choked, sometimes violently. He was no longer able to walk without someone at his side. Some journalists said he began using a wheelchair, though Eleanor claimed he never did. His diction grew slurred. The tone and volume of his voice began to recede, like a radio station fading out of range. He dipped in and out of depression and began to think about quitting his job, or at least taking a leave of absence.

"As for myself," he wrote to O'Leary in January of 1941, "it is getting a little more difficult each day and it will be hard to say how much longer I can carry on. . . . I don't mean to be pessimistic but one cannot help wonder how much further this thing can go and I wish you would again drop a note as to your thoughts and percentage of making a proportional recovery. I also understand how difficult this is."

He continued:

"Don't think that I am depressed or pessimistic about my condition at present. I intend to hold on as long as possible and then if the inevitable comes, I will accept it philosophically and hope for the best. That's all we can do."

CHAPTER 26

HE WAS BASEBALL

Even as Gehrig's body failed, his mind remained clear, his memory sharp. One day that winter, John Kieran of *The Times* dropped by the house in Riverdale. The men sat in the living room. Gehrig's face was withered. He moved slowly and with great difficulty. But as he propped an old scrapbook full of newspaper clippings on his lap, his voice filled with energy.

He gestured toward a picture of the High School of Commerce baseball team that had traveled to Chicago to take on Lane Tech for the high school championship in 1920. It had been a fantastic time in his life. He was seventeen. His body was nearing its physical peak. He was discovering a talent for baseball that, slowly but surely, would help him overcome his shyness and insecurity. The game had taken place at Cubs Park, now known as Wrigley Field. In the bottom of the ninth, with the bases loaded and two outs, Gehrig had smacked a towering home run that, looking back on it, launched his career. But it wasn't the excitement of the journey to Chicago or the glory of the game or the majesty of the home run that Gehrig wanted to talk about now. Instead, he wanted to correct a bit of mythology that had come to surround his performance as a young slugger.

"There's a mistaken impression about that homer," Gehrig told Kieran. "I often see it written that I won the game with that homer. As a matter of fact, it was unimportant. There were two out in the ninth and the bases filled when I hit it, but we were leading 8-6 at the time. So all we got out of it was four runs we didn't need."

He went on to recall his tryout the following year before John McGraw, manager of the Giants. "That was the spring of 1921," he said. "I worked out with the Giants at the Polo Grounds and I think McGraw liked me. But I didn't sign a Giant contract. I planned to go to Columbia in the fall." Gehrig was probably being polite, not mentioning that McGraw failed to recognize the young first baseman's potential. Instead, it was Paul Krichell of the Yankees who saw Gehrig playing for Columbia and gave him his first professional contract. "In 1924," Gehrig said, "when I was in New Orleans with the Yankees, I met McGraw and he called me a contract jumper."

Kieran asked Gehrig about his spectacular performance as a pitcher for Columbia.

"Spectacular is right!" Gehrig said with a chuckle. "I struck out seventeen men in one game. Pretty good, wasn't it? Now I'll tell you the rest of it. We were playing Williams and they beat me, 5-1. I think I must have walked every batter I didn't strike out. I could heave the ball in there pretty fast, but I never knew where it was going."

Throughout his career, Gehrig had always given Kieran and the rest of the sportswriters a difficult time. He had usually been polite and good-natured, but he rarely had much to say about himself. Now, Kieran was so charmed by Gehrig's storytelling and self-deprecating humor that he returned a few weeks later for another trip down memory lane. He found Gehrig seated near a window, having recently scattered some peanuts on the snow and hoping to see his favorite pheasant wander over to gobble them up. This time, Kieran asked Gehrig about some of the framed photos decorating the walls of his house. One picture, taken at Yankee Stadium, showed one runner crossing home plate and another turning the corner at third base.

"I'm the bird turning third," Gehrig

said, laughing loudly.

Kieran said there didn't seem to be anything funny about the picture.

"There isn't?" Gehrig asked. "Look again. Look at that guy on the mound." The pitcher seemed to be staring in Gehrig's direction.

"You can't tell by looking, but you should have heard him. That's [Grover Cleveland] Alexander [of the Cardinals]. He thought he had our number. You know, he beat us three times in the 1926 World Series. That is, he beat us twice and saved the last game. . . . This picture is in the second game of the 1928 Series. First inning. There was Alex, thinking he'd have us feeding out of his hand, as usual. Well, with two on in the very first inning, he threw me one — the first ball — right where I liked it and I smacked it away up in the right-field bleachers. Man, oh man! You should have heard what he called me as I ran around the bases. That's why he's looking at me in the picture. He's pouring it on — and I'm laughing. In fact, I'm still laughing."

Gehrig talked about another picture on the wall, one from game three of the 1927 Series. The picture showed catcher Johnny Gooch of the Pittsburgh Pirates making the tag as Gehrig tried to score on what would have been an inside-the-park home run.

"Combs led off with a single and Koenig beat out a hit," Gehrig said, his recall as sharp as Ty Cobb's spikes. "Ruth — wait a minute, oh, yes — he hit one of those tremendous infield flies. I think Glenn Wright finally caught it. Then I smacked one away out in center and began running. When I got around to third, Art Fletcher chased me in. 'Keep going,' he yelled, and waved me on. . . . I slid in and there was Gooch with the ball. So I had to settle for a triple."

Only Gehrig would display a picture that showed him getting tagged out at the plate. Off the ballfield, he was still a hard man to peg. While he was comfortable now talking about himself, he still wasn't inclined to brag. While he spoke as if he missed the game, he showed no interest in hanging around like some sort of team mascot. While he seemed to have quietly accepted the fact that he was not going to beat his illness, he carried on most of the time as if he had nothing to worry about.

Kieran and other visitors could see he was dying. The weight was melting from his body like winter's last snow on a suddenly warm day. But Gehrig continued to talk about the upcoming baseball season and his great expectations for the 1941 Yankees, saying he fully expected to see them back in the World Series that fall.

The team had given up on Babe Dahlgren and planned to try Joe Gordon at first base in the coming season. "He can't miss!" Gehrig said. "He's really a great ballplayer. Just give him a little time to practice and he'll be a whiz at first base. Maybe he'll make the Yankee fans forget Lou Gehrig."

When he could no longer drive, when he could no longer walk without a cane or hold a pencil or answer the phone, or handle a fork and knife, Gehrig continued to show up for work downtown, at least for a time. Eleanor accompanied him to the office, opened his mail, stamped his signature on letters, and even stuck cigarettes in her husband's mouth. Eventually, though, the effort became too much. On April 14, 1941, Gehrig requested a six-month leave of absence from his post. In a letter to the mayor, he said the doctors were telling him his condition might improve after some rest. If he didn't see any change in five or six months, he wrote, "I will at that time and most regretfully submit, with your permission, my resignation."

Gehrig and O'Leary continued to exchange letters through the winter and into the spring of 1941 — but with one important change. The patient no longer asked his doctor about his chances for survival.

In fact, he no longer mentioned his physical condition at all. Gehrig concerned himself almost entirely with the health problems of his friends and family. Eleanor was suffering from a terrible rash on her scalp and face. She'd tried radiation, but that only seemed to make it worse. Pitzy Katz, the comedian, drank too much and suffered blackouts and had finally agreed to see a doctor. Fred Fisher, the songwriter, was suffering abdominal pain. Bill Jurges, the Giants shortstop, was experiencing dizzy spells that jeopardized his career. Gehrig hoped that O'Leary or some of the other doctors at the Mayo might help.

Meanwhile, visitors to the house obeyed Eleanor's instructions, carrying on as if they fully expected Gehrig to overcome his illness. Gehrig played along, too, telling everyone that he would have to hit rock bottom before he could start climbing back. "I've still got a fifty-fifty chance," he repeated.

"I'm getting better, isn't that right, doc?" he would ask one of the doctors who visited his home to check on his condition. But he winked when he said it.

Meanwhile, paralysis was flattening him. Eleanor recalled:

There was no hope in it anywhere along the line, just downhill going, every day a little bit more downhill. . . . [He] just died away by inches, every day a little bit more, and if you saw him at the end of a week you couldn't remember what he had looked like at the beginning of the week. Every once in a while, when a new symptom came on, when another part of his body fell still on him and became dead, he'd break down somewhat and shake his head and say he didn't think he was going to come out of this thing so well, or say he wasn't so sure he was going to lick it. I would tell him I was sure he would . . . and after a while he'd be back to the way he was, that quiet way of his, that wonderful quiet way of his.

By the time spring set in, when baseball games buzzed on the radio again, buds grew on the trees, and the peacocks began parading across his lawn, Gehrig was fading fast. For months, he had insisted on rising to greet visitors at the door. Now, no longer able to do so, he made jokes. "I'm getting so lazy," he said.

In May, Tommy Henrich, his brother Eddie, and a few sportswriters drove up to Riverdale to visit the former Yankee. Eleanor poured the men glasses of whiskey and led them to a small bedroom on the first floor, a room that had probably been designed as the servant's quarters. Gehrig appeared to be permanently settled there, unable to get out of bed. It appeared to Henrich that Gehrig's weight had slipped to about 125 pounds. He didn't move at all. But somehow he managed to remain upbeat. The men spent an hour at Gehrig's bedside, sipping their drinks and talking baseball.

"I'll never forget what he said as we were going," Henrich recalled. "He said, 'Goodbye, boys, nice of you to come out here. The doc says I'm going to be all right. He said I have to go downhill and hit rock bottom before I come back.' "

The men exchanged uncertain glances.

"He knew," Henrich said. "He knew."

Eleanor poured milk shakes and orange juice into her husband's mouth to keep him from wasting away. It was no use. His ribs showed through his skin; his slender arms sat uselessly at his side; his legs turned to doughy lumps of flesh.

At times, only the strained sound of his breathing indicated that he was alive. When he could no longer speak, he continued to mouth the words: "Fifty-fifty."

By the middle of May, it was clear that little time remained. Day by day, his chest began to rise and fall more slowly, "like a great clock winding down," Eleanor said.

★ ★ ★

At ten o'clock in the morning on Monday, June 2, 1941, Eleanor, Nell Twitchell, and a doctor crowded around the bed. Gehrig was slipping away.

"My three pals," he said, looking up at them. A few minutes later, he fell into a coma.

The day went by. Christina and Henry joined the vigil by their son's bed. His eyes never opened. The light in the room faded. At ten minutes past ten o'clock that evening, he died.

Barrow and his wife were the first to arrive at the house after getting word that Gehrig was gone. Babe Ruth and his wife were next, showing up at about one in the morning, offering their condolences, and then quickly getting back in the car and driving home. The rest of the world had to wait until Tuesday morning to begin paying tribute.

"His death is a loss to me and the entire country," La Guardia said. "He was baseball and everything it stands for," Babe Dahlgren said. "He was a good influence on us young ballplayers," Joe DiMaggio said. "Baseball has lost one of its greatest players of all time," said Rogers Hornsby. "Gehrig was not only a great ballplayer but a real gentleman whose conduct on and off

641

the field set a standard to which all players may well aspire," said baseball's commissioner, Kenesaw Landis. "He was an example of good living, a great athlete, a grand fellow," said his old college coach, Andy Coakley.

Flags flew at half-staff all over New York City and at every baseball stadium in the nation that afternoon. At the Baseball Hall of Fame in Cooperstown, Gehrig's plaque was draped in black cloth. One writer commenting on Gehrig's death quoted a letter by former president Calvin Coolidge, who had lost his own son in 1924, in which Coolidge consoled another bereaved father, reassuring him that both of their boys, "by the grace of God, will be boys through eternity."

Eleanor decided to hold the funeral service at the Christ Protestant Episcopal Church, a small sanctuary across the street from her home in Riverdale. It had room enough for only about two hundred, but she was determined to keep the guest list even smaller than that. Originally, she didn't want any part of the memorial service open to the public. Gehrig's will didn't include any instructions for his funeral, but Eleanor said her husband had always disdained public memorials. Eventually, friends and relatives persuaded her to give New Yorkers an opportunity to pay tribute. On Tuesday afternoon, the day before the funeral, Gehrig's body, dressed in a dark blue, pinstriped suit, was put on view at the Church of the Divine Paternity, at Central Park West and 76th Street. Among the thousands who turned out were five members of the Commerce High baseball team, who carried with them their baseball caps and mitts, as if looking for a game. Babe Ruth showed up, cut through the line, and wept in front of the coffin.

Late in the afternoon, the body was transferred to the Christ Protestant Episcopal Church in Riverdale. By seven o'clock that evening, the line of people waiting to view the body stretched for three blocks. Eleanor could see them from her living room window.

The next morning, June 4, a cool rain pattered the trees. The ivy-covered church glistened in shades of green and gray. Inside, the altar was banked in flowers.

Christina and Henry Gehrig were the first to arrive. They were joined in the pew closest to the altar by Eleanor, Nell Twitchell, and Eleanor's brother, Frank Jr. The Yankees were in Detroit to play the Tigers, but Dickey and McCarthy had flown home to attend the funeral. The game that day was eventually rained out.

The ceremony began promptly at ten

o'clock. About one hundred people clustered inside the church. The service, which lasted about seven minutes, was as simple and straightforward as the public image of the man being remembered. Eleanor sat silently. Christina wept. The Reverend Gerald V. Barry read the Episcopal service for the dead. "The Lord gave and the Lord hath taken away," he said. He paused and announced there would be no eulogy.

"We need none," he said, "because you all knew him."

With that, Gehrig's mahogany coffin, blanketed in red roses, was carried to the hearse. His body was taken to the Fresh Pond Crematory in Queens, the same place his baby sister had been cremated thirty-five years earlier.

As the hearse pulled out of the church driveway and onto the Henry Hudson Parkway, hundreds of strangers stood in the pouring rain along the side of the road, saying goodbye.

EPILOGUE

Back in the summer of 1929, when Gehrig was single and still living with his parents, a young writer named Niven Busch Jr. of *The New Yorker* had come to his house in New Rochelle for an interview. By the summer of 1941, when Gehrig died, Busch was working as a story editor for Samuel Goldwyn, the Hollywood producer. He proposed to his boss that they make a movie about Gehrig's life.

"It's boxoffice poison," Goldwyn said. "If people want baseball, they go to the ballpark."

Busch persuaded his boss to watch newsreels from Lou Gehrig Appreciation Day at Yankee Stadium. The movie producer cried; then he ordered his projectionist to run the film again. Moments later, he phoned an associate in New York and told him to cut a deal with Gehrig's widow. Eleanor sold him the story rights for $30,000.

Goldwyn knew almost nothing about baseball, and the actor he chose to play Gehrig, Gary Cooper, perhaps knew even less. Cooper grew up riding horses in

Montana. It was evident to everyone on the set that he had never swung a baseball bat. He trained with professional players to learn a few fundamentals, but the right-handed actor still couldn't swing convincingly from the left side of the plate. Director Sam Wood used doubles for most of the long shots. Still, he wasn't satisfied. He needed some close-ups that showed Cooper hitting the ball. Finally, a film editor bailed him out with a clever suggestion: Let the actor bat right-handed and run to third base. They would have him wear a reversed Number 4 on his back. Then they would flip the film so it would look as though the actor were swinging from the left side and running to first.

Fortunately for Cooper, there were not a lot of baseball scenes in Paul Gallico's script. Goldwyn wanted a love story, not a baseball movie. He wanted people to see that Gehrig's heroism sprung not from his baseball abilities but from his humility and courage. Teresa Wright, who would soon marry Niven Busch, was cast in the role of Eleanor. Walter Brennan played a sportswriter loosely modeled on Fred Lieb. Babe Ruth, after a crash diet enabled him to fit into the old pinstripes, co-starred as himself.

Eleanor — the real one, not the actress

— played a powerful role behind the scenes. When Gehrig's parents were written into the wedding scene, Eleanor reminded Goldwyn that Christina and Henry hadn't attended the ceremony. She made wardrobe suggestions, too. Finally, in a letter regarding the film's climax, she urged the producer not to depart from the text of her husband's famous farewell speech.

If you were to look at my scrapbooks and see the reaction this simple speech made you would realize how important the wording of the authentic speech is to the picture. The reason the sports writers did not copy it down in full is because it was so touching and spontaneous that the speech was over before they could recover enough to jot it down verbatim. But it was that speech that brought tears to the thousands in the Yankee Stadium and I feel if you should depart from the original you would lose all of the simple charm.

She urged the producer not to leave out any of the people Gehrig thanked that humid day. "You see, the whole charm of the closing scene seems to me to be the fact that Lou thanked everyone even remotely connected with his career for making him the 'luckiest man on earth.' It never occurred to him to give himself credit."

Eleanor was right: None of the writers at the game that day had recorded a full transcript of her husband's remarks. In fact, even the newsreel companies and radio stations failed to save a complete recording. Only four sentences of the original speech survive on tape today. The rest of the text has been pieced together from various newspaper accounts. But Cooper's rendition bore only a loose resemblance to the original. Cooper recited correctly Gehrig's most famous line — "Today, I consider myself the luckiest man on the face of the earth" — but the actor finished his speech with those words, whereas Gehrig used them near the beginning.

By the time the movie was released, American men were going off to war. Goldwyn wanted to be certain that women would buy tickets, so he decided to call the film *The Pride of the Yankees*, not *The Lou Gehrig Story*. In fact, Gehrig's name appeared nowhere on the film's posters. Goldwyn used the Irving Berlin song "Always" to add an extra touch of romance and included a nightclub scene starring the dance team of Velez and Yolanda. The movie was a huge success at the box office and received nine Academy Award nominations. It is still considered one of the best baseball movies ever made.

★ ★ ★

In the summer after their son's death, Christina and Henry Gehrig compiled a long list of grievances against their daughter-in-law. Henry asked if he might have his son's tiny fishing boat, *The Water Wagon*. Eleanor said she intended to sell it. Christina requested some of her son's clothing. Eleanor refused. It's not clear whether Gehrig's parents wanted their son's feisty little dog, Yankee, but Eleanor certainly didn't. "I ordered the hound destroyed after he had made a pass at my mother," she wrote in a letter to Christy Walsh, "but the vet did not have the heart to do away with a healthy dog." Thanks to the vet's intervention, a family in Connecticut adopted the pet.

Gehrig's will, completed two months before his death, at a time when he could no longer sign his name, would prove the biggest source of conflict. A lawyer and two women — probably nurses — witnessed Gehrig's approval of the two-page document. But his parents were skeptical. Gehrig's estate was valued at about $160,000. Christina and Henry were awarded an allowance of $205 a month. Eleanor received $14,000 in bonds and a stock portfolio worth about $50,000. Christina and Henry were allowed to hold on to whatever trophies were in their possession, but only as custodians. Legally, the trophies belonged to Eleanor.

Christina and Henry asked a politically connected friend to help them present a letter of complaint. When Eleanor received the letter, she sent it on to Milton Eisenberg, the lawyer who had handled Gehrig's libel case against the *Daily News*. "I am down here nursing the worst heart break a woman will ever have to bear," she wrote the lawyer from Los Angeles, "but there are certain limits to what I will accept from trouble makers. Please advise me what steps I can take if this outrage persists."

Eisenberg suggested that Eleanor might avoid a lot of stress if she agreed to give the Gehrigs $1,000 or $1,500 for their cooperation with the movie. But in connection with the will, he assured his client she had nothing to worry about. If necessary, Eisenberg wrote, he would remind Christina and Henry that they were still citizens of Germany and that the United States government could freeze their assets with little cause. Eisenberg didn't say why the government might take such action, but in the summer of 1941, with Hitler's troops ravaging Europe and the call for American intervention growing louder, German immigrants were easily intimidated. Christina and Henry eventually hired a lawyer and filed a lawsuit contesting the distribution of their son's estate. They settled the matter out of court. The terms were never disclosed.

Christina and Henry faded from public view not long after their son's death. They left their home in New Rochelle and moved to Mount Vernon, New York. In 1944, they both became citizens of the United States. Two years later, at the age of seventy-nine, Henry was dead. Christina died in 1954, age seventy-two.

Eleanor Gehrig, widowed at the age of thirty-six, never remarried and never had children. She dedicated much of her life to the enrichment of her husband's legacy. For the better part of four decades she appeared at Yankee old-timer games, at Hall of Fame inductions, and at fundraisers for ALS research. But she never settled peacefully into her solitary life. Her drinking, always somewhat heavy, became intense. She died on March 6, 1984, her eightieth birthday. She had no surviving relatives. She bequeathed more than $180,000 to medical research and asked that most of it go toward finding a cure for Lou Gehrig's disease. Her body was cremated and her ashes placed beside those of her husband, in a crypt at Kensico Cemetery in Valhalla, New York. The tombstone contains no inscription and no decoration. Only the balls, bats, and gloves left occasionally in the grass by fans indicate the resting place of a baseball player.

The record Gehrig cherished most was broken on September 6, 1995. Cal Ripken Jr. of the Baltimore Orioles played in his 2,131st game on a warm night in Baltimore in which he went 2-for-4 and hit a home run. He was thirty-five years old, the same age as Gehrig when he began showing symptoms of ALS. President Bill Clinton, Vice President Al Gore, and Joe DiMaggio were at the game. Also in attendance were 260 fans who paid $5,000 each for special box seats near the field. The money went to charity, including a fund for ALS. At the end of an hour-long postgame ceremony on the field at Camden Yards, Ripken stepped to the microphone and said: "Tonight, I stand here, overwhelmed, as my name is linked with the great and courageous Lou Gehrig."

Soon after Gehrig's death, Dr. Israel Wechsler began shutting down his research on vitamin E. The ALS patients that he had written about so enthusiastically were all dead or dying. Wechsler's instincts had been solid. Some doctors still believe vitamin E, a potent antioxidant, holds promise for the treatment of ALS, but as of this writing no one has made good on the theory. Wechsler's big mistake wasn't his hunch. His error was mostly procedural. He failed to include a control group in his studies. If he had administered vitamin E to one group of patients and a placebo to another, he probably would have found that both groups experienced more or less the same results. In a way, he was undone by his own enthusiasm. Those patients who enjoyed brief improvement under his care probably did so because they wanted so desperately to please their doctor.

Today, about five thousand Americans a year are diagnosed with ALS. Scientists still don't know what causes the disease, and they still don't have a cure. Most patients die within two or three years of diagnosis. In other words, not much has changed since 1941. The biggest difference, perhaps, is that the malady is now widely referred to in the United States as Lou Gehrig's disease. Gehrig helped lift this rare and poorly understood malady from obscurity. Countless millions of dollars have been raised for scientific research thanks in good part to his name.

Many neurologists still hang pictures of the ballplayer in their offices and examination rooms. When they break the news to patients with ALS, they almost always invoke his name. "It hits them like a fastball between the eyes," says Dr. Anthony J. Windebank of the Mayo Clinic. "Everyone knows Gehrig died young." But after the initial shock, patients often reflect on Gehrig's response to his diagnosis rather than the outcome of his illness.

ALS is a disease of weakness, but Lou Gehrig's disease is associated with strength — the strength of a stricken man who said he felt lucky.

ACKNOWLEDGMENTS

I could not have written this book without a lot of help.

Thanks, first, to David Black, a great agent and friend. He believed in the power of this story when it was little more than a glimmer of an idea. In David's office, thanks also to Jason Sacher, Joy Tutela, and Leigh Ann Eliseo.

A writer longs for the chance to work with an editor like Robert Bender at Simon & Schuster. From start to finish he has guided me with warm and wise advice. At Simon & Schuster, thanks also to Nancy Inglis, Johanna Li, Victoria Meyer, Rachel Nagler, Emily Remes, and David Rosenthal. Thanks to Linda Stern for her extraordinary copy editing.

I am grateful for the support of George Pollack, Eleanor Gehrig's longtime attorney, who generously shared his recollections and allowed me to review some of his files. He also gave me permission to quote from Gehrig's personal letters. Mrs. Gehrig was fortunate to have such a loyal friend.

One snowy morning in the winter of 2003 I drove to Libertyville, Illinois, to visit David Bushing, a dealer in baseball memorabilia. His basement contained wondrous things, including a hickory bat owned by Babe Ruth and a Brooklyn Dodgers uniform worn by Jackie Robinson in his rookie season. But I had come to see something more mundane: Bushing's collection of auction catalogs. By scanning those catalogs, I hoped to pick up a few more details of Lou Gehrig's life. What size hat did he wear? What did his grade-school graduation pictures look like? Then I experienced a thrilling moment. In a Christie's auction catalog from 1998, I spotted a collection of Gehrig's personal letters that had been preserved by one of his doctors, Paul O'Leary of the Mayo Clinic. With help from Bushing and Seth Swirsky, who taught me about the world of baseball memorabilia, I began my hunt for those letters. I had no idea how many letters were in the collection or what they said. After months of searching, I finally found them. They'd been purchased at auction by James W. Ancel, owner of a Baltimore construction company. After a few long and friendly discussions about baseball and history, Ancel agreed to meet me and hand over copies of the letters, which brought Gehrig to life for me in a way that nothing else had. Jim's a great baseball fan with a powerful respect for the game's past. I can't thank him enough.

Henry Yee, another devoted Gehrig collector, allowed me to review his amazing collection of Gehrig photographs. Barry Halper tipped me to some wonderful pieces of Gehrig memorabilia. Dr. Goodman B. Espy also sent copies of his Gehrig photos.

Interviewing former ballplayers provided another big thrill. Thank you Elden Auker, Harry Danning, Charlie Devens, Vince DiMaggio, Bobby Doerr, Dutch Fehring, Bob Feller, Floyd Giebell, Don Gutteridge, Mel Harder, Ray Hayworth, Tommy Henrich, Bill Hitchcock, Willis Hudlin, Eddie Joost, Ernie Koy, Dario Lodigiani, Al Lopez, Walter Masterson, Bud Metheny, Al Milnar, Buck O'Neill, Claude Passeau, Fred Rice, Phil Rizzuto, Billy Rogell, Marius Russo, Robert Stevens, Johnny Sturm, Gene Thompson, Cecil Travis, Mickey Vernon, Johnny Welaj, and Billy Werber. Special thanks to Janet Klaer for helping me get to know her wonderful father, Johnny Welaj. He and some of the others listed above died before this book went to press. It was my privilege to speak with them and share their stories.

At the Baseball Hall of Fame, thanks to Bill Burdick, Jim Gates, Jeff Idelson, and Susan MacKay. At the Bronx Supreme Court, thanks to Gary Byrenbaum and

Mark Nusenbaum. At Yankee Stadium, thanks to Rick Cerrone and Arthur Richman. At the Metropolitan Opera, thanks to Robert Tuggle. Thanks to Katie Dishman at General Mills and Anne Jewell at Hillerich & Bradsby. Thanks also to Ross Adell, Lewis and Judy Eig, Bill James, Peter Mustich, Jeffery Schams, Scott Schleifer, Leslie Silverman, David Vincent, and Jay Youmans. Thanks to writers Ray Bradbury, Joe Durso, Richard Ben Cramer, Robert Creamer, David Nasaw, and Ken Sobol.

I know now why Lou Gehrig felt so at home in Rochester, Minnesota. The staff at the Mayo Clinic gave me a warm welcome and provided enormous help with this book. Special thanks go to Alexander Lucas, Mayo's archivist, who worked tirelessly and with great attention to detail. At the Mayo, thanks also to Drs. Donald Mulder, Anthony J. Windebank, and Christopher Boes. I am deeply grateful to Dr. J. A. Van Gerpen, a former Mayo Clinic neurologist, now at the Ochsner Clinic in New Orleans, who was drawn to the field by a profound admiration for Lou Gehrig. He patiently answered all my questions about neurology. I am indebted to Hank Woltman and John Woltman for remembrances of their father, Dr. Henry Woltman; to Dr. Harold C. Habein Jr. for sharing the memoirs of his father; and to Nancy Bragdon and Tom Horton for memories of their father, Dr. Bayard Horton. Dr. Louis Linn provided vivid details concerning his father-in-law, Dr. Israel Wechsler.

I had a great team helping me gather newspaper clips from libraries around the country. Thanks to Chase Behringer, Dalia Naamani-Goldman, Alexis Hoffman, Megan Merrill, Peter Nasaw, Joel Nierman, Kenn Ruby, Estee Rivka Schulman, and Pearl Wu. Thanks also to Roger Boye at Northwestern University for helping to find so many of those terrific researchers. Those nine comprised my starting lineup, but I also had some fine pinch hitters. In Norfolk, Clay Shampoe; in Detroit, Dan Shine and Ruthie Miles; in New Orleans, Arthur Schott; at the public library in New Rochelle, Beth Mills; at *The Sporting News*, Steve Gietschier; at LaGuardia Community College, Joe Margolis and Richard Lieberman; at the New York City municipal archives, Brian Andersson and Kenneth Cobb.

I am grateful for the help of many librarians, including those working at the Chicago Public Library; Chicago's Newberry Library; the Chicago Historical Society; the Galter Health Sciences Library; the Olmsted County Historical Society in Minnesota; the St. Petersburg Museum of History; the archives of Hebrew University; the Columbia University Archives and Columbiana Library; the New York Public Library; the New York Transit Museum; the Bronx County Historical Society; and the New York Historical Society. Special thanks to the Society for American Baseball Research, a fantastic organization.

I am grateful to Eleanore Jonas for inviting me to visit the home in New Rochelle where Gehrig and his parents lived. Thanks, also, to Stephen Kaminsky and his family for welcoming me into their home in Riverdale, where Gehrig spent his final years.

My appreciation goes to Bill Deane for scouring my manuscript in search of misstated baseball facts; Kathryn Jolowicz for giving me a great tour of Yorkville; June Herr for helping me identify some of Gehrig's ancestors; Mark Spiegler, Sabine Schleichert, and Hans Peter Voss for assisting in my search for family records in Germany; Elizabeth Angell, Daniela Barberis, and Dr. Lewis Rowland for helping me better understand the history of ALS research; and Ela Kotkowska for translating medical papers from French to English.

I am eternally indebted to Bryan Gruley and Robert Kurson, who read the manuscript with great care and made terrific suggestions. I am also grateful to friends Ron Jackson, Bob Kazel, Josh Prager, and Heidi Trilling, who read portions of the manuscript. Special thanks to five people who have shown faith in me and taught me a lot about writing: Richard Babcock, Joseph Epstein, Kevin Helliker, Mike Miller, and Keith Woods.

I was always at home when I traveled to New York to work on this book. For that, thanks and love to my brother, Matt, his wife, Penny, and their amazing boys, Jake and Ben.

My parents spent an afternoon digging through dusty closets and scaling tall bookshelves at P.S. 132 in Manhattan, trying to help me locate Gehrig's grade-school report cards. We came up empty, but it hardly mattered. As always, my mother and father were there for me all the way, with loving encouragement.

Finally, this book is dedicated to my wife, Jennifer Tescher, who makes everything possible. Her brilliant advice and insights are in evidence on every page. To thank her properly would require another manuscript of much greater length and containing considerably more mush. She and our daughter, Lillian, have made me a very lucky man.

APPENDIX
Lou Gehrig's Career Statistics

ANNUAL STATISTICS

	G	AB	R	H	2B	3B	HR
1923	13	26	6	11	4	1	1
1924	10	12	2	6	1	0	0
1925	126	437	73	129	23	10	20
1926	155	572	135	179	47	**20**	16
1927	155	584	149	218	**52**	18	47
1928	154	562	139	210	47	13	27
1929	154	553	127	166	32	10	35
1930	154	581	143	220	42	17	41
1931	155	619	**163**	**211**	31	15	**46**
1932	156	596	138	208	42	9	34
1933	152	593	**138**	198	41	12	32
1934	154	579	128	210	40	6	**49**
1935	149	535	**125**	176	26	10	30
1936	155	579	**167**	205	37	7	**49**
1937	157	569	138	200	37	9	37
1938	157	576	115	170	32	6	29
1939	8	28	2	4	0	0	0
Lifetime	2,164	8,001	1,888	2,721	534	163	493

Boldface numerals indicate a league-leading total.

WORLD SERIES STATISTICS

	Op	W/L	G	AB	R	H	2B
1926	STL	L	7	23	1	8	2
1927	PIT	W	4	13	2	4	2
1928	STL	W	4	11	5	6	1
1932	CHC	W	4	17	9	9	1
1936	NYG	W	6	24	5	7	1
1937	NYG	W	5	17	4	5	1
1938	CHC	W	4	14	4	4	0
Total			34	119	30	43	8

RBI	SB	CS	Walks	SO	AVG	OBP	SLG
9	0	0	2	5	.423	.464	.769
5	0	0	1	3	.500	.538	.583
68	6	3	46	49	.295	.365	.531
112	6	5	105	73	.313	.420	.549
175	10	8	109	84	.373	.474	.765
142	4	11	95	69	.374	**.467**	.648
126	4	4	122	68	.300	.431	.584
174	12	14	101	63	.379	.473	.721
184	17	12	117	56	.341	.446	.662
151	4	11	108	38	.349	.451	.621
139	9	13	92	42	.334	.424	.605
165	9	5	109	31	**.363**	**.465**	**.706**
119	8	7	**132**	38	.329	**.466**	.583
152	3	4	**130**	46	.354	**.478**	**.696**
159	4	3	**127**	49	.351	.473	.643
114	6	1	107	75	.295	.410	.523
1	0	0	5	1	.143	.273	.143
1,995	102	101	1,508	790	.340	.447	.632

3B	HR	RBI	Walks	SO	AVG	OBP	SLG
0	0	4	5	4	.348	.464	.435
2	0	4	3	3	.308	.389	.769
0	4	9	6	0	.545	.706	1.727
0	3	8	2	1	.529	.600	1.118
0	2	7	3	2	.292	.393	.583
1	1	3	5	4	.294	.455	.647
0	0	0	2	3	.286	.375	.286
3	10	35	26	17	.361	.477	.731

FIELDING

	Position	G	PO	E	FPCT
1923	1B	9	53	4	.933
1924	1B	2	9	0	1.000
	OF	1	1	0	1.000
1925	1B	114	1126	13	.989
	OF	6	9	2	.818
1926	1B	155	1566	15	.991
1927	1B	155	1662	15	.992
1928	1B	154	1488	18	.989
1929	1B	154	1458	9	.994
1930	1B	153	1298	15	.989
	OF	1	2	0	1.000
1931	1B	154	1352	13	.991
	OF	1	3	1	.750
1932	1B	156	1293	18	.987
1933	1B	152	1290	9	.993
1934	1B	153	1284	8	.994
	SS	1	0	0	.000
1935	1B	149	1337	15	.990
1936	1B	155	1377	9	.994
1937	1B	157	1370	16	.989
1938	1B	157	1483	14	.991
1939	1B	8	64	2	.971
Total		2147	19525	196	.991

Source: *Total Baseball*, 8th edition, 2004, SPORT
Media Publishing, Inc.; www.mlb.com; www.baseball-
reference.com

BASEBALL ABBREVIATIONS

AB	At Bats
AVG	Batting Average
CS	Caught Stealing
G	Games Played
H	Hits
2B	Doubles
3B	Triples
HR	Home Runs
OBP	On-base Percentage
R	Runs Scored
RBI	Runs Batted In
SB	Stolen Bases
SLG	Slugging Percentage
SO	Strikeouts
E	Errors
FPCT	Fielding Percentage
PO	Putouts

NOTES

This book relies almost entirely on primary materials: newspapers, periodicals, oral histories, government records, church registers, newsreel footage, photographs, private letters and interviews. Nothing here is invented or interpreted. I have taken no literary liberties. I am deeply indebted to the sports writers who covered Gehrig's career. At the same time, journalistic standards of the day permitted more embellishment than readers today have come to expect. Quotes were polished routinely. Unlikely anecdotes were passed along as fact. I have tried in all instances possible to separate the myth from reality. I've corrected some of the most egregious errors, flagged some of the tales that were difficult to verify or suspicious, and omitted many that were too close to call. In every possible instance facts have been confirmed by multiple sources. When conflicts arose, I put my trust in articles written during Gehrig's lifetime rather than anecdotes told years or decades later. Eleanor Gehrig's scrapbook, contained in the archives at the Hall of Fame, held a wealth of newspaper clippings and photos, some of which did not include dates or headlines. In the following section, when a scrapbook entry lacks a date, a headline, or a newspaper name, I indicate the source with the abbreviation SB. Some newspaper stories listed here carry incomplete citations because they have been reprinted on Web sites or in books without their original headlines. I was fortunate to discover the private letters of Gehrig and his primary physician, Dr. Paul O'Leary of the Mayo Clinic. O'Leary preserved Gehrig's letters, as well as carbon copies of his responses. Years later, one of O'Leary's children sold the letters at auction. The yellowed pages are now in the hands of a memorabilia collector named James W. Ancel, who displays a few of them at his Maryland office and keeps the rest under lock and key. Ancel generously provided me copies of the letters, and Gehrig's estate granted me permission to reprint their contents. I have made a handful of small corrections to Gehrig's spelling and punctuation, simply for the sake of clarity; otherwise the letters are presented exactly as Gehrig wrote them. It is my hope that the letters eventually will become part of a library collection so that everyone can read Gehrig's courageous words.

crowd hushed: Newsreel footage, July 4, 1939; newspaper accounts, July 5, 1939.

For the first time . . . Gehrig was afraid: "Fun-Loving Guy Brings a Smile to Lou's Face," *New York Post,* July 5, 1939.

More than 61,000: Ibid.; "61,808 Fans Roar Tribute to Gehrig," *New York Times,* July 5, 1939.

imperceptible shake of the head: Newsreel footage, July 4, 1939.

Workers moved into position: *Washington Post,* July 5, 1939.

whispered in his ear: Newsreel footage, July 4, 1939.

I. THE SURVIVOR

usually at the local tavern: Eleanor Gehrig and Joseph Durso, *My Luke and I* (New York: Thomas Y. Crowell Company, 1976), p. 31.

seventh of nine children: Church registers, Adelsheim, Germany.

Sophia gave birth: Ibid.

identifying themselves as The Gehrigs: Ibid.

Heinrich left Germany: U.S. citizenship application, 1941.

Anna Christina Fack was born: Church registers, Schleswig-Holstein, Germany.

She left home in May: Ellis Island passenger record, 1900.

She had twenty-five dollars: Ibid.

Their first child, Anna Christina: Birth certificate, New York City Municipal Archives.

242 East 94th Street: Ibid.

Anna Gehrig died in the family apartment: Death certificate, New York City Municipal Archives.

Christina's second child was born: Birth certificate, New York City Municipal Archives.

Sophie Louise . . . was born: Ibid.

roast beef . . . and pie: Gehrig and Durso, *My Luke and I,* p. 32.

hustled Lou out of the house: Ibid., p. 36.

". . . resented the fact . . .": Gehrig and Durso, *My Luke and I,* p. 36.

Sophie . . . became sick: Death certificate, New York City Municipal Archives, 1906.

Christina would boast: Fred Lieb, "The Life of Lou Gehrig," *Baseball Register* (St. Louis: C.C. Spink & Son, 1942), p. 5.

"I don't pretend . . .": Ibid.

"Al Smith cigars . . .": "Lou Gehrig Gives Baseball Full Credit for Rescuing Parents and Self from New York Tenement District," *Sporting News,* December 25, 1930.

2. "BABE" GEHRIG

"Fat": Ibid.

"We kids used to get up and play . . .": Ibid.

"Back in the days . . .": "Gehrig Learned to Hit Homers by Watching Babe Ruth in Action," *SB,* 1927.

"We didn't have a baseball . . .": Lawrence S. Ritter, *The Glory of Their Times* (New York: William Morrow, 1985), p. 205.

"The only way you could hit . . .": Ibid., p. 227.

"Some ballplayers . . .": "Meet Lou Gehrig, a Pretty Fair Country Ball Player," *Washington Post,* June 9, 1940.

mitt for the wrong hand: Gehrig and Durso, *My Luke and I,* 33.

Their neighbors, the Gallaghers: U.S. Census, 1910.

gymnastics club and social hall: Stan W. Carlson, *Lou Gehrig: Baseball's Iron Man* (Minneapolis: Stan W. Carlson, 1940), p. 16.

more taunting than ever: Gehrig and Durso, *My Luke and I,* p. 35.

insisted on knickers: Richard Hubler, *Lou Gehrig: The Iron Horse of Baseball* (Boston: Houghton Mifflin, 1941), p. 16.

"I wanted to play ball . . .": "Lou Gehrig Gives Baseball Full Credit . . . ,"

671

Sporting News, December 25, 1930.

Oliver Gintel . . . claimed: Paul Gallico, *Lou Gehrig: Pride of the Yankees* (New York: Grosset & Dunlap, 1942), p. 44.

"We set to work . . .": Frank Graham, *Lou Gehrig: A Quiet Hero* (New York: G. P. Putnam's Sons, 1942), p. 12.

"No one who went to school . . .": Gallico, *Lou Gehrig: Pride of the Yankees,* p. 43.

the crowd shoved and screamed: Chicago Tribune, June 25, 1920.

"The Gotham boys . . .": "Parade, Autos to Welcome N.Y. Prep Champions," *Chicago Tribune,* June 25, 1930.

Taft slipped away: Chicago Tribune, June 26, 1920.

tucked their uniforms under their arms: New York *Daily News,* June 26, 1920.

"Louis Gherig . . . displayed": " 'World Series' of High Schools On Here Today," *Chicago Tribune,* June 26, 1920.

"The crowd was beginning to wonder": "New York Preps Down Lane Tech in Hitfest, 12-6," *Chicago Tribune,* June 27, 1920.

Keep . . . he told himself: Chicago Tribune, June 27, 1920.

"I couldn't believe I had knocked a ball . . .": "Lou Gehrig, Baseball's Iron Horse," *Dime Sport Magazine,* October 1935.

stuffed it in a drawer: Gehrig and Durso, *My Luke and I,* p. 38.

Dartmouth and the University of Pennsylvania: "Gehrig Learned to Hit Homers . . . ," *SB,* 1927.

Christina wasn't ready: Ibid.

fans overflowed bleachers: "Commerce Beaten by Clinton Eleven," *New York Times,* November 26, 1920.

enrolled in . . . extension program: student transcript, Columbia University.

wearing a sweatshirt: "Lou Gehrig Recalls His Days in the Minors," *Sporting News,* November 9, 1933.

"Life without baseball . . .": "Giants Among Men," *Sports Illustrated,* August 25, 2003.

hit seven balls into the . . . stands: "Gehrig's Shadow Still Hexes First Base," *SB,* 1952.

"did not give me too much attention . . .": "Galloping Down Memory Lane," *Sporting News,* April 22, 1937.

"I have often thought . . .": Ibid.

He didn't own a dinner jacket: Gallico, *Lou Gehrig: Pride of the Yankees,* p. 66.

"Oh, this is all I need": Sam Dana, telephone interview.

"Handsome as he was . . .": Gallico, *Lou Gehrig: Pride of the Yankees,* p. 66.

"He was sorta shyish": Sam Dana, telephone interview.

flunked English and German: Student transcript, Columbia University.

earned Cs on both exams: Ibid.

"Buck O'Neill always . . .": "Life of Lou Gehrig," *Baseball Register,* 1942.

"Lou was stubborn . . .": Ibid.

"I tackled him head-on . . .": Sam Dana, telephone interview.

"Judged by college baseball standards": Graham, *Lou Gehrig: A Quiet Hero,* p. 48.

"And when I saw the way he swung . . .": "Gehrig Learned to Hit Homers . . . ," *SB,* 1927.

Gehrig's name came up: Graham, *Lou Gehrig: A Quiet Hero,* p. 51.

"I had a lot of confidence . . .": Ed Barrow, with James M. Kahn, *My Forty Years in Baseball* (New York: Coward-McCann, 1951), p. 148.

4. THE BEHEMOTH OF BING

"They were rough guys": Bill Werber, telephone interview.

Miller Huggins . . . was in his office: Hubler, *Lou Gehrig: The Iron Horse of Baseball,* p. 30.

socks up to his knees: Photo, New York *Evening Post,* June 14, 1923.

"Get a bat": Graham, *Lou Gehrig: A Quiet*

Hero, pp. 67–70.

"We all knew . . .": Ibid., p. 70.

"Did you ever hear the story . . .": "Lou Gehrig, Baseball's Iron Horse," *Dime Sport Magazine,* October 1935.

"Paddy always took a fatherly interest . . .": "Lou Gehrig Recalls His Days in the Minors," *Sporting News,* November 9, 1933.

"stealer of Babe Ruth's thunder": "60,000 See Hartford Take Two Games from Pittsfield and Gehrig Hit Brace of Homers," *Hartford Courant,* August 12, 1923.

"I couldn't hit . . .": "Galloping Down Memory Lane," *Sporting News,* April 22, 1937.

"I've never seen anyone suffer . . .": Robert Rubin, *Lou Gehrig: Courageous Star* (New York: G. P. Putnam's Sons, 1979), p. 69.

"He looked like a tramp": Ibid.

Krichell . . . took the train to Hartford: Graham, *Lou Gehrig: A Quiet Hero,* pp. 80–82.

"I decided not to quit . . .": "Galloping Down Memory Lane," *Sporting News,* April 22, 1937.

" 'Lou' is already . . .": "Homers by Ted Hauk and Lou Gehrig Bring 4-1 Win Over Bridgeport," *The Hartford Times,* September 1, 1923.

"Lou . . . you have a great career ahead . . .":
Ibid.

"He has shown no . . .": "Gehrig Recalled
By Miller Huggins," *The Hartford Courant,* September 23, 1923.

Gloria Swanson arrived: Graham McNamee,
You're on the Air (New York and
London: Harper & Brothers, 1926), pp.
52–53.

"The crowd is ready, yowling . . .": "Pandemonium on Radio as Fans Cheer
Haines Taming 'Murderers' Row,' " *St.
Louis Post-Dispatch,* October 6, 1926.

*"I don't know which game to write
about . . .":* Jules Tygiel, *Past Time:
Baseball as History* (New York: Oxford
University Press, 2000), p. 71.

5. GOODBYE, MR. PIPP

office clerk at the New York Edison Company:
Lou Gehrig, "Am I Jealous of Babe
Ruth?" *Liberty,* August 19, 1933; "Lou
Recalls Another Spring," *SB,* April 3,
1931.

"The fall dragged along": "Lou Recalls Another Spring," *SB,* April 3, 1931.

"I signed it . . .": Ibid.

twelve dollars in his pocket: "Gehrig Started
Career with $12 in His Pockets," *SB,*
September 19, 1932.

slack-jawed: "Lou Recalls Another Spring," *SB*, April 3, 1931.

"He was a fine boy": John Tullius, *I'd Rather Be a Yankee* (New York: Macmillan, 1986), p. 74.

walk the city's crooked streets alone: "Lou Recalls Another Spring," *SB*, April 3, 1931.

he excused himself: "With Lou in Louisiana," *New York Journal-American*, February 13, 1952.

"Lines were sharply drawn . . .": "Lou Recalls Another Spring," *SB*, April 3, 1931.

"I like that big first baseman": "Fred Clark Says Ghrig [*sic*] Looks Like a Sensation," *Times-Picayune*, March 17, 1924.

"My first thought was to step out . . .": "Lou Recalls Another Spring," *SB*, April 3, 1931.

"When I started the 1924 season . . .": "Lou Gehrig, Baseball's Iron Horse," *Dime Sport Magazine*, October 1935.

using Gehrig as a reserve outfielder: "Yanks to Abandon New Orleans Camp," *New York Times*, January 31, 1924.

Miller Huggins believes . . .": "Gehrig Leaves Yanks to Play Under Option with Hartford," *New York Times*, April 15, 1924.

"clearing the heads": " 'Buster' Gehrig Cele-

brates 21st Birthday By Crashing Out Homer, Double and Triple," *Hartford Courant,* June 20, 1924.

"20 YEARS IN GAME": Detroit Times, September 21, 1924.

added a sharp insult: "Tyger Notes," *Detroit News,* September 22, 1924.

Gehrig worried that he might be traded: "Galloping Down Memory Lane," *Sporting News,* April 22, 1937.

Pipp might be offered to the Browns: "Shocker Bush Trade to Go Through Soon," *Washington Post,* December 13, 1924.

"he is rated by Yankee owners . . .": "Many Booming Yank Rookie for Babe's Title," New Orleans *Times-Picayune,* March 1, 1924.

Huggins was frustrated: "Huggins' 'Broadway Butterflies' Charged with Mutiny in Gossip," *Sporting News,* June 11, 1925.

never complained of recurring headaches: Thomas Pipp and Wally Pipp, Jr., telephone interviews.

"Huggins has arrived . . .": Sporting News, June 11, 1925.

"The old order . . .": "Yankees Defeat Senators, 8-5, and End Losing Streak," *Herald Tribune,* June 3, 1925.

"If you were even half my size . . .": Robert W. Creamer, *Babe: The Legend Comes to*

Life (New York: Simon & Schuster, 1974), p. 293.

"That was the great kick of my career . . .": "Lou Gehrig, Baseball's Iron Horse," *Dime Sport Magazine*, October 1935.

tucked it in his wallet: "Lou Insists Writers Omitted One Game in 1925," *SB*, August 2, 1933.

6. COMING OF AGE

younger women . . . thought her crude: Fred Lieb, *Baseball As I Have Known It* (New York: Coward, McCann & Geoghegan, 1977), p. 174.

"Dear Judge Landis": Archives, National Baseball Hall of Fame and Museum, Cooperstown, New York.

The men were hysterical: Ken Sobol, *Babe Ruth and the American Dream* (New York: Ballantine Books, 1974), p. 9.

"He was just hopeless": Ibid., p. 213.

"Babe is the color . . .": "Cards Fans Jam Streets Getting Game by Radio," *St. Louis Post-Dispatch*, October 3, 1926.

brought soapboxes from home: "World Series Sidelights," *St. Louis Post-Dispatch*, October 5, 1926.

"I ain't got no twenty-five dollars . . .": Ibid.

Lotty Schoemmell jumped into the Hudson: "Woman Begins Swim down the Hudson," *New York Times,* October 11, 1926.

took the ball, rolled it around: "Valiant Alexander Turns Back Threats," *New York Times,* October 11, 1926.

"Hustling is rather overrated . . .": Leo Trachtenberg, *The Wonder Team* (Bowling Green State University Popular Press, 1995), p. 41.

"Now who the hell is Johnny Sylvester?": Robert W. Creamer, *Babe: The Legend Comes to Life,* p. 328.

"It was boring as hell": Ken Sobol, *Babe Ruth and the American Dream,* p. 209.

7. SINNER AND SAINT

"Every time I think": New York Telegram, March 23, 1927.

Yankees had considered trading Gehrig: New York World, February 20, 1927.

Ruth had earned $20,000: "Sports of the Times," *New York Times,* March 1, 1927.

"You can say for me . . .": New York *Daily Mirror,* March 3, 1927.

"widespread neurosis": F. Scott Fitzgerald, "Echoes of the Jazz Age," *Scribner's Magazine,* November 1931.

announced a few rules: New York *Evening Journal,* April 1, 1927.

"unhappy little man": "Miller Huggins, Unhappy Warrior, Overcame Ridicule, Hatred, Prima Donnas to Lead Earlier Yanks to Top," *Sporting News,* November 2, 1939.

"You big, stupid clown": Joe Williams column, *New York World-Telegram,* December 27, 1938.

"This is my year of vindication": Ty Cobb with Al Stump, *My Life in Baseball* (Lincoln and London: University of Nebraska Press, 1993), p. 250.

"The weather was lovely": "Yankees Beat Athletics, 8-3, in Opening Game," *New York Times,* April 13, 1927.

"No question . . .": New York *World,* April 13, 1927.

"Huggins knew what he was doing . . .": New York *Sun,* April 15, 1927.

"This giant of a youth . . .": New York *Evening World,* April 29, 1927.

"Babe Ruth and Buster Gehrig": "Yanks Bow to Senators," *New York Times,* May 24, 1927.

ribs and bottles of booze: John Mosedale, *The Greatest of All* (New York: Warner, 1975), p. 86.

"If you had nine Combses . . .": Trachtenberg, *The Wonder Team,* p. 67.

"This is just an easy park . . .": "Yanks Make Sweep of Detroit Series," *New York Times,* August 27, 1927.

he named one ass Babe: Trachtenberg, *The Wonder Team,* p. 22.

"When we got to the ballpark": Donald Honig, *Baseball America* (New York: Macmillan, 1985), p. 162.

"dancing academies, drug stores . . .": John Kobler, *Ardent Spirits: The Rise and Fall of Prohibition* (New York: Da Capo Press, 1993), pp. 234–235.

"With only a few exceptions . . .": G. H. Fleming, *Murderers' Row* (New York: William Morrow, 1985), p. 13.

looking through the transom: Werber, telephone interview.

"the movie set": Fleming, *Murderers' Row,* p. 14.

ride the roller coaster: Paul Gallico, "Lou Gehrig — An American Hero," *Cosmopolitan,* January 1942.

"He used to come up . . .": Mosedale, *The Greatest of All,* p. 99.

flying cross-country: New York Post, June 16, 1927.

"Gehrig has everything . . .": New York *Telegram,* July 5, 1927.

notch in the barrel of his bat: Hillerich & Bradsby Co. museum and archives.

"There's only one man . . .": New York Evening Journal, July 2, 1927.

"There'll never be another . . .": Ibid.

"and other happenings . . .": New York *World,* July 2, 1927.

"*Every day bring this chronicler . . . .*": "Yanks Are Stopped, but Only by Rain," *New York Times,* August 1, 1927.

"*frolicking, rollicking, walloping . . . .*": "Yanks' Late Spurt Beats Indians," *New York Times,* July 16, 1927.

a second announcer: New York *Sun,* April 14, 1927.

"*I have as much respect . . .*": "I'm Not Trying to Hit Homer — Lou Gehrig," *Literary Digest,* September 27, 1927.

"*I'd rather see Ruth . . .*": New York *Sun,* May 13, 1927.

"*The only real home run hitter . . .*": "Yanks Are Stopped, but Only by Rain," *New York Times,* August 1, 1927.

"*The most astonishing thing . . .*": New York *Daily News,* September 3, 1927.

"*I'm so worried about Mom . . .*": Lieb, *Baseball As I Have Known It,* pp. 174–175.

"*the guy who hit all those home runs*": Paul Dickson, *Baseball's Greatest Quotations* (New York: HarperCollins, 1991), p. 6.

"*Will I ever break this again?*": *New York Evening World,* October 1, 1927.

"*I am so happy to hear . . .*": "Gehrig's Ma Backs Lou," *Los Angeles Times,* October 6, 1927.

"*Go on, you Miljus*": "Yanks Sweep Series, Wild Pitch Beating Pirates, 4-3, in

Ninth," *New York Times,* October 9, 1927.

Phi Delta Theta invited him: "Rah, Rah, Gehrig!" *Pittsburgh Press,* October 6, 1927.

8. BARNSTORMING DAYS

Babe Ruth, the two call girls: Sobol, *Babe Ruth and The American Dream,* 1.

"Meet Lou Gehrig, Gov": Ibid., p. 3.

"There is no room in baseball . . .": widely quoted, date and origin unknown.

children wrapped around his legs: "Boys Jam Trenton Field and Stop Game When Ruth Hits His Third Homer of Day," *New York Times,* October 12, 1927.

"Who cares about winning ballgames?": "Brooklyn's Other Ball Club," *Coronet,* August 1943.

"We don't need any lifeguards here": Ibid.

game was delayed an hour: "36 Baseballs Lost, Ending Ruth Game," *New York Times,* October 14, 1927.

bribed a grocer: "Pitched Best Curve to Ruth," *Washington Post, SB.*

$1,000 at 6 percent interest: "Adios to Ghosts," *Sporting News,* January 20, 1938.

"It was an education . . .": "Innocents Aboard," *Collier's,* April 14, 1928.

"This sturdy and serious lad . . .": "Sports of the Times," *New York Times,* October 26, 1927.

"Hello, Mother": Baseball Hall of Fame, permanent collection.

Babe Ruth of egg laying: "Champ Egg Layer Receives Sultan of Swat Calmly," *Omaha Evening World-Herald,* October 17, 1927.

"He spotted a couple . . .": "The Day the Babe and Lou Were in Omaha," *Omaha Evening World-Herald,* October 16, 1977.

"This isn't Babe Ruth": "Innocents Aboard," *Collier's,* April 14, 1928.

"Geez, kid . . .": Pete Grijalva, telephone interview.

"You guys gave those Pirates . . .": "Innocents Aboard," *Collier's,* April 14, 1928.

stropping motions: Ibid.

first customer was Ruth: Ibid.

200,000 fans: "Ruth, Gehrig Back; Played in 9 States," *New York Times,* November 9, 1927.

"I ain't doin' a thing . . .": Sobol, *Babe Ruth and the American Dream,* p. 24.

"I plan to play . . .": Ibid.

9. A CHARMED LIFE

don't settle for a penny less: "Innocents

Aboard," *Collier's,* April 14, 1928.

"Baseball men were at a loss . . .": "Yanks Sign Gehrig to 3-Year Contract," *New York Times,* January 7, 1928.

Seagram's and ice: Bill Werber, telephone interview.

asked Ruppert for a five-year deal: "Yanks Sign Gehrig to 3-Year Contract," *New York Times,* January 7, 1928.

"I don't see how . . .": Gehrig radio interview, KROC, Rochester, Minnesota, 1939.

"proudest day of my life": "Lou Gehrig Gives Baseball Full Credit . . . ," *Sporting News,* December 25, 1930.

fourth most popular: "Fans Vote Dempsey Most Popular Figure in Sports World," *Washington Post,* January 30, 1928.

Philadelphia Warriors . . . recruited him: "Warriors to Sound Lou Gehrig on Playing Cage Game Here," *Philadelphia Record,* November 14, 1927.

agreed, for $250 fee: Hubler, *Lou Gehrig: The Iron Horse of Baseball,* p. 54.

bizarre competition: "Ball Player Wins Oddest Golf Match," *Washington Post,* November 22, 1925.

Afra of Cosalta: Catalogue, 18th Annual Dog Show, Bronx County Kennel Club, October 16, 1932.

"I hope to crack out sixty-one . . .": "Yanks Squad Rolls Southward in Rain," *New*

York Times, February 26, 1928.

"I'm just learning . . .": Ibid.

Huggins urged his players: Frank Graham, *The New York Yankees: An Informal History* (Carbondale and Edwardsville: Southern Illinois University Press, 2002), p. 141.

"the face plays a very small part . . .": "Yanks Win, 4 to 1, In Series Opener; 63,000 See Game," *New York Times,* October 5, 1928.

Gehrig chuckled: "Looking Around with Lou Gehrig," *New York Times,* March 16, 1941.

"The ball Gehrig hit . . .": "Yanks Sing in Joy Over Routing Cards," *New York Times,* October 6, 1928.

"He hadn't changed a bit": Sam Dana, telephone interview.

10. THE CRASH

Jacob Ruppert was a collector: Graham, *The New York Yankees: An Informal History,* 20; "Jacob Ruppert Major Figure in Trade and Sport," *New York Post,* January 13, 1939; "Ruppert Makes Up with Babe — Dies with Smile," *Daily News,* January 14, 1939.

"I have no intention . . .": Graham, *The New York Yankees: An Informal His-*

tory, pp. 151–152.

"It won't be necessary": Graham, *The New York Yankees: An Informal History*, p. 152.

"I signaled for a fastball . . .": "Bill Dickey . . . A Yankee of Distinction," *Sporting News*, June 13, 1970.

"Listen, Bill, I've been watching . . .": Bill Dickey, "My Roommate, Lou Gehrig" (introduction to Gallico, *Pride of the Yankees*), p. 4.

"I guess he was the best batting coach": Ibid., p. 7.

skies . . . turned gray: Ibid.; "2 Die, 30 Hurt at Yankee Stadium," *Daily News*, May 20, 1929; "2 Die, 100 Hurt in Panic at Yankee Stadium as Rain Stampedes 5,000," *New York Herald-Tribune*, May 20, 1929.

handed out rabbit feet: "Sports of the Times," *New York Times*, June 16, 1929.

"I had a look at Lou Gehrig . . .": Hank Greenberg, *The Story of My Life* (New York: Times Books, 1989), p. 18.

"Lou Gehrig has accidentally . . .": "The Little Heinie," *The New Yorker*, August 10, 1929.

Huggins sat in a rocking chair: "Sports of the Times," *New York Times*, September 27, 1929.

Huggins called a meeting: Graham, *The New*

York Yankees: An Informal History, p. 155.

went upstairs: Ibid., pp. 155–156.

"They're through": Ibid.

"Why is it that any ignoramus . . .": Robert S. McElvaine, The Great Depression (New York: Times Books, 1993), p. 46.

feverish and weak: Ibid., p. 157; "Cold Weather Stops Yankees-White Sox," New York Times, September 1, 1929.

"I guess I'll miss him . . .": "Many Praise Huggins as Clean Sportsman," New York Times, September 26, 1929.

16.4 million shares: McElvaine, The Great Depression, p. 48.

Gehrig had lent Koppisch thousands: Sam Dana, telephone interview.

11. IRON HORSE

"Well, Ruth . . .": Newsreel footage, 1930.

"There is no excuse . . .": "Lou Gehrig, Baseball's Iron Horse," Dime Sport Magazine, October 1935.

"He's got the old-time . . .": "Sports of the Times," New York Times, June 25, 1929.

"He wasn't as outgoing . . .": Bill Werber, telephone interview.

forty packs of chewing gum: Hubler, Lou Gehrig: The Iron Horse of Baseball, p. 94.

took a laxative called Agarol: Gehrig, personal letter to Dr. Paul O'Leary, February 17, 1940.

"If all players were like Gehrig . . .": Hubler, *Lou Gehrig: The Iron Horse of Baseball,* p. 94.

still limping: "Yanks Figure to Take Three out of Four in Series with Kickless Tigers," *New York Evening Post,* May 9, 1930.

"a veritable Iron Horse . . .": "Gehrig's Iron Man Record," New York *Sun,* April 16, 1931.

"It is lively . . .": Charles C. Alexander, *Breaking the Slump* (New York: Columbia University Press, 2002), p. 30.

total income fell: Ibid., p. 15

"Mickey Cochrane . . . lost . . .": Ibid., p. 16.

checked into St. Vincent's: "Gehrig Undergoes Minor Operations," *New York Times,* October 31, 1930.

shaving . . . was banned: Bill Werber, telephone interview.

"Ten Commandments of Baseball": National Baseball Hall of Fame and Museum archives.

"You know, Bill . . .": Graham, *Lou Gehrig: A Quiet Hero,* p. 145.

"emerged not even a fair second": "Gehrig Is Signed By Yanks For Year," *New York Times,* February 14, 1931.

"It might pay Joe McCarthy . . .": "Short

Shots in All Directions," *New York Times,* January 25, 1931.

Lieb paid the commissioner a visit: Lieb, *Baseball As I Have Known It,* p. 198.

Lieb was more humble: Mimi Holloway, Lieb's granddaughter, telephone interview.

Mary was modest: Lieb, *Baseball As I Have Known It,* p. 226; Mimi Holloway, telephone interview.

"Have you seen Lou?": Lieb, *Baseball As I Have Known It,* p. 176.

hiding in a lifeboat: Ibid., p. 177.

Shakespeare's Twelfth Night: "New Rochelle Cast in 'Twelfth Night,' " *New York Times,* June 15, 1934.

took her ice skating: Barrett-Gehrig photo, Mastronet auction catalog, December 2000.

attended the season opener: Ticket stubs and notes from Gehrig, Mastronet auction catalog, December 2000.

"Lou, you know I'm fond . . .": Lieb, *Baseball As I Have Known It,* p. 177.

"You know the game . . .": Ibid., pp. 177–178.

"I could never be another Ruth . . .": "Damon and Phythias of the New York Yankees," *New York World-Telegram,* December 8, 1932.

"Never again . . .": "Ruppert to Cut Ruth's Pay — Babe Not So Sure,"

Sporting News, December 10, 1931.

owners, looking to save: Alexander, *Breaking the Slump,* p. 49.

seeking $40,000 in damages: Stelzle v. Gehrig, New York Supreme Court, County of New York, 1929.

Sunday doubleheader in July: "Yanks Postpone Game," *New York Times,* May 10, 1932.

not called upon to testify: "Gehrig in Court for Suit," *New York Times,* May 10, 1932.

"It was a fairly hard chance . . .": "Lou Gehrig, Baseball's Iron Horse," *Dime Sport Magazine,* October 1935.

"I was still boiling . . .": Ibid.

"You know . . . I think . . .": "Gehrig Again in Home Run Race After Clouting Four," *New York Evening Post,* June 4, 1932.

"They're chiselers . . .": "Babe Airs His Views of Cubs and 'Chiseling,' " *Chicago Tribune,* September 30, 1932.

last Yankee to reach the clubhouse: "Ruth Achieves Aim; Starts 10th Series," *New York Times,* September 29, 1932.

Fans . . . threw lemons: "Yankees Beat Cubs for 3d in Row, 7–5, As 51,000 Look On," *New York Times,* October 2, 1932.

"It's all right there in the papers": Creamer, *Babe: The Legend Comes to Life,* p. 368.

"old Klem has never moved faster": "Scribbled by Scribes," *Sporting News,* October 13, 1932.

told him what he thought: Ibid.

"no trace of the inferiority complex . . .": Lou Gehrig, "Am I Jealous of Babe Ruth?" *Liberty,* August 19, 1933.

12. COURTSHIP

forty dollars a week: Gehrig and Durso, *My Luke and I,* p. 111.

Her boyfriends seemed much less attractive: Ibid., p. 78.

a couple of boarders: U.S. Census, 1910.

F.B. Twitchell Co.: Chicago Park Commission archives.

gross sales of more than $100,000: "Concessions in All South Parks Sold by Board," *Chicago Tribune,* April 1, 1915.

claimed to have won the money: Gehrig and Durso, *My Luke and I,* p. 94.

"Marine Returns to Charge Wife Loves Another": **Chicago Tribune,** October 5, 1919.

followed him around town: Gehrig and Durso, *My Luke and I,* p. 62.

"not less than $4,000 or $5,000": Chicago Park Commission archives.

"I never heard of the Depression": Bill Werber, telephone interview.

disappeared down the block: Gehrig and Durso, *My Luke and I,* p. 136.

"a family hotel": Ibid., p. 139.

"I just wanted to say good night, dear,": Ibid.

"So this was it": Ibid., p. 140.

served at a supper club: Ibid., p. 141.

"They are shown in Comiskey Park . . .": "Lou Gehrig and His Reason for the Grin," *New York Evening Post,* June 20, 1933.

"I couldn't believe my ears . . .": Sobol, *Babe Ruth and the American Dream,* p. 238.

"The published dope": SB, August 2, 1933.

"Formidable . . .": Gehrig and Durso, *My Luke and I,* p. 150.

"Mom is the most wonderful woman in the world": Lieb, *Baseball As I Have Known It,* p. 178.

"Lou played in his 1,348th": "Ruth Drives Homer as Yanks Triumph," *New York Times,* September 29, 1933.

"Gehrig retired at the end . . .": "Yanks Outslug Nats, 11-9," *Daily News,* September 29, 1933.

"Gehrig, whose wedding . . .": *New York Herald Tribune,* September 29, 1933.

about the drapes: Ibid.

gave her age as twenty-seven: Transcript of marriage record, City of New Rochelle.

"Lou asked me to pick you up . . .": Lieb, *Baseball As I Have Known It,* p. 179.

"Freddy, wasn't I . . .": Ibid.

13. OUT OF THE SHADOWS

got up from the dinner table: Gehrig and Durso, *My Luke and I*, p. 160.

turned over most of his savings: Ibid., p. 156.

"I'm no psychologist . . .": Ibid., p. 161.

Abercrombie & Fitch: Ibid., p. 162.

parked his car two blocks away: "Life of Lou Gehrig," *Baseball Register*, 1942.

"She was difficult . . .": Frances Metheny, telephone interview.

"Fans wondered what Larruping Lou . . .": "Gehrig's Four Hits Help Yankees Win," *New York Times*, May 11, 1934.

Cartoon: "His Place in the Sun," *Daily News*, May 12, 1934.

"He's the guy that swiped me": Billy Rogell, telephone interview.

"He was great": Mel Harder, telephone interview.

"It was out there a mile": William Fehring, telephone interview.

skip the pre-game autograph session: "Blow on Head Fails to Daunt Lou Gehrig," *Virginian-Pilot*, June 30, 1934.

"Five big-league teams": Robert Stevens, telephone interview.

"They didn't like each other": Bud Metheny, telephone interview.

rested the pitcher for five days: "Yankees Here Friday," *Norfolk Ledger-Dispatch,* June 28, 1934.

unbuttoned his gray flannel shirt: Photograph, June 28, 1934; Robert Stevens, telephone interview.

"a moderate concussion": "Blow on Head Fails to Daunt Gehrig," *Virginian-Pilot,* June 30, 1934.

"I guess the streak's over now": Robert Stevens, telephone interview.

"The big problem": "No. 2130 Goes on Siding After Long Run," *Sporting News,* May 11, 1939.

Head down, left hand clutching: photograph, *The Detroit Free Press,* July 14, 1934.

"record that promises to endure . . .": "Ruth's Record of 700 Home Runs Likely to Stand for All Time in Major Leagues," *New York Times,* July 14, 1934.

"breathing difficult . . .": "Tigers Halt Yanks to Regain the Lead," *New York Times,* July 15, 1934.

"He wouldn't let me . . .": St. Louis Star-Times, July 24, 1936, *SB.*

Gehrig who insisted: "Tigers Beat Yankees, 12-11 in Ninth and Regain League Lead," *The Detroit News,* July 15, 1934.

"I'm getting out of this game . . .": "Ruth Injured as Yankees Lose; Hit on Leg by Gehrig's Drive," *New York Times,* July 19, 1934.

Ruth complained to Gehrig: Creamer, *Babe: The Legend Comes to Life,* p. 380; Gehrig and Durso, *My Luke and I,* p. 176.

sailed on the Empress of Japan: Gehrig and Durso, *My Luke and I,* pp. 189–190.

"It just is unpleasant . . .": Maury Allen, *Where Have You Gone, Joe DiMaggio?* (New York: Signet, 1975), p. 63.

14. A NIGHT AT THE OPERA

"Singapore, Penang . . .": "Home from World Tour, Gehrig Expected to Ask $35,000 Salary from Yanks," *New York Times,* February 14, 1935.

seventeenth row: Ticket stub, Eleanor Gehrig's scrapbook, Baseball Hall of Fame.

Eleanor became more attentive: "Home from World Tour, Gehrig Expected to Ask $35,000 Salary from Yanks," *New York Times,* February 14, 1935.

"How do I know?": Ibid.

new collection of suits: "Gehrig, Compromising on Pay, Signs Up for Reported $30,000," *Sporting News,* February 21, 1935.

"If I don't get the big dough . . .": Ibid.

"We had no trouble . . .": "Yanks Sign Gehrig for One Year; Salary Reported to Be $30,000," *New York Times,* Feb-

ruary 20, 1935.

"Gehrig . . . it is a pleasure . . .": "Simple Ceremony Crowns New King," *SB,* February 28, 1935.

"That Gehrig is getting to be . . .": Ibid.

240 pounds: "Return from World Tour Finds Babe Ruth Hopeful of Remaining in Baseball," *New York Times,* February 21, 1935.

publicity stunt at Artie McGovern's: Newsreel footage, April 12, 1935.

"Well, night baseball is strictly a show . . .": Gehrig radio interview, KROC, Rochester, Minnesota, 1939.

"I guess I have been very lucky:" "Lou Gehrig, Baseball's Iron Horse," *Dime Sport Magazine,* October 1935.

"no automaton . . .": Gehrig and Durso, *My Luke and I,* pp. 165–166.

saw every performance: Ibid., p. 26.

sobbing in the dark: Ibid., p. 26.

15. THE NEXT BIG THING

proper pronunciation: "Pronunciation of DiMaggio," *New York Times,* March 21, 1936.

"Hey, Joe . . .": Richard Ben Cramer, *Joe DiMaggio: The Hero's Life* (New York: Simon & Schuster, 2000), p. 80.

"DiMaggio will develop . . .": "Gehrig Hits

698

High 'C' Praising DiMaggio," *Sporting News*, March 26, 1936.

$100,000 . . . for Buddy Myer: "Yanks Plan to Stand Pat on 1936 Team," *New York Times*, January 15, 1936.

"Joe became the team's biggest star . . .": Ray Robinson, *Iron Horse: Lou Gehrig in His Time* (New York: W.W. Norton, 1990), p. 216.

first on the team to own a . . . radio: Tommy Henrich with Bill Gilbert, *Five O'Clock Lightning* (New York: Birch Lane Press), p. 35.

"Lou was the perfect team man": Ibid., p. 32.

"He entered the lobby . . .": St. Louis *Star-Times*, July 24, 1936.

"The Olympic Games exploded . . .": "Negro Athletic Representation," *New York Times*, August 29, 1936.

"In the past, I played ball . . .": Baseball notes, *Sporting News*, August 20, 1936.

"I get tired of sitting on cushions . . .": "1876 Hardwood vs. 1936 Cushions," *Sporting News*, June 18, 1936.

seemed embarrassed: "Gehrig Is Honored As Yanks Triumph," *New York Times*, September 20, 1936.

"I had watched Lou Gehrig . . .": Joe DiMaggio, *Lucky to Be a Yankee* (New York: Rudolph Field, 1946), p. 59.

"We were swinging at headlines": Joe Wil-

liams, *The Joe Williams Baseball Reader* (Chapel Hill, N.C.: Algonquin Books, 1989), p. 120.

"There it goes": audiotape of broadcast, October 3, 1936.

practically an intentional walk: "66,669 See Yanks Down Giants, 5-2; Hubbell Is Beaten," *New York Times,* October 5, 1936.

stuffed the ball in his pocket: "Jubilation Reaches High Pitch in Quarters of Yankees After Final Triumph," *New York Times,* October 7, 1936.

16. LORD OF THE JUNGLE

"I guess the public's entitled . . .": "Gehrig Seeks Role as Tarzan in Films," *New York Times,* October 21, 1936.

"Having seen several pictures . . .": "As Tarzan, Gehrig Good Baseball Player — Burroughs," *Los Angeles Times,* November 9, 1936.

"Afraid of animals?": "Gehrig Seeks Role as Tarzan in Films," *New York Times,* October 21, 1936.

"a place where, it seems to us . . .": "Film Gossip of the Week," *New York Times,* October 25, 1936.

"a trifle too ample": "Gehrig Fails to Make Tarzan Club," *Los Angeles Times,* No-

vember 21, 1937.

"Gehrig will entertain . . . .": "DiMaggio's Unsigned Contract Lands Back in Yankee Office," *New York Times,* January 30, 1937.

"I think Lou's making . . . .": "Babe Ruth Discusses Gehrig, Dean, The 1937 Pennant Races — And Golf," *New York Times,* January 27, 1937.

"If it develops . . . .": "Many Marks to Be Sought by Gehrig as He Tries to Extend Playing String," *New York Times,* January 31, 1937.

thought he had a good chance: Ibid.

"But these are not unreasonable . . . .": Bill James, e-mail correspondence, October 22, 2003.

"Honus Wagner . . . there was a wonderful . . . .": "Daniel's Dope," *World-Telegram,* February 4, 1937.

"I have to make you beautiful": Newsreel footage, March 1937.

"And I won't go for . . . .": "Gehrig Signs for Movies, Bars Tarzan Role; Says He Has No Idea of Quitting Baseball," *New York Times,* March 4, 1937.

"I know I'm no actor . . . .": "Lou Hits the Screen," *Sporting News,* March 11, 1937.

"And if there are any love sequences . . . .": Ibid.

Packard convertible for $2,000: canceled

check, October 26, 1936, *The Barry Halper Collection of Baseball Memorabilia* (New York: Sotheby's, 1999), p. 395.

Elks club: Peter Mustich, New Rochelle Elks Club, telephone interview; "Gehrig, Henry L. Jr., Ballplayer," *New York Alive*, July/August 1988.

Dunkel's . . . to get a haircut: "Gehrig, Henry L. Jr., Ballplayer," *New York Alive*, July/August 1988.

Singer pharmacy for a coffee malted: Ibid.

Bruzzese earned twenty-five cents: Dom Bruzzese, telephone interview.

bicycle in the basement: Eleanore Jonas, interview.

negotiations . . . acrimonious: "Gehrig Accepts One-Year Contract," *New York Times,* March 19, 1937.

"Lou is the perennial youth . . .": "Gehrig Given the 'Call' over Foxx by Veteran Critic," *Sporting News,* January 21, 1937.

"If Gehrig ever knocks off": Graham, *The New York Yankees: An Informal History,* p. 234.

"I just hold it . . .": Associated Press, *SB,* May 1, 1937.

never cared much for Dean: Gehrig letter to Paul O'Leary, February 6, 1940.

"Ha! Shucks!": "A Report from a Good Scout," *New York Times,* June 26, 1937.

90-*pound* *marlin:* "Yankee Stars Get Marlin," *New York Times,* August 3, 1937.

"*The first 2,500 are the hardest*": "Yanks Routed, 5-2, Despite 2,500th Hit in Gehrig's Career," *New York Times,* August 22, 1937.

"*I eat a light breakfast . . .*": "Setting the Pace," *SB,* August 3, 1937.

"*That's all there is*": "Nothing up His Sleeve and Little in His Pocket, Has Gehrig," *Sporting News,* September 23, 1937.

"*I don't seem to be timing the ball . . .*": "Gossip of Fourth Game," *Sporting News,* October 14, 1937.

sapped by a cold: Ibid.

expression on his face: Ibid.

17. STRANGE TIMES

trouble with his balance: "Mrs. Iron Horse," *Atlanta Journal,* July 2, 1962.

change in the way . . . swinging the bat: "When McCarthy Learned Gehrig Was Slipping," *New York World-Telegram,* February 7, 1945.

voice popped with energy: Louis Linn, M.D., interview.

not shy about his intelligence: Ibid.

"*The treatment is palliative*": Israel S.

703

Wechsler, M.D., *A Textbook of Clinical Neurology* (Philadelphia and London: W.B. Saunders, 1939), p. 147.

borrowed one of Gehrig's nightshirts: Newspaper Story, *SB.*

benefit for the widow of . . . Healy: "Stars of Radio and Screen in Healy Benefit Tonight," *Los Angeles Times,* January 22, 1938.

telegrams to sportswriters: "This Morning with Shirley Povich," *Washington Post,* January 27, 1938.

"Boy, I never had so much fun . . .": " 'Two-Gun' Lou Gehrig Stars as Rootin', Tootin', Shootin' Hero of the Wild West," *Sporting News,* January 27, 1938.

Kasarskis . . . paper: E. J. Kasarskis and M. Winslow, "When Did Lou Gehrig's Personal Illness Begin?" *Neurology,* Vol. 39, 1989, pp. 1243–1245.

brought home a souvenir: "History Loaded with the Famous Getting Favored Treatment," *New York Post,* August 10, 2003.

"I am a slave to baseball": "Daniel's Dope," *New York World-Telegram, SB.*

"Irrespective of any other players . . .": Ibid.

"a man is entitled to a little rest": "Ruppert Assails DiMaggio's Stand," *New York Times,* March 14, 1938.

unable to have children: Lieb, *Baseball As I*

Have Known It, p. 180.

never got around to it: Joseph Durso, telephone interview.

heat was too much for him: "Initial Workout Staged by Gehrig, *New York Times,* March 16, 1938.

felt lousy: Ibid.

"his cleats stuck": "Gomez and Ruffing Yield Only Three Hits," *New York Times,* March 21, 1938.

"a couple of sore lunch hooks": "Champs' Averages Misleading," *The Sun,* March 26, 1938.

foam rubber: Ibid.

"Of all the movie-struck . . .": *Daily News,* April 25, 1938.

landed . . . on his rear end: "Yanks Turn Back Little Rock, 10-5," *New York Times,* April 10, 1938.

18. THE LONGEST SUMMER

"Every time up there . . .": "Ruffing Shuts Out Senators With 4 Hits, 7-0, as Yankees Open Home Season Before 25,000," *New York Herald Tribune,* April 23, 1938.

struggled even in batting practice: "Players Gossip, Landis Frets, Fans Boo at Picket Line Delay," *New York Herald Tribune,* April 23, 1938.

"DiMaggio is a very ungrateful . . . ": "Ruppert Assails DiMaggio's Stand," *New York Times,* March 14, 1938.

"The Yankees can get along . . . ": "Snub by McCarthy Draws Blast from DiMaggio in Salary Fight," *New York Times,* April 1, 1938.

"Let Lou hit his way back . . . ": "DiMaggio Nudges Gehrig Aside in Shakeup of Yankees," *New York Sun,* May 3, 1938.

"Now, Lou . . . ": Letter from Elizabeth McCarthy, Baseball Hall of Fame archives.

"galloping around the bags . . . ": "Ruffing Captures Third Straight, 5-1," *New York Times,* May 4, 1938.

new volatility: The Sun, May 14, 1938.

"It's just a cold": "Lame Back Menaces Gehrig," *New York Sun,* May 23, 1938.

would be ready to play: "Yankee Game Off; Wicker Released," *Daily News,* May 24, 1938.

changing bats: Hillerich & Bradsby Co. museum and archives.

"Lou, I've got an idea": Gehrig and Durso, *My Luke and I,* p. 206.

"the greatest player of all time": "Lou the Everlasting," *Daily News,* June 1, 1938.

side-by-side photos: "Then and Now," *The Sporting News,* June 1938.

"I like to play baseball": "Gehrig, the 'Iron Man' of Baseball, Now Looks Ahead to

2,500 Games," *New York Times,* June 1, 1938.

"A ballplayer, like any other . . .": "Gehrig Will Be 35 Tomorrow," *New York Post,* June 18, 1938.

"You know, Joe . . .": "When McCarthy Learned Gehrig Was Slipping," *World-Telegram,* February 7, 1945.

"I wouldn't take Lou out . . .": "Yanks Plan Battle Against Invaders to Regain Lead," *Daily News,* July 12, 1938.

"I'd play in this series . . .": "Gehrig Plays 2,045th Game with Fractured Thumb," *Daily News,* July 20, 1938.

"It is my conviction . . .": "Close Fight Turns Pressure on Yanks," *Sporting News,* July 28, 1938.

Speaker sat in the pressbox: "62,753 See Feller Beaten, 6-1, As Yanks Take 3½-Game Lead," *New York Times,* August 6, 1938.

"There was something stumbling . . .": Charlie Wagner, telephone interview.

"He got his legs tangled up . . .": Bob Feller, telephone interview.

"Lou Gehrig has pulled himself out . . .": "Gehrig Goes Back to Old Stance, Clicks," *SB,* August 17, 1938.

two more Louisville Slugger bats: Hillerich & Bradsby Co. museum and archives.

"This fellow Gehrig . . .": "This Fellow Gehrig," *New York Times,* October 1, 1938.

"To my mind . . .": "Much Ado About Lou," *New York Times*, October 8, 1938.

"He didn't look quite right . . .": Richard Lally, *Bombers: An Oral History of the New York Yankees* (New York: Crown, 2002), p. 19.

"hollow shell": "No Means in Sight for Halting Yankees," *New York Times*, October 11, 1938.

"had no oomph": Ibid.

"You'd better look after Lou": Gehrig and Durso, *My Luke and I*, p. 5.

19. LIKE A MATCH BURNING OUT

began to suspect . . . a brain tumor: "Mrs. Iron Horse," *Atlanta Journal*, July 2, 1962; Gehrig and Durso, *My Luke and I*, p. 7.

gallbladder trouble: Gehrig and Durso, *My Luke and I*, p. 5.

Ruth visited: "Ruppert Makes Up with Babe — Dies With Smile," *Daily News*, January 14, 1939.

"He was one of the outstanding sportsmen . . .": "Sports and Business Join in Tribute to Ruppert," *New York Post*, January 13, 1939.

tried golf: Williams, *The Joe Williams Baseball Reader*, p. 70.

"Replying to your letter . . .": Henrich, *Five O'Clock Lightning*, p. 61.

expecting an even steeper reduction: "Gehrig Signed by Yanks at Estimated Salary of $35,000."

"thoroughly satisfied": Ibid.

message from Wattenberg: Lieb, *Baseball As I Have Known It*, p. 228.

"YOU WILL SOON BE CALLED UPON . . .": Ibid., p. 180.

"We were all somewhat startled": Ibid.

"He didn't have a shred . . .": DiMaggio, *Lucky to Be a Yankee*, p. 98.

"a little leg stiffness . . .": "Dickey Joins Yankee Team-Mates In Strenuous Two-Hour Workout," *New York Times,* March 3, 1939.

"The hardest part . . .": "Yankee Pilot Eyes Rookies," *New York Post,* March 1, 1939.

short of breath: "Wanted Quickly! A New Iron Horse," *Daily Mirror,* March 11, 1939.

"pain in his calves": Ibid.

"Father Time . . .": "Father Time Scouting Gehrig," *New York Sun,* March 2, 1939.

"He knew it": Johnny Sturm, telephone interview.

"I never saw a guy . . .": Eddie Joost, telephone interview.

"He'd stoop over . . .": Bill Hitchcock, tele-

phone interview.

"Lou, how do you feel?": Bud Metheny, telephone interview.

"Al, you've caught me before": Al Lopez, telephone interview.

"He isn't hitting the ball well . . .": "Is Gehrig Through?" *New York World-Telegram,* March 17, 1939.

"He runs and throws and bats . . .": "Yankees Wonder About First," *The New York Sun,* March 15, 1939.

"There's still rust . . .": "Yanks Shake Off Slump," *New York Post,* March 20, 1939.

"Gehrig never has been . . .": "Dickey Plays First '39 Game and Leads Attack," *Herald Tribune,* March 20, 1939.

"Gehrig's ambition . . .": "Iron Horse Lou Could Use Some Cast Iron Legs," *New York Post,* March 23, 1939.

"I've been worried since 1925": "Gehrig's Sparse Hitting Makes Him Yankees' Chief Problem," *New York Herald Tribune,* March 21, 1939.

"McCarthy figured a day off . . .": "Yanks Rip KC Farmhands, 14-4," *Daily News,* March 23, 1939.

"all washed up": "The PowerHouse," *Daily News,* March 24, 1939.

"All of a sudden . . .": Robinson, *Iron Horse,* pp. 246–247.

"I will not play Gehrig . . .": "Gehrig Given

Ultimatum," *Daily News,* March 30, 1939.

"Give me a little time": Ibid.

propped a couple of ladders: "DiMaggio Hits 2 As Yankees Win in Slugfest, 22-3," *New York Herald Tribune,* April 1, 1939.

"I'd like to see anyone . . .": "Yanks and Gehrig in Swing," *New York Sun,* April 4, 1939.

"Gehrig's getting stronger . . .": "McCarthy Rates Yanks Better Than His '38 Champions," *New York Sun,* April 6, 1939.

"He wouldn't talk": Ernie Koy, telephone interview.

hit it toward the end of his bat: photograph, *Norfolk Virginian-Pilot,* April 14, 1939.

"whistling drives": "Yankees Elated over Sudden Rejuvenation of Gehrig," *New York Sun,* April 14, 1939.

"It would have been easy . . .": Tommy Henrich, telephone interview.

20. LAST CHANCE

"Never in his palmiest years . . .": "Yanks Blank Red Sox Before 30,278 at Stadium Opener," *New York Times,* April 21, 1939.

"He didn't really rip it": Ted Williams, *My Turn at Bat* (New York: Pocket Books, 1970), p. 97.

"Geez, I wonder what's wrong . . .": Bobby Doerr, telephone interview.

"pretty cheerful for a corpse": "Power House," *Daily News*, April 21, 1939.

"The stroke and everything looked good": Walt Masterson, telephone interview.

tried sneaking out: "Krakauskas Regrets Curve He Threw Joe," *Washington Post*, April 22, 1939.

"He couldn't hardly move": Cecil Travis, telephone interview.

running uphill: "Steve Sundra Holds Senators As Champions Rout Ken Chase," *Herald Tribune*, April 24, 1939.

jeering . . . was gone: "Yankees Shade A's on 3 Hits, 2-1," *New York Herald Tribune*, April 25, 1939.

"He was pretty fast . . .": Dario Lodigiani, telephone interview.

"I wish you would tell . . .": "Yankees Down Athletic Again, 8-4," *Herald Tribune*, April 26, 1939.

"First, I want to tell the fans . . .": "Iron Man Unburdens Himself," *New York Sun*, April 27, 1939.

three new bats: Hillerich & Bradsby Co. museum and archives.

birthdate of an important new industry: "Ceremony Is Carried by Television as Industry Makes Its Formal Bow," *New York Times*, May 1, 1939.

"A hit would have won the ballgame . . .": "Gehrig Voluntarily Ends Streak at 2,130 Straight Games," *New York Times*, May 3, 1939.

"Heavens . . . has it reached that stage?": "No. 2130 Goes on Siding After Long Run," *Sporting News*, May 11, 1939.

"troubled, shaken . . .": Gehrig and Durso, *My Luke and I*, p. 213.

"They don't think I can . . .": Ibid.

21. PITCHERS ONCE FEARED HIS BAT

"Yes, off to a very bad start": "Gehrig Hopeful Despite Slow Start," *Detroit Times*, May 2, 1939.

"It's a black day . . .": "Strain over for Gehrig," *New York Post*, May 3, 1939.

"I haven't been a bit of good . . .": "Gehrig Voluntarily Ends Streak at 2,130 Straight Games," *New York Times*, May 3, 1939.

"a couple of games": "Withdrawal of Gehrig, DiMag Injury Jar Yanks," *Sporting News*, May 4, 1939.

"I've got to remain in baseball": "No. 2130 Goes on Siding After Long Run," *Sporting News*, May 11, 1939.

locker room seemed quiet: "Gehrig's Last Day," *Sports Illustrated,* June 19, 1956.

"Pitchers Once Feared His Bat": "Pitchers Once Feared His Bat," *New York Times,* May 7, 1939.

bent over the water fountain: Ibid.

"The crowd was pretty quiet . . .": Floyd Giebell, telephone interview.

"Lou looks ill . . .": "Bob Tales," *Detroit Evening Times,* May 3, 1939.

"They don't need me . . .": "Gehrig's Last Day," *Sports Illustrated,* June 19, 1956.

22. THE BITTER WITH THE SWEET

"Just think, Lou . . .": "Buoyant Gehrig, Long String Ended, Puzzled over His Batting Decline," *New York Times,* May 4, 1939.

"stripped to the waist . . .": Bob Feller, *Bob Feller's Strikeout Story* (New York: Grosset and Dunlap, 1947), p. 120.

fallen down the . . . staircase: Walt Masterson, telephone interview.

"That's entirely up to Gehrig": "McCarthy, at Fair, Deftly Parries Vexing Query Posed by Youngster," *New York Times,* May 21, 1939.

"Oh, God, Elden": Elden Auker, telephone interview.

"There must be something organically . . .":

Williams, *The Joe Williams Reader*, p. 125.

"I just can't understand": "Buoyant Gehrig, Long String Ended, Puzzled over His Batting Decline," *New York Times*, May 4, 1939.

"These hot days . . . .": "Yanks Beat Chisox, 5-2, for 10 Straight," *Daily News*, May 21, 1939.

"My friends slap me on the back . . .": "Setting the Pace," *New York Sun*, May 22, 1939.

"Lou is a sick man": "Gehrig Sick Man; Will Go to Clinic, Says Yank Coach," *Daily News*, June 2, 1939.

"Just another rumor": "Gehrig Reported Ailing," *New York Times*, June 2, 1939.

"I hadn't made up my mind . . .": "Gehrig Didn't Have a Pain Until That Latest Story Broke," *New York Herald Tribune*, June 4, 1939.

"Oh, it was a sad day": Phil Rizzuto, telephone interview.

concession stand roofs: "Yesterday's Crowd a Record for Yanks in Exhibitions," *Kansas City Star*, June 13, 1939.

"He looked kind of thin . . .": Johnny Sturm, telephone interview.

having trouble walking: Phil Rizzuto, telephone interview.

McCullough . . . remembered: "The Last Game of the Iron Horse: Lou Gehrig in

Kansas City," *Gateway Heritage,* Fall 1982.

choppy air: "Sure Doctors Will Find Out What Ails Him," *Rochester Post-Bulletin,* June 14, 1939.

mussed his hair: photographs, Olmsted County Historical Society.

Kernan drove slowly: "Sports Browser," *Rochester Post-Bulletin,* June 14, 1939.

Gehrig rubbed his chin: Ibid.

Benny Goodman, Eddie Duchin: Dr. Harold C. Habein, Jr., telephone interview.

"a bit clumsy": unpublished memoirs, Dr. Harold C. Habein.

Woltman . . . shunned attention: Dr. Donald W. Mulder, interview; Henry Woltman, Jr., interview; Woltman papers, Mayo Clinic archives.

Woltman would . . . ask the patient: Dr. Donald Mulder, interview; Dr. Joe R. Brown, interview; Woltman papers, Mayo Clinic archives.

handwriting was small: Henry Woltman, Jr., telephone interview.

test his children's reflexes: Dr. Henry Louis Woltman, interview; John Woltman, interview.

"like looking at an orange": Dr. Donald Mulder, interview.

"I don't know any more . . .": "Famed Slugger Meets Former Teammate Here," *Rochester Post-Bulletin,* June 15, 1939.

"Julie? In town here?": Ibid.

"You couldn't help but fall in love . . .": Jay Youmans, interview.

"There's too much loafing . . .": "Lou Addresses Legion League, Hits Softball," *Rochester Post-Bulletin,* June 16, 1939.

a couple of ten-year-old kids: Marilyn Brienholt, telephone interview.

demonstrated his swing: "Lou Addresses Legion League, Hits Softball," *Rochester Post-Bulletin,* June 16, 1939; Nancy Bragden, interview.

Tommy told Gehrig a dirty joke: Nancy Bragden, telephone interview.

cruise on Lake Pepin: "Gehrig Away on Cruise," *New York Times,* June 19, 1939.

"I haven't got the kind of money . . .": "Gehrig's Spirit Unbroken," *New York Post,* June 22, 1939.

daily doses of vitamin B: personal correspondence, Gehrig and Dr. Paul O'Leary.

"I guess I need a drink": Lieb, *Baseball As I Have Known It,* p. 181.

looked like a superhero: Mike Paulios, interview.

"Gentlemen . . . we have bad news": "Paralysis Ends Gehrig's Career," *Daily News,* June 22, 1939.

"They were particularly interested . . .": "Gehrig Has Infantile Paralysis; Can

Never Play Baseball Again," *New York Herald Tribune*, June 22, 1939.

23. LUCKIEST MAN

wouldn't notice his awkward gait: "Yanks of Past and Present, Fans, Writers and Officials to Do Honor to Lou Gehrig," *New York Herald Tribune*, July 4, 1939.

"I'm not going to make that play . . .": "Gehrig Starts New Routine of Baseball Duties," *Herald Tribune*, June 23, 1939.

Associated Press bio: "Gehrig Case is Expected to Spur Research into Baffling Malady," *New York Times*, June 29, 1939.

"Personally, I don't care . . .": "It's Gehrig Day," *San Francisco Chronicle*, July 4, 1939.

"If he had been content . . .": "On Line with Considine," *Washington Post*, July 7, 1939.

Eleanor . . . called one of the doctors: Lieb, *Baseball As I Have Known It*, p. 182.

"Nobody knew what the heck . . .": Tommy Henrich, telephone interview.

privacy of the clubhouse: "Yanks of Past and Present, Fans, Writers and Officials to Do Honor to Lou Gehrig," *New York Herald Tribune*, July 4, 1939.

dreading it: Ibid.

Johnny Welaj Appreciation Day: "Welaj Receives Gifts From Home Town Fans," *Plainfield Courier-News,* July 7, 1939; Johnny Welaj, Lou Welaj, Helen Ward, telephone interviews.

"Has this made much difference . . .": "Wife Brave, Lou Shaken As 61,000 Cheer Gehrig," *Daily News,* July 5, 1939.

"Take those uniforms off . . .": "Setting the Pace," *New York Sun,* July 5, 1939.

keg of beer: "Crowd of 61,808 Pays Gehrig Honor," *New York Daily Mirror,* July 5, 1939.

"I'd give a month's pay . . .": "Fun-Loving Guy Brings a Smile to Lou's Face," *New York Post,* July 5, 1939.

Gehrig stepped gingerly: Newsreel footage, photographs.

"the perfect prototype . . .": "Gehrig Day Epic Event," *New York Post,* July 5, 1939.

"live long in baseball": Ibid.

"In 1927, Lou was with us . . .": Newsreel footage.

afraid . . . Gehrig might collapse: "Lou Gehrig Remembered on His 80th Birthday," Dahlgren interviewed for National ALS Foundation.

mother and father . . . sobbed: "Wife Brave, Lou Shaken As 61,000 Cheer Gehrig," *Daily News,* July 5, 1939.

Eleanor's eyes were dry: Ibid.

"Over 60,000 people . . .": Jim Walls, telephone interview.

"For the past two weeks": First, second, fourth, and last sentences of Gehrig's speech transcribed from newsreel footage; other sentences pieced together from various newspaper accounts.

"Du, Du Liegst Mir im Herzen": "Gehrig Gives Dramatic Speech," *Sunday News*, July 30, 1939.

"Throughout Lou Gehrig's Career": "Down in Front," *New York Herald Tribune*, July 5, 1939.

never been more frightened: "Fun-Loving Guy Brings a Smile to Lou's Face," *New York Post*, July 5, 1939.

"Feel my undershirt": "Tribute to Lou Gehrig Is Unparalleled in History of Baseball," *New York Sun*, July 5, 1939.

24. THE BUREAUCRAT

thirty thousand letters: Jack Sher, "Meet Lou Gehrig, a Pretty Fair Country Ball Player," *Washington Post*, June 9, 1940.

"I hate like hell . . .": Gehrig-O'Leary correspondence, December 12, 1939.

"He was very impressive . . .": Donna Ivins, telephone interview.

"the greatest institution . . .": Gehrig-

O'Leary correspondence, undated, probably July 16, 1939.

referred . . . half a dozen friends: Gehrig-O'Leary correspondence, July 14, 1939.

"Just a line to say hello": Gehrig-O'Leary correspondence, undated, probably July 16, 1939.

teammates averted their eyes: DiMaggio, *Lucky to Be a Yankee,* p. 101.

"At the beginning of this trip . . .": Ibid., 102.

"The doctors at the clinic . . .": "Gehrig Returns to Clinic for 'Routine Check-Up,'" *SB,* August 21, 1939.

O'Leary . . . there to meet him: "Gehrig Returns for Treatment at Clinic," *Rochester Post-Bulletin,* August 21, 1939.

"The general condition . . .": "Gehrig Quits City After Being Told He Is Definitely Better," *Rochester Post-Bulletin,* August 23, 1939.

"I've been feeling right along . . .": Ibid.

$30,000 to lend his name: "Gehrig Considering Offers of New Job," *New York Times,* October 10, 1939.

$750 a week to greet: "Gehrig, in Parole Job, Calls It 'Greatest Thrill of Life,'" *Daily Mirror,* October 12, 1939.

"I have forwarded your request . . .": New York City Municipal Archives.

"It all boils down to . . .": Ibid.

"We don't go out and overpower . . .":

"Down in Front," *New York Herald Tribune,* September 13, 1939.

"So we went over to help": Eddie Joost, telephone interview.

"Beer Barrel Polka": "DiMaggio's Base Running Is Praised as Yanks Celebrate," *New York Times,* October 9, 1939.

25. OUR BOY IS PRETTY DISCOURAGED

set out to go fishing: "Gehrig, in Parole Job, Calls It 'Greatest Thrill of Life,' " *Daily Mirror,* October 12, 1939.

"I think I'm going to get a bigger kick . . .": "Lou Gehrig Steps Up to Bat in New Job — Helping Kids Who Got a Tough Break," *New York Post,* October 12, 1939.

"pheasants roamed the lawns . . .": Gehrig and Durso, *My Luke and I,* p. 223.

new dog: Eleanor Gehrig's personal correspondence; Louise Goode, telephone interview.

"We always want Lou to feel . . .": "Yanks Never to Use Gehrig's 'No. 4' Again; Veteran Put on Retired List, Not Released," *New York Times,* January 7, 1940.

"The history of medicine . . .": Dr. Bayard

T. Horton, "Musings on Medical Research with a Note on My Last Talk with Dr. Will," *Staff Meetings of the Mayo Clinic,* Vol. 37, No. 12, p. 334.

"make the lame to walk . . .": David Goldblatt, M. D., "True Believer, Bayard Taylor Horton," *Seminars in Neurology,* Vol. 8, No. 4 (December 1988), p. 339.

"like a cat . . .": Ibid.

histamine might even help pitchers: Gehrig-O'Leary correspondence.

colleagues were skeptical: Dr. Frederick Moersch, unpublished memoirs, Mayo Clinic archives.

planned to saturate Gehrig's body: Gehrig-O'Leary correspondence.

"I wish I knew, Eleanor . . .": letter from O'Leary to Eleanor, January 9, 1940.

first visited . . . Wechsler: Wechsler, "The Treatment of Amyotrophic Lateral Sclerosis with Vitamin E (Tocopherols)," *American Journal of Medical Sciences* Vol. 200 (1940), pp. 765–778.

office reeked of genius: Dr. Louis Linn, interview.

"That's not for you": Ibid.

wealthy woman visited: Ibid.

Joseph Fuchs: Ibid.

"When first seen": Wechsler, "The Treatment of Amyotrophic Lateral Sclerosis with Vitamin E (Tocopherols)."

"Unless I am a rotten judge . . . .": Gehrig-O'Leary correspondence, February 4, 1939.

" *. . . publicity-crazed ape . . .* ": Gehrig-O'Leary correspondence, February 6, 1940.

"Wechsler said he has experimented . . . .": Gehrig-O'Leary correspondence, February 4, 1939.

"He mellowed considerably . . . .": Gehrig-O'Leary correspondence, February 11, 1940.

earning Gehrig's confidence: Gehrig-O'Leary correspondence, March 20, 1940.

arrived at nine: "Gehrig Thinks He Is Winning," *SB*, January 30, 1941.

"You've been in your share of trouble . . . .": Robinson, *Iron Horse*, p. 267.

"It came just at a time . . . .": "Gehrig Thinks He Is Winning," *SB*, January 30, 1941.

"From what I am going to write": Gehrig-O'Leary correspondence, March 31, 1940.

Wechsler, who wrote to Dr. Woltman: Ibid., May 5, 1940.

This report — eventually published: "The Treatment of Amyotrophic Lateral Sclerosis with Vitamin E (Tocopherols)."

tip of his left thumb: Gehrig-O'Leary correspondence, May 5, 1940.

"The Yankees, who for the past . . .": "Has 'Polio' Hit the Yankees?" *Sunday News,* August 18, 1940.

"yellow bastard": Gehrig-O'Leary correspondence, August 23, 1940.

"greatly injured . . .": Henry Louis Gehrig vs. News Syndicate Co., Bronx Supreme Court, 1940.

signed . . . in a hand so shaky: Copy of agreement contained in Baseball Hall of Fame archives.

O'Leary urged Gehrig to quit: Gehrig-O'Leary correspondence, January 17, 1941.

Eleanor often invited guests: Gehrig-O'Leary correspondence; Gehrig and Durso, *My Luke and I,* p. 21.

"Oh . . . I can't complain . . .": "On the Line with Considine," *Washington Post,* December 8, 1940.

O'Leary . . . to meet with Gehrig's parents: Gehrig and Durso, *My Luke and I,* pp. 223–224.

eating was becoming increasingly difficult: Eleanor Gehrig letter to O'Leary, January 13, 1940.

26. HE WAS BASEBALL

"There's a mistaken impression . . .": "Fanning with Lou Gehrig," *New York*

Times, November 22, 1940.

"I'm the bird . . .": "Looking Around with Lou Gehrig," *New York Times*, March 16, 1941.

stuck cigarettes in her husband's mouth: "Mrs. Lou Gehrig Recalls the 'Iron Man's' Great Fight for His Life," *St. Louis Daily Globe-Democrat*, September 20, 1941.

"I've still got a fifty-fifty chance": "Lou Gehrig Was Hopeful to the End," *New York Post*, June 3, 1941.

"I'm getting better . . .": "Mrs. Lou Gehrig Recalls the 'Iron Man's' Great Fight for His Life," *St. Louis Daily Globe-Democrat*, September 20, 1941.

"There was no hope in it . . .": Ibid.

"I'm getting so lazy": Memoirs of an unnamed sportswriter, Hall of Fame archives.

Henrich . . . drove up to Riverdale: Tommy Henrich, telephone interview.

milk shakes and orange juice: Gehrig and Durso, *My Luke and I*, p. 162.

"Fifty-fifty:" "Lou Gehrig Was Hopeful to the End," *New York Post*, June 3, 1941.

clear that little time remained: "Gehrig Dies Suddenly; Famed as Yank Star," *Daily News*, June 3, 1941.

"like a great clock winding down": Ibid.

Barrow and his wife were the first to arrive: "Lou Gehrig Dies at 37; Yankee Star

14 Years," *New York Herald Tribune,*
June 3, 1941.

Babe Ruth . . . next: "Ruth at Gehrig
Home," *New York Times,* June 3, 1941.

"His death is a loss . . .": "La Guardia and
Baseball Chiefs Pay Tribute to Gehrig's
Memory," *New York Times,* June 3,
1941.

"He was baseball . . .": Ibid.

"He was a good influence . . .": Ibid.

"Baseball has lost one of its . . .": Ibid.

"Gehrig was not only a great . . .": "A Fine
American, Lehman Declares," *New
York Times,* June 4, 1941.

"He was an example of good living . . .":
Ibid.

"by the grace . . . boys through eternity":
"Lou Gehrig Was the True Sportsman
. . . ," *Washington Post,* June 6, 1941.

dark blue . . . suit: "Gehrig Funeral This
Morning," *Daily News,* June 4, 1941.

Church of the Divine Paternity: "Sorrowful
Crowd in Final Tribute," *New York
Times,* June 4, 1941; "Thousands Go
Past His Bier in 2 Churches," *New
York Herald Tribune,* June 4, 1941.

"The Lord gave . . .": "Farewell to an Idol,
Lou Gehrig," *New York Post,* June 4,
1941.

"We need none": "Funeral Service for
Gehrig Is Held," *New York Times,* June
5, 1941.

"It's boxoffice poison": A. Scott Berg, *Goldwyn: A Biography* (New York: Riverhead Books, 1989), p. 370.

The movie producer cried: Ibid., p. 371.

Eleanor . . . played a powerful role: Letter from Christy Walsh to Samuel Goldwyn, March 23, 1942.

"If you were to look at my scrapbooks . . .": Letter from Eleanor Gehrig to Samuel Goldwyn, April 16, 1942.

Goldwyn wanted to be certain: Berg, *Goldwyn: A Biography,* p. 372.

long list of grievances: Milton Eisenberg letter to Eleanor Gehrig, August 7, 1941.

"I ordered the hound destroyed . . .": Eleanor Gehrig letter to Christy Walsh, January 31, 1942.

Gehrig's will: Copy of will, Baseball Hall of Fame archives.

"I am down here nursing . . .": Eleanor Gehrig letter to Milton Eisenberg, July 26, 1941.

$1,000 or $1,500: Milton Eisenberg letter to Eleanor Gehrig, August 7, 1941.

freeze their assets: Ibid.

Christina and Henry . . . filed a lawsuit: Henry Gehrig and Christina Gehrig vs. Eleanor T. Gehrig, Supreme Court of the State of New York, August 16, 1943.

bequeathed more than $180,000: George Pollack, attorney, interview.

"Tonight, I stand here . . .": "Orioles' Ripken Goes to Work and Steps Into History Books," *New York Times,* September 7, 1985.

"It hits them like a fastball . . .": Dr. Anthony J. Windebank, Mayo Clinic, interview.